Fundamentals of Telecommunications

AND

Networking for IT

Riki Morikawa

George Mason University

Kendall Hunt
publishing company

Kendall Hunt
publishing company

www.kendallhunt.com
Send all inquiries to:
4050 Westmark Drive
Dubuque, IA 52004-1840

Copyright © 2018 by Riki Morikawa

ISBN 978-1-5249-5207-5

Published in the United States of America

Dedication

To my loving family, Sue, Kristy, Katie, Kimi, and Boo.

ABOUT THE AUTHOR

Dr. Riki Morikawa teaches courses in telecommunications, wireless networking, and satellite communications at the George Mason University, Volgenau School of Engineering. He has over thirty-five years of experience as an electrical engineer working in the federal government, and has gained expertise in the development of highly complex strategic and tactical secure communication systems. During his tenure working within the intelligence community, he has received numerous awards and recognitions for his technical contributions toward mission including the Career Intelligence Medal. As a former executive-level manager for the Central Intelligence Agency, his philosophy for sustained technical excellence centers around an engineer's ability to dissect complex systems and to analyze these parts by applying sound fundamental math and physics theories by which all systems are governed. After his retirement from the federal service, he became a full-time faculty member at GMU and has brought this same philosophy into the classroom, ensuring that students learn how to dissect and analyze the many aspects that together, comprise today's modern IT offerings.

Prior to entering government service as a civilian employee, Dr. Morikawa served eight years in the military as a Naval Flight Officer onboard U.S. Navy P3-C Anti-Submarine Warfare aircraft. He earned a B.S. in Electrical Engineering from the University of Colorado (Boulder), an M.B.A. from George Washington University in D.C., and a Ph.D. in Information Technology from George Mason University.

CONTENTS

PREFACE

This is the first edition of the *"Fundamentals of Telecommunications and Networking for IT"* textbook intended primarily for undergraduate IT students within an engineering school or college. However, this textbook is also applicable for courses taught to students at either the undergraduate and graduate level within non-ECE curricula such as ISM business. The motivation for this book is based upon the needs of the average IT student, who require a working knowledge of telecommunications, but not a need for in-depth engineering theories like their ECE counterparts. In searching for an adequate textbook for a telecommunications course specifically addressing the needs of the IT student, I found that existing textbooks either catered to the electrical engineering student, presenting complex theories through lengthy mathematical proofs, or written at a high-level for business students. IT curricula tend to cover a wide landscape of technologies that overlap ECE, CS, and ISM disciplines. Basic theories in communication sciences are the foundations that provide the IT student with the tools for understanding the technologies that make up this broad discipline. Without the need for prerequisite courses in advanced math, physics, or electrical engineering, this textbook attempts to provide communications principles with a focus on the details needed by the average IT student in order to be successful within their selected concentration.

In this textbook, concepts are presented in a manner that intentionally avoids the use of lengthy mathematical derivations. Instead, basic communications theories are presented using simple trigonometric and logarithmic functions that describes the relationships between key variables. In this manner, students are taught the science behind telecommunications prior to learning how these concepts are actually applied to IT systems.

Chapter one introduces electrical and electromagnetic signaling basics by first describing the fundamental concepts of current, voltage, resistance, power, and power density and the effects of attenuation through conductive guided and free space mediums. Basic principles of optical signals are discussed and how they differ from electrical and RF signals. In addition, the decibel is introduced as a common metric used in telecommunications.

Chapter two covers analog modulation techniques and the differences between baseband, passband, and broadband signals. Trigonometric equations are introduced to show how changes in the amplitude, frequency, and phase of a carrier wave are used to modulate information, and how the resulting modulated carrier waves appear in the time domain. Students are also introduced to the importance of viewing modulated carrier signals and their associated bandwidths in the frequency domain.

Chapter three introduces digital communications and builds upon the modulation techniques covered in chapter two by discussing ASK, FSK, and PSK. In addition, digital line coding using basic examples such as NRZ, Bipolar AMI, Manchester, B8ZS, are introduced. Analog-to-digital (ADC) PCM is covered along with the Nyquist Sampling Theorem, quantization bit depth, and the effects of signal aliasing and quantization noise. Digital compression, error control, network timing, and TDM are covered, as well as Hartley's Law and the concept of M'ary modulation.

Chapter four discusses both guided and unguided mediums. Guided mediums such as UTP, coaxial and fiber optic cables, and unguided systems such as microwave, free space optics, and satellite communications are covered. Signal noise, signal-to-noise ratios, thermal noise, and the Shannon-Hartley theoretical capacity formula are presented.

Chapter five is an in-depth review of RF wireless concepts that include popular technologies used in today's telecommunication systems such as MIMO, spread spectrum, and OFDM. Link equations are introduced that describe Friis Free Space Losses, antenna gain, transmit and receive power, and the importance of carrier-to-signal power ratios on Eb/No and digital bit rate capacity.

Based upon chapters one through five, the following chapters six, seven, and eight begin the discussion of how these fundamental concepts are applied to communications networks. Chapter six starts with basic centralized and decentralized LAN architectures and the definitions for DTE and DCE. Several Ethernet specifications are covered as examples of how conductor diameters and line coding methods determine bit rates, as well as the difference between shared and switched Ethernet LANs. Popular WLAN and WPAN standards are included as wireless network examples.

Chapter seven begins with a brief regulatory history of the PSTN, and describes the evolution toward the PDN and WAN. Popular WAN standards are covered including Carrier Ethernet. Methods used to access high-speed digital networks such as DSL, CATV, PONs, and WLL are discussed in chapter eight.

Chapter nine is dedicated to the Internet and begins with a brief history of the Internet and the PC. Similar to chapter nine, chapter ten is dedicated to mobile cellular networks and the evolution from first-generation analog cellular systems to today's fourth-generation digital packet switch-based networks. In addition, cellular fifth generation requirements are touched upon.

As mentioned earlier, the scope of topics that can be considered part of IT spans all seven layers of the OSI Reference Model, and all types of communications architectures. Since this textbook is about telecommunications, emphasis is principally on the lower four layers of the OSI model. IT security is not a topic covered in this book. Instead, it is left for other textbooks and courses to address the importance of digital security.

The advances made in telecommunications have been dramatic and continuous. Any course developed to cover such a fast paced and changing topic needs constant refreshing, and therefore providing supplemental material on current innovative efforts should always be considered. This textbook attempts to provide the student with the basic foundations of communications which rarely change, thus providing the student with a foundational understanding of how and why communications works, and what limitations exist. This basic knowledge is invaluable to the student wishing to begin a career in the dynamic field of IT.

Fundamentals of Telecommunications

AND

Networking for IT

CHAPTER 1

Fundamental Principles of Communications

"Most of the fundamental ideas of science are essentially simple, and may, as a rule, be expressed in a language comprehensible to everyone."
Albert Einstein, http://www.brainyquote.com/search_results.html?q=science+fundamentals&pg=1

1.1 INTRODUCTION

Today's communication systems involve a complex mixture of proprietary and nonproprietary technologies that span software, firmware, and hardware. Systems typically combine both analog and digital techniques, which in turn involve an array of protocol standards that describe everything from data framing to physical interfaces. This complex picture combined with the fast pace of innovation and the offering of new capabilities by service providers and manufacturers only serves to further complicate our understanding of modern communication systems.

Due to a constant barrage of system offerings and an ever-growing list of new acronyms that describe new or relabeled capabilities, new IT graduates and managers are faced with the hurdle of understanding what these technologies offer, and how they might be applied in support of their organizations.

Basic to understanding current and new communications technologies is the understanding of the physical laws and theories that govern the principles of communications. As an example, knowing the basic idea of how radio waves are created and propagated gives you a better appreciation of the challenges faced by the cellular phone industry in their quest to provide greater data throughput and quality video programming.

In this chapter, we will discuss the basic theories of electrical and electromagnetic signals, and optics. We end the chapter by introducing basic measures used in communication systems such as the decibel, as well as fundamental concepts regarding the exchange of information between two communicating parties.

1.2 INTRODUCTION TO THE OSI REFERENCE MODEL

The digital communications between two or more entities involve numerous interface and protocol specifications. At the physical level, these specifications include the type of medium, whether copper wire, optical fiber, or radio frequency (RF) waves. It must also detail the type of electrical signal, the medium's impedance or resistance to the signal, the direction of flow of information, and so on. In addition to the physical specification, there must be an agreement regarding the framing

```
┌─────────────────────────────┐
│    7. APPLICATION LAYER      │
├─────────────────────────────┤
│    6. PRESENTATION LAYER     │
├─────────────────────────────┤
│    5. SESSION LAYER          │
├─────────────────────────────┤
│    4. TRANSPORT LAYER        │
├─────────────────────────────┤
│    3. NETWORK LAYER          │
├─────────────────────────────┤
│    2. DATA LINK LAYER        │
├─────────────────────────────┤
│    1. PHYSICAL LAYER         │
└─────────────────────────────┘
```

FIGURE 1.1 The OSI seven-layer reference model.

of digital information in the form of logical 1s and 0s. If we consider the Internet, as an example, where multiple service provider networks are involved, then additional complexity is introduced since most networks involved will operate using their own network parameters or protocol standards. In an attempt to organize this complex mix of protocol standards and their functions, the *International Organization for Standardization (ISO)* developed the *OSI (Open Systems Interconnection) Reference Model*. The purpose of the *OSI Reference Model* is to categorize the various functions that are required of protocols used for digital communications, by aligning them to a layered architectural framework. It should be noted, however, that the seven-layer model (fig. 1.1) is a reference framework that assists us in understanding the functions of adopted protocols, but it is not a mandatory framework used for development purposes. As an example, the TCP/IP protocol suite does not align perfectly into the OSI model; yet we use the OSI framework to better understand the functions related to the TCP/IP suite of protocols (e.g., IP is an OSI layer 3 protocol used for end-to-end network communications).

Physical Layer 1. Layer 1 of the OSI model represents the physical layer. We might think of the physical layer as representing the physics behind the communications. In this layer, the type of medium is described, whether copper twisted pair (TP), coaxial cable, fiber optic, wireless radio frequency, or free-space optics (FSO). Layer 1 also includes the mechanical and electrical interface specifications of the transmitter and receiver to the medium itself. As an example, both the physical dimensions and electrical characteristics of an RJ-45 connector interfacing twisted pair copper wires are considered parts of the physical layer 1 specification. Parameters of the electrical, electromagnetic, or optical signal are described in this layer. Parameters include methods of *line coding* binary logical data (1s or 0s), digital modulation techniques, the coding and decoding of analog and digital information, signal power transmission, interface impedance,[1] and many other parameters necessary for connectivity. The initial framing of logical data is also considered a function of this layer (e.g., Ethernet). Data framing enables the differentiation of the header information, which contains source/destination addresses and other information used to enable network communications, from the actual payload containing user data. By doing this, both transmitter and receiver understand where a dataword begins and where it ends, as opposed to seeing a stream of seemingly endless logical 1s and 0s.

---

[1] Impedance is the combination of resistance and reactance found in a conductive medium that oppose signal current and voltage, thus causing signal attenuation. Reactance is a combination of the capacitive and inductive properties that are present in the medium when the direction of current changes over time (e.g., signal current).

Data Link Layer 2. Layer 2 describes the communications between nodes within a common network. In a *common network* (data link network), all connected nodes share a common protocol standard and set of rules that are assigned and managed by a single organization. This enables full control of the network by the organization or service provider, and avoids the need for protocol conversions when data is exchanged between nodes within the same network. As an example, an Ethernet local area network (LAN) is administered and managed by the organization that is served by the LAN. Network service providers offer common network services in the form of wide area networks (WANs) that are offered to subscribers. However, if a node in one common network wishes to communicate with a node in a different common network, then the network layer 3 of the OSI model gets involved, and a protocol conversion at the data link layer 2 is typically required.

Network Layer 3. Today, it is common for devices on one common (layer 2) network such as Ethernet to require access to other devices or servers on different common networks. Enabling devices to communicate across different common networks is the job of network layer 3 protocols. The best known of these protocols is the Internet Protocol (IP), which provides end-to-end connectivity over numerous data link layer 2 networks. Since the network layer depends upon the protocols residing at layer 2 below, coordination between the two layers is necessary. As an example, if a node on an Ethernet LAN wishes to communicate outside of its own network, it must map its layer 2 medium access control (MAC) address to a layer 3 IP address. By doing this, Ethernet can direct the communications through a network gateway that is connected to the external destination network.

Transport Layer 4. Network layer 3 protocols enable data to be sent from the source node to the destination node over different underlying networks at the data link layer 2. Above the network layer, the transport layer 4 has several responsibilities that include the establishment of connection-oriented or connectionless communication sessions between end points, and the identification of the application to which the data is intended. Today, computers and servers are capable of multi-tasking applications. As an example, an FTP session may work concurrently with a web browser or e-mail exchange. As such, multiple communications sessions may occur simultaneously. Transport protocols such as the Transport Control Protocol (TCP) and User Datagram Protocol (UDP) ensure that the data received at the network layer 3 level is sent to the proper application within the computer. TCP, which is a connection-oriented protocol, also ensures that sessions (e.g., data flow control and delivery assurances) are established between the proper source and destination applications. TCP and UDP are two examples of layer 4 protocols that are commonly used on the Internet.

Session Layer 5. Session layer 5 is not used as often as the other layers described above. Some data exchanges require that special sessions between end points be established to provide unique features or higher reliability than that provided by lower layers. Some examples include e-commerce, transaction processing, and messaging. The session layer enables greater control over a particular session. In some cases, this greater control can be provided by software applications operating at the application layer 7.

Presentation Layer 6. Many types of data formats can be exchanged between communicating end-points. The presentation layer 6 identifies the specific format that the data is following, as well as service that should be performed, such as data decryption. Data formats can include images (.jpg, .tiff, .gif, etc.), text (ASCII, extended ASCII, Unicode, etc.), video (.mpg, .wma, etc.), audio (.mp3, etc.), and other format types.

Application Layer 7. The application layer is where the application program resides. The application program is the intended destination for the data. Applications can be multimedia for human interface, or machine-to-machine (M2M).

With the definitions of the seven layers that make up the OSI Reference Model, we now have a framework by which we can begin to describe the complex interactions that must take place between communicating endpoints over several networks.

As an example in fig. 1.2, a user on Ethernet LAN 1 desires to send data to a user residing on Ethernet LAN 2. In order to establish a connection, the data must traverse two service provider layer 2 networks A and B, which operate on different protocols. In addition, since IEEE 802.3 describes a family of Ethernet-based specifications, there is no guarantee that Ethernet LANs 1 and 2 will operate on the same exact specification (e.g., 100Base-T compared to 1000Base-T). Since LAN 2 is not reachable within the LAN 1 common network, a network layer 3 protocol is required. The user on LAN 1 must know the network layer address of the user on LAN 2. This destination network address is part of the header that is appended to the user data to create the network layer packet. Since the destination address is not reachable on LAN 1, the packet is sent to a network gateway connected to service provider A's common data link network. At the gateway, LAN 1's data link layer envelope is removed

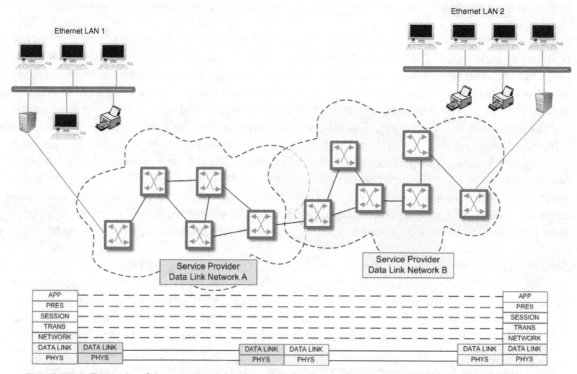

FIGURE 1.2 Example of data communications across disparate layer 2 networks. Below the network diagram, the OSI RM stack is depicted showing the connection between the communicating nodes on LANs 1 and 2. The solid lines indicate a direct connection through the networks, while the dashed lines indicate virtual connections that depend upon layers below.

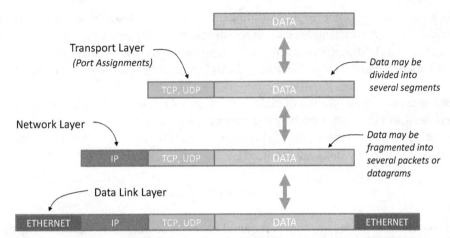

FIGURE 1.3 Appending data headers that represent protocol layers. As data is received by the transport layer 4, a TCP or UDP header is appended. Next, the network layer 3 IP header is appended to enable end-to-end delivery of the IP packet over disparate data link layer common networks. Finally, a data link layer 2 envelope is added to enable data transmission within the common network.

and replaced by A's data link envelope. The packet traverses A's data link network, until it reaches the gateway to service provider B's data link network. Like before, A's data link layer envelope is exchanged for B's envelope. Finally, after traversing B's network, it reaches LAN 2's gateway and again exchanges B's data link envelope for LAN 2's Ethernet envelope. Since the destination network layer address remains unchanged throughout the packet's journey through several layer 2 common networks, LAN 2's gateway server is able to map the destination layer 3 address to the correct layer 2 users Ethernet address for delivery. Once the data link frame reaches the user on LAN 2, the Ethernet envelope is removed and the data is delivered to the upper layers of the destination node.

Data produced by computer applications are prepared for network transmission by appending header information to the data at layers 4, 3, and 2. In fig. 1.3 a transport layer 4 header is appended to the data providing information regarding the application that the data is intended for. In the case of TCP and UDP, source and destination ports identify specific applications such as file transfer, email, web browser, or other user-defined application. Next the network layer 3 header is appended identifying source and destination IP addresses. This enables the end-to-end packet delivery across different data link layer 2 networks. Finally, the layer 2 header is appended enabling the data frame to traverse across the common network. In order to ensure proper delivery, layers 2 and 3 source and destination addresses are mapped to one another through protocols to be discussed in a later chapter. It should be noted that throughout this process, data is fragmented into segments and packets as it moves through the various layers.

1.3 INTRODUCTION TO NETWORKS

A basic description of a network is a set of nodes that are interconnected through some physical medium, whether guided (i.e., wire or fiber optic) or unguided (radio frequency or free space optics), that is used to facilitate communications between those nodes. "Node" is a general term that describes a connection point for network links. Of course, we know that networks have highly complex architectures in which nodes can represent routers, switches, gateway servers, and so on, all operating at various OSI protocol layers. However, in order to better understand the implementation of today's modern networks, we will first discuss some simple networking concepts.

Let's consider a network that consists of eight nodes (fig. 1.4). Each node in the network is required to communicate with every other node in the network. As such, each node must have a dedicated link to every other node in the network. This is termed a *full mesh network*. By using equation (1.1), we can determine how many links are required for our eight-node network.

$$X = \frac{N(N-1)}{2} = \text{number of links required} \tag{1.1}$$

X represents the number of links or trunks required between devices or nodes, and N is the number of devices/nodes in our network. For our eight-node network, this equates to 28 links.

$$X = \frac{8(7)}{2} = 28 \text{ links}$$

Therefore, our full mesh network will require 28 links to support eight nodes. While having a dedicated link between each node presents very high overall network reliability, the cost associated with purchasing the high number of links is a disadvantage. In addition, if we were to add a ninth node to our network, we would be required to add additional eight links. So extensibility of full mesh networks is poor.

In most cases, we do not need to have the high reliability offered by a full mesh network. It is more cost-effective to build only the number of links needed to meet network reliability[2] requirements for a specified purpose. Figures 1.5(a) and 1.5(b) are two examples of *partial mesh networks*.

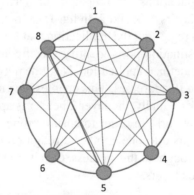

FIGURE 1.4 Full mesh connected network. Each communicating node is connected to every other node.

---

[2] Network reliability provides the percentage of time that the network is fully operational. This is dependent upon numerous factors such as the mean time between failures (MTBF) of critical pieces within the network.

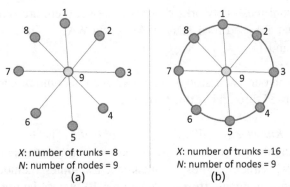

FIGURE 1.5 Examples of partial mesh networks. The number of trunks used typically depends upon the network reliability required.

Network devices such as switches enable links to be shared by more than just the directly connected nodes. As an example, in fig. 1.5(b), while nodes 1 and 3 have no direct connection, data can be sent through either node 2 in one direction or nodes 8, 7, 6, 5, and 4 in the opposite direction. In order to do this, each node must be able to read the destination address of the data so that it can move the data to the next link. The network device that reads the address of the data frame and places it onto the correct link is called the switch.

A switch is a device that is connected to two or more nodes within a network. It has the ability to read the destination address of a received data frame, and make the appropriate connection to an outgoing switch port based upon this address. The concept of switching goes back to the earliest days of the public switched telephone network (PSTN) where telephone operators would make manual connections to the appropriate trunk lines in order to service their customers' calls. Doing this enabled the average telephone user to connect to any telephone in the network, while minimizing the number of trunk lines needed between users. More discussion regarding the PSTN is found in chapter 7.

Returning to fig. 1.5(a), we see that the network is in a physical star configuration. A switching node, 9, has been added, with links reaching out to each node. If node 1 wishes to send data to node 3, it must first go to the switch located at node 9. The switch inspects the data frame to determine the destination address, and then transmits the data through the appropriate switching port that interfaces to the link connected to node 3. By using this configuration, we only need eight links plus an additional switching node located in the center. This results in a major decrease in the number of links required when compared to the full mesh network. Of course, the disadvantage is that this network has a *single point of failure* which is node 9. Failure of the central switching node essentially brings down the entire network.

By adding additional links between adjacent nodes as in fig. 1.5(b), an improvement in reliability is realized. Now if the central node 9 fails, data can still be transmitted to each node. However, each node is required to have switching capability similar to the central node.

Today, partial mesh networks are used extensively. The Internet is an example of a partial mesh network that is resilient to both nodal or link failures.

Besides the full and partial mesh networks described above, there are other physical and logical network architectures that are used for LANs, MANs, and WANs. These will be discussed in further detail in chapters 6 and 7.

Before going any further in our discussion of networks and telecommunications, we need to define a few terms that will be used throughout this textbook.

Data, Information, and Knowledge—What we communicate. The terms data, information, and knowledge all have different meanings, and are organized in a hierarchical manner. At the lowest level is data. Data is raw, without context or meaning. Examples include binary logical 1s and 0s from a computer or analog signals from a transmitter. By itself, data provides no real insights. Information is at the next level in the hierarchy. With information, accumulated data provides context that can be interpreted. As examples, binary data in the form of Unicode gives you symbols and words with meaning. Telemetry data can be aggregated into information that represents the status of hardware, firmware, or software. Finally, the top of the hierarchy is knowledge. Knowledge is information that is "actionable." As an example, imagine a satellite that is drifting away from its assigned position. The telemetry sent by the satellite is received by an operator at a ground station, who then interprets the information, and makes a corrective maneuver based upon knowledge.

Links, Channels, Trunks, and Circuits—Are they all the same? Many of these terms can be used interchangeably with slight differences in meaning depending upon the type of communication systems you are referring to. As an example, a link is a connection between two or more nodes, however, this could also be referred to as a channel, especially when referring to a wireless link. Of course, you are probably saying to yourself that your cable television box provides channels through a wired or guided medium and you would also be correct. As you might have concluded, many of these terms overlap, so the best we can do is define what they typically refer to.

A communications *link* exists between two or more nodes in order to exchange analog or digital information. When two endpoints are communicating, we refer to this as a *circuit*. Circuits represent a complete communications path, end-to-end, between entities and are comprised of several links. *Trunks* are similar to links except that they support multiple users. While a link typically serves a single communicating pair (e.g., client and server), trunks support multiple connections. When we think of telephone trunks between switching offices, we typically think about multiple simultaneous calls that are aggregated onto the medium. Finally, channels, similar to links, typically support a single communications pair, or in the case of a broadcast, a single station from a radio broadcast tower. Of course, when we consider the definition of *virtual* connections, we see that the above definitions become a bit more ambiguous.

Virtual and Physical Connections. OSI layer 1 describes the physical connection between communicating devices. As discussed previously, the physical layer is comprised of the actual transmission medium and equipment used to communicate. By digitizing our communications, we can place multiple users on a single physical link or channel by separating user data frames by time. When the link is shared among multiple users, each user is said to have a *virtual* connection vice a connection that is physically dedicated. In most cases, the user is oblivious to the fact that the physical connection is being shared with other users.

Multiplexer. Combining multiple user connections into a single aggregate is called multiplexing. User connections, or channels, can be separated through channel frequency assignments or by time. Combining multiple frequency channels onto a single medium is termed *frequency division multiplexing (FDM)*, while combining user data by time slot assignments is termed *time division multiplexing (TDM)*. More will be said about multiplexing in later chapters.

Guided and Unguided Mediums. A transmission medium consists of the material or nonmaterial context in which the signal propagates. When medium such as copper twisted pair, coaxial cable, or fiber optic cable is used to send a signal, it is termed a *guided* medium. If, on the other hand, free space is used (i.e., radio or optical waves that travel through the air or the vacuum of space), then the term used is *unguided* medium.

Switches and Routers. Nodes connect communication links together in the form of a network. Nodes consist of network devices used to switch connections through a network. End devices such as terminals or servers are also considered nodes. As discussed earlier, *switches* read the destination address of incoming packets or data frames, and send these packets to the appropriate output port and connected link. Traditional switches operate at the OSI data link Layer, but today there are many switches that can operate on both OSI layers 2 and 3. The job of a layer 2 (L2) switch is to ensure that data is sent to the destination node within the data link common network. Layer 3 (L3) switches provide the functionality of traditional L2 switches, with the added functionality of a high-speed network layer router. *Routers* operate at the OSI network layer 3 and typically have greater intelligence than a traditional L2 switch. As a L3 device, the job of the router is to help ensure end-to-end connectivity between the source and destination end nodes. The ability to ensure an end-to-end connection at the network layer is required despite the presence of multiple disparate common networks in the layer below. Therefore, routers within a network must communicate to one another in order to exchange critical network status and *reachability* information. More will be discussed about routers and switches in a later chapter.

Transmitter, Receiver, and Transceiver. *Transmitters* send analog or digital signals through guided or unguided mediums. *Source* is another term used to describe a transmitter. A *receiver* receives the signal from a transmitter and is also called a *destination* or *sink*. The combination of a transmitter and receiver into a single device is termed a *transceiver*.

Full-duplex, Half-duplex, and Simplex. Communications between two or more entities occur in three basic ways. With one-way "simplex" communications, the source sends transmissions to one or more receivers over a single channel or circuit, with no expectation of a response back from the receiver. An example of simplex communications is broadcast radio or television. With "half-duplex" (HDX), communications occur between two or more entities over a single circuit or channel. Since the channel is shared between all users, only one user can send a transmission at a time. Push-to-talk (PTT) radios are an example of HDX communications where an RF channel is shared between communicating parties. If two or more PTT operators attempt to transmit at the same time, interference is heard and communications are disrupted. With "full-duplex" (FDX) communications, communicating entities can send and receive simultaneously. FDX communications typically involve separate frequency channels or circuits that provide different send and receive paths. This enables users to transmit and receive at the same time. However, analog telephone communications over a single *unshielded twisted pair (UTP) local loop* are an exception where FDX communications are possible. In this case, we are able to talk and listen simultaneously over a single wire pair even though our transmit and receive signals are being combined on the shared guided medium (i.e., local loop). Two reasons why this is possible involve the use of a telephone device called a *magnetic hybrid*,[3] which helps to separate and combine transmit and receive analog voice signals between the network and the user, and the human ear's ability to separate the transmit and receive analog signals during a phone conversation.

1.4 ELECTRICAL SIGNALS

1.4.1 The DC Circuit

In order to understand how modern communication systems work, it is helpful to discuss some basic ideas about electricity. The three major components of an electrical circuit are current, voltage, and resistance. *Ohm's law* [equation (1.2)] describes the relationship between these components.

$$V \text{ (volts)} = I \text{ (amperes)} \times R \text{ (ohms)} \qquad (1.2)$$

Figure 1.6 depicts a simple DC (direct current) electrical circuit showing voltage, current, and resistance. Current (*I*) is the flow of electrons through a conductive material such as copper and is measured in units of *amperes*. Voltage (*V*), also termed *electromotive force (emf)*, represents the potential energy existing between two points within a circuit and is measured in units of *volts*. For example, a battery has potential energy between its positive and negative terminals. When this potential energy is connected to a load, current flows from the battery to the load creating power. Resistance (*R*), measured in *ohms* (Ω), describes *resistance* to the flow of current through a conductive wire and through an attached load such as a motor or light bulb. In the DC circuit depicted in fig. 1.6, voltage remains constant and the flow of current remains in a single direction.

Two other basic elements of an electrical circuit are *capacitance* and *inductance*. A capacitor stores an electrical charge between parallel plates of opposite voltage polarity. Capacitance is typically represented by the letter "*C*" and measured in units of *farads*. As current flows into a capacitor,

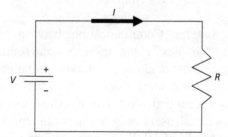

FIGURE 1.6 Basic DC electrical circuit. In a DC circuit, current only flows in one direction.

---

[3] Telephone hybrid magnetic coils are used to interconnect four-wire (two pair) analog network links to two-wire (one pair) customer local loops. Telephone networks typically separated transmit from receive signal in order to amplify these signals separately through the network. The local loop is the dedicated wire pair servicing the customer.

it slowly builds up potential energy or voltage over time. When current is removed, the capacitor dissipates this stored energy over time. Therefore, capacitors are time and source dependent. Inductors are similarly source and time dependent; however, the energy stored in an inductor will resist any changes in current traveling through the inductor. Inductance is represented by the letter "*L*" and is measured in units of *henrys*.

The 12-volt battery in our automobile represents an *independent* source that provides power to the circuit. Of course, if we want to send electrical signals that represent information, there must be changes in voltage and current that correspond to the information we wish to send. In this case, the changes in voltage and current are dependent upon the information, and therefore we call this a *dependent* or *controlled* source. *Transducers*[4] such as a microphone take acoustic voice and change it to an electrical signal. We will discuss how we deal with changing voltage and currents in our circuit, but first we discuss the concept of power.

Electrical *power* is measured in units of watts, and represents the amount of energy (in joules) expended over a time. We can define this relationship in equation (1.3).

$$P(\text{watts}) = \frac{\text{energy(joules)}}{\text{time(seconds)}} \qquad \textbf{(1.3)}$$

Power in a DC circuit is dissipated by the resistor in the form of heat. Equation (1.4) is used to determine the amount of power in a resistor given either the voltage across or current through the resistor itself. Keep in mind that the wire used to connect electrical components together also has resistance, typically measured in *ohms* per unit length (e.g., 1 Ω/m). So for any conductive medium such as copper twisted pair wire, the copper itself has a measurable resistance that is dependent upon the length and diameter of the wire.

$$P = VI = I^2 R = \frac{V^2}{R} \qquad \textbf{(1.4)}$$

1.4.2 The AC Circuit and Signal Representation

In an alternating current (AC) circuit, current flow is constantly changing directions, and voltage is constantly changing polarity (fig. 1.7). Changing voltage or current can change in a *periodic* manner such as a repeating sinusoid, or in a *nonperiodic* manner such as an information signal (e.g., voice). An example[5] of a periodic signal is the utility power servicing our homes. It is a periodic source where both voltage and current change in a predictable sinusoidal manner, typically at a rate of 60 or 50 cycles per second or *Hertz*[6] (Hz).

---

[4] Transducers are devices that change one form of signal energy into another. As an example, transducers in communication systems are used to convert acoustic, thermal, or optical signals into electrical signals represented by changes in voltage and current.

[5] AC signals used in this example provide 60 Hz utility power; however, we will see in chapters 2 and 3 that periodic sinusoidal waves are also used extensively in telecommunication systems. The principles behind each are identical.

[6] Named after the 19th-century physicist Heinrich Hertz. One Hz (Hertz) equals the number of cycles of a periodic wave in one second (i.e., cycles per second).

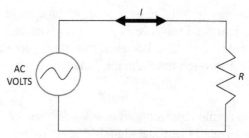

FIGURE 1.7 AC electrical circuit.

A 60 Hz wave is shown in fig. 1.8. The *x*-axis is time (seconds) and the *y*-axis represents voltage. The sinusoidal wave in fig. 1.8 is a *sine* wave; however, we could have easily used a *cosine* wave in this example. The importance is that a periodic wave repeats itself continuously. One cycle of the sine wave (i.e., the point at which the sine wave begins to repeat itself) has a time measure called the *period* of the wave, represented by *T*. In the case of fig. 1.8, the period of the sine wave is $T = 0.0167$ s. At any point in time, represented by the variable *t*, we can determine the actual value of the sine wave in volts by solving the sine wave equation (1.5).

$$v(t) = A \sin(2\pi ft \pm \phi) \tag{1.5}$$

$$f \text{ (frequency of the wave in Hz)} = \frac{1}{T} \tag{1.6}$$

A represents the *peak amplitude* of the sine wave, *f* is the frequency of the wave which equals $1/T$ in equation (1.6), *t* is the time variable, and ϕ is the phase angle of the sinusoid. Wavelength is

60 Hertz sine wave

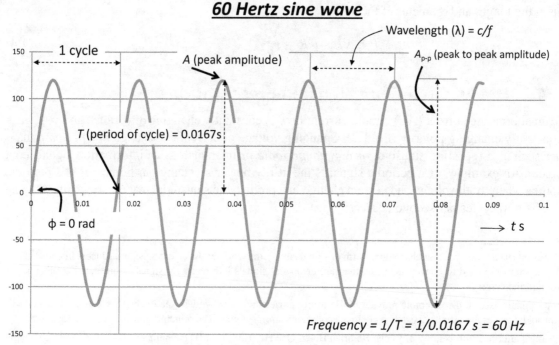

FIGURE 1.8 60 Hz signal showing voltage versus time (seconds).

measured between the peak amplitudes of a periodic wave (also equal to the length of one sinusoidal cycle) in units of length such as meters. Wavelength and frequency are related by equation (1.7). As we can see, wavelength and frequency are inversely proportional to one another by the *speed of light through a vacuum,* meaning that as frequency increases, wavelength decreases.

$$\text{Wavelength } (\lambda) = \frac{c(\text{speed of light})}{f(\text{Hz})} \text{ (Hz), where } c = 3 \times 10^8 \text{ m/s}^7 \qquad \textbf{(1.7)}$$

Example 1.1: In fig. 1.8, given $A = 120$ V, what is the frequency of the sine wave in Hz, and the voltage at $t = 0.004175$ s? (Assume phase angle $\phi = 0$.)

Answer: By looking at the sine wave in fig. 1.8, we see that one cycle ends at $T = 0.0167$ s. By using equation (1.6), the frequency of this sine wave is

$$f(\text{Hz}) = \frac{1}{T} = \frac{1}{0.0167 \text{ s}} = 59.88 \text{ or approximately } \underline{60 \text{ Hz}}$$

Using equation (1.5),

$$v(t) = A \sin(2\pi ft \pm \phi) = 120 \sin(2\pi(60)0.004175) = \underline{120 \text{ V}}$$

Since $t = 0.004175$ s is 1/4 of T, we see that peak amplitude occurs at t, which is consistent with fig. 1.8.

The sinusoidal waveform can shift along the horizontal time axis. This shift along the horizontal axis is called the *phase shift* of the sinusoid and it determines the position of the wave with respect to time in units of *degrees* or *radians*. We know that the time it takes for the sinusoidal wave to complete one cycle is equal to the period, T, in seconds. Another way we can visualize this concept is to think of a sinusoidal wave as a point traveling in a circle, continuously repeating itself. The sinusoidal waveform travels in a clockwise direction around the circumference of the circle in one period, T seconds (fig. 1.9). Completion of one-quarter of the wave equals $T/4$ seconds. Half of the wave is completed in $T/2$ seconds, and so on, until the full wave is completed in T seconds.

Now, instead of using time, let's think of our circle as divided into degrees and/or radians, similar to a compass (fig. 1.10). At the beginning of the sinusoidal wave, our point is at the top of the compass at $0°$ (0 rad). At $T/4$ seconds, our wave is at $90°$ ($\pi/2$ rad), at $T/2$ seconds at $180°$ (π rad), at $3T/4$ seconds at $270°$ ($3\pi/2$ rad), and at T seconds $360°$ (2π rad). The phase angle in degrees or radians essentially tells us where the periodic wave cycle begins. Since we defined the wave in fig. 1.10 as a *sine wave*, we observe that the cycle begins at $t = 0$ s, which corresponds to $0°$ (0 rad). Therefore, our phase angle is $0°$ (0 rad). We can use either radians or degrees when describing phase shifts and can easily convert between the two using the relationship $180° = \pi$ rad. By knowing the phase angle in rads or degrees, we can use equations (1.5) to plot the sinusoidal response over time. *Note: In this text, we will use radian measure vice degrees.*

---

[7] We can also represent 3×10^8 m/s using the notation 3E8 m/s, where "E" is the exponent (i.e., 10 to the power of E). In this text, we will use both notations.

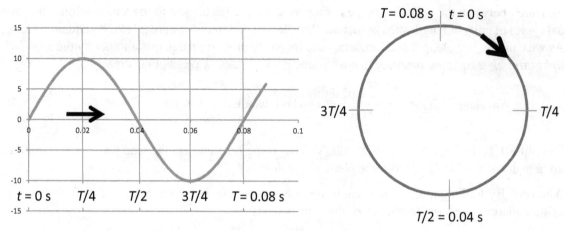

FIGURE 1.9 Sinusoidal wave can be represented by a circle.

Example 1.2: Determine the equation for the waveform in fig. 1.10.

Answer: First, determine the frequency of the wave. $T = 0.08$ s; therefore, $f = 1/T = 1/0.08 = 12.5$ Hz. The peak amplitude of the wave is 10 V. The sine wave begins at $t = 0$, so the phase angle is also zero. When applying equation (1.5), we can convert degrees to radians using the following relationship.

$$\text{radians} = \frac{\pi \,(\text{radians})}{180 \,(\text{degrees})} \times \underline{\quad}(\text{degrees})$$

The final equation that describes this waveform is, $v(t) = 10 \sin(2\pi(12.5 \text{ Hz})t + 0 \text{ rad})$

Now let's say that our sine wave is shifted to the right in time so that the beginning of the wave starts $T/4$ seconds later than before. The beginning of the sine wave in fig. 1.11 is now $t = 0.02$ s later, which shifts our phase angle by $-90°$ or $-\pi/2$ rad (negative sign denotes a shift of the wave

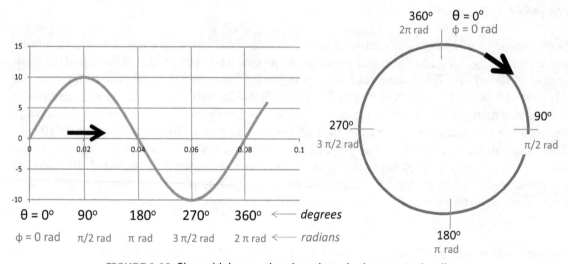

FIGURE 1.10 Sinusoidal wave showing phase in degrees and radians.

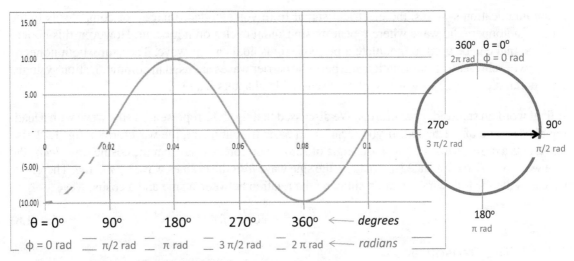

FIGURE 1.11 Lagging sine wave with a phase angle, $\phi = -\pi/2$ rad $= -1.57$ rad.

to the right). We say that this sine wave at $\phi = -\pi$ rad is *lagging* the previous sine wave. The equation that represents the sine wave in fig. 1.11 is now

$$v(t) = 10 \sin\left(2\pi(12.5 \text{ Hz}) - \frac{\pi}{2}\right) = 10 \sin(2\pi(12.5 \text{ Hz}) - 1.57)$$

If we instead shift the sine wave in fig. 1.10 to the left so that the cycle begins $T/4$ seconds prior to $t = 0$ (i.e., $t = +T/4$), then our phase angle becomes $\phi = +\pi/2$ rad $= +1.57$ rad and the equation representing the sine wave in fig. 1.12 becomes

$$v(t) = 10 \sin\left(2\pi(12.5 \text{ Hz}) + \frac{\pi}{2}\right) = 10 \sin(2\pi(12.5 \text{ Hz}) + 1.57)$$

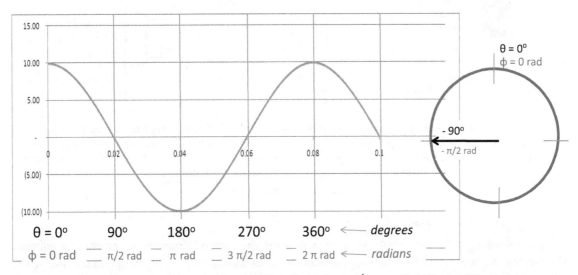

FIGURE 1.12 Leading sine wave with a phase angle, $\phi = +\pi/2$ rad $= +1.57$ rad.

In communication systems, the electrical signal from voice, video, images, or computer is in the form of a nonperiodic wave where repeating sinusoidal cycles do not occur. However, this nonperiodic signal can be used to modulate a periodic sinusoidal carrier wave. Therefore, both nonperiodic waves representing information and periodic carrier waves are used in communication systems. The modulation of carrier waves will be discussed in chapters 2 and 3.

A final word on sinusoidal waveforms. We discussed that fig. 1.12 represents a sine wave with a leading phase angle of +1.57 rad. If you recall from basic trigonometry, the waveform in fig. 1.12 also represents a *cosine wave* with a phase angle of zero. Therefore, we say that the cosine wave *leads* the sine wave by $\pi/2$ rad, or stated alternately, the sine wave *lags* the cosines wave by $\pi/2$ rad. Therefore, we can write the following equation showing the relation between a sine and a cosine wave:

$$v(t) = A \sin\left(2\pi ft + \frac{\pi}{2}\right) = A \cos(2\pi ft) \tag{1.8}$$

1.4.2.1 The Transducer

A *transducer* is a device that changes a signal's energy from one form to another form (e.g., optical to electrical, acoustic to electrical, etc.). As an example, in fig. 1.13 a speaker talks into a transducer called a microphone. By speaking, an acoustic pressure wave is created that begins to vibrate air molecules along its path to the microphone. The microphone detects the pressure of the acoustic wave front, and converts this energy into changes in resistance within the microphone. This has the effect of changing the voltage and current as a function of the acoustic wave. Therefore, an electrical signal is created that accurately represents the acoustic information received. The electrical signal propagates through the circuit until it reaches another transducer, which is the speaker. The speaker converts the electric signal back into an acoustic one through the use of permanent magnets and a speaker diaphragm which vibrates according to the changes in the electrical signal's current.

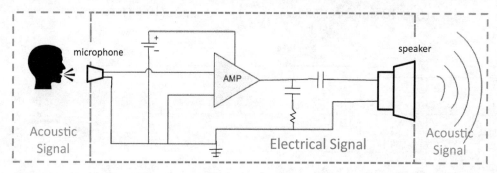

FIGURE 1.13 The transducer (i.e., microphone) converts acoustic voice energy to an electrical signal consisting of changes in voltage and current. The electrical signal travels through the circuit until it reaches another transducer, this time the speaker. The speaker then converts the electrical signal back into an acoustic signal which our ears can detect.

Head icon © Arcady/Shutterstock.com

1.4.3 Modeling the Communications Transmission Line

Electrical signals, whether they are periodic or nonperiodic, involve changes in current and voltage. The fact that we now have a time varying element increases the complexity of our circuit analysis when compared to the simple DC case. As a result, differential equations and phasor math using complex numbers are typically applied to accurately determine power, current, voltage, and impedance. *Impedance* in AC circuits is represented by a complex[8] number involving resistance and reactance, and is represented by equation (1.9). In other words, it is the contribution of both real resistance (R) and the varying reactance from elements such as inductors (L) and capacitors (C). Similar to resistance in a DC circuit, impedance "*impedes*" the current flow within AC circuits. Since communications involve both periodic (e.g., carriers) and nonperiodic waves, we typically use the term *impedance* when discussing communication systems. Readers are encouraged to delve further into these specific concepts; however, for the purposes of this discussion, we will not go further into the mathematical representations.

$$Z(\text{Impedance}) = R \text{ (resistance)} + jX \text{ (reactance)}, \text{ where } j = (-1)^{1/2} \quad \textbf{(1.9)}$$

Let's review what we've learned so far. An electrical communications system involves the transmission of information in the form of an electrical signal. This signal can be periodic, as in the case of a carrier wave (to be discussed in chapter 2), or nonperiodic in the case of a voice or video stream. In order to create an electrical signal from an acoustic, thermal, or photonic, source, we use transducers which change the energy of the signal from one form to another. Once the electrical signal is created based upon source information, it travels through the communications circuits. Elements such as voltage, current, impedance, inductance, and capacitance characterize how our signal will behave as it propagates through the circuit.

As an example, consider the case of an unshielded twisted pair copper cable.[9] Two wires (i.e., one pair) are used to transmit an electrical signal. As mentioned previously, the wire will have a value of resistance (R) and inductance (L), the later created by the changes in current flowing through the wires. Although each wire is electrically insulated by a dielectric material, they will nonetheless interact electromagnetically with one another thus creating capacitance (C) between the wires. These values are a function of wire diameter, dielectric insulation, and wire length. The flow of current is therefore impeded by both the resistive value of the wire (R), and the reactive values of inductance and capacitance and is represented by impedance[10] (Z). Note that R, L, and C of the conductor are not discrete elements, but are continuous throughout the length of the wire. Therefore, as the length of wire increases, so does the values of R, L, and C, which means that they have a greater impact over our electrical signal. This makes common sense since we know that the longer the wire, the more impedance encountered which impedes the flow of signal current, thus weakening the overall electrical signal. With this information, we can model our transmission circuit as shown in fig. 1.14.

In fig. 1.14, *Vs* is a dependent electrical signal source that represents changes in voltage and current which are proportional to the information signal we are sending. As current flows through the wire, a magnetic field is created that surrounds each wire. This magnetic field interacts with the electrical signal and is represented by the inductance of the wire, labeled L (inductance). The wire itself has

---

[8] Impedance is represented by the complex number Z (impedance) $= R$ (resistance) $+ jX$ (reactance). Note that $j = (-1)^{1/2}$ and therefore reactance is called the ***imaginary*** part of the complex number.

[9] Concepts described here are applicable for any guided transmission system using two conductors, whether in a balanced configuration such as TP, or single signal wire with separate ground such as a coaxial cable.

[10] The impedance value of a line is used to characterize the line. Matching the impedance of an antenna, connector or other device to the impedance of the line is critical in order to avoid signal reflection and distortion.

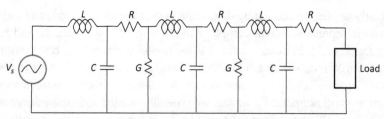

FIGURE 1.14 Transmission line representation of a communications transmission line. *Vs* represents a dependent signal source, *L* is the inductance of the line, *R* is resistance, *C* is the capacitance that exists between the two wires, and *G* is conductance, also considered the leakage current across the capacitor.

resistance as discussed previously, and this is represented by the letter *R* (resistance). *C* (capacitance) represents the interaction between the two wires within the pair, which creates a voltage potential. Given this interaction, selection of the dielectric material is critical for signal quality and propagation. Finally, conductance, *G*, which is essentially the opposite of resistance, represents leakage current through the capacitor, *C*. These elements are continuous across the entire length of the conductor.

The transmission line model gives us several insights about the propagation of an electrical signal through a wire.

- We see that impedance, made up of both resistive and reactive values, increases as the length of our communications line increases, which in turn contributes to signal attenuation.
- The reactive elements inherent within our transmission line causes signal voltage and current phase angles to differ, thereby effecting our signal power calculations.
- As signal frequency increases, the resistive part of impedance decreases, but the reactive part increases. Therefore, a signal traveling through any conductive material will have different characteristics depending upon signal frequency. As an example, frequency increase results in an increase of signal attenuation as well as an increase in the capacitive interaction between adjacent wires (i.e., causing interference or *crosstalk* between wires).
- Dielectric material used to insulate wires will help reduce wire interaction, however this is dependent upon the type of dielectric material as well as signal frequency.
- The impedance value of a conductive wire is a function of the physical wire diameter, length and type of insulation (dielectric). Larger wire diameters present lower signal resistance than smaller diameter wires. Therefore, wires with larger diameters can transmit more information over longer distances and with less resistance than smaller diameter wires.
- The type of conductive material is also critical since transmission line values are specific to the conductive material used (e.g., copper is a better conductor than aluminum).

1.4.4 Signal Power

A key goal of any communication systems is to transmit a signal with sufficient power to ensure reception by the receiver at the other end. If our transmission system was purely resistive (i.e., no reactive capacitance or inductance) and our signal DC, then power would simply be equal to voltage multiplied by current as in equation (1.4). Of course, we know that a communications signal varies in voltage and current over a conductive medium that has inherent reactive properties. If we want to determine signal power requirements under these conditions, we need to consider the effects of both a changing electrical signal and the impact of reactive components within the transmission medium.

Before we discuss how AC signal power is determined, we need to define a few concepts first. For simplicity we use a periodic cosine wave as our signal. In this case, both current and voltage signals are cosines, and we can determine the *instantaneous voltage and current* measurements at a specific time, *t*, by solving equations (1.10) and (1.11). Applying equation (1.12) gives us the *instantaneous power* of the signal. However, measuring a single instantaneous point in time does not tell us what the average power over time is; which is more useful. So we want to know what our average value of voltage, current, and power is. Unfortunately, if we were to simply take the mean of a cosine wave, the mean would equal zero,[11] and this would also not be useful. A popular way of determining average values of current and voltage is the RMS (root-mean-square) method. With this method, you first square the value of the voltage and current cosine signals, which results in all values becoming positive. You then take the mean of the squared cosine, and finally the square root of the mean. We denote RMS voltage and current signals as V_{RMS} and I_{RMS}, respectively. Simplifying the RMS method of current and voltage results in equations (1.13) and (1.14).

$$v(t) = V_p \cos(2\pi ft) \tag{1.10}$$

$$i(t) = I_p \cos(2\pi ft - \theta), \text{ where } \theta \text{ is the phase angle}$$
$$\text{difference between voltage and current} \tag{1.11}$$

$$p(t) = v(t) \times i(t) = [V \sin(2\pi ft)] \times [I \sin(2\pi ft - \theta)] \tag{1.12}$$

$$V_{\text{RMS}} = \frac{V_P}{\sqrt{2}}, \text{ where } V_P \text{ is peak voltage} \tag{1.13}$$

$$I_{\text{RMS}} = \frac{I_P}{\sqrt{2}}, \text{ where } I_P \text{ is peak current} \tag{1.14}$$

AC power is comprised of three related components that can be described in a diagram we call the *power triangle* in fig. 1.15. The first power component *P (in watts)* is termed *real* or *true* power, and

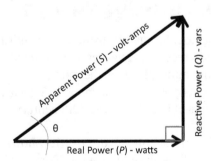

FIGURE 1.15 The Power Triangle.

---

[11] Half of a cosine wave is above zero, and therefore has a positive value, while the other half is below zero with a negative value. Therefore, the average value of the cosine wave over a single period, *T*, equals zero.

it represents the useful power needed to send the signal [equation (1.15)]. Maximizing true power is our goal. The second power component Q is called *reactive power* and is measured in units called var, which stand for *volt-ampere-reactive*[equation (1.16)]. Reactive power exists when reactive elements such as capacitance and inductance are present. Reactive power does not perform work; however, its presence decreases the amount of real power available in our system. In addition, the existence of reactive elements causes the phase angle, θ, between voltage and current signals to become out-of-phase from one another. The third component termed *apparent power* is a mathematical combination of real and reactive power measured in volt-amps[equation (1.17)]. *Note: The phase angle θ is the difference between voltage signal phase angle and current signal phase angle. Voltage is typically used as the reference when determining phase angle difference.*

$$\text{Real Power: } P = V_{\text{RMS}} I_{\text{RMS}} \cos\theta \text{ (watts)} \tag{1.15}$$

$$\text{Apparent Power: } S = V_{\text{RMS}} I_{\text{RMS}} \cos\theta \text{ (volt-amps)} \tag{1.16}$$

$$\text{Reactive Power: } Q = V_{\text{RMS}} I_{\text{RMS}} \cos\theta \text{ (var)} \tag{1.17}$$

From fig. 1.15, we see a cosine relationship between real and apparent power, equation (1.18) that we call the *power factor, PF*. PF gives us a metric to determine if our power transfer is efficient and maximized. For example, if voltage and current phases are aligned, then the difference in phase angle between the two is $\theta = 0$. This means that S(volt-amps) = P(watts), resulting in a resistive circuit. As such, all of available power is real power in watts (i.e., best case). However, if $\theta = 90°$ (or π rad), then our power is all reactive, which means no real power to perform work is available (i.e., worst case). Therefore, the closer PF can get to a value of 1, the better power transmission.

$$\text{Power Factor (PF)} = \cos\theta = \frac{P}{S} \tag{1.18}$$

In summary, we know that transmission lines will have reactive elements. When sending a periodic or nonperiodic signal, these reactive elements cause voltage and current phase angles to differ. As a result, the power available to the system (i.e., apparent power) is reduced to real and reactive components. Real power in watts is desirable, but is reduced by the existence of reactive power in var, which is not useful for the transmission of our signal.

1.5 ELECTROMAGNETIC WAVE THEORY

In section 1.4, we learned that electrical signals transmitted through a conductive wire can represent information between a sender and a receiver. However, if we wanted to transmit information through an unguided medium such as the atmosphere or the vacuum of outer space, how could this be accomplished? The answer is based upon electromagnetic (EM) wave theory and it was first discovered by the English physicist Michael Faraday in the 19th century.

In 1831, Faraday made one of his most significant discoveries showing that a moving magnetic field will cause an electrical current to flow through a wire. Conversely, a changing current whether periodic or nonperiodic, traveling through a conductive wire will produce both an electrical and magnetic (EM) field in free space around the wire. This relationship was later placed into a series of important equations by James Clerk Maxwell in 1864 called "Maxwell's Equations." These equations describe the phenomenon of electromagnetism and are taught even today to university students around the world who study physics and engineering.

MAXWELL'S EQUATIONS

During the 19th century, the Scottish physicist James Clerk Maxwell developed a series of elegant equations that describe the highly complex phenomena of electromagnetism. Known simply as "Maxwell's Equations," they placed into mathematical form the numerous observations made by physicists such Michael Faraday. Maxwell's equations were used by Albert Einstein in developing his famous "special theory of relativity."

Today, Maxwell's equations are integral to the understanding of antennas and electromagnetic wave propagation, and are taught to advanced college students in electrical engineering and physics.

In fig. 1.16 (a), current flow through a conductive wire creates an EM field that surrounds the wire. When an electrical signal represents information such as voice, it produces an EM field whose changes are proportional to the changes in the electrical signal, fig. 1.16(b). Therefore, the propagating EM wave carries information in the form of changes within the EM field. As the EM wave travels in free space, it will experience attenuation in signal strength. At the receiver, the EM wave encounters a receive antenna and a current is produced through the Faraday Effect, that is proportional to the EM wave. The electrical signal originally produced by the sender is now in the receive system for further processing. We will discuss more about electrical signal and EM propagation in chapter 4.

As mentioned earlier, information signals are nonperiodic; however, we can think about the human voice as being a complex combination of periodic sinusoidal waves operating simultaneously at different frequencies. The average human voice operates over a frequency range between 300 Hz and 3 kHz. This range can be thought of as the *frequency bandwidth*, which can be determined by subtracting the lowest frequency from the highest frequency in the range, see equation (1.19).

$$\text{Frequency Bandwidth (BW)} = f_{\text{Highest Freq.}} - f_{\text{Lowest Freq.}} \tag{1.19}$$

Let's consider the case of telephony. The public switched telephone network (PSTN) identifies a frequency bandwidth of 4 kHz for normal voice grade transmission. Whether we transmit voice

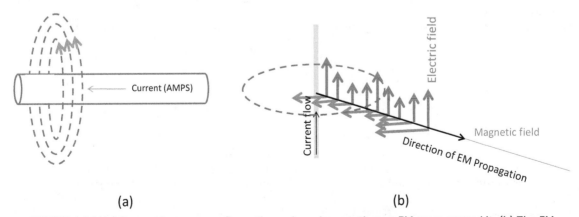

(a)   (b)

FIGURE 1.16 (a) Current in amperes flows through a wire creating an EM wave around it. (b) The EM wave created is comprised of an electrical field and magnetic field that are perpendicular to one another. The direction of propagation is outwardly, 360° around the wire.

through guided medium or as an EM wave through free space, our transmission would occupy a bandwidth of approximately 4 kHz. However, if the transmission medium were shared with other users, as in the case of free space, then users would interfere with one another since they would be operating on the same frequencies. Using only a single frequency would be impractical since only one conversation could take place at any given time. The solution would be to have every pair of communicating users operate on different channels, similar to the separate channels on a radio station. This where *modulation* and *carrier frequencies* come in.

Carriers are periodic sinusoidal waves that are used to "carry" information from sender to receiver at a specified frequency. Modulation is the process of taking our information signal, and using this signal to modify certain aspects of our carrier wave such as the *amplitude*, *frequency,* or *phase angle*. Once the carrier has been modified by the information[12] signal, we need only transmit the carrier frequency itself. Once the carrier is received, it goes through a *demodulation* process, which turns the carrier back into the original information signal. Now, if we wish to share the same medium[13] with multiple communicating users, we simply assign a different carrier frequency to each communicating pair.

The allocation of frequencies within the electromagnetic spectrum, shown in fig. 1.17, is managed and regulated by international organizations such as the International Telecommunications Union (ITU), as

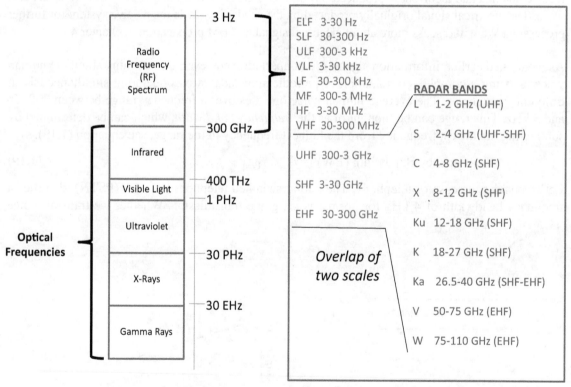

FIGURE 1.17 The Electromagnetic Spectrum. Note the overlap in designations within the RF spectrum—UHF, SHF, and EHF have further designations as "Radar Band" frequencies.

---

[12] In this text, we will also refer to the information signal as the *message.*

[13] Note: We can modulate information signals on either guided or unguided medium.

TABLE 1.1   Hertz Conversion.[14]

1 kHz (kilo)	1E3 Hz
1 MHz (mega)	1E6 Hz
1 GHz (giga)	1E9 Hz
1 THz (tera)	1E12 Hz
1 PHz (peta)	1E15 Hz
1 EHz (exa)	1E18 Hz
1 ZHz (zetta)	1E21 Hz

well as national agencies such as the Federal Communications Commission (FCC). Frequency and bandwidth allocations are assigned to particular uses such as AM and FM radio, cellular phone services, terrestrial microwave communications, satellite communications, as well as navigation, radar, and many more. Licensing to operate on these frequencies is required by regulators in order to avoid interference between operators. However, the exception to the licensing requirement exists for devices operating at the designated *Industrial, Scientific, Medical (ISM)* frequency bands (e.g., 2.4 GHz and 5 GHz) such as IEEE 802.15 WiFi routers. Devices operating in the ISM bands do not require specific license, however, the devices themselves must meet transmission specifications outlined by the regulatory agency.

Modulating a carrier signal with an information or message signal enables us to transmit the message on the carrier frequency. Both the transmitter and receiver must be tuned to the carrier frequency in order to complete the communications. The *unmodulated* carrier is a sinusoidal wave form with minimal bandwidth. When we modulate the carrier with information, the bandwidth of the signal increases. This increase is dependent upon the amount of information being transmitted. As an example, a video signal will occupy more frequency bandwidth than a voice signal. Regulatory agencies assign carrier frequencies in order to manage and control RF transmissions. In the case of ISM frequencies, no licensing is required; however device manufacturers must ensure that their products meet strict regulatory guidelines which are designed to minimize interference.

Frequency measurements are represented by the number of cycles per second. One cycle per second is called a Hertz (Hz), named after the German physicist Heinrich Rudolf Hertz who confirmed the validity of Maxell's equations in the late 1880's. Table 1.1 shows common units used to describe frequency. Note that the unit Hz is capitalized in honor of Heinrich Hertz's contribution towards our understanding of electromagnetic wave theory.

1.5.1 Power Density

In section 1.4.4, we discussed transmission power through guided medium in units of watts [equation (1.15)]. However, when signal power is transmitted from an antenna through free space, we have to take into consideration the signal spreading at the surface of the wave front as it propagates outwardly. The spreading of signal power over a surface area, given in units of meters squared in this case, is

---

[14] E.g., 1 GHz = 1×10^9 Hz = 1E9 Hz

proportional to the distance the signal travels. Therefore, the further the signal travels, the weaker the signal per unit surface area, resulting in signal attenuation. This concept can best be illustrated using the *ideal isotropic antenna* in fig. 1.18. An ideal isotropic antenna is a theoretical concept that describes the antenna as a single point. The signal pattern emanating from the isotropic antenna is in the shape of a perfect sphere where the signal power resides at the surface area of the sphere. As the signal continues to propagate away from the antenna, the sphere's surface area increases and the signal power spreads and weakens as distance from the antenna increases. In equation (1.20), transmitted power in watts is divided by the surface area of a sphere (i.e., area of sphere $= 4\pi d^2$, where d is the radius of the sphere), and is termed *power density* which is given in units of watts per meter squared.

$$\text{Power density, PD} = \frac{p}{4\pi d^2}, \text{(watts/m}^2) \tag{1.20}$$

Power (watts) is transmitted from the ideal isotropic antenna in fig. 1.18. At a distance from the antenna of $D1$ meters, the power density equals, $\text{PD} = \frac{p}{4\pi D1^2}$ in watts/m². As the signal continues to propagate outwardly, it reaches distance $D2$ meters. At this point, the power density of our signal is now, $\text{PD} = \frac{p}{4\pi D2^2}$ in watts/m². Since $D2 > D1$, the power density measured at $D2$ is less than the power density measured at $D1$.

Example 1.3: The transmitted power from an ideal isotropic antenna is 10 W. What is the power density, PD, measured at a distance of 100 meters from the transmitting antenna?

Answer: By applying equation (1.20),

$$\text{Power density, PD} = \frac{p}{4\pi d^2} = \frac{10 \text{ W}}{(4*\pi*(100 \text{ m})^2)} = \underline{79.58\text{E-6}} \text{ (watts/m}^2)$$

While building an ideal isotropic antenna is not possible, it provides a metric for comparing the effectiveness of real-world antennas. More will be discussed on this topic in later chapters.

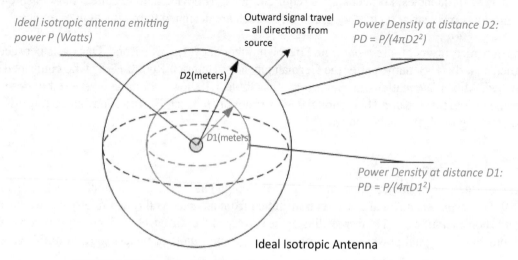

Ideal isotropic antenna emitting power P (Watts)

Outward signal travel – all directions from source

Power Density at distance D2: PD = P/(4πD2²)

D2(meters)

D1(meters)

Power Density at distance D1: PD = P/(4πD1²)

Ideal Isotropic Antenna

FIGURE 1.18 The Ideal Isotropic Antenna. Power density propagation.

1.6 OPTICAL SIGNAL BASICS

Today, optical systems are used extensively because of the high data rates that can be supported. This is principally due to the higher frequencies associated with optical signals compared to RF signals. While both RF and optical signals are electromagnetic waves, some of their behaviors differ in key ways. While RF exhibits wave-like features, light behaves with the characteristics of both a wave and a particle.

As discussed previously, electrical current traveling through a wire produces an EM wave that propagates outwardly. When this EM wave encounters another electrical conductor such as an antenna, it produces an electrical current proportional to the EM wave. A light source also produces an EM wave, however light consists of photons, or quanta of energy, which are electrically neutral in charge. Because of charge neutrality, light encountering a conductive antenna will not produce an electrical current. This also means that, unlike RF signals, light signals are immune from electromagnetic interference (EMI) from broadband sources such as lightening, electrical machinery, or interfering RF signal harmonics.

In the 1800s, Thomas Young conducted an experiment in which he aimed a light source through two thin linear openings (i.e., double-slits) toward a screen in order to observe the behavior of the light. At the time, some physicists believed that light behaved as a particle, while others believed that light behaved like a wave. Young conducted an experiment to determine which behavior was true. In his experiment, Young theorized that if light behaved as a particle, the light on the screen would appear as just two slits of light on the screen. However, if instead light behaved as a wave, then a wave pattern would appear on the screen. What Young observed was the appearance of wave patterns which demonstrated that light diffracted as a wave does. As a result, the wave theory of light was accepted among physicists for many years. However, in the 1900s, Max Planck theorized that light also behaved like a particle while conducting research on discrete values of light energy called *quanta*. Planck's discoveries gave rise to the discipline of quantum theory in physics and led to the idea that photons also traveled as bundles of energy (quanta) similar to the way particles travel, vice as a *continuous* wave of photons. Both observations are correct and today it is accepted that light behaves as both a wave and a particle, thus giving rise to the *dual nature* of light.

It goes without saying that optical signals are very different from RF signals. Major differences include:

- Optical communications are immune from RFI (radio frequency interference) since photons are neutral in charge.
- RF waves are produced by signal current or electrons traveling through a conductor, while optical signals are produced by photons from light sources which carry information. Because of these fundamental differences, the design of RF transmitters and receivers are very different from the optical light *sources* and *detectors*.
- Optical signals operate at much higher frequencies (THz or 10^{12} Hz range) than RF frequencies (3 KHz to 300 GHz range). The higher optical frequencies enable greater information carrying capacity over RF, but also higher signal attenuation and the need for more precise alignments between optical source and detector (i.e., line of sight, LOS).

TABLE 1.2   ITU-T Optical Transmission Bands (Window).

Band	Wavelgnth (nm)		Frequency (THz)	
	From	To	From	To
850 Band	810	890	370.37	337.08
O (Original Band)	1260	1360	238.10	220.59
E (Extended Band)	1360	1460	220.59	205.48
S (Short Wavelength Band)	1460	1530	205.48	196.08
C (Conventional Band)	1530	1565	196.08	191.69
L (Long Wavelength Band)	1565	1625	191.69	184.62
U (Ultra Long Wavelength Band)	1625	1675	184.62	179.10

Similar to RF designations, the ITU-T (International Telecommunication Union—Telecommunications) has organized and designated certain *optical wavelength windows* as shown in Table 1.2. When we refer to optical communications, we refer to the wavelength and the wavelength *window*[15] it occupies. This is similar to referring to frequencies and frequency bandwidth when discussing RF channels. Recall the inversely proportional relationship between frequency and wavelength in equation (1.7).

1.7 BASIC METRIC USED IN COMMUNICATION SYSTEMS—THE DECIBEL

A decibel is a relative measure between two quantities that is used to compare values, typically against some standard. As a ratio, a decibel is dimensionless (i.e., it has no units) although it is typically referenced to a unit of measure such as a watt. **Decibel** measure is widely used to compare audio levels in sound systems, audible noise attenuation or noise production levels, and telecommunications signal and noise power levels. Essentially, any two values that you want to compare can be turned into a decibel value. In equation (1.21), X and Y represent the two values you are comparing, $\log_{10}$ refers to the fact that you are working in decimal (base 10) logarithmic format, and Z is the resulting decibel value. The two values compared share the same unit of measure.

$$Z \text{ dB (decibels)} = 10\log_{10}\left(\frac{X}{Y}\right) \tag{1.21}$$

In telecommunications the decibel ratio values for *X and Y* in equation (1.21) must share common units even though the ratio itself is unitless. A reference unit is commonly used as the denominator *Y* to ensure an "apples to apples" comparison of the two values. As an example, signal power can be referenced to a unit power of 1 watt (W). The decibel value is then appended with a *dBW*. Likewise, the decibel value of a signal power referenced to 1 milliwatt (mW)[16] would be represented by *dBm*.

---

[15] A wavelength window is determined by subtracting the lowest wavelength from the highest wavelength identified.

[16] Many other references are used in telecommunications. 1 watt (dBW) and 1 mW (dBm) are common references.

We can also take other measureable properties of a system and convert them to a decibel ratio by applying other unit references. As an example, antenna gain can be referenced to the gain of an *ideal isotropic antenna*, which after converting into a decibel value, would be identified by **dBi**. Therefore, if an antenna gain value was 50 dBi, you would know that the gain of the antenna was compared to the gain of an ideal isotropic antenna (i.e., ratio of the antenna gain to that of the ideal isotropic antenna). More will be said in later chapters regarding antenna gains.

By using the logarithmic relationship in equations (1.22) and (1.23), we can convert from nondecibel to decibel values and back.

$$\text{If } Y = \log_b X, \text{ then } X = b^y \tag{1.22}$$

$$\text{If } Y(\text{dBs}) = 10\log_{10}X, \text{ therefore, } X = 10^{(Y/10)} \tag{1.23}$$

Example 1.4: Given a transmitter power, P_{TX}, with an output power of 30 W, what is the decibel value when referenced to 1 W (i.e., what is the decibel power in dBW)?

Answer: $[P_{TX}] = 10\log_{10}(30 \text{ W}/1 \text{ W}) = \underline{14.77 \text{ dBW}}$

(Note: The brackets that appear around [P_{TX}] are our short-hand notation identifying this as a decibel value. This notation will be used throughout this text.)

The above decibel ratio referenced to 1 W, or dBW, tells us that this P_{TX} in watts is being compared to the unit value of 1 W. If we were instead given the decibel power value of $[P_{TX}] = 14.77$ dBW, we could easily obtain the actual transmitted power in watts by following the steps below.

1. Given $[P_{TX}] = 10\log_{10}(X \text{ W}/1 \text{ W}) = 14.77$ dBW, we know that this value is referenced to 1 W.
2. By dividing each side of the equation by 10, we get:

$$\log_{10}\left(\frac{X\text{W}}{1 \text{ W}}\right) = \frac{14.77}{10} = 1.477$$

3. In order to eliminate the logarithm from our equation, we raise 10 to the value appearing on each side of the equal sign.

$$\frac{X}{1 \text{ W}} = 10^{1.477} = 30$$

4. Multiply each side of the equation by 1 W.

$$X = 30 \times (1 \text{ W}) = \underline{30 \text{ W}}$$

So what is the advantage of using decibel logs when determining how much signal power actually appears at the receiver? First we need to review some basic logarithmic relationships such as in equations (1.24) and (1.25).

$$\log(XYZ) = \log(X) + \log(Y) + \log(Z) \tag{1.24}$$

$$\log\left(\frac{X}{Y}\right) = \log(X) - \log(Y) \tag{1.25}$$

Equation (1.24) tells us that the product of $X*Y*Z$, when placed into logarithmic notation, can be added vice multiplied. Equation (1.25) tells us that X divided by Y, when converted into log form,

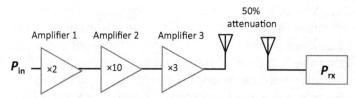

FIGURE 1.19 Power, P_{in}, goes through several amplification stages and attenuation prior to reaching the receiver at power P_{rx}.

becomes a simple subtraction problem. In other words, using decibel values enables you to use simple addition and subtraction when determining values, such as power within a complex multi-stage telecommunication system. In addition, since we are using logarithmic values, we can deal with very large or very small values more easily. Consider the following example.

Example 1.5: Figure 1.19 shows that the power input (P_{in}) into the system undergoes several levels of amplification (shown by the triangles), before it is transmitted through the air. The signal experiences attenuation loss of 50% before it reaches the receiver. Determine the power level in watts that reaches the receiver (P_{rx}) given the following: $P_{in} = 8.2$ mW, amplifier 1 doubles the input signal P_{in}, amplifier 2 takes the output from amplifier 1 and multiplies it by 10×, amplifier 3 takes the output signal from amplifier 2 and triples it before transmission.

Solution 1: First, we solve the problem without the benefit of using logarithmic math. This means that we must solve a series of multiplication problems.

Answer (not taking advantage of decibel format): $P_{rx} = (((P_{in} \times 2) \times 10) \times 3) \times 50/100 = 246$ mW

As we see for this simple example, we are faced with a nested multiplication problem combined with a percentage problem. In a more realistic example, we would be required to take into account many more variables in order to arrive at our solution. Since telecommunication systems are subject to numerous factors that change dynamically over time (e.g., noise, weather, attenuation, data rates, etc.), complexity grows very quickly as solutions must be revised with changes in variables.

Next we take advantage of logarithmic math by converting our variables to decibels. By doing these decibel conversions, our problem can be solved using simple addition and subtraction. This also allows us to solve problems (e.g., link calculations) using simple tools such as common spreadsheet applications to add and subtract values as they change.

Solution 2: First, we convert all of the values in fig. 1.19 into decibel values. By working with logarithms, we simplify our calculations.

Answer (using decibel format):

$[P_{rx}](\text{dBmW}) = [P_{in}] + [\text{Amp1}] + [\text{Amp2}] + [\text{Amp3}] + [\text{FSL}]$

$[P_{rx}](\text{dBmW}) = 10\log_{10}\left(\dfrac{8.2 \text{ mW}}{1 \text{ mW}}\right) + 10\log_{10}2 + 10\log_{10}10 + 10\log_{10}3 + 10\log_{10}0.5$

$\qquad = 9.14 \text{ dB} + 3 \text{ dB} + 10 \text{ dB} + 4.77 \text{ dB} - 3 \text{ dB} = 23.91 \text{ dBmW}$

(Note: For amplification and attenuation, the values are compared to the unit value of 1.)

Once the independent variables are converted into decibel format, determining P_{rx} above becomes a trivial addition or subtraction problem.

By applying equation (1.23), we can check our answer: **$P(mW) = 10^{(23.91 dBmW/10)} = 246$ mW**, which is the same power we calculated in the first solution above.

Since we converted each of the system variables into decibel format, we can now easily accommodate for dynamic changes within our system by simply modifying the changed variable and adding/subtracting it back into our overall solution.

As an example, let's say we wish to remove the ×10 amplifier 2 from our system. In addition, we discover through measurement that the attenuation of our signal is actually 60% vice 50%. To solve for these changes, we simply subtract the ×10 amplifier and change attenuation to 60% in decibel form.

$$[P_{rx}](dBmW) = [P_{in}] + [Amp1] + [Amp3] + [FSL]$$

$$\text{Attenuation of 60\%: } 10\log_{10}(1 - 0.6) = 10\log_{10}(0.4) = -3.98 \text{ dB}$$

$$[P_{rx}](dBmW) = 10\log_{10}\left(\frac{8.2 \text{ mW}}{1 \text{ mW}}\right) + 10\log_{10}2 + 10\log_{10}3 + 10\log_{10}(0.4)$$

$$P_{rx} (dBmW) = 9.14 \text{ dB} + 3 \text{ dB} + 4.77 \text{ dB} - 3.98 = \underline{12.93 \text{ dBmW}}$$

$$\text{or } P(mW) = 10^{(12.93 \text{ dBmW}/10)} = 19.63 \text{ mW}$$

In telecommunication systems, power levels in decibels are typically referenced to 1 W, 1 mW (1E-3 W), or 1 microwatt (1E-6 W). Table 1.3 compares watts, milliwatts, dBW, and dBm. You can

TABLE 1.3 Typical reference powers used in telecommunication systems.

1 Watt = 1E3 mW = 1000 mW
1 mW = 1E-3 W = 0.001 W

Watts	mW	dBW	dBm	
1	1.00E+0.3	0	30	
10	1.00E+0.4	10	40	
100	1.00E+0.5	20	50	
1000	1.00E+0.6	30	60	dBm = dBW + 30
10000	1.00E+0.7	40	70	
100000	1.00E+0.8	50	80	
1000000	1.00E+0.9	60	90	
0.001	1	−30	0	
0.01	10	−20	10	
0.1	100	−10	20	
1	1000	0	30	dBm = dBW − 30
10	10000	10	40	
100	100000	20	50	
1000	1000000	30	60	

see a pattern appear between dBW and dBm, in which the difference between the two is 30 dB. This gives us a simple conversion method between dBm and dBW:

$$\_\_\_\_\_\text{ dBm} = \text{dBW} + 30$$

$$\_\_\_\_\_\text{dBW} = \text{dBm} - 30$$

Example 1.6: Convert 20 W to milliwatts.

Solution: 20 W × 1000 (mW/W) = <u>20,000 mW</u>

Example 1.7: Convert 20 dBW to dBm.

Solution: 20 dBW + 30 = <u>50 dBm</u>

Example 1.8: Convert 120 W to dBm

Solution (a): Convert 120 W to mW: 120 W × 1000 (mW/W) = 120,000 mW

Convert 120,000 mW to dBm: $10\log_{10}\left(\dfrac{120,000 \text{ mW}}{1 \text{ mW}}\right)$ = <u>50.79 dBm</u>

Solution (b): Convert 120 W to dBW: $10\log_{10}\left(\dfrac{120 \text{ W}}{1 \text{ W}}\right)$ = 20.79 dBW

Convert 20.79 dBW to dBm: 20.79 dBW + 30 = <u>50.70 dBm</u>

Example 1.9: Convert 3000 mW to dBW

Solution (a): Convert 3000 mW to W: 3000 mW ÷ 1000 (mW/W) = 3 W

Convert 3W to dBW: $10\log_{10}\left(\dfrac{3 \text{ W}}{1 \text{ W}}\right)$ = <u>4.77 dBW</u>

Solution (b): Convert 3000 mW to dBm: $10\log_{10}\left(\dfrac{3000 \text{ mW}}{1 \text{ mW}}\right)$ = 34.77 dBm

Convert 34.77 dBm to dBW: 34.77 dBm − 30 = <u>4.77 dBW</u>

Besides simplifying link calculations, there are other reasons for using decibels in telecommunications such as the ability to view large variations on a logarithmic scale, and an ability to compare values to a reference. The decibel is used widely in telecommunications, so an understanding of what it means is critical.

KEY TERMS

alternating current (AC)	dielectric	EMI (electromagnetic
attenuation	direct current (DC)	interference)
capacitance (farads)	electromagnetic	frequency bandwidth
current (amperes)	spectrum	guided and unguided
decibel (dB)	electromagnetic wave	mediums

full and partial mesh network	local area network (LAN)	radar bands
full-duplex, half-duplex, simplex	modulation	resistance (ohms)
	multiplexer	transducer
Hertz (Hz)	Ohm's Law	transmitter, receiver, transceiver
ideal isotropic antenna	optical signal (source, detector)	sinusoidal signal (amplitude, frequency, phase)
impedance	optical wavelength window	
inductance (henrys)	OSI Reference Model	switches and routers
ISM band (Industrial, Scientific, Medical)	periodic and aperiodic	virtual connection
	power density	volt-ampere (VA)
line of sight (LOS)	power (watts)	volt-ampere-reactive (var)
link, circuit, trunk	power factor (PF)	voltage (electromotive force)

CHAPTER PROBLEMS

1. Describe the role of the *OSI Reference Model* in modern digital communication systems. Why is it used?

2. Select the true statement(s) regarding the OSI Reference Model.
   a. OSI RM consists of four layers
   b. ISO developed the OSI Reference Model to assist in the conceptualization of how protocols and interface standards work together to enable digital communications
   c. The OSI Reference Model is intended for analog communications only
   d. All of the above are true

   Answer: b

3. Which OSI Reference Model layer would you see electrical or optical signals being exchanged on the medium?
   a. Layer 1—Physical
   b. Layer 2—Data Link
   c. Layer 3—Network
   d. Layer 4—Transport

   Answer: a

4. What does the *physical layer* (layer 1) of the OSI model describe?
   a. The physical layer describes the type of communications medium used between transmitter and receiver.
   b. The physical layer can include descriptions of how data frames are assembled.
   c. The physical layer is where the mapping between electrical or electromagnetic signals and logical data.
   d. All of the above describe layer 1.

   Answer: d

5. The *data link layer* (OSI layer 2) describes network end-to-end connectivity. An example of a data link network is the Internet.
   a. True
   b. False

   Answer: b

6. Which OSI Reference Model layer describes communications protocols within a "common" network (e.g., Ethernet LAN)?
   a. Layer 1—Physical
   b. Layer 2—Data Link
   c. Layer 3—Network
   d. Layer 4—Transport

   Answer: b

7. The OSI data link layer (Layer 2) identifies the standards and specifications used to communicate within a "common network" (e.g., 100BaseT Ethernet). However, the data link layer does not provide end-to-end network connectivity over disparate common networks.
   a. True
   b. False

   Answer: a

8. Network layer protocols (OSI layer 3) enable data to be transported over common networks.
   a. True
   b. False

   Answer: a

9. Which of the following protocols belong to the *transport layer* (OSI layer 4)?
   a. Internet Protocol (IP)
   b. Transport Control Protocol (TCP)
   c. ASCII text
   d. None of the above

   Answer: b

10. In a full mesh network of 30 nodes, how many links would need to exist between all nodes?

    Answer: 435 links

11. Today, service providers only implement "full mesh" networks because of the need for high-speed reliable communications, and because the cost of physical communication links are very low.
    a. True
    b. False

    Answer: b

12. Service providers select the number of links within a *partial network* based upon reliability and availability requirements.
    a. True
    b. False

    Answer: a

13. What is a virtual connection/circuit?
    a. Virtual circuits are ones that are available virtually all of the time
    b. Virtual circuits are physical circuits that are dedicated to communicating users
    c. Virtual circuits are shared physical circuits
    d. None of the above.

    Answer: c

14. Push-to-talk radios (e.g., CB radios), operate in half-duplex mode.
   a. True
   b. False

Answer: a

15. FM broadcast radio is an example of:
   a. Simplex communications
   b. Half-duplex communications
   c. Full-duplex communications
   d. Complex communications

Answer: a

16. What is true regarding Ohm's Law?
   a. Given a 10 Ω resistor, as voltage increases, current decreases
   b. Given a 10 Ω resistor, as voltage increases, current increases
   c. An increase in resistance causes an increase in current
   d. None of the above are true

Answer: b

17. Power in watts is related to voltage, resistance, and current.
   a. True
   b. False

Answer: a

18. What is the purpose of a transducer?
   a. They are used to transform potential energy into power (watts)
   b. Transducers were invented by Michael Faraday, who used these devices to create electric motors
   c. They transform one type of energy into another type of energy (e.g., acoustic signals into electrical signals and vice versa)
   d. None of the above are correct

Answer: c

19. The period of a sinusoidal waveform is $T = 1\mathrm{E}-6 = 1 \times 10^{-6}$ s. What is the frequency and wavelength of the waveform?
   a. 1 Hz, 3E8 m
   b. 1 kHz, 3E5 m
   c. 1 MHz, 300 m
   d. 1 GHz, 0.3 m

Answer: c

20. The period of a sinusoidal waveform is $T = 1\mathrm{E}-3 = 1 \times 10^{-3}$ s. What is the frequency and wavelength of the waveform?
   a. 1 Hz, 3E8 m
   b. 1 kHz, 3E5 m
   c. 1 MHz, 300 m
   d. 1 GHz, 0.3 m

Answer: b

21. A measured carrier phase angle is 180°. What is the phase in radians?
    a. 0 rad
    b. $3\pi/2$ rad
    c. 0.1 s
    d. π rad

Answer: d

22. The period of a carrier wave is $T = 0.01$ s. Determine the frequency and wavelength of the carrier wave.
    a. $f = 10$ Hz, $\lambda = 3E8$ m
    b. $f = 100$ Hz, $\lambda = 3E7$ m
    c. $f = 100$ Hz, $\lambda = 3E6$ m
    d. $f = 10$ Hz, $\lambda = 3E7$ m

Answer: c

23. 1,000,000,000 Hz (1E9) is equivalent to:
    a. 1000 kHz
    b. 10 GHz
    c. 1 GHz
    d. 1 THz

Answer: c

24. 1,000,000 Hz (1E6) is equivalent to:
    a. 1000 kHz
    b. 10 MHz
    c. 1 MHz
    d. 1 GHz

Answer: c

25. 1000 MHz (1000E6) is equivalent to:
    a. 1000 kHz
    b. 10 GHz
    c. 1 GHz
    d. 1 THz

Answer: c

26. A carrier wave has an amplitude of 3.4 V, a frequency of 10 MHz, and +1.57 rad phase angle.
    Select the correct carrier wave equation.
    a. $c(t) = 10 \cos(2\pi*3.4*t-1.57)$
    b. $c(t) = 3.4 \cos(2\pi*10E6*t + 1.57)$
    c. $c(t) = 3.4 \cos(2\pi*10*t + 1.57)$
    d. None of the above are correct

Answer: b

27. A carrier wave has an amplitude of 5 V, a frequency of 10 kHz, and -1.57 rad phase angle.
    Select the correct carrier wave equation.
    a. $c(t) = 10 \cos(2\pi*5*t -1.57)$
    b. $c(t) = 5 \cos(2\pi*10*t +1.57)$
    c. $c(t) = 5 \cos(2\pi*10E3*t -1.57)$
    d. None of the above are correct

Answer: c

28. A carrier wave has an amplitude of 2.5 V, a frequency of 125 kHz, and zero phase angle. Select the correct carrier wave equation.
    a. $c(t) = 5 \cos(2\pi * 125 * t + 0)$
    b. $c(t) = 125 \cos(2\pi * 2.5 * t + 0)$
    c. $c(t) = 2.5 \cos(2\pi * 125E3 * t + 0)$
    d. None of the above are correct

Answer: c

29. A carrier wave has an amplitude of 5 V, a frequency of 1 MHz, and zero phase angle. Select the correct carrier wave equation.
    a. $c(t) = 1E6 \cos(2\pi * 5 * t)$
    b. $c(t) = 5 \cos(2\pi * 1E6 * t)$
    c. $c(t) = 5 \cos(2\pi t)$
    d. None of the above are correct

Answer: b

30. Describe the difference between *impedance* and *resistance*.

31. Describe the *power triangle*.

32. A signal has a frequency range from 300 MHz to 1 GHz. What is the frequency bandwidth in Hz?
    a. 1300E6 Hz
    b. 700 GHz
    c. 700E6 Hz
    d. 130 MHz

Answer: c

33. Acoustic signals are exactly the same as electromagnetic (EM) signals. As such, RF (radio frequency) channels propagate acoustically.
    a. True
    b. False

Answer: b

34. There is no difference between an acoustic signal and an electrical signal. Acoustic and electrical signals are used extensively in satellite communications.
    a. True
    b. False

Answer: b

35. Select the correct statement regarding acoustic and electrical signals
    a. Acoustic wave propagate at the speed of light (3E8 m/s)
    b. Electrical waves depend upon the existence of air molecules in order to propagate
    c. Transducers are required to turn acoustic signals into an electrical signal
    d. Acoustic signals are electrical signals

Answer: c

36. An EM wave consists of an electrical wave and a magnetic wave separated by 90°. An EM wave is created when a current travels along a wire.
    a. True
    b. False

Answer: a

37. Radio frequency (RF) signals propagate as an electromagnetic (EM) wave. Optical signals behave as both a wave and as a particle as it propagates. Although optical waves possess this "wave-particle duality," they are still considered EM waves.
    a. True
    b. False

Answer: a

38. Only RF signals are considered part of the electromagnetic spectrum. Optical signals consist of photons which behave as a wave and a particle (wave-particle duality), thus optical signals are not considered part of the EM spectrum.
    a. True
    b. False

Answer: b

39. Optical signals are not considered part of the EM spectrum.
    a. True
    b. False

Answer: b

40. Select the correct statement regarding EM (electromagnetic) waves.
    a. EM waves are created when current flows through a conductor
    b. The Right-hand rule is used to describe the direction of rotation of an EM field
    c. The EM wave is comprised of an electric field and a magnetic field that are perpendicular to one another
    d. All statements are correct

Answer: d

41. Select the correct statement regarding power density.
    a. For an unguided signal, power density decreases as it travels away from the transmitter
    b. For an unguided signal, power density increases as it travels away from the transmitter
    c. For an unguided signal, power density does not change as it travels away from the transmitter
    d. None of the above are correct

Answer: a

42. Antennas are used to transmit and receive signals. Both EM and acoustic signals can be captured by an antenna.
    a. True
    b. False

Answer: b

43. RF and optical signals are both EM waves. Therefore, you can collect an optical EM wave using an RF antenna.
    a. True
    b. False

Answer: b

44. Regarding EM signal propagation from an ideal isotropic antenna; the transmitted power spreads over the surface area of a sphere, with the sphere's radius equal to the distance measured from the antenna.
    a. True
    b. False

Answer: a

45. Determine the decibel value of 30 W, referenced to 1 W.

Answer: 14.77 dBW

46. Determine the decibel value of 100 mW, referenced to 1 mW.

Answer: 20 dBm

47. Determine the watt value of 22 dBW.

Answer: 158.49 W

48. Determine the milliwatt vale of 39 dBm.

Answer: 7943 mW

CHAPTER 2

Analog Communications

"We believe that the next generation of powerful mobile companies have a deep understanding of the world as a unified whole, where digital and analog experiences affect each other rather than transporting analog experiences into the digital realm."

Evan Spiegel, co-founder and CEO of Snapchat, http://www.brainyquote.com/quotes/quotes/e/evanspiege662176.html

2.1 INTRODUCTION

We live in an analog world where all of our human senses receive and process information in a continuous, nondiscrete manner. As examples, rainbows have an infinite number of shades between basic colors, and sounds can have an infinite number of pitches. So communicating in analog form is natural for us to do.

Analog signals are continuous; where incremental changes occur in an infinite manner over a period of time. In contrast, digital signals have discrete values over a period of time. The clock provides us with a good example of the differences between these two. An analog clock has hands that represent hours, minutes, and seconds. The hands move continuously from one point in time to another, with an infinite number of values or steps inbetween each point. If we were to graph the movement of the second hand over one minute, we would see a continuous sinusoidal plot as in fig. 2.1. The time

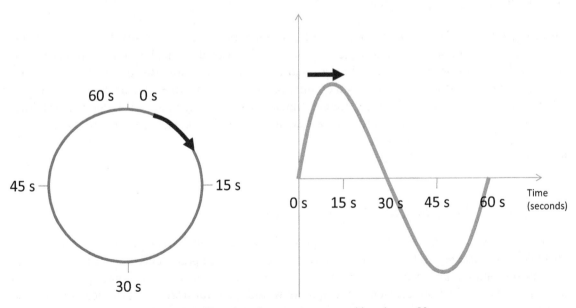

FIGURE 2.1 The plot of an analog second hand over 60 s.

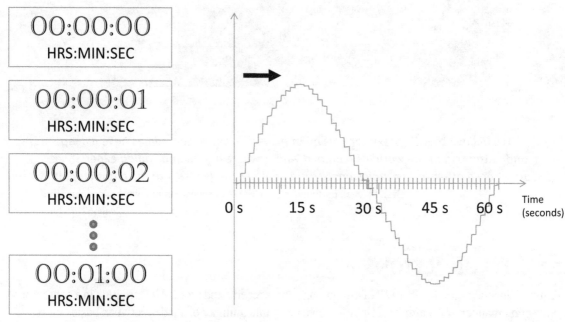

FIGURE 2.2 The plot of a digital clock over 60 s.

plot on the right is continuous and the sine wave repeats itself every 60 s. Figure 2.2 shows a digital clock where the countdown of seconds is discrete in increments of one second between time points. The plot on the right is very different from the plot in fig. 2.1, and it shows us that there are no values inbetween seconds. We could, however, increase the accuracy of our digital clock by making the increments smaller such as 0.1 s, but there will always be slight differences between our analog and digital clock.

The first *public switched telephone network* (PSTN), radio broadcasts, television broadcasts, telemetry and control, and two-way radio systems were entirely based upon analog signals. Today, digital signal technologies are incorporated into a majority of these systems. But this is not to say that analog signals and information have been eliminated. As analog creatures, we must still receive our information in analog form. Unguided communication systems such as WiFi, cellular, satellite, microwave, etc., still rely upon sinusoidal carriers to transfer digital data. So while digital data has a firm foothold in our telecommunication systems, we will always be integrating it with analog technologies.

2.2 ANALOG COMMUNICATIONS

In the early days of the analog PSTN, the telephone instrument transformed our acoustic voices into an analog electrical signal for transmission over conductive wire pairs. This electrical signal made its way through an analog network comprised of switches, trunk lines, and multiplexers. Upon arriving at the destination receiver, the telephone would then transform the electrical signal back into an acoustic voice.

We know that the human voice has a frequency range between 100 Hz and 8 kHz. However, telephone engineers discovered that a frequency bandwidth between 300 Hz and 3.4 kHz was sufficient to accurately represent human speech on the PSTN. The frequency bandwidth of 3.1 kHz[1] was rounded up to 4 kHz, and it allowed for "voice recognition" during calls. Voice recognition meant that users could recognize the voice of the person they were conversing with. For typical voice applications, 4 kHz bandwidth remains the standard for analog voice transmissions.

However, if nothing more is done to the 4 kHz electrical signal, you would quickly run into several limitations:

- Signal transmissions operating at the same frequencies over the same, shared medium would interfere with one another. You would not be able to combine multiple voice channels onto a single trunk line between switches.
- For radio frequency (RF) signals (unguided transmission within a common geographic area), operating within the same 4 kHz band, channels would interfere with one another resulting in severe signal interference and degradation.
- For RF communications, if you did not raise the transmitted frequency well above the 4 kHz range, you would encounter physical limitations such as need for very large antenna sizes and expensive high-power transmission facilities.

Since it is not practical to only allow one radio broadcast channel in a given broadcast area, or allow a single voice signal to occupy an entire trunk line between switches, *modulation* techniques were developed to raise each channel signal to a higher, unique carrier frequency. This would allow them to be combined together in a noninterfering basis. This process is called ***modulation/demodulation (MODEM)*** and ***frequency division multiplexing (FDM)***. We discuss these in the following sections.

2.2.1 Analog Modulation

The modulation process involves taking a single information or message signal, which we term the ***baseband***[2] *signal*, and raising its frequency to an even higher frequency by combining it with a ***carrier wave***. The modulated signal is sometimes called the ***passband*** signal, which describes the modulated signal after it has passed through the system's frequency band-pass filter. If multiple baseband signals are modulated so that each passband frequency is different, then our transmitted signals will not interfere with one another and we can aggregate or ***multiplex*** these signal channels together using *frequency division multiplexing*. The multiplexed output, which is the aggregate of all combined channels, is termed the ***broadband***.

Figure 2.3 shows a simplified modulation process. The baseband, which represents the message or information signal, is typically ***aperiodic***, which means that there are no repeating patterns

---

[1] Voice recognition frequency bandwidth: 3.4 kHz − 300 Hz = 3.1 kHz. This bandwidth is rounded up to 4 kHz for practical applications.

[2] Baseband signals can be either analog or digital. Chapter 3 discusses techniques that are used to modulate an analog carrier with digital information in order to create a passband.

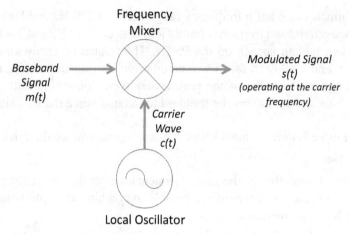

FIGURE 2.3 Modulation Process.

within the signal itself. This makes sense considering voice, video, or other information media, are not periodic in nature. The baseband is raised to a higher frequency by mixing it with a *periodic* sinusoidal *carrier* wave. The frequency oscillator controls the actual frequency of the carrier wave. By mixing the baseband signal with the carrier wave, baseband information is impressed onto the carrier wave resulting in a modulated signal that operates at the original carrier frequency. Since the modulated carrier wave contains the message, receivers need only tune into the carrier frequency for reception. The received modulated carrier signal goes through a demodulation process which separates the carrier wave from the message signal, thus resulting in the recovery of the baseband.

To understand how the modulation process works, we go back to our sinusoidal equation. The unmodulated carrier wave can be represented by the sinusoidal wave in equation (2.1). Recall that a sinusoid can be described using a sine or cosine waveform.[3] A_c is the carrier amplitude, f_c is the carrier frequency, and ϕ_C is the phase angle in radians.

$$c(t) = A_c \cos(2\pi f_c t + \phi_c) \tag{2.1}$$

The carrier wave, $c(t)$, is a *periodic* sinusoidal wave which differs from our message baseband signal which is *aperiodic*. However, for the purposes of observing how the message baseband signal modulates the carrier, we will use the periodic message wave, $m(t)$ in equation (2.2). Note that in this case, the information contained in the message is represented by changes in amplitude, A_m. The amplitude of our message wave $m(t)$ is A_m and the message wave frequency is f_m. To simplify our discussion, we assume that $\phi_C = 0$ rad.

$$m(t) = A_m \cos(2\pi f_m t) \tag{2.2}$$

The message wave, $m(t)$, can impress its information onto the carrier wave, $c(t)$, by modifying its amplitude, frequency, or phase angle as shown in fig. 2.4. When $m(t)$ modifies A_c of the carrier, it is

---

[3] The sine and cosine waves are separated by a phase angle of 90° or $\pi/2$ rad.

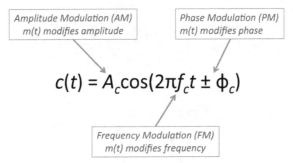

FIGURE 2.4 Basic modulation of carrier wave.

called *amplitude modulation (AM)*. When $m(t)$ modifies the carrier's frequency, f_c, it is called *frequency modulation (FM)*. Finally, when $m(t)$ modifies ϕ_c, it is called *phase modulation (PM)*.

2.2.1.1 Amplitude Modulation

With amplitude modulation (AM), an analog message wave, $m(t)$, which represents information as changes in amplitude A_m, will impress its information as changes in the amplitude of the carrier. This is the modulation technique used for AM radio which operates between 535 kHz and 1.7 MHz. Unfortunately, RF noise and interference is manifested as unwanted changes in signal amplitudes, thus impacting the quality of AM broadcasts. As such, AM techniques are susceptible in a noisy RF environment. We have all experienced the sometimes poor sound quality and noise while listening to our favorite AM broadcast channel.

If we want our carrier amplitude, A_c, in equation (2.1) to accurately represent the changes in our analog message, $m(t)$, we need to combine both $c(t)$ and $m(t)$. In our modulated carrier $s(t)$, equation (2.3), we see that A_c is combined with $m(t)$ thus producing amplitude changes in the modulated carrier based upon the message.

$$s(t) = [A_c + m(t)]\cos(2\pi f_c t \pm \varphi_c) = [A_c + A_m \cos(2\pi f_m t)]\cos(2\pi f_c t \pm \varphi_c) \tag{2.3}$$

We obviously desire to have $s(t)$ received with minimal signal distortion, and the amount of distortion we may expect is related to the ratio of message to carrier amplitudes. In other words, we want to know how the amplitude changes in the message compare to the amplitude changes of the carrier. This ratio is called the **AM modulation index** which is represented by the Greek letter μ in equation (2.4). An index[4] between 0 and 1 provides the correct level of modulation with minimal distortion. An index greater than 1 is considered **overmodulation**, and results in transmit signal phase reversals. This in turn causes a corresponding increase in frequency bandwidth (i.e., increase in number of sidebands seen in the frequency domain) and signal distortion. As a result, there is a higher chance of interfering with adjacent operating channels.

$$\mu = \frac{A_m}{A_c}, \text{ where } 0 \le \mu \le 1 \tag{2.4}$$

---

[4] The AM Index between 0 and 1 can also be viewed as a percentage of modulation from 0% to 100% modulation.

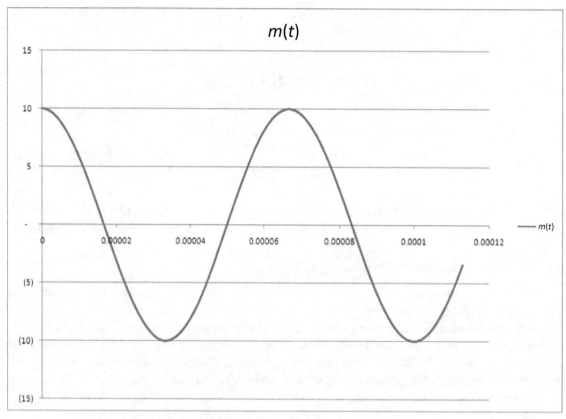

FIGURE 2.5 **Message wave** $m(t)$ **where** $A_m = 10$ V, $f_m = 15$ kHz, $\varphi_m = 0$

In order to include the modulation index into equation (2.3), we rearrange equation (2.4) to solve for A_m and substitute the result into equation (2.3).

$$A_m = \mu A_c$$

$$s(t) = [A_c + \mu A_c \cos(2\pi f_m t)]\cos(2\pi f_c t \pm \varphi_c)$$

$$s(t) = A_c [1 + \mu \cos(2\pi f_m t)]\cos(2\pi f_c t \pm \varphi_c) \qquad \textbf{(2.5)}$$

Equation (2.5) represents the modulated carrier signal, $s(t)$, with the modulation index included.

To illustrate the AM concept, let's consider the following example. Figure 2.5 shows our message wave, $m(t)$, which has an amplitude of 10 V and a period $T = 0.0000667$ s. For simplicity, we set our phase angle $\phi_m = 0$. Since we know the period of the wave, we can easily determine the frequency which is $f_m = 1/T = 15,000$ Hz. The message wave is written below.

$$m(t) = A_m \cos(2\pi f_m t \pm \varphi_m) = 10 \cos(2\pi 15 \text{ kHz}*t)$$

Our carrier wave shown in fig. 2.6 has a much higher frequency which is $f_c = 1/T = 100,000$ Hz = 100 kHz. With a carrier amplitude of $A_c = 10$, and $\phi_c = 0$ rad, our carrier equation becomes:

$$c(t) = A_c \cos(2\pi f_c t \pm \varphi_c) = 10 \cos(2\pi 100 \text{ kHz}*t)$$

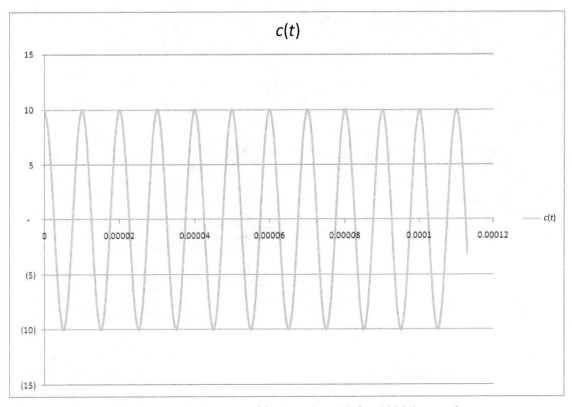

FIGURE 2.6 Carrier wave, c(t), where $A_c = 10$, $f_c = 100$ kHz, $\varphi_c = 0$

Our message wave, $m(t)$, modulates the amplitude of $c(t)$, and therefore the modulated carrier signal, $s(t)$ is written below.

$$s(t) = A_c \left[1 + \mu \cos (2\pi f_m t)\right]\cos(2\pi f_c t)$$

$$= 10[1 + 1\cos(2\pi 15 \ kHz^*t)]\cos(2\pi 100 \ kHz^*t),$$

$$where \ \mu = \frac{A_m}{A_c} = \frac{10}{10} = 1$$

Figure 2.7 shows both $m(t)$ and $s(t)$ graphs in the time domain. We observe how the $s(t)$ changes as the input message wave, $m(t)$, changes. The AM index, $\mu = A_m/A_c = 10/10 = 1$, is within the required range of $0 \leq \mu \leq 1$, therefore distortion will not be a problem and $m(t)$ can be recovered from the transmitted signal $s(t)$.

Let's now consider what happens when the modulation index, μ, is greater than 1 thus creating a condition for over modulation. In fig. 2.8, we dramatically increase our index to $\mu = 10$.

Figure 2.8 shows distortion in $s(t)$ caused by the high index. Changes in $s(t)$, which represents changes in $m(t)$, are not as pronounced as when $\mu = 1$; therefore, it is much more difficult, if not possible, for the receiver system to recover $m(t)$.

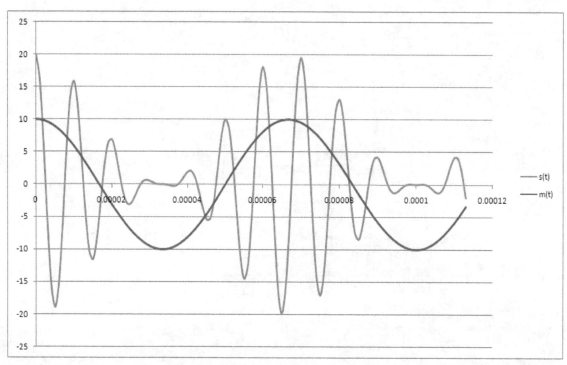

FIGURE 2.7 The higher frequency signal wave, $s(t)$, represents the modulate carrier. The lower frequency message wave represents $m(t)$.

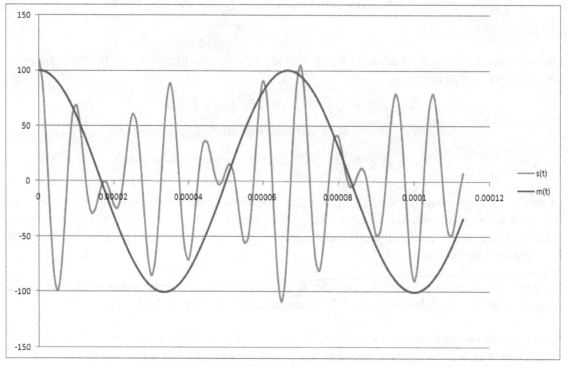

FIGURE 2.8 $s(t)$ and $m(t)$, with an AM index of $\mu = 10$.

Next we want to determine how our modulated carrier appears in the frequency domain. Considering that our transmitted signal shares a common medium with other transmitted signals, the bandwidth of each signal becomes critical. Channels operate on different carrier frequencies separated by a ***guard channel*** which are unused spectral spaces residing inbetween adjacent channels used to avoid inter-channel interference. We know that a modulated carrier will have an associated frequency bandwidth, so we need to make sure that the bandwidth does not unintentionally overlap with an adjacent channel bandwidth in order to prevent signal interference. In other words, we need to know how much capacity in Hertz our signal occupies.

By manipulating $s(t)$, we find that our signal actually consists of two main frequency bandwidths called ***sidebands***. We will use the following ***trig identity: cosA*cosB = (1/2)[cos(A − B) + [cos(A + B)]*** to determine the sideband frequencies and approximate bandwidth of our signal in the frequency domain. Starting with equation (2.3), we manipulate it to take advantage of the trig identity as seen below.

$$s(t) = (A_c + m(t))\cos(2\pi f_c t)$$

$$= (A_c + A_m\cos(2\pi f_m t))\cos(2\pi f_c t)$$

$$= A_c \cos(2\pi f_c t) + A_m [\cos(2\pi f_c t)^*\cos(2\pi f_m t)]$$

$$= A_c \cos(2\pi f_c t) + \left(\frac{A_m}{2}\right) [\cos(2\pi f_c t - 2\pi f_m t) + \cos(2\pi f_c t + 2\pi f_m t)]$$

$$= A_c \sin(2\pi f_c t) + \left(\frac{A_m}{2}\right) \cos2\pi t(f_c - f_m) + (A_m/2)\cos2\pi t (f_c + f_m)$$

The equation tells us that there will be two frequency bands: a ***lower sideband*** at $f_c - f_m$, and an ***upper sideband*** at $f_c + f_m$. Figure 2.9 shows these two information bands represented in the frequency domain. Note that f_m represents the highest frequency contained within the message signal. These sidebands are essentially mirror images of one another and therefore each contain the entire

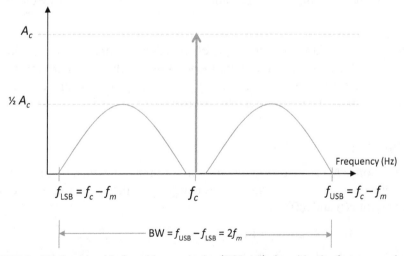

FIGURE 2.9 AM double side band large carrier (DSB-LC) signal in the frequency domain.

message $m(t)$. As such, communication systems can take advantage of several modes of AM transmissions based upon these sidebands:

- Double Side Band Large Carrier (DSB-LC): This describes the fundamental amplitude modulation method that is represented by the equations above. In the frequency domain, the carrier and both sidebands are transmitted and received resulting is a bandwidth equal to $2f_m$.
- Double Side Band Suppressed Carrier (DSB-SC): With DSB-LC described above, the carrier is transmitted even though is does not carry information. While this simplifies the receiver's demodulation process, it results in the inefficient use of transmit power. By removing the carrier frequency and sending just the two sidebands which carry information transmit power efficiency is improved. The later is what is done using DSB-SC, which distributes transmit power to just the two sidebands. In this case, the modulated signal equation becomes $s(t) = m(t)[\cos(2\pi f_c t)]$.
- Single Side Band (SSB): Each of the two sidebands carry identical information, therefore, by just sending one sideband, power and bandwidth is conserved. The single sideband (SSB) bandwidth becomes half of the DSB bandwidth (BW $= f_m$). However, the fidelity of the signal is also less than that of double sideband systems.

Understanding how much bandwidth is being occupied by the modulated carrier signal is critical, especially for unguided medium such as wireless. Regulating organizations such as the FCC (Federal Communications Commission) are specific regarding transmission frequency, frequency bandwidth, and transmit power for all wireless communication systems.

2.2.1.2 Angular Modulation

Angular modulation describes both frequency and phase modulation techniques. With *frequency modulation (FM)*, the message $m(t)$ is captured as changes in the carrier frequency, f_c. In *phase modulation (PM)*, $m(t)$ is captured as changes in the carrier phase angle φ_c. While FM and PM describe different ways to impress $m(t)$ onto $c(t)$, both impact the phase angle of the carrier with respect to the message, and hence both are termed ***angular modulation*** techniques.

Because angular modulation does not attempt to change carrier amplitude as AM does, these techniques are less vulnerable to additive noise components within the RF environment. However, the cost for better noise performance is the need for greater frequency bandwidth, as well as more complexity in the design of the transmitter and receiver.

2.2.1.2.1 Frequency Modulation

Frequency modulation (FM) is an analog modulation technique in which the message wave $m(t)$ is represented by changes in the carrier wave's frequency. Like the AM case, we will use the same equations to represent $c(t)$ and $m(t)$.

$$c(t) = A_c \cos(2\pi f_c t \pm \varphi_c), \tag{2.1}$$

$$m(t) = A_m \cos(2\pi f_m t \pm \varphi_m), \text{ where } \varphi_m = 0 \tag{2.2}$$

If we wish to represent the message wave as carrier frequency changes, then we must convert message amplitudes into carrier frequency changes [i.e., $m(t)$ is represented by changes to f_c]. This conversion is accomplished by a device called the ***voltage controlled oscillator (VCO)***, which is designed to convert input voltages into output frequency changes. To represent the VCO in our modulated signal equation, we use the term k_{vco}, which represents the VCO's frequency sensitivity in terms of a Hz to input voltage ratio (Hz/V). As an example, if $k_{vco} = 10$ (Hz/V), then we know that for every 1 V of change in our message, our frequency would change 10 Hz.

As with AM, it is important to have a ***FM modulation index***[5] that provides some measure of signal quality or fidelity. However, unlike the AM index which provides the percentage of modulation from 0 to 1 (or 0% to 100%), the FM index, β_{FM}, tells us how much the carrier frequency is allowed to change per message wave. The peak frequency deviation from the carrier's center frequency is Δf. The FM index β_{FM} is the ratio of Δf to the highest frequency of the message, f_m. From equation (2.6), we see that the term Δf (Hz) also equals k_{vco} (Hz/V) * A_m (V).

$$\beta_{FM} = \frac{\Delta f}{f_m} = \frac{(k_{vco}A_m)}{f_m} \tag{2.6}$$

Since we want $m(t)$ to modulate the carrier wave's frequency, we can write the following equation $s(t)$:

$$s(t) = A_c \cos[2\pi f_c t + 2\pi k_{vco} \int m(t)dt]$$

You will note that the $s(t)$ equation shows that our message, $m(t)$, is integrated over time. In simplified terms, the message amplitude over time is quantized so that conversion into Hertz is possible using k_{vco} (Hz/V). In the following steps, we derive the FM modulated carrier signal equation $s(t)$,[6] equation (2.7).

$$s(t) = A_c \cos[2\pi f_c t + 2\pi k_{vco} \int A_m \cos(2\pi f_m t)dt]$$
$$= A_c \cos[2\pi f_c t + 2\pi k_{vco} A_m \int \cos(2\pi f_m t)dt]$$
$$= A_c \cos\left[2\pi f_c t + \left(\frac{2\pi k_{vco} A_m}{2\pi f_m}\right) \sin(2\pi f_m t)\right]$$
$$= A_c \cos\left[2\pi f_c t + \left(\frac{k_{vco} A_m}{f_m}\right) \sin(2\pi f_m t)\right]$$
$$s(t) = A_c \cos[2\pi f_c t + \beta_{FM} \sin(2\pi f_m t)] \tag{2.7}$$

We can now use equation (2.7) to plot an FM modulated carrier in the time domain given $c(t)$ and $m(t)$. As an example, we are given a $k_{vco} = 900$ (Hz/V), $f_c = 150$ kHz, $f_m = 50$ kHz, and $A_m = A_c = 100$ V. The FM index is $\beta_{FM} = (k_{vco}*A_m)/f_m = (900*100)/50$ kHz = 1.8. In fig. 2.10, we see that $s(t)$ changes frequencies in synch with the amplitude changes in $m(t)$, and therefore the receiver will be able to extract $m(t)$ from the modulated carrier signal.

---

[5] Note: For FM radio broadcasts, β_{FM} is typically a number between 1 and 5.

[6] $\int \cos(2\pi f_m t)dt = \left(\frac{1}{2\pi f_m}\right) \sin(2\pi f_m t)$

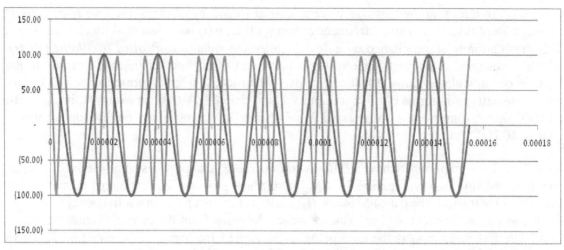

FIGURE 2.10 The modulated carrier wave, $s(t)$ in blue, is modulated by the message wave, $m(t)$, in red.

Now let's make it more difficult for the receiver to extract $m(t)$ by drastically lowering k_{vco} to 1 (Hz/V). In other words, there will only be 1 Hz of change for every 1 V of message amplitude. This results in a very low FM index $\beta_{FM} = (k_{vco} * A_m)/f_m = (1 * 100)/50\,\text{kHz} = 2\text{E} - 3$. In fig. 2.11, our modulated signal wave $s(t)$, shows no discernable changes based upon our message wave.

In equation (2.6), we see that β_{FM} is proportional to Δf, or the amount of frequency deviation. This has a direct impact on the bandwidth occupied by the FM signal. Based upon the bandwidth occupied, we can classify our FM signal as either ***narrrowband FM*** or ***wideband FM***. We know that the bandwidth occupied by any signal is dependent upon the bandwidth of the message wave and the desired fidelity of the signal. As an example narrowband FM, which is sufficient for voice communications, has a modulation index of $\beta_{FM} < 0.5$. In contrast wideband FM, with a $\beta_{FM} > 0.5$, is better suited for the transmission of FM broadcasts where greater signal fidelity is required.

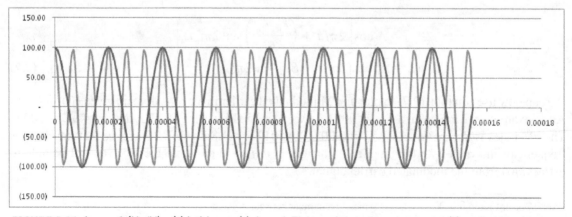

FIGURE 2.11 $k_{vco} = 1$ (Hz/V), $c(t)$ in blue, $m(t)$, in red. The modulated carrier wave $s(t)$ no longer changes frequency to accurately represent $m(t)$.

TABLE 2.1   Bessel function coefficients. Sideband amplitudes as a function of FM index β_{FM}.

β_{FM}	J_0	J_1	J_2	J_3	J_4	J_5	J_6	J_7	J_8	J_9	J_{10}
0.5	0.94	0.24	0.03								
1.0	0.77	0.44	0.11	0.02							
2.0	0.22	0.58	0.35	0.13	0.03						
3.0	−0.26	0.34	0.49	0.31	0.13	0.04	0.01				
4.0	−0.40	−0.07	0.36	0.43	0.28	0.13	0.05	0.02			
5.0	−0.18	−0.33	0.05	0.36	0.39	0.26	0.13	0.05	0.02		
6.0	0.15	−0.28	−0.24	0.11	0.36	0.36	0.25	0.13	0.06	0.02	
7.0	0.30	0.00	−0.30	−0.17	0.16	0.35	0.34	0.23	0.13	0.06	0.02

In the frequency domain, the FM signal produces an infinite number of side frequencies[7] making it difficult to accurately determine bandwidth. However, as the side frequencies extend further from f_c, the amplitude diminishes to the point where it becomes negligible. We can apply either Bessel functions or Carson's rule to approximate bandwidth in the frequency domain.

Bessel functions help us determine the frequency and amplitude of side bands in the frequency domain based upon the modulation index β_{FM}. For narrowband signals where $\beta_{FM} < 0.5$, bandwidth is similar to that of an AM signal. Two predominant sidebands are located either side of f_c therefore, the narrowband FM bandwidth is BW $= 2f_m$. As β_{FM} increases, additional sideband frequencies appear therefore increasing the total bandwidth. This makes sense since β_{FM} increases as frequency deviation increases, thus causing the modulated signal to occupy greater bandwidth.

Table 2.1 shows Bessel function values (J_n) against FM index values β_{FM}. If we normalize the carrier amplitude to a unit value of 1, then J_0 through J_{10} represents the percentage values of each side frequency with J_0 representing the carrier amplitude, J_1 representing the first side frequency amplitude at f_m, J_2 representing the second frequency amplitude at the harmonic frequency of $2f_m$, and so forth.

Figures 2.12 through 2.14 correspond to $\beta_{FM} = 0.5$, $\beta_{FM} = 1.0$, and $\beta_{FM} = 5.0$. While the harmonic frequencies produced by the modulated signal are infinite, there comes a point in the frequency domain where the nth-order harmonic contribution is insignificant and can therefore be filtered from our signal.

---

[7] AM signal sidebands are also extensive when observing the frequency domain. If the AM index goes over 1 (i.e., over modulation), sidebands become significant.

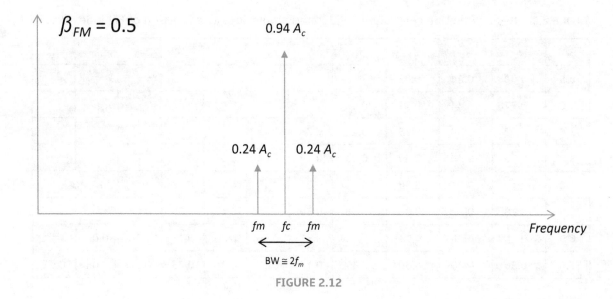

FIGURE 2.12

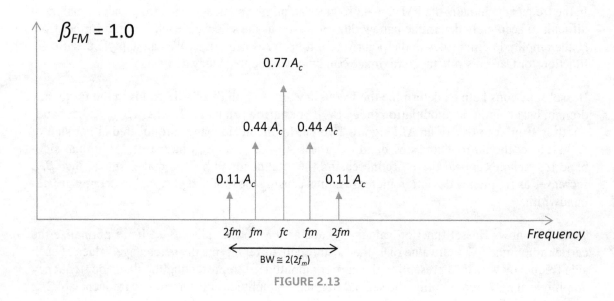

FIGURE 2.13

A second method used to approximate the FM signal bandwidth is by using ***Carson's Rule***, equation (2.8).

$$\mathrm{BW_{FM}} = (f_c + f_m + \Delta f) - (f_c - f_m - \Delta f) = 2f_m + 2\Delta f = 2f_m + 2\beta = 2f_m(1 + \beta) \tag{2.8}$$

In equation (2.8), approximate bandwidth is a function of f_m and β_{FM}. β_{FM} is directly proportional to the frequency deviation Δf, so the greater the carrier is allowed to swing either side of center, the greater the frequency bandwidth the signal will occupy. Frequency bandwidth for an FM modulated carrier signal is depicted in fig. 2.15.

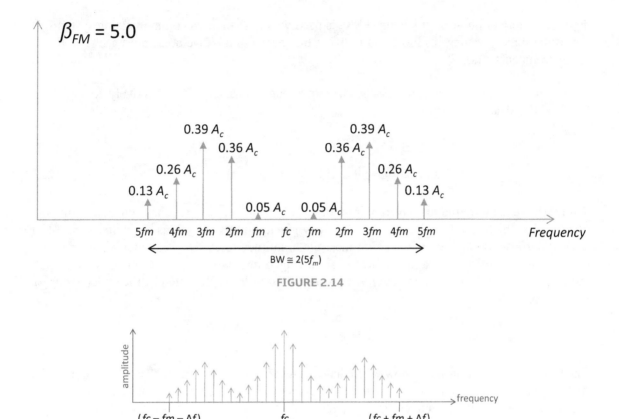

FIGURE 2.14

FIGURE 2.15 Carson's Rule—FM bandwidth, BW$_{FM}$ shown in the frequency domain.

There are several observations regarding FM:

1. Since noise impairments such as radio frequency interference (RFI) are typically induced as amplitude impacts to the signal, FM is less vulnerable to RFI than AM signals
2. Fidelity of the modulated signal is dependent upon Δf, which has a direct impact to frequency bandwidth.
3. When comparing AM and FM[8] bandwidths, we see that BW$_{FM}$ > BW$_{AM}$ or $2f_m(1 + \beta) > 2f_m$

2.2.1.2.2 Phase Modulation

Phase modulation (PM), like FM is considered an angular modulation technique. However, unlike FM, the message $m(t)$ modulates the carrier's phase angle vice frequency. PM along with its

---

[8] Applying Carson's Rule to FM.

digital counterpart phase shift keying (PSK) is used widely in modern communication systems. It shares the same advantage as FM of minimizing the impact of additive noise presence (i.e., forms of electromagnetic noise).

We will use our carrier, $c(t)$, and message $m(t)$ equations (2.1) and (2.2), respectively, to derive the PM modulated carrier equation.

$$c(t) = A_c \cos(2\pi f_c t + \phi_c) \tag{2.1}$$

$$m(t) = A_m \cos(2\pi f_m t \pm \varphi_m), \text{ where } \varphi_m = 0 \tag{2.2}$$

With PM, we are required to convert amplitude change in $m(t)$ to carrier phase changes using the constant k_P which stands for the phase sensitivity given in units of radians per volts. k_P serves a similar purpose as k_{VCO} did in changing message amplitude to carrier frequency changes; however, in the case of k_p, message amplitudes are changed into carrier phase changes. Based upon the value of k_P, we can determine our **phase modulation index** represented by the Greek letter μ_P in equation (2.9).

$$\mu_P = k_P A_m \tag{2.9}$$

The following derivation shows how we include μ_P into our phase modulated carrier equation. The first step is to include $m(t)$ into the carrier $c(t)$; however, we need to multiply $m(t)$ by k_P in order to convert amplitude changes into carrier wave phase shifts.

$$s(t) = A_c \cos(2\pi f_c t + k_P m(t))$$

$$s(t) = A_c \cos(2\pi f_c t + k_P A_m \cos(2\pi f_m t))$$

We can now substitute $k_P A_m$ with μ_P, which results in our PM signal equation (2.10).

$$s(t) = A_c \cos(2\pi f_c t + \mu_P \cos(2\pi f_m t)) \tag{2.10}$$

Determining the exact phase angle of a carrier signal is difficult since both transmitter and receiver must be able to determine the starting point for each carrier cycle. As a solution, a differential method for determining phase angles is used based upon the phase shifts from one symbol to the next vice determining the actual phase of the carrier itself.

In addition, since the phase angle of one carrier wave cycle is a maximum of 2π rad, phase ambiguity[9] can be experienced at large values of k_P. However, this can be overcome with devices such as a frequency multiplier which allows for the use of larger PM indices.

---

[9] Methods used to address phase ambiguity are beyond the scope of this text.

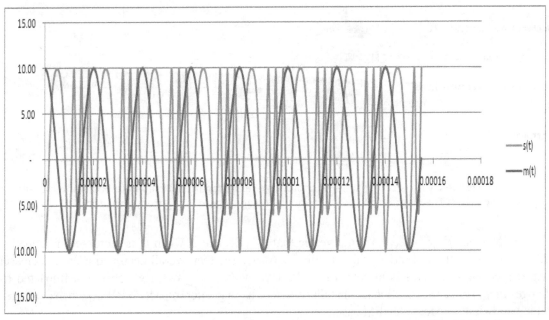

FIGURE 2.16 Phase Modulation where $s(t) = 10 \cos(2\pi \ 200 \ \text{kHz} \ t + 3 \cos(2\pi \ 50 \ \text{kHz} \ t))$.

We use the following information to plot the PM signal in the time domain:

$$\text{Message: } m(t) = A_m\cos(2\pi f_m t) = 10 \cos(2\pi \ 50 \ \text{kHz} \ t)$$

$$\text{Carrier: } c(t) = A_c\cos(2\pi f_c t \pm \phi) = 10 \cos(2\pi \ 200 \ \text{kHz} \pm \phi)$$

Phase Modulation (PM) Index: $\mu_p = k_P A_m = 0.3 \times 10 = 3$, where $k_P \ (\text{rad/V}) = 0.3$

$$\text{Modulated Carrier: } s(t) = A_c\cos(2\pi f_c t + \mu_P\cos(2\pi f_m t))$$
$$= 10\cos(2\pi 200 \ \text{kHz} \ t + 3\cos(2\pi 50 \ \text{kHz} \ t))$$

In the frequency domain, the modulated PM signal is similar to the FM spectrum; however, there are some observable differences. If you consider the FM index, $\beta_{\text{FM}} = (k_{\text{vco}}A_m)/f_m$, we find that as the modulating frequency, f_m, increases, β_{FM} decreases and the number of side frequencies also decreases as per Table 2.1. This results in a decreased occupied bandwidth. On the other hand, the PM index, $\mu_P = k_P A_m$, is only dependent upon message amplitude, so an increase in f_m does not result in a decrease of the number of sideband frequencies. In fact, if there is an increase in f_m, the spacing of side frequencies[10] (i.e., f_m, $2f_m$, $3f_m$, . . .) within the PM signal would actually increase causing an increase in occupied bandwidth.

The PM bandwidth equation (2.11) can be compared to the FM bandwidth equation (2.8). We see that an increase in f_m has a greater impact on the PM signal bandwidth than the FM signal bandwidth. This difference becomes evident when comparing the modulation indices of the FM and PM techniques.

---

[10] Side frequencies appear as a function of message frequency harmonics on either side of the carrier frequency.

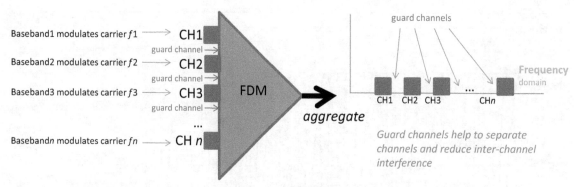

FIGURE 2.17 Frequency Division Multiplexer depicting the aggregation of separate baseband modulated carriers. The diagram on the right shows the aggregate in the frequency domain.

For the FM index $\beta_{FM} = (k_{VCO}A_m)/f_m$, we see that β_{FM} decreases when f_m is increased. In equation (2.8) we replaced the FM index with equation (2.6). We see that overall occupied BW_{FM} decreases with decreasing β_{FM}. This is in contrast to the PM index $\mu_P = k_P A_m$, which is not impacted by changes in f_m. However, equation (2.11) tells us that f_m has a greater impact on BW_{PM} when compared to the bandwidth impact in the FM case.

$$BW_{PM} = 2f_m(1 + \mu_p) = 2f_m(1 + k_P A_m) \tag{2.11}$$

$$BW_{FM} = 2f_m(1 + \beta) = 2f_m\left(1 + \frac{k_{VCO}A_m}{f_m}\right) = 2(f_m + k_{VCO}A_m) \tag{2.8}$$

2.3 FREQUENCY DIVISION MULTIPLEXING

Analog and digital baseband messages can be aggregated together using frequency division multiplexing (FDM) in which each baseband channel modulates different carrier frequencies. The frequency multiplexer then combines these modulated channels, ensuring spacing between channels by use of **guard channels**. The purpose of the guard channels is to prevent adjacent channel interference. Figure 2.17 depicts the multiplexing process and how the aggregated channels appear with guard channel separation in the frequency domain. At the receiving side, a **demultiplexer**, separates the aggregate back into separate baseband modulated carriers, which are then forwarded to separate demodulators.

KEY TERMS

amplitude modulation (AM)	frequency domain	multiplexer/demultiplexer
AM modulation index	frequency division	phase modulation (PM)
analog signal	multiplexing (FDM)	PM modulation
angular modulation	frequency	index
baseband, passband,	modulation (FM)	radio frequency (RF)
broadband	FM modulation index	sideband
Bessel function	guard channel	time domain
carrier wave	MODEM (modulator/	voltage controlled
digital signal	demodulator)	oscillator (VCO)

CHAPTER PROBLEMS

1. The human voice is an analog acoustic signal with a frequency range from 300 to 3400 Hz.
   a. True
   b. False

Answer: a

2. Modulation is a process of taking a baseband signal and raising it to higher frequency passband signal. Demodulation is the reverse process of recovering the baseband from the passband.
   a. True
   b. False

Answer: a

3. Multiple analog frequency channels can be combined into a broadband signal using frequency division multiplexing (FDM) techniques.
   a. True
   b. False

Answer: a

4. The modulated carrier frequency is what is transmitted and received. The baseband signal must be recovered through a demodulation process at the receiver.
   a. True
   b. False

Answer: a

5. A signal that has been modulated to a higher frequency is called:
   a. Baseband
   b. Broadband
   c. Passband
   d. Message

Answer: c

6. In AM, information on a carrier is represented by changes in the carrier frequency amplitude.
   a. True
   b. False

Answer: a

7. Select the correct equation that represents an AM signal.
   a. $s(t) = A_c[1 + \mu_{AM} \cos(2\pi f_m t)] \cos(2\pi f_c t)$
   b. $s(t) = A_c \cos[2\pi f_c t + \beta_{FM}*\sin(2\pi f_m t)]$
   c. $s(t) = A_c \cos[2\pi f_c t + \mu_p \cos(2\pi f_m t)]$
   d. $c(t) = A_c \cos(2\pi f_c t \pm \varphi)$

Answer: a

8. If the AM index, μ, is between 0 and 1, the distortion of the signal will be minimized.
   a. True
   b. False

Answer: a

9. Given the following AM signal, determine the carrier wave's amplitude (A_c) and frequency (f_c), the message signals frequency (f_m), and the modulation index (μ): $s(t) = 2.5[1 + 0.5\cos(2\pi100E3\ Hz*t)]\cos(2\pi1E9\ Hz*t)$
   a. $A_c = 2.5, f_c = 100\ kHz, f_m = 1\ GHz, \mu = 0.5$
   b. $A_c = 2.5, f_c = 1\ GHz, f_m = 100\ kHz, \mu = 0.5$
   c. $A_c = 0.5, f_c = 1\ GHz, f_m = 100\ kHz, \mu = 5$
   d. $A_c = 0.5, f_c = 1\ GHz, f_m = 2\ kHz, \mu = 5$

Answer: b

10. Given the following AM signal, determine the carrier wave's amplitude (A_c) and frequency (f_c), the message signals frequency (f_m), and the modulation index (μ): $s(t) = 3[1 + 0.6\cos(2\pi100E3\ Hz*t)]\cos(2\pi1E9\ Hz*t)$
   a. $A_c = 3, f_c = 100\ kHz, f_m = 1\ GHz, \mu = 0.6$
   b. $A_c = 3, f_c = 1\ GHz, f_m = 100\ kHz, \mu = 0.6$
   c. $A_c = 0.5, f_c = 1\ GHz, f_m = 100\ kHz, \mu = 6$
   d. $A_c = 0.5, f_c = 1\ GHz, f_m = 2\ kHz, \mu = 6$

Answer: b

11. Given the following AM signal, determine the carrier wave's amplitude (A_c) and frequency (f_c), the message signals frequency (f_m), and the modulation index (μ): $s(t) = 5[1 + 0.25\cos(2\pi2E3\ Hz*t)]\cos(2\pi1E9\ Hz*t)$
   a. $A_c = 5, f_c = 1\ GHz, f_m = 2\ kHz, \mu = 0.25$
   b. $A_c = 5, f_c = 2\ kHz, f_m = 1\ GHz, \mu = 0.25$
   c. $A_c = 0.25, f_c = 1\ MHz, f_m = 1\ kHz, \mu = 5$
   d. $A_c = 0.25, f_c = 1\ MHz, f_m = 2\ kHz, \mu = 5$

Answer: a

12. Given the following AM signal, determine the carrier wave's amplitude (A_c) and frequency (f_c), the message signals frequency (f_m), and the modulation index (μ): $s(t) = 10[1 + 0.5\cos(2\pi1\ kHz*t)]\cos(2\pi1\ MHz*t)$
   a. $A_c = 0.5, f_c = 1\ kHz, f_m = MHz, \mu = 1$
   b. $A_c = 10, f_c = 1\ MHz, f_m = 0.5\ kHz, \mu = 1$
   c. $A_c = 1, f_c = 1\ MHz, f_m = 1\ kHz, \mu = 0.5$
   d. $A_c = 10, f_c = 1\ MHz, f_m = 1\ kHz, \mu = 0.5$

Answer: d

13. Viewing a signal in the time domain gives you the profile of the signal over time, while viewing the signal in the frequency domain tells you the frequency bandwidth that the signal occupies. Viewing a signal in both domains is important when determining the overall quality of the signal.
   a. True
   b. False

Answer: a

14. What is the frequency bandwidth for an AM DSB-LC signal?
   a. Bandwidth $= f_m$
   b. Bandwidth $= 2f_m$
   c. Bandwidth $= 3f_m$
   d. Bandwidth $= 4f_m$

Answer: b

15. What is the frequency bandwidth for an AM SSB signal?
    a. Bandwidth $= f_m$
    b. Bandwidth $= 2f_m$
    c. Bandwidth $= 3f_m$
    d. Bandwidth $= 4f_m$

Answer: a

16. FM and PM are both considered "angular modulation" techniques. As such, these modulation techniques are completely interchangeable (i.e., you can modulate with FM and demodulate the same signal with PM)
    a. True
    b. False

Answer: b

17. Frequency Modulation (FM) requires that the amplitude changes in a message signal are converted into carrier frequency changes.
    a. True
    b. False

Answer: a

18. Select the correct equation that represents an FM signal.
    a. $s(t) = A_c[1 + \mu_{AM} \cos(2\pi f_m t)] \cos(2\pi f_c t)$
    b. $s(t) = A_c \cos[2\pi f_c t + \beta_{FM}*\sin(2\pi f_m t)]$
    c. $s(t) = A_c \cos[2\pi f_c t + \mu_p \cos(2\pi f_m t)]$
    d. $c(t) = A_c \cos(2\pi f_c t \pm \varphi)$

Answer: b

19. Select the correct equation that represents a PM signal.
    a. $s(t) = A_c[1 + \mu_{AM} \cos(2\pi f_m t)] \cos(2\pi f_c t)$
    b. $s(t) = A_c \cos[2\pi f_c t + \beta_{FM}*\sin(2\pi f_m t)]$
    c. $s(t) = A_c \cos[2\pi f_c t + \mu_p \cos(2\pi f_m t)]$
    d. $c(t) = A_c \cos(2\pi f_c t \pm \varphi)$

Answer: c

20. A voltage controlled oscillator (VCO) is used to convert message amplitudes into carrier frequency changes.
    a. True
    b. False

Answer: a

21. What does the FM modulation index, β, tell us.
    a. How much the phase of the carrier frequency is allowed to change
    b. What the phase of the message signal is in relation to the carrier frequency
    c. How much the carrier frequency is allowed to deviate from center
    d. All of the above

Answer: c

22. Bessel functions are used to help determine the amplitude of FM sidebands in the frequency domain.
    a. True
    b. False

Answer: a

23. FM signals are more vulnerable to RFI than AM signals.
    a. True
    b. False

Answer: b

24. Given the following equation for an FM signal, select the correct information below:
    $s_{FM}(t) = 3\cos[(2\pi 280\ khz*t) + 3\sin(2\pi 4000\ Hz*t)]$, $k_{VCO} = 2000\ (Hz/V)$
    a. FM index, $\beta = 9$, message amplitude, $A_m = 3$ V
    b. FM index, $\beta = 3$, message amplitude, $A_m = 6$ V
    c. FM index, $\beta = 3$, message amplitude, $A_m = 3$ V
    d. FM index, $\beta = 9$, message amplitude, $A_m = 6$ V

Answer: b

25. Given the following equation for a FM signal, select the correct information below:
    $s_{FM}(t) = 9\cos[(2\pi 250\ Mhz*t) + 8\sin(2\pi 4\ kHz*t)]$, $k_{VCO} = 3E3\ (Hz/V)$
    a. FM index, $\beta = 9$, message amplitude, $A_m = 6$
    b. FM index, $\beta = 9$, message amplitude, $A_m = 10.67$ V
    c. FM index, $\beta = 8$, message amplitude, $A_m = 10.67$ V
    d. FM index, $\beta = 8$, message amplitude, $A_m = 6$ V

Answer: c

26. Determine your FM bandwidth given the following: FM index $\beta = 5$, frequency of your message is $f_m = 4000$ Hz.
    a. 4 kHz
    b. 12 kHz
    c. 24 kHz
    d. 48 kHz

Answer: d

27. What is the bandwidth in the frequency domain for a FM modulated carrier signal with the following:
    $\beta = 2.5$, highest modulating frequency $f_m = 20$ kHz.
    a. BW = 50 kHz
    b. BW = 40 kHz
    c. BW = 140 kHz
    d. BW = 20 kHz

Answer: c

28. Given the following equation for a PM signal, select the correct information below:
    $s_{PM}(t) = 5\cos[(2\pi 300\ MHz*t + \cos(2\pi 4\ kHz*t)]$, $k_P = 0.2$
    a. PM index, $\mu_p = 2$, message amplitude, $A_m = 16.67$ V
    b. PM index, $\mu_p = 1$, message amplitude, $A_m = 5$ V
    c. PM index, $\mu_p = 3$, message amplitude, $A_m = 6$ V
    d. PM index, $\mu_p = 6$, message amplitude, $A_m = 5$ V

Answer: b

29. Given the following equation for a PM signal, select the correct information below:

$s_{PM}(t) = 3\cos[(2\pi 300 \text{ MHz}*t + 5\cos(2\pi 4 \text{ kHz}*t)], k_P = 0.3$

    a. PM index, $\mu_p = 5$, message amplitude, $A_m = 16.67$ V

    b. PM index, $\mu_p = 6$, message amplitude, $A_m = 16.67$ V

    c. PM index, $\mu_p = 3$, message amplitude, $A_m = 6$ V

    d. PM index, $\mu_p = 6$, message amplitude, $A_m = 5$ V

Answer: a

30. With PM, the message amplitude and frequency are directly related to bandwidth.

    a. True

    b. False

Answer: a

31. When frequency division multiplexing (FDM) is used, guard channels are NOT required inbetween frequency channels.

    a. True

    b. False

Answer: b

CHAPTER 3

Introduction to Digital Communications

"It is not the strongest of the species that survive, nor the most intelligent that survives. It is the one that is the most adaptable to change."

Charles Darwin (https://robllewellyn.com/digital-transformation-quotes)

3.1 INTRODUCTION

Chapter 2 introduced us to the differences between *analog* and *digital* communications, as well as the concepts of **baseband,**[1] **passband,** and **broadband**. In this chapter, we focus our attention on digital communication techniques. In particular, we discuss how logical data (0s and 1s) can be modulated onto sinusoidal carriers in order to form passband signals, and how logical data can be line coded into an electrical baseband signal. In addition, analog-to-digital and digital-to-analog signal conversion is covered through a discussion of pulse code modulation (PCM) techniques.

While digital communication systems require the use of computers and intelligent networking devices, thus making them more complex than analog systems, it has numerous advantages in terms of noise elimination, data compression, digital security, network survivability, and network efficiency.

3.2 DATA ENCODING

When we think of digital communications, we think of streams of logical 1s and 0s moving along guided or unguided mediums. However, a stream of 1s and 0s are meaningless unless we can group the data into bytes and frames, and map these groupings to meaningful symbols such as text, pixels, voice, video, or machine-to-machine (M2M) computer languages. This mapping between symbols, such as the letter "A" or pixel value, to bytes[2] of data is called *encoding*.

The specific mapping between logical data and symbols is dependent upon the type of information being sent. As an example, popular text encoding standards such as ASCII Extended (American Standard Code for Information Interchange Extended) consists of an 8-bit pattern that represents a single symbol. With 8 bits, we are able to represent $2^8 = 256$ different symbols which include the alphabet, numbers, and other symbols used in text exchanges. A newer text encoding scheme, Unicode, which was developed by the *Unicode Consortium*, consists of several schemas such as

---

[1] Baseband signals can be either analog or digital. This chapter discusses techniques that are used to modulate an analog carrier with digital information in order to create a passband.

[2] While a byte can represent any number of bits, the common definition used in computing is that a byte consists of 8 bits. *Code units* can be any number of bits according to the specific encoding standard used (e.g., Unicode byte is 16 bits long).

UTF-16. UTF-16, which is widely used on the Internet today consists of 16-bit code units that enables the representation of $2^{16} = 65,536$ symbols.

Images have several encoding schemes such as *True Color* which consists of 24 bits, divided into three bytes, with each byte representing one of three basic colors (i.e., blue, green, and red)[3] that are associated with the pixel. Each byte represents up to 256 shades for a basic color. All three bytes combined can represent a rainbow of up to $2^{24} = 16,777,216$ colors, which is considered the maximum number of color levels that the average human eye can discern.

Likewise, audio, video or machine-to-machine (M2M) also have their own digital encoding schemes that uniquely maps byte or code units to a desired symbol.

It's obvious that a shared encoding scheme must exist between communicating entities. However, in order to transmit logical 1s and 0s through guided or unguided medium it must be turned into an electrical, electromagnetic, or optical signal. Sections 3.3 and 3.4 discusses two methods by which this can be accomplished.

3.3 DIGITAL DATA MODULATION OF AN ANALOG CARRIER

In chapter 2, we discussed AM, FM, and PM modulation techniques which involved impressing analog information onto a sinusoidal carrier wave. We can use these same techniques to modify a carrier wave with a digital message wave. As an example, digital messages can modulate sinusoidal carriers by impressing information on the carrier's amplitude (*amplitude shift keying, ASK*), frequency (*frequency shift keying, FSK*), or phase (*phase shift keying, PSK*). In the case of QAM (*quadrature amplitude modulation*), the amplitude and phase of two carriers operating at the same frequency but separated by a phase angle of $\pi/2$ rad, are modulated using a combination of both ASK and PSK. This enables a single symbol using QAM modulation to take on numerous signaling levels, which results in increased capacity in bits per second of the signal. More will be said about signaling level, symbol rate, and its relationship to bit rate capacity.

Let's first look at a simplified version of ***amplitude shift keying (ASK)*** called *on-off keying (OOK)* shown in fig. 3.1. The digital message, $m(t)$, modulates the carrier, $c(t)$, which operates at frequency f_c. Whenever $m(t)$ is a logical "1," the carrier amplitude, A_c, is equal to a specific voltage which in this example is 5 V in fig. 3.1. When $m(t)$ is a logical "0," then $A_c = 0$ V.

$$m(t) \in \{0, 1\}, \text{ where } m(t) \text{ is either a logical "1" or "0"} \tag{3.1}$$

$$c(t) = A_c \cos(2\pi f_c t \pm \phi) \tag{3.2}$$

Logical data in "1s" and "0s" are obviously different than electrical signals which are changes in signal voltage, frequency, or phase. Therefore, logical data must be mapped to electrical *symbols*, which carry these changes as an electrical signal between communicating entities. In fig. 3.1, a symbol equals two sinusoidal periods of the carrier wave which take on one of two amplitude

---

[3] Depending upon the color standard, a pixel can consist of other basic color sets such as magenta, cyan, and yellow.

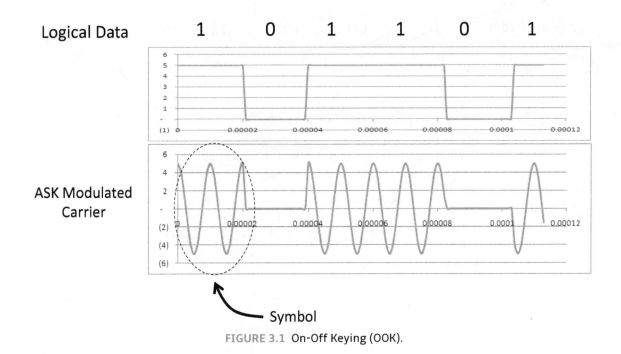

Logical Data

ASK Modulated
Carrier

Symbol

FIGURE 3.1 On-Off Keying (OOK).

levels, 0 V or 5 V. The symbol amplitude maps to a logical "0" or "1". It should be noted that a symbol in this example is equal to two periods of $c(t)$; however, symbols can be represented by any number of carrier cycle periods ($T = 1/f_c$) depending upon the particular technique or standard being applied.

The number of **symbols per second** transmitted by the electrical signal is termed the **baud** rate. In the case of fig. 3.1, we see that there is a one-to-one relationship between bit and symbol. The bit can have one of two values "1" or "0". Likewise, the symbol can have one of two values, +5 V or 0 V. If "M" is the number of values or levels that a symbol can have, then in fig. 3.1, $M = 2$ and the *data rate in bits per second equals the baud rate in symbols per second*. However, this one to one relationship is *not always the case*. As an example, in fig. 3.2, a single electrical symbol, represented by four cycles, can take on values of -5 V, -2.5 V, $+2.5$ V, and $+5$ V. With $M = 4$, each symbol can have one of four different values, with each symbol value mapped to two bits of data (-5 V = "01," -2.4 V = "00," $+2.5$ V = "10," $+5$ V = "11"). Therefore, for every one symbol transmitted, two bits of data are sent, resulting in a data rate that is twice the baud rate. Depending upon the sophistication of our send and receive equipment, we can increase "M" to gain even greater ratios of data rate over baud rate.

Hartley's Law gives us an easy way to determine data rate gains given a baud rate, S, and number of levels per symbol M [eq. (3.3)]. The number of bits that can be represented by a single symbol is given by the equation, **N(bits per symbol) $= log_2 M$**. Note that a binary log is used in Hartley's equation since we are working with binary data. The log identity in equation (3.4) can be used to directly enter the equation into a standard calculator configured for base 10 math.

$$C(\text{bps}) = S\ (\text{baud}) \times \log_2 M \tag{3.3}$$

$$\text{Log identity: } \log_2 M = \frac{\log_{10} M}{\log_{10} 2} \tag{3.4}$$

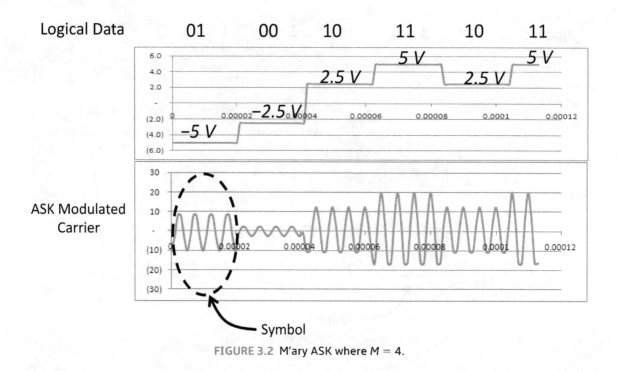

FIGURE 3.2 M'ary ASK where $M = 4$.

Example 3.1: Determine the data rate in bits/s given a baud rate of 2400 symbols/s and an $M = 32$.

Solution: For a 2400 baud signal, we know that each symbol can take on one of 32 signaling levels ($M = 32$). Applying Hartley's equation gives us the following:

$$N(\text{bits/symbol}) = \log_2(32) = 5 \; \textit{bits/symbol}$$

$$C(\text{bps}) = 2400 \text{ baud} \times \log_2(32) = \underline{12,000 \text{ bps}}$$

$$\text{or } C(\text{bps}) = 2400 \text{ baud} \times \left(\frac{\log_{10}32}{\log_{10}2}\right) = \underline{12,000 \text{ bps}}$$

With *frequency shift keying (FSK)* logical data is similarly mapped to electrical symbols. However, in FSK, symbol values equate to changes in frequency vice amplitude changes as in ASK. Figure 3.3 shows that a symbol can take on one of two different frequencies, f_1 or f_2, which are mapped to logical "0" and "1," respectively. In the case of fig. 3.3, the number of different frequency levels that a single symbol can take is $M = 2$. We can add additional frequency values per symbol as seen in fig. 3.4 where $M = 4$.

In *phase shift keying (PSK)*, logical data is impressed by changing the carriers phase angle. PSK, like FSK, is an angular modulation technique that, when viewed on a spectrum analyzer, can look similar to one another. However, as discussed in chapter 2, PSK and FSK modulation techniques use different mechanisms to modulate information onto the carrier and therefore cannot be used interchangeably for signal modulation/demodulation.

In any phase modulation technique, it would be difficult for the receiver to determine the exact phase of the carrier without a mutual reference point in time; therefore, differential phase changes

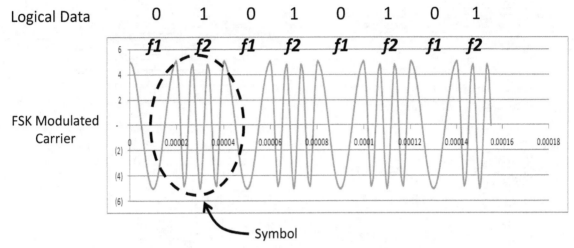

FIGURE 3.3 Frequency Shift Keying (FSK), M = 2.

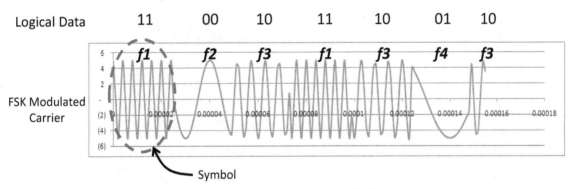

FIGURE 3.4 Frequency Shift Keying (FSK), M = 4.

are used instead. As an example, fig. 3.5 depicts an $M = 2$, PSK modulated signal where a logical "1" is seen as a phase shift of π rad (180°), and logical "0" a shift of 0 rad (0°). So the receiver need only see the phase shift of the carrier to determine if a logical "1" or "0" was sent.

Similar to other modulation techniques, a single PSK symbol can have more than two signaling levels or values (i.e., $M \geq 2$ or ***M'ary modulation***[4]). As an example, fig. 3.6 depicts an $M = 4$, PSK modulated signal where values equate to: 45° → "11," 135° → "10," 225° → "00," and 315° → "01." $M = 4$ PSK modulation is referred to as ***quadrature phase shift keying (QPSK)***, while $M = 2$ PSK is termed ***binary phase shift keying (BPSK)***.

Similar to FM and PM, FSK and PSK both have inherent advantages over amplitude modulation techniques. In particular, additive noise products that impact the amplitude of the carrier thus causing severe degradation to AM and ASK modulated signals, do not impact FSK and PSK signals.

---

[4] M'ary modulation is a term used for a modulation method in which a symbol represents multiple bits (e.g., $N > 2$ bits per symbol), or $M > 2$.

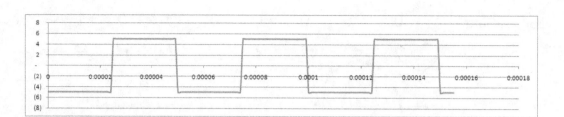

Logical Data   0   1   0   1   0   1   0

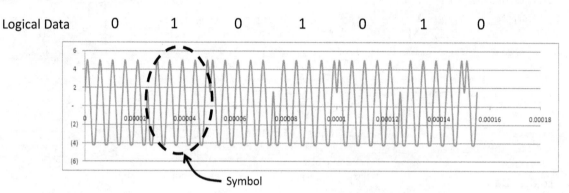

Symbol

FIGURE 3.5 Phase Shift Keying (PSK), $M = 2$.

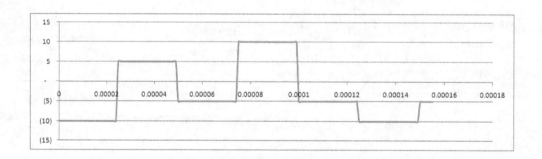

Logical Data   00   10   01   11   01   00   01

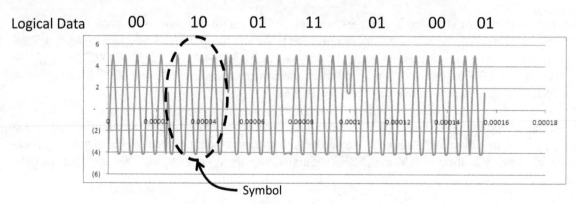

Symbol

FIGURE 3.6 Phase Shift Keying (PSK), $M = 4$.

This is because information is captured as frequency changes or phase angle shifts vice amplitude changes. The result is greater immunity from the effects of additive noise products. The tradeoff, however, is in the bandwidth occupied. Both FSK and PSK modulated signals typically occupy more frequency bandwidth than ASK signals.

Quadrature amplitude modulation (QAM) incorporates both ASK and PSK techniques. It is comprised of two carriers operating at the same frequency but separated by 90° or $\pi/2$ rad. Once each carrier is modulated, they are combined and transmitted as a single carrier. The advantage of QAM over the application of a single modulating technique is its ability to represent a greater number of bits per symbol as a combination of both amplitude and phase angles of the carriers. QAM easily supports *M'ary modulation*, which leads to improved data rate capacity. The best way to illustrate how QAM works is to consider the constellation map in fig. 3.7.

The QAM constellation map in fig. 3.7 is shown for $M = 8$. The two concentric circles represents two different amplitudes (ASK), while the intersecting lines show phase angles at 0 (or 2π), $\pi/2$, π,

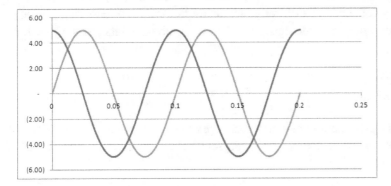

Two sinusoidal waves
- *Same frequency*
- *Separated by $\pi/2$ rad*

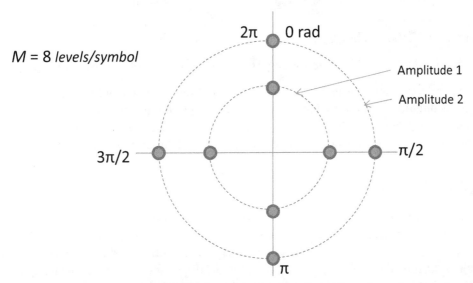

FIGURE 3.7 Quadrature Amplitude Modulation (QAM). QAM consists of two carriers of the same frequency, but separated by $\pi/2$ rad. The constellation diagram shows $M = 8$.

$M = 16$ *levels/symbol*

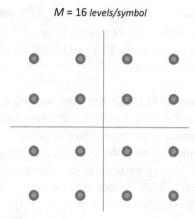

FIGURE 3.8 16 QAM, $M = 16$ *levels/symbol.*

and $3\pi/2$ rad. The solid dots show the various values that a single QAM symbol can have (i.e., in this case one of eight values, or $M = 8$). Of course, we can add additional amplitudes and phase angles in order to increase M levels per symbol, thus increasing our data rate capacity. Hartley's Law can be applied to determine the data rate capacity and the number of bits per symbol for a given value of M.

$$C(\text{bps}) = \text{Baud} \times \log_2 M, \text{ where } \log_2 M = \textit{no. of bits per symbol}$$

$$N(\text{bits/symbol}) = \log_2 M = \log_2 8 = 3 \textit{ bits/symbol}$$

As an example, fig. 3.8 shows a QAM method in which there are $M = 16$ levels/symbol or 16 QAM. If we wish to know how many bits a single symbol represents, then we use the second part of Hartley's equation:

$$N(\text{bits/symbol}) = \log_2 M = \log_2 16 = \left(\frac{\log_{10} 16}{\log_{10} 2}\right) = \underline{4 \text{ bits/symbol}}$$

If given a baud rate of 2400 symbols/s, then our data rate capacity is:

$$C(\text{bps}) = \text{baud} \times \log_2 M = 2400 \text{ baud} \times \log_2 16 = 2400 \text{ symbols/s} \times 4 \text{ bits/s} = \underline{9600 \text{ bps}}$$

These are some basic examples of how we modulate digital data directly onto an analog carrier. There are other modulation techniques that are beyond the scope of this chapter; however, they follow the same ideas of directly modifying the carrier wave with digital information. Next we will discuss how an electrical baseband signal can represent logical data through *line coding*.

3.4 LINE CODING

In addition to modulating digital data onto an analog sinusoidal carrier, we can also impress logical 1s and 0s directly onto an electrical signal to create a *digital baseband*. A prime example is the Ethernet LAN (local area network) in which 1s and 0s are directly **line coded** as an electrical signal onto a common, shared medium. The difference between the digital modulation of an analog carrier and line coding is that the former produces a *passband* signal transmitted at the higher carrier frequency, whereas line coding produces an electric *baseband* signal.

In order for logical "1s" and "0s" to be exchanged on a medium, they need to be mapped to an electrical signal, or *symbol*, consisting of voltage and current changes. This is termed *line coding*, and the representation of logical data is dependent upon the actual standard being implemented. Multiple line coding standards have been developed to address particular strengths or weaknesses, with each having various tradeoffs in performance depending upon the application. However, the typical traits of a good line code includes the efficient use of frequency bandwidth and transmit power (i.e., transmission efficiency), and the existence of signal transitions that enable clock synchronization using received data.

In the following sections, we discuss five line coding methods: non-return to zero (NRZ), bipolar alternative mark inversion (Bipolar AMI), Manchester line coding, bipolar with eight-zero substitution (B8ZS), and 4B5B. While there are numerous other line coding methods that exist and are being developed, these five basic techniques give you an idea of how line coding is used.

3.4.1 Non-Return to Zero

Digital clocks are used by both the transmitter and receiver to synchronize data exchanges over a circuit. The clock provides the timing for the electrical signal as well as a reference that defines the beginning and end of a data frame. With the *non-return to zero (NRZ)* line coding method shown in fig. 3.9, we see the relationship between the logical data, clock, and NRZ line coded signal. A logical "1" equates to a $+V$, and a logical "0" to a $-V$; therefore, a single symbol can have one of two values (i.e., $M = 2$). Since the electrical signal can have either a $+V$ or $-V$ value, it is called a *bipolar* signal. This is in contrast to a signal that has $0\,V$ as one of its values which is called a *unipolar* signal (fig. 3.10).

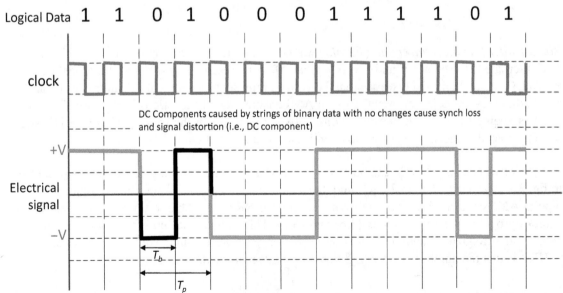

NRZ (Non-Return to Zero) Line Coding

FIGURE 3.9 Non-Return to Zero (NRZ).

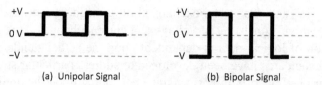

(a) Unipolar Signal   (b) Bipolar Signal

FIGURE 3.10 (a) Unipolar signal shown with values of +V and 0 V. Unipolar signals may also have the values of 0 V and −V. (b) Bipolar signals shown having both +V and −V values.

The darker outline of the signal in fig. 3.9 shows one period, Tp, of the electrical signal, and the time it takes to transmit a single bit in T_b seconds, which is called the **bit-time**. The data rate can then be determined by equation (3.5).

$$R(\text{bps}) = \frac{1}{T_b} \tag{3.5}$$

In this case, the time it takes to transmit one bit also equals the time it takes to transmit one symbol, or $T_b = T_{symbol}$.

We can also determine the highest signal frequency by observing how the signal changes over time. In fig. 3.9, the signal shows the characteristics of a repeating cycle with a period of T_p when the logical data has consecutive changes of "0" and "1." This gives us the highest frequency of the signal as

$$f_{(\text{NRZ}, M=2)} = \frac{1}{T_p} = \frac{1}{2T_b} = \frac{1}{2T_{symbol}} \tag{3.6}$$

A weakness of NRZ line coding occurs when a long string of just logical "1s" or "0s" are transmitted. As you can see in the figure, consecutive "1s" or "0s" results in a signal being transmitted with no transitions. As a consequence, since the data received cannot be used to keep the receive timing accurate, synchronization between the transmitter and receiver may drift.

3.4.2 Bipolar Alternate Mark Inversion (AMI)

Bipolar alternate mark inversion (Bipolar AMI) is a bipolar line coding method in which logical "1s" alternate between a +V and −V. A logical "0" is represented by 0 V and therefore is considered a DC signal. In fig. 3.11, we see that the voltage representing a logical "1" alternates regardless of whether they are adjacent or not. Bipolar AMI ensures signal transitions in the case of consecutive "1s" being transmitted; however, consecutive "0s" result in the transmission of a DC signal which can lead to the same synchronization issues as discussed with NRZ.

The period of one signal cycle can be readily observed when transmitting consecutive logical "1s." In fig. 3.11, we see that $T_b = T_{symbol}$, and that $T_p = 2T_b = 2T_{symbol}$. Therefore, the frequency of the bipolar AMI signal is similar to the frequency for the NRZ signal based upon T_p. We can see this similarity by comparing equations (3.6) and (3.7). This tells us that both NRZ and bipolar-AMI have similar frequency bandwidth and power efficiencies. The advantage of bipolar-AMI compared to NRZ is that the number of signaling transitions has increased.

$$f_{(\text{B-AMI}, M=2)} = \frac{1}{T_p} = \frac{1}{2T_b} = \frac{1}{2T_{symbol}} \tag{3.7}$$

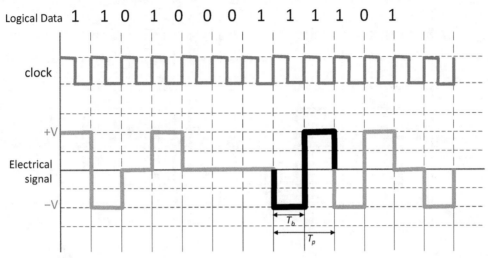

FIGURE 3.11 Bipolar Alternate Mark Inversion (Bipolar AMI).

3.4.3 Manchester

Manchester line coding was designed to ensure that a signal transition takes place in the middle of the clock cycle for every bit sent. This enables receive clocks to continuously synchronize with the incoming signal despite the presence of long string of "1s" or "0s" being received. Instead of coding logical data as discrete voltage values, logical data mapping is accomplished through the transition from one voltage to another. So a voltage transition from −V to +V equates to a logical "1," while a transition from +V to −V represents a logical "0." From fig. 3.12, we see that even when consecutive "1s" and "0s" exist, signal transitions always take place.

While the Manchester line coding technique ensures signaling transitions, it is not as efficient a coding scheme as either NRZ or bipolar AMI in terms of frequency bandwidth. By observing the signal when consecutive "1s" or "0s" are sent in fig. 3.12, we can determine the bit-time, signaling period, and highest signal frequency.

$$T_b = T_p \tag{3.8}$$

$$f_{\text{Manchester}} = \frac{1}{T_p} = \frac{1}{T_b} = \frac{1}{T_{symbol}} \tag{3.9}$$

When we compare equation (3.9) above with equations for NRZ [equation (3.6)] and bipolar AMI [equation (3.7)], and compare their frequencies, we see that $f_{\text{Manchester}}$ requires twice the bandwidth as either the other two [equation (3.10)].

$$f_{(\text{NRZ}, M = 2)} = f_{(\text{B-AMI}, M = 2)} = \frac{1}{2T_{symbol}}$$

or

$$2f_{(\text{NRZ}, M = 2)} = 2f_{(\text{B-AMI}, M = 2)} = \frac{1}{T_{symbol}}$$

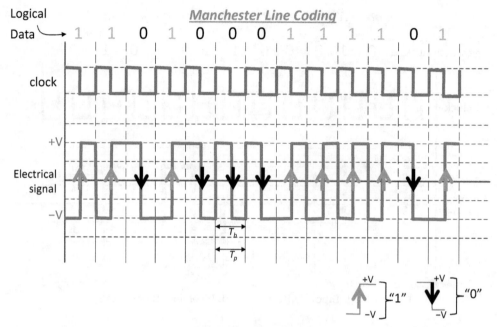

FIGURE 3.12 Manchester.

From equation (3.9), we can compare the bandwidth required by each line coding method:

$$\frac{1}{T_{symbol}} = 2f_{(NRZ, M = 2)} = 2f^{(B\text{-}AMI, M = 2)} = f_{(Manchester, M = 2)} \tag{3.10}$$

In other words, Manchester requires twice the frequency bandwidth to send a single symbol when compared to NRZ or bipolar AMI. Conversely, this means that NRZ or bipolar AMI is a more bandwidth efficient method than Manchester line coding.

3.4.4 Bipolar with Eight-Zero Substitution (B8ZS)

Bipolar with eight-zero substitution (B8ZS) is an improvement over bipolar AMI. As you recall from section 3.4.2, bipolar AMI ensures that signal transitions exist when consecutive "1s" are sent, thus enabling receive clock recovery and synchronization. However, this was not the case for AMI when consecutive "0s" are sent. B8ZS uses alternating voltages when sending logical "1s" which is similar to bipolar AMI, but adds a ***bipolar violation*** sequence when eight consecutive "0s" are detected. In fig. 3.13, we see that a logical sequence of eight zeros is replaced by a bipolar violation signaling sequence of −V, +V, 0 V, +V, −V starting with the fourth bit. This particular bipolar violation sequence was inserted because the previous logical "1" sent was mapped to a −V. Doing this ensures alternate marks for consecutive "1s" are maintained. Had the previous value been +V, then the sequence would have been +V, −V, 0 V, −V, +V. By inserting bipolar violations into string of eight consecutive "0s," B8ZS always ensures that signaling transitions will take place.

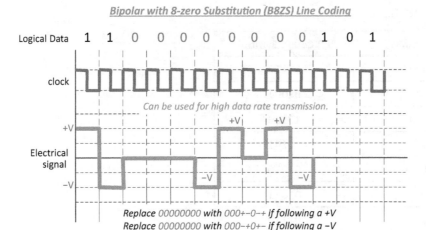

FIGURE 3.13 Bipolar with Eight-Zero Substitution (B8ZS).

3.4.5 4B5B

The line coding techniques discussed thus far deal with the mapping of logical data to electrical signaling levels or voltage transitions. Sending long strings of consecutive "1s" or "0s" is undesirable since this could lead to lost synchronization between transmit and receive clocks when using methods such as NRZ or bipolar AMI. Applying Manchester ensures that signaling transitions always exist, but at the cost of higher bandwidth requirements. B8ZS also ensured signaling transitions, but at the cost of higher complexity.

4B5B involves a different approach that is applied prior to the logical data being line coded into electrical symbols. On the digital side prior to line coding, any logical sequence containing long strings of consecutive "1s" and "0s" are avoided through data mapping, thus eliminating the need to compensate for a lack of signal transitions during the line coding process. The 4B5B technique involves the mapping of four-bit datawords into five-bit codewords. The four-bit dataword represents the actual data or information we wish to send, while the codeword represents the five-bit sequence (i.e., four-bit dataword plus one additional bit) that is actually transmitted. The four-bit dataword represents $2^4 = 16$ "real" data or information bit combinations. By adding an additional bit to the dataword, we have a total of $2^5 = 32$ possible permutations which we term codewords. Since only 16 of the 32 codewords are mapped to real dataword bit sequences, the remaining 16 codewords do not have to be used (i.e., codewords that can be avoided altogether). We can then eliminate two codewords that are represented by all "0s" or "1s" (i.e., codewords "00000" and "11111"). Therefore, if we wish to send the dataword "0000 0000," we would actually send the codeword "11110 11110" using 4B/5B coding described in table 3.1, thus ensuring signal transitions for synchronization purposes. Likewise, if we sent "1111 1111," the codewords sent would be "11101 11101" instead. Once coded using 4B5B, we could use a simpler line coding technique such as NRZ to line code and transmit our data. Table 3.1 represents the mapping between four-bit datawords to five-bit codewords.

However, there is a drawback when using 4B5B. Since we send a five-bit codeword for every four-bit dataword sent, we incur an overhead penalty of 20%. This means that the transmission contains

TABLE 3.1   4B5B.

4B Data	5B Coded Symbol
0000	11110
0001	01001
0010	10100
0011	10101
0100	01010
0101	01011
0110	01110
0111	01111
1000	10010
1001	10011
1010	10100
1011	10110
1100	11010
1101	11011
1110	11100
1111	11101

only 80% (4 bits/5 bits) real information bits, with the remainder realized as overhead (i.e., 1 bit/5 bits = 20% overhead). Despite the additional overhead requirement, 4B5B and other similar encoding methods such as 8B/10B, are used extensively in data communication systems.

3.5 DIGITAL REPRESENTATION OF ANALOG INFORMATION

Working with digital signals comes with a great number of benefits including the ability to apply digital encryption technologies to enhance communications security, data compression to increase efficiency, and noise elimination through the use of repeaters. However, there are numerous types of analog information that we wish to send through digital networks, such as speech, music, video, and images. Therefore, methods have been developed to transform analog information into digital representations for communications purposes. The two steps in this process involve the sampling of an analog signal, and the quantization of the sample by applying a bit sequence representation. This *analog-to-digital (ADC)* process results in a digital stream of logical "1s" and "0s." The reverse process, or *digital-to-analog (DAC)* process, then recovers the analog information from the digital data.

Since analog signals are continuous, we need to sample the signal at various points in time as a first step in the digitization process. For each sample of the analog signal we take, we must apply a bit sequence to represent the amplitude of the signal. The process of mapping this bit sequence to the intensity or amplitude of the analog signal is called **quantization** and the number of bits we apply to each sample is termed the **bit-depth**. Since we are attempting to *quantize* a signal comprised of infinite levels into a discrete sequence of bits, we will always encounter a mismatch between the values of the quantized digital sample and actual analog sample. This mismatch between analog and digital values is termed **quantization error**. The greater bit-depth we apply to each sample the smaller our quantization error, and the smaller the bit-depth the larger the quantization error.

In order to ensure that we collect the minimum number of samples needed to accurately represent the original analog signal, we use the **Nyquist sampling theorem** [eq. (3.11)]. The Nyquist sampling theorem tells us that if we have a sample rate (i.e., number of samples taken of the analog signal per second) that is greater than or equal to twice the frequency bandwidth of the analog signal, then we can faithfully represent the signal in digital form. As such, once the digital signal is received and converted back into an analog signal, it will closely approximate the original analog signal. However, if our sampling rate falls below the Nyquist sampling theorem rate, then our signal will **alias**, which essentially means that our sampled signal will not be a faithful representation of the original analog signal.

$$f_s(samples/s) \geq 2 \times \text{BW, } \textit{where BW represents bandwidth in Hertz} \qquad \textbf{(3.11)}$$

In order to effectively digitize an analog signal, we must sample the signal according to *Nyquist*, and then apply the proper *bit-depth* to ensure that we can recreate the analog signal from the digital signal transmitted. The device used to perform the ADC and DAC processes is called a **coder-decoder (CODEC)**.

Example 3.2: Let's consider a simple illustration. We take the simple sine wave, $c(t) = 15sin(2\pi 20t)$ in fig. 3.14, which has a frequency of 20 Hz and a peak amplitude of 15 V. We will convert this into a digital stream using the Nyquist sampling theorem and apply a bit-depth of 3 bits/sample.

Applying Nyquist: $f_s \geq 2 \times 20$ Hz = 40 samples/s.

Our frequency is 20 Hz = 20 cycles/s, therefore, we can determine the number of samples that should be taken per single cycle of the sine wave:

$$40 \text{ samples/s} \div 20 \text{ cycles/s} = 2 \text{ samples/cycle}$$

Figure 3.14 shows that we take two samples per cycle. The first at a peak amplitude of 15 V at time 0.0125 s, and the second at time 0.0375 s when the sine wave is at −15 V. To the left of the *Y*-axis is our three-bit encoding scheme.[5] Our three-bit encoding scheme gives us $2^3 = 8$ permutations that can be specifically mapped to certain voltage levels. In this example, we've decided to map our bit pattern to the following: "000" = +20 V, "001" = +15 V, "010" = +10 V, "011" = 5 V, "100" = −5 V, "101" = −10 V, "110" = −15 V, "111" = −20 V.

---

[5] The encoding scheme (i.e., mapping of a bit sequence to voltage levels) varies depending upon the standard and specifications applied. In this case, we have assigned three bits to voltage levels sequentially for illustration purposes only. It does not follow a specific published standard.

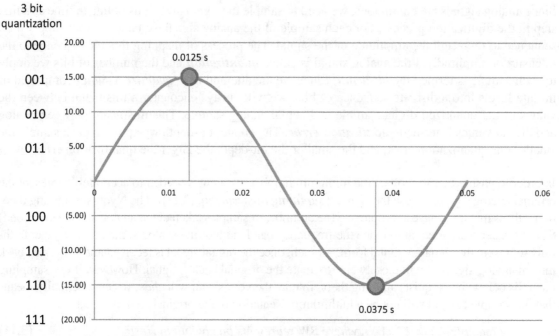

FIGURE 3.14 Sampling a simple sine wave using f_s = 40 samples/s and bit-depth of 3.

Note: Our three-bit scheme does not allow for the representation of 0 V, and therefore, if our sample equaled 0 V, we would be forced to quantize to the nearest mapping which would be either "001" or "100" (i.e., +5 V and −5 V, respectively). As such, selecting either "001" or "100" would result in a 5 V quantization error.

Our three-bit value at the first sample is "001" which equates exactly to +15 V, and our second sample is "110" which equates exactly to −15 V. In this rather unusual case, our quantization error at each sample is 0 V. The two samples indicate the positive and negative peaks of the sine wave and therefore the receive CODEC has enough information to accurately decode the digital stream "001 110" and recover the original sine wave signal.

Now we consider a case in which we encounter quantization error, also termed *quantization noise*. We once again follow the Nyquist sampling theorem to determine the number of samples we need to perform; however, we find that our analog peak amplitude value does not neatly fit into our encoding scheme.

Example 3.3: Our analog signal is now the sine wave, $c(t) = 12 \sin(2\pi 20t)$ in fig. 3.15, which has a frequency of 20 Hz and a peak amplitude of 12 V. We once again apply the same bit-depth of 3 bits/sample.

Applying Nyquist: $f_s \geq 2 \times 20$ Hz = 40 samples/s.

Figure 3.15 shows that there is no three-bit code representing 12 V. The nearest bit code is "010" which represents 10 V. Therefore, we have a 2 V quantization error. The same is seen at $t = 0.0375$ s

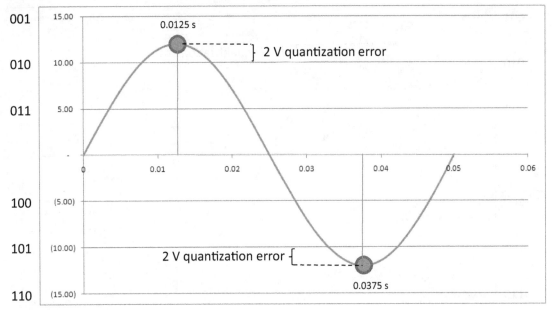

FIGURE 3.15 Quantization Error.

where our analog signal is equal to -12 V. The code nearest to this value is "101" which represents -10 V, therefore, once again we have a quantization error of 2 V. We can reduce this error by adding additional bits to our code, which increases the number of amplitude values we can represent, thus reducing quantization error.

Now let's consider a case in which we ignore Nyquist altogether, which results in the aliasing of our signal.

Example 3.4: Our analog signal remains the same as in example 3.3, $c(t) = 12 \sin(2\pi20t)$. The frequency is 20 Hz with a peak amplitude of 12 V. We apply the same three-bit encoding scheme. However, this time we ignore the Nyquist sampling theorem.

Ignoring Nyquist: $f_s = 20$ samples/s $<$ Nyquist sampling theorem

Although our frequency is 20 Hz requiring a sampling rate ≥ 40 samples/s, we purposely use 20 samples/s instead. The number of samples per single cycle of the sine wave:

$$20 \text{ samples/s} \div 20 \text{ cycles/s} = 1 \text{ sample/cycle}$$

Figure 3.16(a) shows that we take only one sample per cycle at the peak amplitude, 12 V, of the sine wave. The three-bit code, "010," assigned results in a 2 V quantization error as in example 3.3. Therefore, the only code bits sent is "010" which maps to $+10$ V. Since our digital encoded signal does not change, it does not contain sufficient information to recreate the analog signal and the result after decoding is a single $+10$ V signal that does not vary over time, see fig. 3.16(b). This $+10$ V decoded signal does not accurately represent the original analog sine wave sent, demonstrating that our signal has experienced severe *aliasing*.

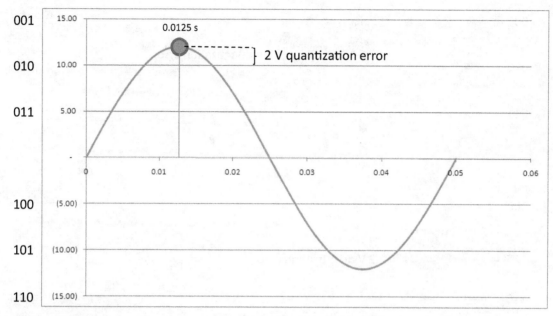

(a) Single sample taken per cycle

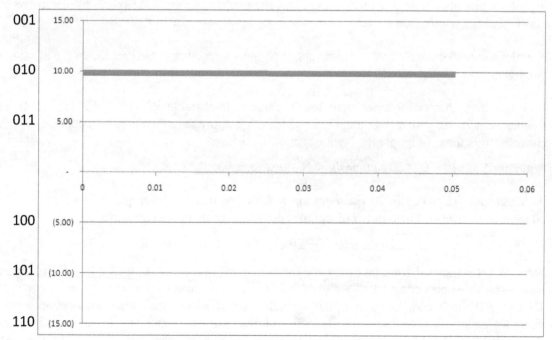

(b) Recovered aliased signal after decoding

FIGURE 3.16 Signal aliasing and quantization error.

3.5.1 Pulse Code Modulation (PCM)

Pulse code modulation is a method by which we convert a voice grade signal with a frequency bandwidth of 4 kHz, into an uncompressed digital signal. Nyquist tells us that we must sample the analog voice grade stream at approximately double the frequency bandwidth in order to avoid "aliasing" the signal which results in distortion at the other end. So our Nyquist sampling rate is $f_s \geq 2 \times$ BW or 2×4000 Hz $= 8000$ samples/s.

Next, we need to assign a bit sequence to represent the analog amplitude (e.g., voltage) of our signal per sample. In the case of PCM, 8 bits are allocated to each sample. This means that the number of voltage levels that we can encode with 8 bits or 1 byte is $2^8 = 256$ permutations, with each permutation mapping to a unique voltage level.[6]

Since you have to transmit 8 bits of voice data for every sample, the capacity in bits per second required to send an uncompressed digital voice grade signal becomes

$$8 \text{ (bits/sample)} \times 8000 \text{ (samples/s)} = 64 \text{ kbps}$$

In voice technologies, this uncompressed voice grade 64 kbps data rate is known as a ***digital signal zero (DS0)***, and is a building block for communications standards such as Channelized T-1 and SONET. These standards will be discussed in a later chapter.

By following Nyquist, PCM avoids signal aliasing, and although the use of 8 bits per sample ($M = 256$) will cause some quantization error, it is not severe enough to prevent accurate voice grade digital transmission from occurring. ***Differential Pulse Code Modulation (DPCM)***, dramatically reduces the data rate capacity needed for transmission by decreasing the bit depth per sample from 8 to 4 bits. This is accomplished by only transmitting the differences detected from one sample to the next. This is useful for voice signals where changes between samples are not significant, thus reducing the required capacity from 64 kbps to 32 kbps. However, in situations where the difference between samples occur at a more dramatic rate, ***Adaptive Differential Pulse Code Modulation (ADPCM)*** can be applied where the bit depth per sample can dynamically change as the differences between samples are detected.

3.6 DIGITAL COMPRESSION

In section 3.5.1, we digitized a 4 kHz voice grade signal using PCM which resulted in an *uncompressed* 64 kbps digital signal. An *uncompressed digital signal* refers to a signal in which every sample taken is included as part of the final digital signal. However, when considering typical voice, video, image, text, etc., there are typically numerous redundant samples, including those samples containing no information, that can be eliminated prior to transmission. This decreases the transmission throughput required. As an example, analog voice conversations are inherently inefficient considering the pauses between spoken words during an average two-way conversation. By applying an uncompressed technique such as PCM, these pauses are digitized along with the actual voice samples, and are included as part of the 64 kbps transmission. This results in an inefficient use of available bandwidth capacity. However, if we eliminate the samples taken where no speech takes place, we decrease our data rate requirement and increase overall transmission efficiency. Through a technique called ***digital speech interpolation***, we can take advantage of these conversational void areas to insert additional data.

---

[6] *Note: The formula $2^N = M$ (voltage levels), where N equals the number of bits.*

Digital compression techniques such as the one briefly described above are used to decrease the size of digital files for storage and transmission. There are several ways to eliminate unneeded or redundant bits. As an example, in a digital image or video, each pixel has a bit-depth[7] that represents a particular shade of color. If the background of an image or video has a uniform color that does not change, then it is not necessary to send each redundant[8] pixel. Instead, you could include a byte that informs the decoder that a pixel is being repeated a specific number of times, thus eliminating the need to actually send the redundant data. In a word document, you might encounter frequently used words or phrases that can be abbreviated. Since each letter, number, or symbol in a word document is encoded to an 8 (e.g., extended ASCII) or 16 (e.g., Unicode) bit word, then using abbreviations which are known to both send and receive applications, can easily decrease the data that must be transmitted. Web HTML pages present yet another example of how data exchanges can be minimized through the use of well-structured forms and elements that are known and preprogrammed into browser applications. If HTML or XML elements are known and defined, then only the data required to fill the forms need be sent.

Essentially, any information that is in digital format can be *compressed* to reduce file size for storage or to achieve bit-rate reduction. Depending upon the application of the data, compression can either be *lossy* or *lossless*. A *lossless* compression technique recovers all of the original data when uncompressed, whereas a *lossy* compression technique permanently loses some of the original data when uncompressed. The selection of which type of compression technique to use depends upon whether data loss can be tolerated or not. As an example, for typical images on a web page, resolution quality is not a major concern so lossy compression techniques can be applied in order to achieve bit-rate reduction. On the other hand, a medical MRI used for patient diagnosis must have high resolution and lossless compression in order to be free from artifacts for diagnostic reasons.

Table 3.2 lists some of the popular lossy and lossless compression techniques. It should be noted that this list is just a sample of what it available, and that many of the more popular formats may have multiple versions associated with it.

TABLE 3.2 Lossy and Lossless Compressions Methods.

Lossy Compression	Lossless Compression and Uncompressed Formats
Image: • Joint Photographic Experts Group (JPEG) **Video:** • Moving Picture Experts Group (MPEG-1, MPEG-2, MPEG-4) • Digital Video (DV) • (HDV), 2003 • Windows Media Video (WMV) • H.264 **Audio:** • MPEG Audio Layer-3 (MP3) • MPEG Audio Layer-4 (MP4) • Ogg • Advanced Audio Coding (AAC) • Audio Coding 3 (AC3)	**Image:** • Tagged Image File Format (TIFF) • Portable Network Graphics (PNG) • Microsoft BMP (uncompressed) • Better Portable Graphics (BPG) • RAW format • Graphics Interchange File (GIF) **Video:** • RAW (uncompressed) • High-Definition Multimedia Interface (HDMI) **Audio:** • Windows Wave (WAV), (uncompressed) • Windows Media Audio (WMA) • Free Lossless Audio Codec (FLAC) • Apple Lossless Audio Codec (ALAC)

---

[7] True Color has a bit-depth of 24 bits/pixel. This is considered the maximum bit-depth that the normal human eye can discern.

[8] Redundant data is also termed "white space."

3.7 ERROR CONTROL

When we consider the transmission of binary data, especially at high data rates, we will inevitably encounter errors induced by environmental and system noise products. An error which changes, or *flips*, one or more bits within a byte or frame causes erroneous data and information to be transmitted and received. As such, it is essential in digital communications to identify and/or correct these errors. This is the objective of *error control*.

Since we cannot be absolutely certain when or how many bit errors will occur, we must deal with the probabilities that bit errors may be experienced. ***Bit error rates (BER)*** is a term used to describe the probability of bit errors encountered over a given transmission system. As an example, over a wireless link, a typical BER is 10^{-5}, which translates to the probability of experiencing one bit error in 10^5 bits transmitted. On a typical guided electrical link, a BER of 10^{-9} might be experienced, while on a fiber optic link, the probability of errors is much less from a BER of 10^{-12} to 10^{-15}. The actual BER experienced depends upon numerous system factors such as transmission power, modulation scheme, medium selection, noise environment, data rate, and bandwidth selection. Therefore, adjusting any one of these variables will affect the actual BER experienced.

Error control consists of two parts: ***error detection*** and ***error correction.*** Both error detection and correction involve the addition of bits which are used to help identify and/or correct the erroneous bits (fig. 3.17). The actual data that we wish to send is termed the ***dataword*** and we typically represent the number of bits in the dataword as **k** bits. When we add additional bits for error control purposes, the combination of dataword and the additional bits is termed the ***codeword*** which is **n** bits long. Therefore, the number of error control bits added equals **$n - k$**. Various error detection and error control algorithms are used to determine the actual sequence and length of the $n - k$ bits which are added to the dataword.

3.7.1 Error Detection

As the term implies, the job of error detection is to detect, but not correct, errors in the data received. The simplest example is the addition of even or odd parity bits. With even parity, the number of logical "1s" within a codeword should sum to an even number. Upon receipt of a

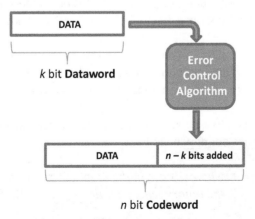

FIGURE 3.17 Error Control Process.

codeword, if the sum of logical "1s" were not even, then we would know that an error has occurred. As an example, if we have the seven-bit ASCII dataword "1101011" and implement even parity, then we would add a "1" parity bit to the dataword in order to make the sum of "1s" within the codeword even, "11010111." Upon receipt of the codeword in this example, if the number of bits sum to an odd number such as "11000111," then we know that an error has occurred during transmission and that we should not use the received codeword. Likewise, if we implement odd parity, then the parity bit added in our example dataword would be a "0," which would make the codeword "11010110." While this is a very simple algorithm to implement, it has short comings as an error detection method. As an example, with a single added parity bit, if we were to encounter more than one bit error in the dataword, then the an erroneous dataword would be mistaken for a legitimate one, see examples 3.5 and 3.6.

Example 3.5: Using even parity for a seven-bit ASCII word results in the codeword "11010111" being transmitted. During transmission, a single bit flip occurs resulting in the codeword "11000111" being received. The receiver detects the error and rejects the codeword as not being legitimate.

Example 3.6: Using even parity for the same dataword in example 3.5 results in the same codeword "11010111" being transmitted. During transmission, two bit errors occur resulting in the codeword "10000111" being received. The receiver sums the "1s" as even and determines that the codeword is legitimate even though two errors have occurred making the data received erroneous.

In the case of examples 3.5 and 3.6, we can surmise that the probability of a single bit error occurring is greater than the probability of two or more bit errors occurring. So single parity error detection may be sufficient on a highly reliable transmission system in which the occurrence of two or more bit errors in a codeword is rare.

In most cases where error detection methods are used on telecommunication systems, simple parity bit checking is not sufficient. A better error detection method is **_cyclic redundancy check (CRC)_** in which a predetermined polynomial shared by both sender and destination, is divided into the dataword prior to transmission. The mathematical _remainder_ resulting from the division operation is then appended to the end of the dataword thus creating a codeword, and transmitted. Upon receipt of the codeword (i.e., dataword plus mathematical remainder), the destination end divides the received codeword using the same shared polynomial. If the remainder from this operation is zero, then no errors are present in the received codeword. However, if a remainder is present after the operation, then the destination end knows that it has received an erroneous codeword. Example 3.7 demonstrates how the CRC method works.

Example 3.7: You plan to use CRC-5 (meaning that the highest order polynomial is x^5) as your error detection method. Your shared polynomial is $x^5 + x^4 + x^2 + 1$. The dataword is 1010001101. What **_frame check sequence (FCS)_** do you append to your dataword?

The polynomial can be mapped to a binary sequence, and we can use binary division to determine our remainder, which becomes our appended FCS.

$x^5 + x^4 + 0 + x^2 + 0 + 1$, _where 0's are in the x^3 and x^1 positions indicating zero value_
1   1   0   1   0   1, _the binary representation of our CRC-5 polynomial_

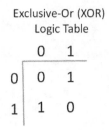

Exclusive-Or (XOR)
Logic Table

	0	1
0	0	1
1	1	0

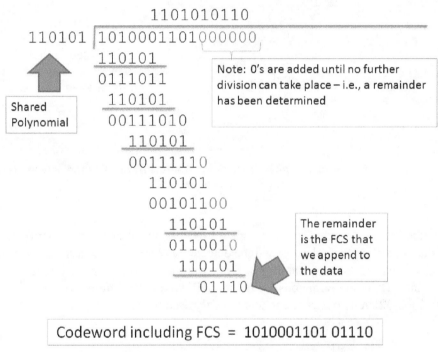

FIGURE 3.18 CRC-5, determining the FCS.

Next, we take the binary representation of our polynomial value and divide this into the dataword by using the *exclusive-or (XOR)* function, see fig. 3.18. The remainder of this operation becomes the FCS which is then appended to the dataword for transmission to the destination.

Example 3.8: You receive the codeword in 101000110101110 with an appended CRC-5 FCS. Your shared polynomial is $x^5 + x^4 + x^2 + 1$. Does the received codeword contain errors?

As in example 3.7, we will use binary math to determine if an error has been detected. We convert the shared polynomial to the binary equivalent 110101. Next, we divide this binary number into the entire codeword received (i.e., data plus FCS), see fig. 3.19. The division operation results in zero remainder, and therefore CRC has not detected an error in our codeword.

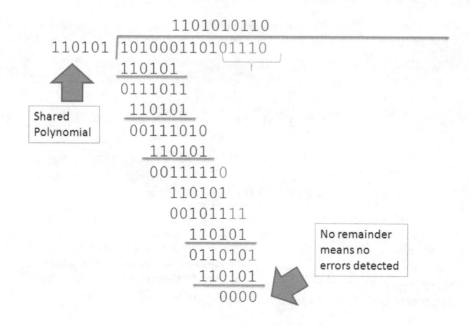

FIGURE 3.19   CRC-5 codeword received is checked for errors by dividing the polynomial into the received codeword.

The CRC method is much better in detecting the presence of bit errors than parity bit checking; however, it does not mean that all errors will be detected. Error detection is stated in terms of probabilities, and you have a high probability of detecting these errors when using CRC, but not an absolute certainty. There are numerous forms of CRC which use different orders of polynomials. CRC-16 and CRC-32 are two versions that are widely used today.

3.7.2 Automatic Repeat Request (ARQ)

Once an error has been detected in a data block or *frame*, retransmission needs to take place. ***Automatic Repeat Request (ARQ)*** is a method in which a *request for retransmission* is sent automatically by the receiver upon the detection of an error. Three version of ARQ are commonly used:

Stop-and-wait ARQ. With this ARQ method, the transmitter sends a single data frame at a time and waits for the receiver to send either a *positive acknowledgment*, *"ACK,"* indicating that the data has been received without error, or a *negative acknowledgment*, *"NACK,"* indicating that the frame was received with errors. The frame being transmitted is placed into a buffer to facilitate retransmission in the event that a NACK is received. If an ACK is received, the transmitter buffer is cleared to make room for the next frame. Since the data frame, ACK or NACK can be lost during transmission, the transmitter starts a timer for each frame sent. If no acknowledgments are received at the expiration of the timer, or ***time-out period***, the transmitter assumes that either the frame or the acknowledgment has been lost and resends the unacknowledged data frame. However, in the event that it was a positive ACK that was lost, then retransmission would lead to a duplicate frame being sent. As such, the receiver must be able to handle duplicate frames.

Throughput inefficiencies are inherent with this method since the transmitter must always wait for acknowledgments before sending the next frame. To improve efficiency when used in a full-duplex circuit, acknowledgments are placed into the header of data frames (i.e., *piggy-backing method)*. In addition, greater efficiencies can be realized when using larger data frame sizes.

Go-back-N (GBN) ARQ. The *"Go-back-N"*ARQ protocol improves efficiency by allowing several data frames to be sent without the need to acknowledge each frame individually. GBN enables the transmission of a ***window*** which is comprised of N number of frames that are sequentially labeled. Sequential numbers assigned to each frame within a window are represented by a field of n binary bits within the frame header. Therefore, if $n = 3$ bits, then the sequence of numbers that can be assigned to frames are from 0 to $(2^n - 1)$, or a repeating sequence from 0 to 7. However, to avoid any confusion caused by overlapping sequence numbers during transmission a ***window size***, N, is used to define the maximum number of frames that can be sent by the transmitter. In the case of the example above, the window size is limited to $N = (2^n - 1)$, or $N = 7$ frames per window. The *window size* determines the transmitters' buffer size since it must be prepared to resend any frame within the transmitted window (i.e., ability to store unacknowledged frames).

Since frame transmission is continuous, the receiver must respond with positive acknowledgment, ***ready-receive (RR)***, or negative acknowledgment, ***reject (REJ)***, that are labeled with the identifying frame number, n.

As the frames are sent in sequence, the transmitter places these frames into a buffer. Upon successful receipt of the sent frames, the receiver sends an RR with the last successful frame sequence number identified. Since an acknowledgment can occur in the middle of window, only the frames positively acknowledged are removed from the buffer thus allowing additional frames to enter and to be transmitted. This ***sliding window*** concept allows for the continuous flow of data, vice waiting for the end of each window transmission before sending an acknowledgment. Receipt of a RR tells the transmitter that all frames previously received, including the one which is being acknowledged, has been received successfully, and the transmitter then clears these frames from the buffer. However, if the destination end receives an erroneous frame, it sends a REJ which identifies the erroneous frame number. Upon receipt of the REJ, the transmitter not only resends the erroneous frame, but all subsequent frames sent after the REJ frame was identified. Similar to the *Stop-and-wait ARQ*, a *time-out period* is initiated with the transmission of each frame. Therefore if a RR or REJ is lost, the retransmission of frames subsequent to the last received RR will be automatically resent.

Example 3.9: Our window size, N equals 7 frames $(N = 7)$, which is represented by $n = 3$ bits or sequential numbers from 0 to 7 $(n = 2^3 - 1)$.

1. Transmitter: The first window of 7 frames is sent: frame-00 to frame-06 (transmit buffer contains frame 00 to 06).
2. Receiver: Frame-00, frame-01, and frame-02 are received correctly, therefore a RR-02 is sent letting the transmitter know that all frames up to and including frame-02 have been received correctly.
3. Transmitter: Upon receipt of RR-02, frame-00, frame-01, and frame-02 are cleared from the buffer to make room for the next sequence of frames labeled frame-07, frame-00', and

frame-01' (*sliding window*—in this example, 00' and 01' indicates that the *sequence number is reused* to represent the next frames to be sent and entered into the buffer). Frames 07, 00', and 01' are then sent (transmit buffer now contains frames 03 to 07, 00', and 01').

4. Receiver: Frame-03, however, is found to have either one of two problems: (a) frame-03 is found to be incorrect, or (b) frame-03 is never received, but frame-04 is received out-of-sequence, leading the receiver to believe that frame-03 has been lost. In either case, the receiver responds with a REJ-03.

5. Transmitter: Upon receipt of REJ-03, frame-03 and all subsequent frames sent after frame-03 are retransmitted (i.e., frames 03 through 07, 00', and 01' are sent and remain in the buffer).

6. Receiver: Frame-03 and frame-04 are received successfully and a RR-04 is sent.

7. Transmitter: RR-04 is received and frames 03 and 04 are cleared from the buffer to make room for frames 02' and 03'. Frames 02' and 03' are transmitted (transmit buffer contains frames 05 to 07, 00' to 03').

8. Receiver: Frame-05 and frame-06 are received successfully, and a RR-06 is sent.

9. Transmitter: RR-06 is never received. Therefore, at the expiration of the *time-out period*, the transmitter assumes that either (a) all of the data from the last positively acknowledged frame-04 has never been received, or (b) any positive or negative acknowledgment from the receiver has been lost. In any case, since it cannot be sure what has happened, it resends all subsequent frames following the last known successful frame identified by RR-04 (i.e., frames 05 through 07, 00' to 03' are resent).

Selective-reject, Selective Repeat ARQ. By only having to resend the individual frames received in error, vice all frames transmitted subsequent to the identified erroneous frame, we gain efficiency in how we use the available transmission bandwidth. This is the goal of ***selective-reject, selective-repeat ARQ***. Similar to GBN, the sliding window concept and sequence numbers are used to label both frames and acknowledgments. As frames within a window are transmitted, they are entered into the *transmit buffer*. As the frames are received, they are also entered into the *receiver's buffer*. If a single frame in the middle of the window is received in error, it is identified by sequence number and a ***selective-reject (SREJ)***, or negative acknowledgment, is sent. While the correct frames received prior to the SREJ can be purged from the receive buffer, all frames received after the rejected frame must remain. Upon receipt of the SREJ at the transmitter, it resends just the erroneous frame identified by the SREJ, and also maintains all subsequently transmitted frames within its buffer until a positive acknowledgment, RR, is received.

Select-reject ARQ is a more complex method than the other two, requiring that both transmitter and receiver maintain buffers and the ability to quickly and properly sequence frames as erroneous frames are identified and resent. In addition, buffer sizes must be reduced to prevent confusion regarding the assignment of sequential frame numbers. As an example, individual frame rejects could cause an overlap of identical frame sequence numbers within the buffer leading to confusion. To prevent this from happening, the window size must be reduced to a maximum of one half of the available sequence numbers, n bits (e.g., if $n = 3$ bits, sequence numbers can be from 0 to 7; however, the window size should be no more than half of the available sequence numbers, or $N \leq 2^{(n-1)} = 2^{(3-1)}$ or $N \leq 4$ frames per window).

3.7.3 Error Correction

While detecting and requesting retransmission of data received in error is sufficient for many communication systems, it leads to inefficiencies especially over shared mediums that have significant propagation delays, or are designed for simplex communications only. As an example, due to the great distances between earth stations and geosynchronous satellites, propagation delays between communicating ground sites can take as long as 0.25 s per round trip. With such long delays, waiting to respond to acknowledgments and retransmissions severely slows data throughput. One way we can avoid this overhead is to add a sufficient amount of redundant data along with our information to enable both a high probability of error detection and correction of the transmitted data. This is the idea behind *forward error correction (FEC)*. By using FEC, we can avoid the continuous cycle of acknowledgment and retransmission.

To understand how redundant parity bits support error correction, let's consider a simple example based upon the *"majority vote"* method. As described previously, our information, or *dataword*, is k bits long, while the *codeword* containing both dataword and redundant parity bits, is n bits long. Our dataword size in this example is $k = 1$ bit ($2^1 = 2$ datawords), and codeword is $n = 3$ ($2^3 = 8$ codewords). In Table 3.3, the only legitimate codewords are 000 and 111. All other remaining codewords are redundant and will inform the receiver that an error has occurred. If a "000" has been sent, but a "001" is received, then the error detection scheme counts the number of "0" and "1" bits within the codeword. Since the number of "0" bits in this case is two, which is greater than the number of "1" bits, then we conclude that the original dataword sent must be a "0." The premise here is that the probability of experiencing a single bit error in the codeword is higher than experiencing two bit errors. However, if we were unlucky in this example, we could have experienced two bits errors instead, thus erroneously changing our received dataword value. As mentioned, this is a very simple example. Obviously, error detection and correction algorithms used today are much more sophisticated and effective.

FEC codes are classified as either *block* or *convolutional* codes. A *block code* is one in which the codewords are treated as blocks of data, with the parity bits appended to each codeword.

TABLE 3.3   Simple majority vote error correction $(n, k) = (3, 1)$ using a *repetition code.*

Dataword	Codeword
0	000
	001
	010
	011
	100
	101
	110
1	111

A *linear block code* is one in which any combination of two legitimate codewords within a scheme results in another legitimate codeword. This is in contrast to a *convolutional code* in which the data continuously enters a shift register where parity bits are placed at various positions within the codeword as it is processed. In practice, convolutional codes are better at error correction than linear block coding methods, and the use of hardware shift registers makes implementation straightforward.

Let's look at a simplistic *linear block code* example where we have a three bit dataword, $k = 3$, a codeword where $n = 4$, and $n - k = 1$ parity bit. With $k = 3$, we can represent $2^3 = 8$ actual datawords, and with $n = 4$, we can represent $2^4 = 16$ codewords. However, only 8 of the 16 codewords map to legitimate datawords. We carefully select[9] 8 of the possible 16 codewords to map to real data by determining the *Hamming distance* between all possible pairs of codewords. When comparing two codewords, the *Hamming distance* refers to the number of places where the digits differ. As an example if we compare two legitimate codewords from Table 3.4, 0101 and 1111, we see that the two words differ in the first and third most significant digits from the left. Therefore, the Hamming distance is 2. This means that two "bit flips" or errors need to take place in one of the codewords in order to confuse it with another legitimate codeword. If we were to determine the Hamming distance between all possible combinations of codewords in Table 3.4, we would see that the *minimum Hamming distance*[10] for this particular $(n, k) = (4, 3)$ code is 2.

TABLE 3.4 Linear block code example showing only the legitimate codewords. All other codewords are considered redundant and will flag an error if received.

Dataword (k)	Codeword (n)	Parity bit (n − k)
000	0000	0
001	0011	1
010	0101	1
011	0110	0
100	1001	1
101	1010	0
110	1100	0
111	1111	1

[9] Actual determination of the selected codewords is a process involving a series of matrix multiplications using what is termed a *generator* matrix and *parity check* matrix. This process helps to ensure the selection of an orthogonal codeword set that is used to for correct error detection and correction. A detailed description of this process is beyond the scope of this text.

[10] When we compare codewords 0000 and 1111, we find that the Hamming distance is 4. However, we want to find the minimum distance among all possible combinations of codewords, which is 2. This tells us that two bit errors in specific positions within a codeword could transform it into another legitimate codeword that would not be detected as an error.

From this information, we can make several observations regarding the relative strength of our coding scheme.

1. There are $2^k = 2^3 = 8$ possible datawords and $2^n = 2^4 = 16$ possible codewords of which only 8 of the possible 16 codewords are mapped to datawords. The remaining 8 codewords are considered redundant, and if received will flag that a bit error has occurred.

2. Codewords mapped to datawords are selected to ensure linearity, which means that the combination of any two legitimate codewords via XOR logic, results in another legitimate codeword.

3. During receipt, a codeword that is not mapped to a dataword, is determined to be redundant and is subsequently flagged as an error (note: since there are 8 of 16 redundant codewords, there is good chance that an error during transmission will be flagged).

4. By determining the Hamming distance between all possible combinations of legitimate codewords, we find that the minimum Hamming distance is 2. This means that at least two bit errors in specific bit positions will have to occur before an erroneous codeword is mistaken for a legitimate one. Since the probability of two bit errors in a codeword is less than the probability of a single bit error, we have a higher probability of flagging erroneous codewords. Once an error has been flagged, an error correcting algorithm is used to determine what the probable correct codeword sent was.

There are numerous *block coding* schemes used today. One of the most often used is the ***Reed-Solomon Code*** which encodes blocks of 8 bit symbols, vice bits, and is used as an FEC method for devices such as Compact Discs (CDs), Digital Versatile Discs (DVDs), and hard disk drives. Reed-Solomon codes are best applied in situations where *burst* errors, i.e., those impacting more than a single bit at a time, can be expected. Other examples of block codes are Hamming Code, Golay and BCH, the descriptions of which are beyond the scope of this text.

With *convolutional codes*, an information bit stream is clocked through a register that is K bits in length. As the bits move through the register, coded bits are produced though a series of logical XOR gates, and are placed throughout the stream of data. This is in contrast to appending parity bits at the end of each dataword as in the case of block coders. Parameters for convolutional codes are similar to those of block codes (i.e., n codewords and k datawords), but with the addition of the constraint length K, or (n, k, K). So as datawords enter a K constraint register, redundant $n - k$ bits are added continuously throughout the produced codeword. Upon receipt by the distant end, the received bit stream is placed into a receive register and a reverse process recovers the dataword. While convolutional codes are straightforward to implement, the decoding process especially for long messages, can be complex. As such, the *Viterbi* decoding method, which offers a simpler method for decoding convolutional codes, is often used.

3.8 NETWORK TIMING BASICS

When communicating digitally over any communications link, it is critical to have accurate timing resources (clock references) in order to ensure the proper identification of frames, and the bits within the frame. As covered in section 3.4 on line coding, a symbol can indicate a binary value by a specified voltage or the transition of voltages during a given clock cycle. Therefore, understanding where the symbol begins and ends in time is critical to being able to decode the symbol into a logical bit or number of bits.

There are a number of strategies used to provide reference timing to a network. The higher the data rate capacity expected on a network, the more accurate the timing needs to be. This makes sense when we compare the bit-times associated with low and high capacity networks. As an example, at 1 Mbps, the bit-time is $1/1E6 = 1E-6$ seconds per bit, compared to 1 Gbps where the bit-time is $1/1E9 = 1E-9$ seconds per bit. A reference clock with an accuracy to work only with 1 Mbps rates would not have the accuracy required to reference a faster 1Gbps link.

Below describes types of timing and data synchronization methods.

Asynchronous. With asynchronous data timing, start and stop bits or frames are used to identify the beginning and end of each information segment transmitted. Separate transmit and receive reference clocks are still required to separate bits, but the need to have identical timing is not as critical. Received data buffers are used to store each start/stop frame until it is ready for further processing.

Synchronous. Synchronous timing requires that the transmit and receive clocks are identical. This is typically accomplished by distributing a master clock source to all nodes within the operating network. A synchronization bit pattern precedes each frame during transmission to enable the receiver to identify the start of the frame.

Isochronous. A data stream can be sent without specific reference to a clock. Instead, as the data is received, the receiver recovers the timing from the data rate itself. Therefore, the receiver synchronizes its own clock using the incoming data stream. Since the actual transmit and receive clocks are likely to be dissimilar, buffers must be used.

Plesiochronous. When nodes within a network use clocks that are very close in timing, but do not meet the full definition of synchronous clocks, it is called *plesiochronous*. In a network using this type of timing method, clock slips are expected to occur, especially when long strings of data are sent and received. As such, buffers are required to address clock slips caused by timing errors.

3.9 TIME DIVISION MULTIPLEXING (TDM)

Digital data can be aggregated by using either frequency division multiplexing (FDM), time division multiplexing (TDM), or a combination of both TDM and FDM. We saw in the previous chapter that analog channels can only be aggregated using FDM. However, with digital data, we can separate information in the time domain by dividing data streams into time slots. In fig. 3.20, we see digital baseband signals 1, 2, 3, to n, with each baseband assigned its own unique time slot. However, we would need to make sure that the aggregate data capacity from the multiplexer had sufficient bandwidth to support all of the incoming baseband time slots.

As an example, let's say that all of these channels represented uncompressed PCM voice at 64 kbps each. Each time slot 1 through n, would need to be transmitted at 64 kbps, which means that the

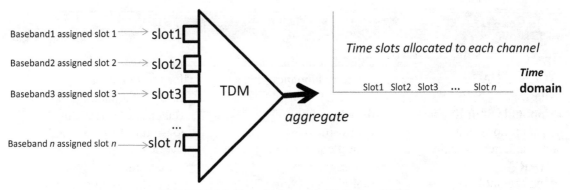

FIGURE 3.20 Time Division Multiplexing (TDM).

aggregate would need to support a minimum of 64 kbps × n (number of time slots) in capacity, otherwise the voice data channels would suffer delay. Therefore, the aggregate must have sufficient frequency bandwidth to support all of the time slots.

In analog voice conversations, we know that a significant amount of bandwidth is taken up by pauses between actual speech. If we digitized a voice conversation, we can fill these pauses with additional voice data, thus be able to support more than one conversation per frequency channel. In fig. 3.21, we can take each frequency channel and divide it to support several more digital basebands, thus multiplying the number of voice calls that can be supported, and increasing our spectral efficiency. As we will see in chapter 10 when we discuss cellular phone systems, this is the reason why service providers upgraded from analog *first generation (1G)* to digital *second generation (2G)* systems.

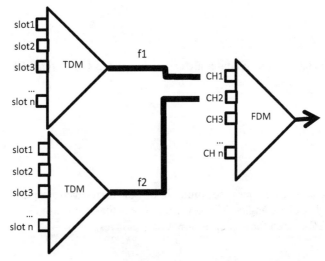

FIGURE 3.21 Time division multiplexing (TDM) applied to each frequency division multiplexing (FDM) channel.

KEY TERMS

4B5B	constellation diagram	line coding
ADC and DAC	cyclic redundancy check	linear block code
Aliasing	(CRC)	M'ary modulation
Amplitude Shift Keying	data encoding	Manchester line coding
asynchronous timing	dataword	non-return to zero (NRZ)
automatic repeat request	digital compression (lossy,	Nyquist sampling
(ARQ)	lossless)	theorem
Baud (symbol rate)	digital signal zero (DS0)	phase shift keying (PSK)
bipolar alternative mark	error control (detection,	plesiochronous timing
inversion (bipolar AMI)	correction)	pulse code modulation
bipolar with eight-zero	forward error correction	(PCM)
substitution (B8ZS)	(FEC)	quadrature amplitude
bit-depth	frequency shift keying	modulation (QAM)
bit error rate (BER)	(FSK)	quantization
bit-time	Hamming distance	quantization noise
coder/decoder	Hartley's Law	symbol
codeword	isochronous timing	synchronous timing

CHAPTER PROBLEMS

1. A signal that is shifted to a higher frequency by mixing it with a carrier is termed as _____.
   a. Baseband
   b. Passband
   c. Broadband
   d. Aggregate

   Answer: b

2. Logical data (1s and 0s) from a computer are coded into an electrical signal which we call the
   _____.
   a. Baseband
   b. Passband
   c. Broadband
   d. Aggregate

   Answer: a

3. PM and PSK modulation techniques are similar in that the carrier wave captures information/message as a series of changing phase angles. The key difference is that PM is used for continuous/analog messages, while PSK is used for digital information/messages.
   a. True
   b. False

   Answer: a

4. Select the correct statement(s) regarding QAM.
   a. QAM consists of two carriers operating at the same frequency
   b. Using QAM, information is captured on the carrier(s) in the form of amplitude and phase shifts
   c. QAM with $M = 8$ can represent 3 bits/symbol
   d. All of the above are correct

Answer: d

5. Calculate the data rate for a 2400 baud signal where each symbol can take on one of two levels ($M = 2$)
   a. 2400 bps
   b. 4800 bps
   c. 9600 bps
   d. 2400 kbps

Answer: a

6. Calculate the data rate for a 1200 baud signal where each symbol can take on one of eight levels ($M = 8$)
   a. 2400 bps
   b. 4800 bps
   c. 3600 bps
   d. 9600 kbps

Answer: c

7. Calculate the data rate for a 9600 baud signal where each symbol can take on one of two levels ($M = 2$)
   a. 2400 bps
   b. 4800 bps
   c. 9600 bps
   d. 9600 kbps

Answer: c

8. A symbol can take on one of 256 signaling levels. How many bits can be represented by a single symbol?
   a. $N = 2$
   b. $N = 4$
   c. $N = 6$
   d. $N = 8$

Answer: d

9. A symbol can take on one of 64 signaling levels. How many bits can be represented by a single symbol?
   a. $N = 2$
   b. $N = 4$
   c. $N = 6$
   d. $N = 8$

Answer: c

10. Applying 128 QAM modulation ($M = 128$), with a Baud rate of 7200, select the correct result below:
    a. $N = 4$ bits/symbol, C(bps) = 28.8 kbps
    b. $N = 5$ bits/symbol, C(bps) = 36 kbps
    c. $N = 6$/symbol, C(bps) = 43.2 kbps
    d. $N = 7$/symbol, C(bps) = 50.4 kbps

Answer: d

11. You are using QPSK modulation in which a symbol can take on one of four values ($0, \pi/2, \pi, 3\pi/2$ rad). How many bits can be represented by a single symbol?
    a. $N = 1$
    b. $N = 2$
    c. $N = 3$
    d. $N = 4$

Answer: b

12. Select the correct statement regarding modulation techniques.
    a. With FM and FSK modulation techniques, analog or digital information is modulated onto the carrier wave as changes in frequency
    b. The FM Index indicates the amount that the carrier wave can change in frequency when representing information
    c. Neither statement is correct
    d. Both a and b are correct

Answer: d

13. What is the Nyquist sampling rate for a frequency bandwidth equal to 88 kHz?
    a. $f_s \geq 88,000$ samples/s
    b. $f_s \geq 176,000$ samples/s
    c. $f_s \geq 176$ samples/s
    d. $f_s \geq 176E6$ samples/s

Answer: b

14. You are converting an analog signal into a digital one. The analog signal has a bandwidth of 8800 Hz, and you have a bit-depth of 6. What data rate will you need to support (i.e., no data compression techniques are used)?
    a. 316.8 kbps
    b. 52.8 kbps
    c. 105.6 kbps
    d. 8800 bps

Answer: c

15. What is the Nyquist sampling rate for a frequency bandwidth equal to 20,000 Hz?
    a. 64 samples/s
    b. 20,000 samples/s
    c. 40,000 samples/s
    d. 10,000 samples/s

Answer: c

16. Select the correct statement regarding pulse code modulation (PCM).
    a. If the Nyquist sampling theorem is not followed, the signal will experience aliasing
    b. Quantization error, also known as quantization noise, occurs when there is a mismatch between the mapping of an analog signal's amplitude and the digital quantization level represented by bits (i.e., bit-depth)
    c. CODECs (coder, decoders) are analog-to-digital (AD) and digital-to-analog converters.
    d. All of the above are correct

Answer: d

17. ADPCM and DPCM, like PCM, always have a bit-depth of 8 bits.
    a. True
    b. False

Answer: b

18. ADPCM provides better performance than DPCM when the analog signal being sampled varies dramatically in amplitude from one sample to the next.
    a. True
    b. False

Answer: a

19. Regardless of the bit-depth applied during the A-D process, you will always experience some amount of quantization error.
    a. True
    b. False

Answer: a

20. Which line coding method codes logical "1s" and "0s" as +v and −v, voltages.
    a. NRZ
    b. Manchester
    c. Bipolar AMI
    d. B8ZS

Answer: a

21. ASCII Extended is an encoding method used to map logical "1s" and "0s" to symbols.
    a. True
    b. False

Answer: a

22. CRC is an error detection method using a shared polynomial operation between transmitter and receiver. This operation creates a frame check sequence which is used by the receiver to determine if bit errors have occurred.
    a. True
    b. False

Answer: a

23. Manchester is a method where logical 1s and 0s are line coded as low-to-high and high-to-low voltage transitions.
    a. True
    b. False

Answer: a

24. Which multiplexing technique can be used with analog signals?
   a. FDM
   b. TDM
   c. Spread spectrum
   d. All techniques can be used with analog signals

Answer: a

25. DSI (digital speech interpolation) is a digital technique that takes advantage of the normal pauses in human speech to insert additional data.
   a. True
   b. False

Answer: a

26. Digital communications require that the transmit and receive clocks are in synchronization with one another. When clocks are out of synch, data errors can occur.
   a. True
   b. False

Answer: a

27 . Which method is used to ensure receive clock synchronization by mapping four-bit words into five-bit representations?
   a. B8ZS
   b. AMI
   c. 4B/5B
   d. DSI

Answer: c

28 . Which timing/data synchronization method uses start and stop bits when transmitting digital data?
   a. Asynchronous
   b. Synchronous
   c. Isochronous
   d. Plesiochronous

Answer: a

29. Select the correct statement(s) regarding "Error Control."
   a. With "Error Detection," additional bits are added to the dataword to help identify bit errors experienced during transmission
   b. With "Error Correction," redundant bits are added to the dataword to help identify and correct bit errors experienced during transmission
   c. Error control provides probabilities of experiencing errors, vice an absolute certainty of experiencing errors
   d. All of the above are correct

Answer: d

30. Which multiplexing technique can be used with both analog and digital basebands?
    a. CDMA
    b. FDMA
    c. TDMA
    d. Spread spectrum

Answer: b

31. Which multiple access technique can be used with analog basebands?
    a. FDMA
    b. TDMA
    c. CDMA
    d. Both FDMA and TDMA

Answer: a

32. What can be done to compress digital data in order to reduce bandwidth?
    a. Remove "white space"
    b. Abbreviate commonly used characters
    c. Remove commonly used format information
    d. All of the above

Answer: d

CHAPTER 4

Transmission System Fundamentals

4.1 INTRODUCTION

The ability to successfully transmit information in the form of either a baseband or modulated carrier (passband) depends upon several parameters such as the type of information being sent, transmission power, electrical or electromagnetic (EM)noise environment, modulation or line coding techniques, frequency, frequency bandwidth, and the communications medium. As the communications signal propagates through any guided or unguided medium, it is subjected to multiple transmission impairments in the form of noise, signal delays, and attenuation. Matching a transmission medium to the overall communications system is one of many key considerations.

In this chapter, we discuss the typical transmission impairments faced by guided and unguided communication systems such as noise, signal attenuation, propagation, and processing delays. We also introduce the key concept of *signal-to-noise ratio (SNR or S/N)* and *noise floor*, as well as some of the techniques used to compensate or eliminate noise from our systems.

4.2 NOISE IN COMMUNICATION SYSTEMS

When we communicate electronically, electrical and EM noise products are always present across the entire electromagnetic spectrum. This presents a significant problem for our receiver system, making it difficult to identify and recover the original transmitted signal. In the time domain, noise can occur as an impulse of very short duration (e.g., electrical power spike or lightening), or it can be persistent over long periods of time (e.g., thermal noise). In the frequency domain, noise can appear as narrow band interference or can exist over the entire frequency spectrum. If we understand the types of noise products that are predominant in any particular system, then we can devise ways to compensate for it.

Key to understanding how noise impacts our ability to communicate is the **signal-to-noise ratio (SNR or S/N)**. The *signal-to-noise ratio*[1] *(SNR)* represents the ratio of signal power in watts, S, over noise power in watts, N, and it gives us a valuable metric in determining whether sufficient signal power exists at the receiver to overcome the noise. This ratio is often represented in decibel values. The noise power, N, within the SNR equation represents sources that appear continuous over a wide frequency spectrum (*wideband*), and over time. This *noise floor*, also called the *additive white Gaussian noise*[2] *(AWGN)*, includes thermal noise, noise caused by the radiation from the earth, sun, and other cosmic sources.

$$SNR = \frac{S}{N} \text{ (watts)} \tag{4.1}$$

$$SNR \text{ (dB)} = [SNR] = [S] - [N] = 10\log_{10}S - 10\log_{10}N \tag{4.2}$$

Notice in equation (4.2) that we use brackets [] to denote a decibel value. This notation will be used throughout this textbook.

In addition to AWGN, there may be other noise components that have similar characteristics that also contribute to the overall *noise floor* figure. In practice, communications engineers will perform spectral surveys around proposed radio frequency (RF) communications sites in order to determine the practical noise floor that exists during certain times of the day. A device called a spectrum analyzer is used to detect the noise floor within the frequency bandwidth of interest. With the measured noise floor value known, the signal power needed at the receiver can be determined. Determining the SNR required to meet certain specifications is key in designing an operable communications link. In this text for reasons of simplification, we will treat the noise floor as equaling *thermal noise*.

Example 4.1: Given a detected power at the receiver of $S = 1 \times 10^{-7}$ mW = 1E−7 mW *(note: "E" stands for the exponent −7)*, and a measured noise floor of $N = 1 \times 10^{-10}$ mW = 1E−10 mW. Determine the SNR in mW and dBm.

Answer:

$$\frac{S}{N} = \frac{1 \times 10^{-7} \text{ mW}}{1 \times 10^{-10} \text{ mW}} = \underline{1000 \text{ mW}}$$

$$[SNR] = \frac{S}{N} \text{ (dBm)} = 10\log_{10}\left(\frac{S}{1 \text{ mW}}\right) - 10\log_{10}\left(\frac{N}{1 \text{ mW}}\right)$$

$$= 10\log_{10}\left(\frac{1 \times 10^{-7} \text{ mW}}{1 \text{ mW}}\right) - 10\log_{10}\left(\frac{1 \times 10^{-10} \text{ mW}}{1 \text{ mW}}\right)$$

$$= -70 \text{ dBm} - (-100 \text{ dBm}) = \underline{30 \text{ dBm}}$$

Figure 4.1 depicts a *narrowband* signal, S, and noise floor, N, in the frequency domain. Under normal operating conditions, S is much greater than N thus providing sufficient signal power over the

---

[1] Signal-to-noise ratio is typically measured as the received signal strength over the noise floor. The noise floor includes noise products that are consistent over the operational frequency and time frame. A major component is thermal noise.

[2] "Gaussian noise" refers to the normal distribution of noise power density over time.

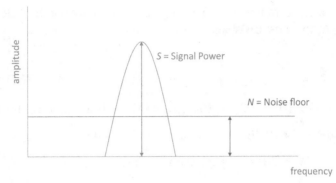

FIGURE 4.1 Signal-to-Noise Ratio.

noise floor, SNR,[3] to enable reception. However, there will inevitably times when the noise floor rises, thereby reducing SNR making the power, S, at the receiver less distinguishable from the surrounding noise. Therefore, engineers will design power transmitters that can temporarily increase power output in order to increase S. This additional power is called the ***link margin***, and it provides a way to handle temporary decreases in SNR due to rising noise floors or increased signal power attenuation caused by phenomena such as weather.

4.2.1 Thermal Noise

Thermal noise (aka Johnson or Nyquist[4] Noise) is caused by the agitation of electrons which exists in all electronic components. It spans the entire frequency spectrum and is dependent upon temperature. As temperature increases, so does the agitation or activity of electrons thus resulting in increased *thermal noise power*. An increase in thermal noise power impacts our ability to distinguish the signal from background noise. Since thermal noise exists in all electronic devices, the noise produced cannot be eliminated, and therefore sufficient signal power must be received in order to effectively overcome the effects of noise.

The formula for thermal noise power is given in equation (4.3), where N is thermal power in watts, k is Boltzmann's constant (1.38×10^{-23} J/K), T is temperature given in Kelvin degrees, and B is the bandwidth in Hz.

$$N \text{ (watts)} = kTB \tag{4.3}$$

Equation (4.4) is the thermal power formula given in decibels referenced to 1 W.[5]

$$N \text{ (dBW)} = [N] = 10\log_{10}(k) + 10\log_{10}(T) + 10\log_{10}(B) \tag{4.4}$$

---

[3] When using instrumentation, the signal power measured is usually a combination of S and N. In other words, the measured signal is actually equal to $S + N$, and not just S. Therefore, engineers will use the equation $(S + N)/N$ in practice; however, the difference between S/N and $(S + N)/N$ values is typically very small. In this text, we will only consider S/N.

[4] Named after engineers John B. Johnson and Harry Nyquist, who first measured and theorized the existence of thermal noise.

[5] Recall that X dBW $= 10 \times \log_{10}(Y \text{ W}/1 \text{ W})$, therefore, this equation is referenced to 1 W.

Example 4.2: Given a temperature of 295 K degrees and a bandwidth of 36 MHz, what is the thermal noise power, N, in watts, dBW and dBm?

Answer:

N (watts) = $(1.38 \times 10^{-23}$ J/K$) \times (295$ K$^o) \times (36 \times 10^6$ Hz$)$ = $\underline{1.46 \times 10^{-13}}$ W

N (dBW) = $10\log_{10}(1.38 \times 10^{-23}$ J/K$) + 10\log_{10}(295$ K$) + 10\log_{10}(36$ K^o 10^6 Hz$)$

$\quad\quad\quad = -228.6$ dB $+ 24.70$ dB $+ 75.56$ dB $= \underline{-128.34}$ dBW

N (dBm) = -128.34 dBW $+ 30 = \underline{-98.34}$ dBm

Example 4.3: Given a received signal power of $S = -82$ dBm, noise temperature of 270 K degrees, and a signal bandwidth of 36 MHz, determine the decibel value of SNR?

Answer:

N (watts) $\quad = (1.38 \times 10^{-23}$ J/K$) \times (270$ K$^o) \times (36 \times 10^6$ Hz$)$ = $\underline{134.14 \times 10^{-15}}$ W

N (dBW) $\quad = 10\log_{10}(1.38 \times 10^{-23}$ J/K$) + 10\log_{10}(270$ K$^o) + 10\log_{10}(36 \times 10^6$ Hz$)$

$\quad\quad\quad\quad = -228.6$ dB $+ 24.31$ dB $+ 75.56$ dB $= \underline{-128.73}$ dBW

N (dBm) $\quad = -128.73$ dBW $+ 30 = \underline{-98.72}$ dBm

$[SNR]$ (dBs) = $[S] - [N] = -82$ dBm $- (-98.72$ dBm$)$ = $\underline{16.72}$ dB

***Thermal noise power density*, *No*,** is thermal noise power normalized to a 1 Hz bandwidth. This is a convenient metric used when doing link analysis calculations, a topic that will be discussed in a later chapter. The formula for No is essentially the same as N, except with $B = 1$ Hz, which results in equations (4.5) and (4.6).

$$No \text{ (watts)} = kT \quad\quad\quad\quad\quad\quad\quad\quad (4.5)$$

$$No \text{ (dBW)} = 10\log_{10}(k) + 10\log_{10}(T) \quad\quad\quad (4.6)$$

Example 4.4: Given the same information as in example 4.2, what is the noise power density, No, in watts, dBW, and dBm?

Answer:

No(watts) = $(1.38 \times 10^{-23}$ J/K$) \times (295$ K$)$ = $\underline{4.07 \times 10^{-21}}$ W

No(dBW) = $10\log_{10}(1.38 \times 10^{-23}$ J/K$) + 10\log_{10}(295$ K$)$ = -228.6 dB $+ 24.70$ dB $= \underline{-203.9}$ dBW

N(dBm) $\quad = -203.9$ dBW $+ 30 = -173.9$ dBm

4.2.2 Other Noise Sources

When designing a communication link, we typically design using a noise floor that is continuous and predictable over time and frequency spectrum. This enables us to design a system that satisfies our communications needs without over designing it to accommodate unpredictable noise events. For noise that occurs on a periodic or unpredictable basis, engineers design transmitters that provide

additional link margin to compensate for periods of either higher noise power or higher signal attenuation. However, even when a healthy link margin exists, noise and attenuation can reduce received
SNR to the point that prevents successful communications from taking place. Since communications
link outages cannot always be prevented, engineers must determine what *availability*[6] and *reliability*[7] requirements are needed for a given application. For communications that must be highly available, path redundancy and use of highly reliable components are critical. For other systems where
outages are tolerated for short periods, the system can be designed to meet lower availability and
reliability requirements. The following describes some common types of noise.

Impulse Noise. In the time domain, impulse noise is characterized by its very short duration. In the
frequency domain, it can either appear as narrow band or wideband interference. Its occurrence is
unpredictable and therefore not used as part of the noise floor when designing the communications
link. Sources of impulse noise are electrical machinery, power lines, electronics, atmospheric noises
such as lightning, etc. Impulse noise is more devastating to digital links than analog ones. On digital
links, the use of error control methods is used to help counter the data loss caused by impulse noise.

Intermodulation (IM) Noise. *Intermodulation* noise (aka, intermodulation distortion) occurs when
two or more frequency channels operate through a nonlinear device such as a transmitter power
amplifier or receiver amplifier. The result is an undesired mixing (i.e., addition and subtraction of
harmonic components) of frequency channels resulting in the creation of new unwanted frequencies. Intermodulation can also occur when a receive antenna and nonlinear amplifier on one system
accidently captures the transmit signal from another adjacent communications system. Transmit
and receive filters are commonly used to minimize the effects of IM. A subset of IM is called *passive IM (PIM)*, in which passive nonlinear components act to combine two or more frequencies
creating additional undesired frequency products. Passive components are typically caused by
mechanical devices such as coaxial connectors, antennas, isolators, and even mechanical joints on
antenna towers where oxidation has taken place. The overall impact of PIM is much less a concern
than IM produced by active components.

Cochannel Interference (CCI). When the same communications frequency is used by two systems that are adjacent to one another, then the probability of experiencing *cochannel interference
(CCI)* is high. In a WLAN system where access points (APs) can share the same operating frequencies, it is critical to carefully plan both the physical location and frequency assignments of the APs.
The same careful planning is required when architecting cellular systems, especially in fourth-
generation systems where the goal is to use all available system frequencies in every cell regardless
of the cell's physical placement. In this later case, close coordination between cellular base stations
is required to prevent CCI between adjacent cells.

Crosstalk. An electrical signal traveling through a wire creates an electromagnetic field as discussed in chapter 1. If two or more wires, each carrying an electrical signal, are in close proximity

---

[6] Availability is the percentage of time over a year that a system is available for communications. As an example, an availability of 0.9 equates to a system that is available 90% of the time throughout the year, which includes system outages
caused by maintenance, system failure, or weather.

[7] The reliability of a system is the probability that the system will operate successfully over time without a major outage.
Reliability is sometimes given in hours of operation before system failure.

to one another, then their EM fields will couple thus creating a noise called ***crosstalk***. In a bundle of unshielded twisted pair (UTP) copper wires, each pair is twisted in a helical pattern at different ratios in order to reduce the crosstalk between adjacent wire pairs. Shielding of wires can also be used to reduce crosstalk.

4.3 DIGITAL COMMUNICATIONS CAPACITY

When we consider analog communications, we know that greater frequency bandwidth is associated with greater information carrying capacity. A frequency bandwidth of 4 kHz, which is classified as a *narrowband* signal, provides voice grade quality over telephone lines, while a larger analog bandwidth of 6 MHz enables the transmission of a television broadcast channel. Like the analog system, we want to understand the relationship between frequency bandwidth and data rate capacity in a digital communications system.

Our understanding of digital communications capacity comes from the early 20th-century work of Harry Nyquist, Ralph Hartley, and Claude Shannon. In an attempt to better understand the relationship between the telegraph system and frequency bandwidth, Nyquist determined that the number of symbols that can be sent is equal to, or less than, twice the frequency bandwidth [eq. (4.7)].

$$S \text{ (symbols/s)} \leq 2B, B \text{ is bandwidth in Hertz} \tag{4.7}$$

Recall from section 3.3 that a single symbol can represent more than one data bit provided that the symbol can take on a value of M greater than or equal to 4 values per symbol (i.e., $M \geq 4$). Hartley provided us with an equation to help us understand this relationship:

$$\text{Hartley's Law: } C(\text{bps}) = S \text{ (baud}^8) \times \log_2 M \tag{3.3}$$

As a consequence, the Nyquist equation was modified to address data rate capacity based upon ***Hartley's Law*** where a single symbol, S, can have multiple values. Equation (4.8) is called the Hartley "*idealized*" capacity, where C is the maximum data rate in bits per second, B is the bandwidth in Hz, and M represents the number of levels possible per symbol.

$$C(\text{bps}) = 2B \times \log_2 M \tag{4.8}$$

However, equation (4.8) does not take into consideration the effect of noise within the transmitting environment. Therefore, Shannon took Hartley's work a step further to come up with an equation based upon both bandwidth and SNR. The result is shown in equation (4.9) which is known as the ***Shannon-Hartley Theoretical Capacity***. This equation gives us the maximum "*theoretical*" data rate capacity achievable given bandwidth, signal strength, and noise.

Figure 4.2 shows the Shannon-Hartley threshold line that represents the maximum theoretical data rate achievable given a system's frequency bandwidth and SNR. The y-axis represents data rate capacity normalized to 1 Hz, and the x-axis represent the SNR in decibel value. The points making

---

[8] Baud = symbols per second.

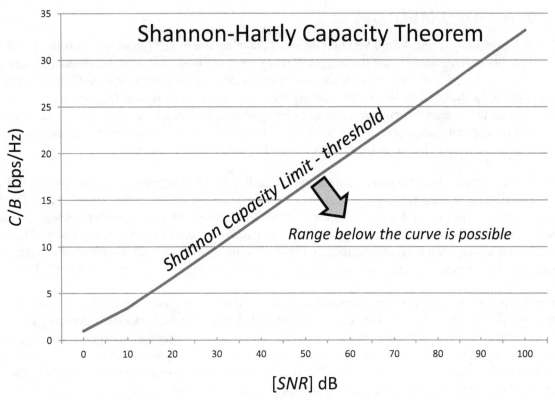

FIGURE 4.2 The graph shows the Shannon-Hartley theoretical capacity line as a function of bit rate per Hz and signal-to-noise ratio in decibels. Only values below the Shannon capacity line are achievable, with points on the line representing the absolute theoretical maximum rates. The greater the sophistication of the modulation techniques (i.e., M'ary modulation where "M" increases in levels per symbol) the closer we get to achieving the maximum theoretical capacity.

up the threshold line represents the theoretical maximum data rate given bandwidth and SNR. All points falling below the threshold line are achievable, while points above the line are not theoretically possible. Since there are many factors involved, realizing this theoretical maximum is extremely difficult. However, achieving the Shannon-Hartley capacity is the ultimate goal of communications and IT engineers.

$$C(\text{bps}) = B \times \log_2(1 + SNR) \tag{4.9}$$

Example 4.5: Determine the Shannon-Hartley maximum data rate capacity given the following: $B = 36$ MHz, SNR = 100.

Answer: $C(\text{bps}) = B \times \log_2(1 + SNR) = 36\text{E}6 \text{ Hz} \times \log_2(1+100) = 36\text{E}6 \text{ Hz} \times \log_2(101)$

Note: Using the following logarithmic identity, $\log_b X = \left(\dfrac{\log_{10} X}{\log_{10} b}\right)$

$$C(\text{bps}) = 36\text{E}6 \text{ Hz} \times \left(\frac{\log_{10} 101}{\log_{10} 2}\right) = 239{,}695{,}613 \text{ bps} = \underline{239 \text{ Mbps}}$$

4.4 GUIDED MEDIUM

When Samuel Morse and Alfred Vail first invented the telegraph in 1837, iron wire was used as the medium between stations. Since the telegraph wires were not protected from harsh environments, they would expand and contract with extreme temperatures causing breakage. Not only did iron wires break easily, but they also rusted causing them to become an unavoidable maintenance issue. It was soon discovered that copper wires were better able to withstand the harsh environment, and it quickly replaced iron as the choice medium. Copper also possessed molecular properties that enabled it to conduct electricity better than most other affordable[9] materials.

Today, the transmission of signals within a guided medium can be electrical, electromagnetic (EM), or optical. One of the advantages of transmitting over guided medium is that signals transmitted over separate wires or cables can be isolated from one another. Of course, with electrical or EM waves, crosstalk must be prevented by twisting wire pairs or by shielding the cable, or both. This is in contrast to unguided RF transmissions that share a common medium and therefore must separate channels by frequency, time, or spread spectrum technologies in order to prevent IM or CCI.

In guided systems, signal power *attenuation* is the weakening of signal strength as it propagates through the medium. Attenuation, which is also called ***insertion loss***, is often identified by the manufacturer in terms of decibels per unit distance. The amount of attenuation experienced depends upon the signal frequency, wire diameter, number of connectors or splices, and the noise reduction technique[10] applied. As an example, the *TIA (Telecommunications Industry Association)/EIA (Electronics Industries Alliance) standard 568-B.2* specifies insertion loss, propagation delay, and crosstalk in twisted pair cabling such as Cat5e, Cat6, Cat7, etc. This standard provides guidance for determining expected decibel loss per 100 m lengths as a function of signal frequency and wire diameter; the later typically identified by an *AWG (American Wire Gauge standard)* number. Figure 4.3 shows that typical decibel attenuation per 100 m increases as frequency increases in Cat5e UTP. It should be noted that an increase in attenuation as frequency increases is common for signals propagating in all guided and unguided mediums.

Chapter 1, section 1.4, described how guided transmission lines can be modeled. In this model, we found that *impedance*[11] characterizes the line, and this impedance must be matched by devices that are connected to the line itself. By doing this, destructive signal reflections[12] can be avoided within the guided medium. A mismatch in impedance causes ***return loss***, which is also typically measured in decibels per unit length.

---

[9] Silver is slightly better than copper at conducting electricity; however, the price for gaining slightly better conductivity would be unjustified in most applications.

[10] Noise reduction techniques can include the shielding of the medium or use of balanced signals.

[11] The flow of current within a conductor is impeded by both the resistive value of the wire (R), and the reactive values of inductance and capacitance (X) and is represented by impedance (Z).

[12] In an ideal communications link, impedance values of the line are matched by all connectors and devices thus allowing the signal to travel from transmitter to receiver. However, if a mismatch of impedance values is encountered by the transmitted signal due to mismatched connectors or devices, then the signal will reflect back toward the transmitter causing interference. This ultimately results in distortion of the received signal.

FIGURE 4.3 Typical unshielded twisted pair insertion loss (attenuation) per 100 m.

In addition to *attenuation (insertion loss)* and *return loss*, signals will have associated propagation delays that are determined by the *speed of light* through the medium, the *circuit length*, and *processing delays* within the circuit.

The maximum speed at which light can travel occurs in a vacuum at 3×10^8 (3E8) m/s. In all other materials such as air, water, glass, copper[13] (i.e., electrical and EM signal speed), etc., it is lower. The **refractive index** which is unique to each material enables us to determine the maximum speed of light through that material. The equation of the refractive index, n, is given in equation (4.10).

$$Refractive\ Index,\ n = \frac{c}{V_s},\ where\ c = 3E8\ m/s,\ V_s = speed\ of\ light\ through\ the\ material \qquad \textbf{(4.10)}$$

The refractive index, n, for the vacuum of space is $n = 1$, since $c = V_s$. In air, $n = 1.000293$, therefore, the speed of light through air is, $V_s = c/n = $ 3E8 m/s $\div$ 1.000293 = 2.99E8 m/s, which is slightly slower than the speed of light in a vacuum.

Example 4.6: Given the refractive index for a single mode fiber optic core made of pure silica is $n = 1.444$ (at a wavelength of 1500 nm). What is the speed of light through this core? What would be the propagation delay in seconds for a signal traveling through 100 km with a processing delay of 5 μs?

---

[13] The speed of light in a metal is actually the speed of the electromagnetic wave through the metal. In metals, the refractive index can be misleading since it can be less than 1. However, the speed of an EM wave through copper, as an example, is approximately 70% to 90% of the maximum speed of light in a vacuum (i.e., it is not faster than the maximum).

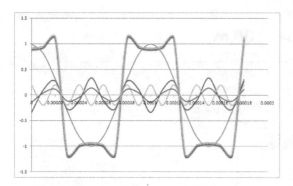

(a) Transmitted digital signal. Signal Bandwidth consists of 1st, 3rd, 5th, and 7th harmonics, with all harmonics in phase. The resulting signal is shown as the bold waveform which appears as a square wave.

(b) Received distorted digital signal. Now the 1st, 3rd, 5th, and 7th harmonics are all out-of-phase from one another. The resulting signal received is shown as distorted digital data.

FIGURE 4.4 Distortion of a digital signal.

Answer: $Vs(\text{pure silica}) = \dfrac{c}{n} = \dfrac{3E8 \; m/s}{1.444} = \underline{207.76E6 \; m/s}$

Propagation Delay (s) $= \dfrac{100E3 \; m}{207.76E6 \; m/s} + (5E-6s) = (481.32 \times 10^{-6} \, s) + (5 \times 10^{-6} \, s) = \underline{486 \; \mu s}.$

In analog communications, propagation delays can be annoying; however in digital links, it leads to the distortion of the signal pulses called ***delay distortion***. A modulated carrier containing information will have a given bandwidth that spans from the highest frequency to the lowest frequency. The transmitted signal starts off with all frequency components within the band in phase with one another. However, when the signal arrives at the receiver, the various frequency components making up the transmitted bandwidth are no longer in phase thus causing the received digital pulses to appear distorted (see fig. 4.4). The received distorted signal will typically go through an *equalization* process to help eliminate signal pulse distortion.

4.4.1 Twisted Pair (TP)

Twisted pair (TP) cables are widely used in both analog and digital communications. Today, local loop connections between a residence and telephone central office (CO) still use ***unshielded twisted pair (UTP)*** to carry both analog voice and digital data. UTP is also widely used with *Ethernet local area networks (LANs)* because of its low costs and ease of installation. While it is not ideal for high capacity communications, the implementation of sophisticated *M'ary modulation* techniques enables twisted pair cables to support higher data rate applications (i.e., up to 1 Gbps) over short distances.

As the name describes, twisted pair uses two wire conductors in a ***balanced configuration*** to support communications. This is in comparison to an ***unbalanced configuration*** (e.g., coaxial cable) in which only a single conductor is used. Both balanced and unbalanced guided media are used extensively in today's telecommunication systems.

So what do these terms actually mean? . . . and why are they important for telecommunications?

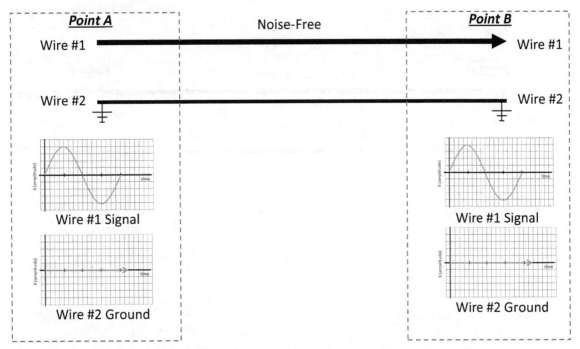

FIGURE 4.5 Unbalanced two-wire circuit in a noise-free environment.

The answers to these questions reside in how each handles noise. As we know, *electromagnetic (EM) noise* from numerous sources in the environment will degrade signal quality, sometimes to the point where the distant end receiver cannot distinguish the signal from the noise itself. The *signal-to-noise ratio (SNR)* is an important measure that helps determine whether a signal can be reliably received. Recall that the signal-to-noise ratio in decibels is given by equation (4.2), and is rewritten below.

$$SNR(\text{dB}) = [SNR] = 10\log_{10}\left[\frac{(\text{signal power})}{(\text{noise power})}\right] \qquad \textbf{(4.11)}$$

From equation (4.11), it can be seen that as noise increases SNR decreases and reception eventually degrades to nothing. By reducing or eliminating EM noise from the signal's environment, our ability to receive signals reliably improves.

Balanced and unbalanced circuits handle this noise problem in different ways. To illustrate, consider a simple two-wire *unbalanced* guided medium system similar to the one that existed in the early days of the telegraph. One-wire conductor carried the signal while the second conductor provided a common reference point to ground for the entire circuit. Figure 4.5 illustrates an unbalanced two-wire transmission system in a RF "noise-free" environment. We use a simple sine wave to represent the signal being transmitted from point "A" to point "B."

In a noise-free transmission environment, the signal is not degraded by any RF noise it encounters along the transmission path or at the receiver. This, of course is an ideal case, and we know that thermal noise will always exist and must be considered. In addition, we know that the received signal, *S*, experiences a certain amount of attenuation based upon transmission frequency and distance. Both negatively impacts SNR.

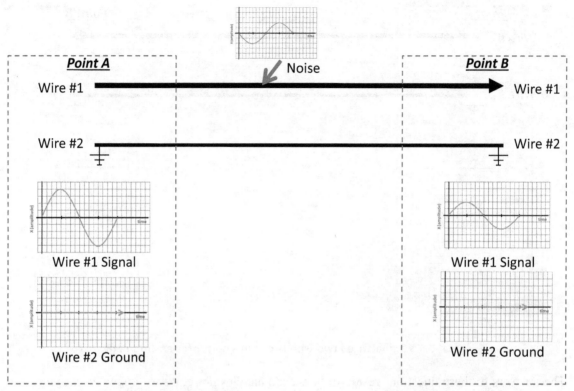

FIGURE 4.6 Noise introduced to a two-wire unbalanced circuit.

To make our example more realistic, let's introduce a simple and discrete frequency noise source[14] that is the same frequency as the signal, but with different amplitudes and phase angles.

Signal: $s(t) = 4 \sin(2\pi ft)$

Noise: $n(t) = 2 \sin(2\pi ft + 180°)$

In figure 4.6 we see that in the unbalanced case when no EM shielding exists, the noise element adds detrimentally to the signal element resulting in a lower signal level, thus lower SNR, received at the point B receiver. To reduce our signal loss, we can configure our two-wire model as a balanced signal pair.

In a balanced configuration the signal is transmitted over two conductors, with each signal essentially being the mirror image of the other (i.e., both signals are polar opposites). Because EM noise tends to be of a single polarity, it affects the balanced signal on each conductor differently. The differences between the two received signals can then be combined at the receiver to eliminate the noise element, thus recovering the original signal transmitted (fig. 4.7).

---

[14] Noise sources are complex and therefore cover a frequency bandwidth vice a discrete frequency. For this specific explanation, however, we choose a very simple "pure" or discrete frequency noise source to simplify the description.

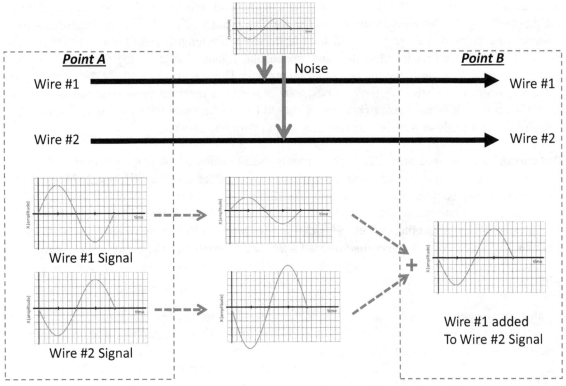

FIGURE 4.7 Balanced media results in noise cancellation.

Four-wire media is typically used for full-duplex data communications, while two-wire[15] provides half-duplex communications. Like two-wire, four-wire is configured as a balanced signal providing full duplex communications with two conductors used for transmit data, and the other two conductors used for receive data.

"*Twisted* pair" describes the helical twisting of the two conductors that make up a single pair. This is done to prevent crosstalk between adjacent wire pairs within a bundle of wires. As an example, Cat5E cable consists of eight-wire conductors paired into four pairs. In order to prevent crosstalk between the four Cat5E pairs, different twist ratios are used within the bundle. The different twist ratios also mean that each pair has different conductor lengths, with highest twist ratio pairs having longer lengths than the lower twist ratio pairs. When just one pair is used for either transmit or receive paths, the different lengths between cable pairs do not impact communications. However, in order to increase transmission capacity, certain specifications call for the use of more than one-wire pair within a single bundle in the transmit and receive directions. This means that two-wire pairs (four conductors) will be used for transmit, while the other two pairs are used for receive. The different length pairs sending data in parallel can lead to signal distortion.

---

[15] We will see in later chapters that techniques can be applied to enable a two-wire pair to provide full-duplex communications through use of FDM and devices such as magnetic hybrids.

As an example, we know that the signal travels at the speed of light dictated by the refractive index for the medium. Say we elect to use two-wire pairs within a Cat5e cable to transmit in parallel; however, we know that these pairs will have different cable lengths based upon differing twist ratios. Since both signals travel at the same speed, the signal carried by the shorter length pair reaches the receiver slightly before the longer length pair. This means that parts of the digital signal pulse are received at slightly different times, thus causing the received pulse to be distorted. This type of distortion is termed *delay skew* and it should be compensated for by using techniques that delay received signals so that their arrival times align with one another.

Basic *unshielded twisted pair (UTP)* is commonly used in many of today's digital systems. While the noise reduction capability of balanced signals is effective for many applications, shielded[16] TP performance may be required for situations where the use of balanced circuits is not enough to reject EMI (electromagnetic interference). Conductive shielding can be configured around each pair, around the entire bundle, or both. *Shielded twisted pair (STP)* surrounds each signal pair with a conductive shield, whereas *screened twisted pair (ScTP)* surrounds the entire cable bundle with conductive material. In either case, a correctly connected shield will shunt EMI safely to ground without disruption to the signal.

Finally, the diameter of the conductive wire determines the capacity that the medium can support, as well as the distance that the signal can travel. For typical Ethernet data applications using TP, Cat5e is common with a wire diameter equal to AWG 24. Cat5e is used for 10/100 Mbps LANs (i.e., 10/100BaseT). Cat6 and Cat7 cables have an increased wire diameter, AWG 23, and can be used for higher capacity communications such as 1000BaseT or 10 GbE. *(Note: AWG stands for the American Wire Gauge which is a measure of the diameter of a wire. The larger the AWG number, the smaller the wire diameter. In the example above, Cat6/7 wire has a smaller AWG number, but larger wire diameter compared to Cat5e).*

Twisted pair is easy to manufacture and install; however, the data rate capacity is limited and physical security from wire taps is extremely poor.

4.4.2 Coaxial Cable

Coaxial cable is an example of an *unbalanced* guided medium in which the center signal conductor is protected by an outer layer shield connected to ground. Figure 4.8 shows how noise current is shunted harmlessly to ground. In this case, the signal is not degraded by the noise.

Widely used today for cable television distribution, coaxial cables have a more complex construction than TP as can be seen in the cross-section in fig. 4.9. Therefore, the manufacturing costs are higher. A single center conductor is used to carry the signal in an unbalanced configuration. The diameter, or gauge, of the center conductor can vary in size depending upon the frequency of the signal and required transmission capacity. Since coaxial conductors have a larger diameter than TP, it is able to support

---

[16] The "shielding" is made of conductive material separated from the signal conductor by dielectric material. The shield is connected to an electrical ground, effectively shunting any noise current harmlessly to ground and away from the signal itself.

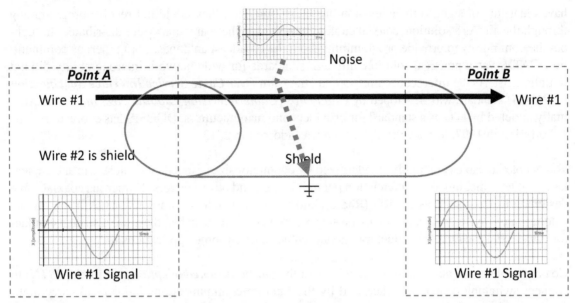

FIGURE 4.8 Coaxial Cable. RF Noise is intercepted by the coaxial cable outer shield and shunted to ground.

higher transmission frequencies and greater data rate capacities compared to TP. The center conductor is surrounded by a dielectric material[17] that isolates the signal conductor from the outer shielding. The dielectric constant of the material used as the insulator contributes to the overall impedance value of the line itself. Surrounding the insulator is the conductive shield which prevents electromagnetic interference (EMI) from entering the center conductor by shunting this RF interference to ground. In all coaxial installations, it is critical to ensure that the shield is properly connected to ground, otherwise the shielding will allow EMI to leak into the center conductor causing signal distortion. Finally, an outer jacket surrounds the shield which protects the entire cable from the environment.

When we think of coaxial cable applications, we typically think of the cable television industry or **CATV (Community Antenna Television)**. CATV had its origins as a way for communities in mountainous or rural areas to receive television broadcasts. Since many residences in these areas did not

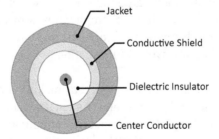

FIGURE 4.9 Parts of a Coaxial Cable.

---

[17] Polyethylene and Teflon are commonly used dielectric materials in coaxial construction.

have clear line of sight to the television broadcast antennas, they could not receive programming through the air. As a solution, coaxial cables connected to these antennas were distributed throughout the community to provide programming from the broadcast antennas. For numerous communities, CATV was a practical solution although standards for wide network interoperability did not initially exist. As the Internet became popular, the ***Data Over Cable Service Interface Specification (DOCSIS)*** standard was developed by *CableLabs (Cable Television Laboratories, Inc.)*, and eventually adopted by ITU as a standard for providers and manufacturers. DOCSIS has evolved from its 1.0 offering in 1997, to DOCSIS 3.1 which was adopted in 2013.

Today coaxial cables are highly standardized by conductor sizes, impedance, dielectric and capacitance values, shielding type, attenuation per unit length, and others factors. Numerous coaxial cable designations exist such as the RG (Radio Guide) series, which is common for CATV and home entertainment systems. In addition to the single conductor coaxial cable, there are also dual conductor (twin-axial) and triple conductor (triaxial) cables used in some applications today.

Coaxial cables have also be used extensively in the ***public switched telephone network (PSTN)*** to connect switching centers together, and by the satellite communications industry to carry high-frequency signals from earth station antennas to earth station terminal equipment. Early forms of Ethernet, ***10Base5*** and ***10Base2***, also adopted coaxial cables as the shared medium, however, because of the need for special coaxial connectors and terminators, and the difficultly of implementation, it soon gave way to TP LANs. As such, these Ethernet standards are now obsolete even though their performance was superior to that of TP-based Ethernet LANs of the time.

Coaxial cables have advantages over twisted pair (TP) when it comes to data rate capacity, noise rejection through shielding, and security from physical intrusion due to its more complex structure. However, the disadvantages when compared to TP include higher costs for manufacturing and installation.

4.4.3 Fiber Optic (FO) Cable

Investigating the use of light as a way to communicate optically goes back to the days of signal fires, lanterns, and semaphore systems. However, when we consider today's modern optical communication systems, the origin goes back to Alexander Graham Bell's experimentation with the *photophone* in 1880. In Bell's experiment, sound vibrated a mirror which was exposed to sunlight. As the mirror vibrated, it essentially modulated the sunlight, which would be captured and turned back into sound at the receiver device. Bell's photophone was mechanical in nature, which is in contrast to today's optical systems that consist of sophisticated laser light sources and detectors that transmit and receive modulated light waves of information.

Optical light operates at the 10^{12} Hz, or THz, range, thus making it an ideal medium for high data rate communications. There are several benefits and challenges when working with optical systems. Advantages include an ability to support high-capacity communications as a consequence of the high frequencies involved, and the optical signal's immunity from RFI (radio frequency interference). One disadvantage includes the need for direct line of sight (LOS) between source and detector, thus making it an unsuitable medium for unguided broadcast systems. Another disadvantage is the higher complexity compared to traditional electrical communication systems, which stems from the need to convert between electrical and optical signals at both ends of the optical medium. While this later disadvantage adds complexity, the promise of greater data rate capacity overrides many concerns, thus making it a clear choice for high-capacity applications. Today, the use of fiber optic cable is growing rapidly, and is commonly deployed as a local loop connection between the PSTN Central Office and numerous homes and businesses.

Light travels in straight lines, so we need a way to bend it within a guided fiber optic cable. The solution involves the refractive indices of the materials used. **Snell's Law** states that when light rays strike the boundary of two materials with different *refractive indices*, then the difference in the *speed of light* between the materials will bend the light rays at the interface of the two materials. Snell's Law can be observed when placing a spoon into a glass of water. Due to the difference in the speed of light in water and air, the spoon will appear to bend, or **refract**. In fig. 4.10(a), we see that the light ray hits the interface between air and water at the **angle of incidence**, which is measured from a normal line perpendicular to the interface between the two materials. The amount that the light bends in the water is also measured from the normal line and is called the **angle of refraction**. The relationship between these variables is given by Snell's Law equation (4.12), where $\theta 1$ is the *angle of incidence*, $\theta 2$ is the *angle of refraction*, $n1$ and $n2$ represent the refractive indices, and $v1$ and $v2$ equate to the speed-of-light in the two materials respectively.

$$\frac{\sin\theta 1}{\sin\theta 2} = \frac{v1}{v2} = \frac{n2}{n1} \tag{4.12}$$

In fig. 4.10(b), if we continue to increase the *angle of incidence*, we will eventually arrive at a **critical angle** for that material, at which point the light rays completely reflect back into the material. This phenomenon is called **total internal reflection (TIR)**, and it is the principle behind how the fiber optic cable works.

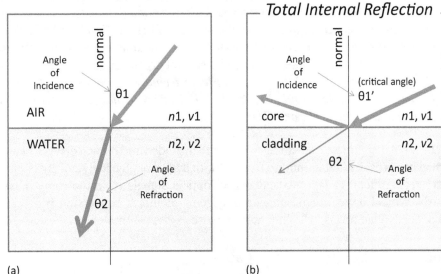

FIGURE 4.10 Snell's Law of Refraction. (a) Light entering the interface between two materials with different *refractive indices, n*, will cause the light to refract. (b) When the *angle of incidence* is at the *critical angle, total internal reflection (TIR)* will occur.

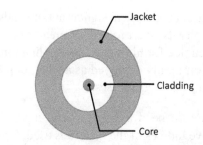

FIGURE 4.11 Parts of a fiber optic cable.

To take advantage of TIR, fiber optic cables, as shown in the cross section in figure 4.11, are constructed with an optical core made of either glass or plastic, and surrounded by a cladding made from similar optical material, but with a different refractive index from that of the core. Doing this enables TIR to occur between the core and the cladding boundary. As long as the optical signal is reflected back into the core by the core/cladding interface, the fiber optic cable can be bent without losing the signal that is propagating within the core.

In the construction of fiber optic cable, materials are selected so that the refractive index of the cladding is less than that of the core. This means that the speed of light in the core is less than the speed of light in the cladding [see equation (4.13), *where n = refractive index, c = speed of light, V = speed of light in the material*].

$$n\text{(cladding)} < n\text{(core)}, \text{ if } n = \frac{c}{V}, \text{ then } V\text{(cladding)} > V\text{(core)} \qquad \textbf{(4.13)}$$

There are two major types of fiber optic cables: ***multimode fiber (MMF)*** and ***single mode fiber (SMF)***. Multimode fiber cables can have either a ***step index*** or ***graded index*** refractive core. MMF is typically used for short distance communications, whereas single mode fibers have much better propagation characteristics and are used for long distance communications such as transoceanic links. Standards for fiber optic cables are produced by several organizations including the *International Standards Organization (ISO), International Electrotechnical Commission (IEC), Telecommunications Industry Association and Electronics Industries Alliance (TIA/EIA)*, and the *International Telecommunications Union (ITU)*.

Fiber optic cables have significant advantages over other guided mediums because of the higher information carrying capacity and immunity from RFI. In addition, physical security is much better since it is extremely difficult to tap into and collect optical signals from the cable. However, as stated previously, typical optical communication systems require a conversion process between electrical and optical signal forms, which in turn increases system complexity.

4.4.3.1 Multimode Fiber (MMF) Optic Cable

The diameter of a MMF core can be either 50/125 μm or 62.5/125 μm. The first number represents the core diameter in micrometers (i.e., 50 or 62.5 μm), while the second number represents the diameter in micrometers of the cladding (i.e., 125 μm).

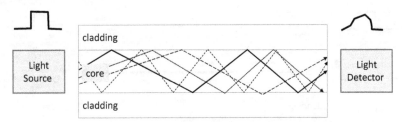

FIGURE 4.12 Multimode Fiber (MMF), Step Index core.

With *step index* MMF, the core's refractive index throughout the core is uniform, which means that light travels at the same speed of light in straight lines as it propagates within the core itself. In fig. 4.12, we see that light rays take different paths as it propagates through the core. These multiple paths of light represent multiple *modes* by which the light travels through the fiber. The speed of light is the same for all modes of light within the core; however, the path lengths differ, thus the different modes of the transmitted pulse reach the receive detector at slightly different times causing *modal dispersion,* distortion, of the transmitted pulse. This is similar to *delay skew* seen in TP, which causes signal distortion. *Modal dispersion* limits data capacity and signal distance.

Signals propagating in step index MMF experiences high attenuation and modal dispersion and therefore is typically limited to distances of 5 km or less.

To improve the performance of MMF, **graded index cores** were developed in which the refractive index within the core gradually decreases in value as it approaches the cladding (see fig. 4.13). Therefore, the speed of light is not uniform across the core, but gradually increases, thus refracting the signal in a sinusoidal pattern as it moves towards and away from the cladding. This has the effect of curving the signal gracefully, thus reducing, but not eliminating, attenuation and modal dispersion. While *graded index MMF* performance is better *than step index MMF*, it's performance is not as good as SMF which we discuss next.

4.4.3.2 Single Mode Fiber (SMF) Optic Cable

Largely credited with the development of **single mode fiber (SMF)**, Charles K. Kao received half of the *2009 Nobel Prize* for his achievements in fiber optics communications. Envisioning that fiber optic communications would connect all of the continents through under ocean cables, his vision is today's reality. SMF, unlike MMF, has a much smaller core diameter of 9 μm, with a cladding core of 125 μm (i.e., 9/125 μm) compared to MMF 62.5/125 μm and 50/125 μm. The extremely small

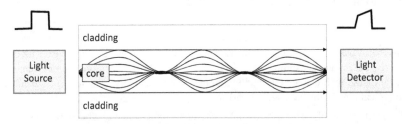

FIGURE 4.13 Multimode Fiber (MMF), Graded Index core.

FIGURE 4.14 Single Mode Fiber (SMF). The received pulse shows some distortion caused by chromatic dispersion, but this distortion is much less than the modal dispersion experienced in step or graded index MMF.

core diameter means that only a single mode of light propagates through the cable, see fig. 4.14. Since multiple modes of light are not present, modal dispersion does not exist, and attenuation is far less than with MMF. The superior performance of SMF enables the transmission of optical broadband signals over much greater distances before it must be amplified.

Communications over SMF can be impacted by *chromatic dispersion*, however these impacts are minimal. An optical signal consists of several wavelengths with the optical transmission **window** defined as the band between the highest wavelength and the lowest wavelength. This concept is similar to frequency bandwidth in the RF domain. The separate optical wavelengths making up the transmission window travels from source to detector at slightly different times, thus causing the dispersion of signal wavelengths This phenomena is called **chromatic dispersion**. While *chromatic dispersion* also exists in MMF, the effects of modal dispersion and attenuation overwhelm any impact caused by chromatic dispersion.

4.4.3.3 Light Sources, Detectors, and Amplifiers

In the simplest form of optical communications, **on-off keying (OOK)** is used as a modulation technique. This method uses the presence or absence of light power to represent data, and as such, simple light sources and detectors can be used. Because optical light *coherency*[18] is not critical, this method is termed *noncoherent detection*, which simplifies the job of both optical source and detector. Non-coherent detection has been used for many years with both optical fiber cables and free space optical (FSO) transmission systems. However, as the demand for higher data rates has grown, modulation techniques that are more *spectrally efficient*[19] such as *M-ary phase-shift keying (MPSK)* and *M'ary quadrature amplitude modulation (M-QAM)* are in greater use. These *coherent detection* methods require more complex *coherent* light sources such as lasers, which add complexity to both light sources and optical detectors. However, the higher capacity optical links typically justify the complexity and associated costs for many applications.

---

[18] *Coherency* means that wavelengths making up the transmitted light *window* are all in phase with one another and add together constructively. Lasers are an example of a highly coherent light source. Noncoherent light sources have wavelengths that are not in phase with one another and therefore add destructively. Examples of noncoherent light sources include LEDs, and typical light bulbs (i.e., white light).

[19] *Spectral efficiency* is a measure of the information rate per Hertz. Higher spectral efficiency means that higher data rates can be achieved for a given bandwidth.

In addition to applying sophisticated modulation techniques, the multiplexing of several information light sources through *wavelength division multiplexing (WDM)* and *dense[20] wavelength division multiplexing (DWDM)*, have also been used to enable the aggregation of multiple wavelengths channels for transmission on a single SMF optical cable. These techniques are used extensively by communications service providers. WDM and DWDM techniques are similar in concept to frequency division multiplexing (FDM) in RF communications. This process combines, or *multiplexes*, several signal channels, or optical wavelengths, together into a single aggregated output.

The selection of *light sources* and *light detectors* are as critical as selecting the right optical fiber, since it is the job of these devices to transform electrical signals into optical ones and back again. Transmission distance, required data rate, modulation, and multiplexing techniques all help to determine the complexity of light source and detector required. As an example, for a short distance, low capacity link, an inexpensive LED light source combined with a simple detector using OOK modulation over MMF cable is sufficient. For high-capacity transoceanic communications, a more sophisticated laser light source and detector using M'ary modulation and DWDM over SMF cables are required.

There are basically two major categories of light sources: **light emitting diodes (LEDs)** and **laser diodes (LDs)**. Each of these categories has different characteristics that differentiate their performance as described in Table 4.1. In all performance categories laser diodes are superior to LEDs,

TABLE 4.1   Optical light source parameters for LEDs and laser diodes.

Parameter	LED	Laser Diode
Speed - *the on and off rise/fall time of the light (faster rise/fall times are better)*	Slow speed	Fast speed
Power - *the optical power or brightness (higher power is better)*	Low power	High power
Spectral Width - *the width or number of the wavelengths within the light beam (narrow spectral width is better)*	Wide width	Narrow width
Coupling Efficiency - *the efficiency of the coupling between light source and fiber cable (higher coupling efficiency is better)*	Low coupling efficiency	High coupling efficiency
Light Coherence - *the extent that all wavelengths are synchronized in phase with one another (higher light coherence is better)*	Noncoherent	High coherency
Light Beam Directionality - *extent by which the light beam lines up with the fiber core at the interface (High directionality is better)*	Low directionality	High directionality
Cost - *manufacturing and complexity of installation*	Low	High

---

[20] As the name suggests, dense WDM aggregates a greater number of signals (i.e., optical wavelengths, also called "colors of light") than WDM.

and therefore they are used in long distance high data rate communication links. There are several types of laser diodes made of different materials such as *gallium arsenide (GaAs), aluminum gallium arsenide (AlGaAs), indium phosphate (InP)* semiconductor materials, each with their own desirable properties.

The most common *light detectors* are the **photo intrinsic negative (PIN)** diode and the **avalanche photo diode (APD)** semiconductors. For each photon detected, one or more electrons are produced by the detectors semiconductor material. PIN detectors, which are inexpensive and less capable then APDs, transform photons into electrons but do not amplify the signal. The more complex and costly APD detectors have increased signal sensitivity and an ability to amplify the optical signal by increasing the number of electrons associated per detected photon. This essentially amplifies the detected optical signal during conversion to an electrical signal.

Optical signals, similar to electrical and RF signals, will attenuate over distance. Therefore, amplification is required for transmissions over long distances. The use of *digital repeaters*, which receive distorted signals and *repeat* them as new digital pulses, are a common method to extend the distance of optical signals. Using this method, the attenuated optical signal received by the digital repeater is first converted into an electrical signal where it undergoes the digital repeating process. This results in the recreation of the original digital signal, which is then amplified and converted back into an optical signal, and placed back onto the fiber cable. However, this **optical-electrical-optical (OEO)** process, while effective, adds signal processing delays and complexity. **Optical amplification** avoids the OEO process by simply amplifying the incoming optical signal without going through the OEO process. A number of optical amplification methods exist. One of better known methods includes the use of erbium molecules that are introduced into amplifying segments of the fiber optic cable. Called an *Erbium-Doped Fiber Amplifier (EDFA)*, this amplification method uses an external laser pump to excite the erbium atoms, which in turn amplifies the optical signal. Another optical amplification method, *Raman Amplification*, uses a laser pump directed in the opposite direction of signal travel. Doing this creates an interaction between the laser energy, optical signal, and the crystalline lattice of the fiber core, resulting in the amplification of the optical signal.

4.5 UNGUIDED MEDIUM

Unlike guided mediums where channels can be isolated using separate physical circuits, unguided medium is shared, and therefore transmission channels have the potential of interfering with one another. As discussed previously, modulated RF carriers occupy a bandwidth of frequencies in the frequency domain. To help prevent adjacent channel interference (i.e., overlap of adjacent channel bandwidths), guard channels are inserted in-between carrier channel frequencies to create separation. The use of band pass filters on transceivers limit the frequency band transmitted and received, which in turn decreases the possibility of interference. In addition, regulatory organizations such as the *Federal Communications Commission (FCC)*, limit transmit power for both licensed and unlicensed frequencies. However, even with these measures in place, unguided medium communications can suffer from environmental noise and other transmission impediments that must be addressed.

When communicating through free space, there are three classic models of signal propagation: *direct line of sight (LOS)*, *skywave*, and *ground wave*. We will discuss these models since they are

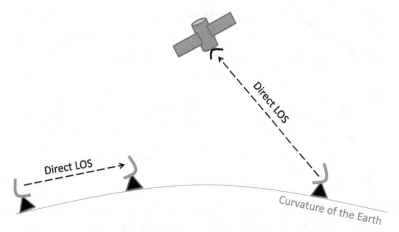

FIGURE 4.15 Direct Line of Sight (LOS) Communications. When both communicating stations are located on the ground, LOS is limited by the curvature of the earth. However, direct LOS for earth to satellite communications is not similarly limited.

central to our understanding of RF propagation. However, it should be pointed out that today's typical wireless and cellular links, which are much shorter in range, do not always fit into a single traditional model (i.e., signals often propagate according to a combination of these models).

When the path of a transmitted signal is direct LOS, the signal travels without encountering obstacles either man-made or terrestrial. **Direct LOS**[21] communications between transceivers on the ground have limited propagation distances due to the curvature of the earth (i.e., distance to the horizon). As an example, equation (4.14) gives us the visual LOS distance from an antenna to the horizon. This distance depends upon the antenna's height in meters and the radius of the earth (6371 km). However, when communicating from an earth ground station to an orbiting satellite, this LOS distance increases dramatically since the earth's horizon is not a factor (see fig. 4.15).

$$\text{Distance to horizon in kilometers, } d \approx 3.57 \times h^{1/2}, \tag{4.14}$$

where h is the height of the antenna in meters.

Skywave propagation takes advantage of the **ionosphere** and ground to create a *waveguide effect* that enables a transmitted signal to follow the curvature of the earth over great distances by reflecting between both. The ionosphere is the upper most layer of earth's atmosphere residing above the *troposphere* at approximately 90 km to about 400 km above the earth's surface. Within the ionosphere are clouds of free electrons that have no uniform distribution, and which tend to attenuate, refract, and reflect signals depending upon signal frequency. The ionosphere is ionized by the sun's UV rays; therefore, the characteristics and altitude of this layer differ between daytime and night. During the daytime, the ionosphere can be divided into four layers, each having different ionization concentrations. The upper most layers, and the most ionized, are referred to as the F1 and F2 layers.

---

[21] For LOS RF communications, we must consider the heights of both transmit and receive antennas, as well as signal refraction.

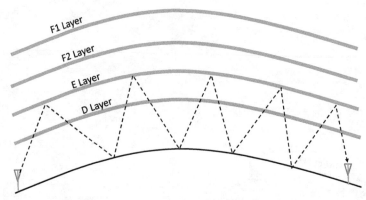

FIGURE 4.16 Skywave Propagation extends signal distance beyond the earth's curvature using a waveguide effect for frequencies less than 30 MHz.

Below the F layers are the E and D layers which reside closer to the earth's surface. At night, these four layer essentially become two, the F and E layers.

Higher signal frequencies transmitted from the ground can penetrate into the upper layers more easily than lower frequencies. As such, lower frequencies, typically under 30 MHz, are reflected back to ground, thus enabling these signals to propagate beyond the horizon despite the curvature of the earth. This *waveguide* phenomenon makes it possible for amateur HF radio operators to communicate with other operators halfway around the globe (fig. 4.16).

However, the nonuniform density of the electrons in each of the layers, combined with the differing characteristics of the ionosphere between day and night, makes it difficult to predict signal propagation characteristics. Therefore, an operator in the United States may be able to contact an operator in Tokyo on one day, but unable to contact the same operator the following day due to the unpredictable characteristics of the ionization layer.

Ground wave propagation is similar to *skywave* propagation in that it follows the earth's curvature for short distances at low frequencies between 3 and 30 MHz. Unlike a skywave, ground waves consist of the combination of several propagation methods such as direct LOS, diffraction, and reflection. Ground waves are typically used for RF broadcasts.

Today's unguided communication systems, such as wireless LAN (WLAN) and cellular, operate in the GHz frequency range and therefore their propagation models do not fit neatly into the lower frequency skywave or ground wave models. As such, it is useful to look at the variables that effect a signal's propagation during transmission.

Figure 4.17 shows several wireless propagation modes. Transmission frequency plays a major role in determining how these modes effect overall communications. As an example, rain droplets impact higher frequencies more than lower frequencies. Line of sight (LOS) transmission becomes more critical at higher frequencies than at lower frequencies. Reflection from the Ionosphere occurs with lower frequencies rather than higher frequencies. Below is a description of various propagation modes.

Direct Line of Sight (LOS). As discussed, direct LOS means that your transmission propagates through free space unimpeded by any obstacles. The higher the transmission frequency, the greater the need for LOS. As an example, microwave communication links using directional antennas at GHz frequencies are specifically designed for direct LOS transmission.

Scattering. When a signal encounters an object such as rain droplets, small particles, trees, etc., the signal reflects in multiple directions, thus weakening the signal strength that eventually reaches the receiver. As an example, the effect of rain is especially detrimental at the higher frequencies (e.g., $\geq$ GHz frequencies) where the wavelength of the signal approaches the size of the rain droplet.

Diffraction. As a signal encounters an object with a relatively sharp edge or corner (e.g., building, terrain such as a hill, etc.), it will change directions, or diffract, around the object. This appears as a bending of the actual signal itself, and is one of the ground wave propagation modes.

Reflection. Reflection occurs when a signal encounters a relatively smooth surface that is many times larger than the signal wavelength. There are many examples of beneficial signal reflection including ionospheric skywave reflection, parabolic antenna reflection towards a transmitting direction, and passive RF reflectors designed to redirect signal energy. However, when we consider multiple reflections of a single signal within an urban environment, multiple path, or *multipath*, reflections can cause severe signal distortion. This will be the subject in a later chapter.

Refraction. Refraction is the bending of the signal caused by an interface between two materials of differing refractive indices. In fig. 4.17, we see that signal refraction occurs at the interface between the atmosphere and the vacuum of space. We also discussed how refraction in fiber optic cables was the key to achieving TIR, which is the key principle behind FO communications.

Absorption. Absorption is essentially the transfer of RF signal power into heat. This occurs when the transmitted signal encounters material which essentially *absorbs* the signal power. A microwave signal encountering rain will not only experience scattering, but also absorption.

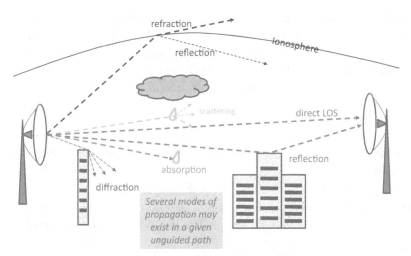

FIGURE 4.17 Multiple variables and impairments can impact unguided signal transmission.

Unguided mediums are typically easier to implement than guided mediums since they do not require the installation of wire runs within a building, or the digging of trenches between buildings or under streets and sidewalks. In some situations, the use of unguided medium may be the only choice based upon user mobility requirements (e.g., cellular services), satellite communications, communications to and within remote areas where infrastructures are nonexistent, etc. In contrast to guided medium, frequency licensing is required for many communication systems except for those operating in the *ISM unlicensed bands* such as WLAN or Bluetooth. Disadvantages include the limited frequency spectrum available to users, as well as the poor physical security posed by the shared medium, which allows anyone to tune into any transmitted signal. Higher carrier frequencies and use of directional antennas reduce the vulnerability to signal interception, but do not eliminate it. Therefore, the use of encryption techniques and methods are critical for any unguided communications.

4.5.1 Microwave Communications

Microwave communications consist of high-frequency carriers operating in the SHF and EHF frequency bands (i.e., 3 GHz to 300 GHz). The high operating frequencies enable microwave links to carry significant amounts of information, thus making them ideal for point-to-point broadband communications. However, higher operating frequencies translate into smaller wavelengths, which makes the signal more vulnerable to weather (e.g., rain droplets, particulates in the air), due to signal scattering and absorption. In addition, higher frequencies suffer from greater attenuation over distance, as well as require greater LOS, when compared to lower frequencies. To compensate for both attenuation and LOS requirements, microwave systems use parabolic antennas that concentrate signal power within a directional beam aimed toward the receive antenna. The width of the beam is measured in degrees at the focal point and is called the antenna ***beamwidth***. In practice, the width of the beam is measured at the half power points, or 3 dB, as shown in equation (4.15), where $\theta_{(3\,dB)}$ is the beamwidth in degrees, λ is the signal wavelength, and D is the diameter of the parabolic antenna. It is noted that both λ and D have the same unit measure (i.e., both in meters or feet).

$$\text{3 dB Antenna beamwidth: } \theta_{(3\,dB)} \approx 70(\lambda/D) \tag{4.15}$$

In fig. 4.18(a), a parabolic transmit antenna directs its beam toward the receiving parabolic antenna. Beamwidth in degrees is measured to where RF power is reduced by 50% or 3 dB. This beamwidth also represents the area, or ***Fresnel zone***, between communicating antennas where direct LOS exists. In the planning of microwave links, engineers ensure that the Fresnel zone is clear of any obstructions, thereby avoiding unwanted signal reflection or diffraction.

4.5.2 Satellite Communications

Satellite communications have the advantage of covering large areas of the earth's surface, which makes them ideal for long distance point-to-point links or broadcast communications. Earth station and satellite links typically operate in the VHF, UHF bands, including the L, S, C, X, Ku, K, and Ka radar bands.[22] In addition, satellites are also able to communicate to one another through ***cross links***, which can operate at much higher frequencies, including the optical range. As an example,

---

[22] Upper UHF, SHF, and EHF bands overlap with the L through W radar bands as discussed in chapter 1.

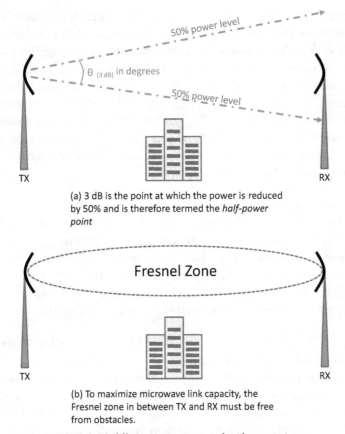

(a) 3 dB is the point at which the power is reduced by 50% and is therefore termed the *half-power point*

(b) To maximize microwave link capacity, the Fresnel zone in between TX and RX must be free from obstacles.

FIGURE 4.18 Microwave communications system.

Iridium satellite cross links operating at the Ka-band are used to handoff calls from one satellite to another as they pass from horizon to horizon, thereby preventing service disruption.

The satellite era began in October 1957 when the Soviet Union launched the very first orbiting satellite called Sputnik 1. While Sputnik 1 only carried a simple radio beacon, it initiated a space race rivalry between the Russians and Americans during the Cold War. Fearing the launch of nuclear warheads from outer space, development of missiles that could breach into space was initially the primary objective. However, soon both sides realized the benefit of using satellites to spy upon one another, and this led to the development of more sophisticated satellite systems. Soon, these advancements were shared with the public for communications, broadcasting, weather tracking, search and rescue (SAR), navigation, imagery, and telemetry. Today, technological advancements continue to be made as satellites have become an integral part of our daily lives.

Satellites revolve around the earth in one of four primary orbits that are distinguished by their approximate altitudes above the earth's surface: ***Low earth orbit (LEO)*** 180 to 2,000 km, ***medium earth orbit (MEO)*** 2,000 to 35,780 km, ***geostationary earth orbit (GEO)*** 35,780 km, and ***highly elliptical orbit (HEO)*** whose orbit altitude changes as it progresses through its revolution around the earth.

The plane of the circular[23] LEO and MEO orbits can be parallel to the earth's equator, the plane intersecting north and south poles, or any inclination[24] in-between. A complete revolution of these orbits is shorter in time than the rotation of the earth; therefore, these satellites seen from a vantage point on the earth's surface will appear to move across the sky. As the satellite vanishes below the horizon, service to a user on the ground will cease. Therefore if continuous uninterrupted service is required, a constellation of many satellites is required so that one or more satellites are always in view of the user. *Iridium* consisting of 66 LEO satellites is an example of a constellation that provides continuous user service anywhere in the world. The *GPS (Global Positioning Satellite)* system operated by the United States Air Force is an example of a MEO constellation that provides continuous positioning information to users globally.

HEO satellites, similar to LEO and MEO, will appear to move from horizon to horizon when observed on the ground. However, HEO orbits are elliptical, not circular, which means that the speed at which the satellite crosses the sky will change depending upon where the observer is located. As an example, HEO satellites are designed to have a long dwell time over the north pole, thus providing longer service in the northern pole area than in the southern pole area. This is due to the greater altitude that the satellite travels at the north pole, called the *apogee*[25] of the orbit, than the much smaller altitude, or *perigee*, at the southern pole (see fig. 4.19).

For LEO, MEO, and HEO satellite systems, there must be satellite earth stations that provide satellite tracking, command, and control inputs, as well as telecommunication services to users. Since these types of satellites do not appear stationary to an observer on the ground, several geographically dispersed earth stations may be needed. Some satellites may also be equipped with a data store and forward capability that enables the downlink of collected data and the uplink of satellite commands when in view of the system earth station. This allows the satellite to operate during periods in which it is not in view of any earth station. In addition, some satellite systems use crosslinks to transfer data from one satellite to another within the constellation, until the data reaches a satellite that is in view of an earth station.

A geostationary orbit (GEO) is unique in that it revolves in synchronization with the earth's rotation. As such, a GEO satellite appears in a single position in the sky when observed from the ground. This makes GEO satellites ideal for broadcasting and point-to-point communications. However, while there may be numerous LEO, MEO, and HEO satellites at different altitudes, only one geostationary orbit exists. In order for the GEO satellite to appear motionless in the sky, it must revolve in an equatorial plane, and must be at an altitude of approximately 35,780 km.

---

[23] It should be noted that circular satellite orbits are not perfectly circular due to anomalies of the earth and the gravitational pulls from the moon and sun. Therefore, there is always a certain amount of ellipticity in all satellite orbits.

[24] The inclination of a satellite orbit is the angle, measured in degrees, of the orbital plane from the equator.

[25] Apogee is the greatest distance of the satellite's orbit from the earth. Perigee is the closest point within the satellite's orbit, or altitude, to the earth. These terms are not unique to HEO satellites, and are used for all satellites, including the moon as referenced from the earth.

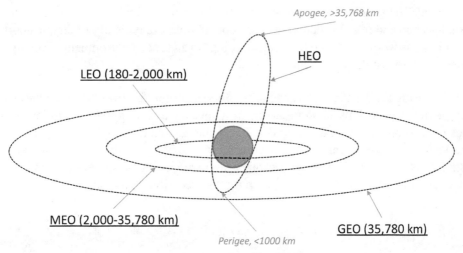

FIGURE 4.19 Satellite Orbits.

Any deviation in inclination or altitude will cause the satellite to appear to drift from its position in the sky. Since all GEO satellites have the same altitude around the equator, the longitudinal position, termed *orbital slot,* is treated as a limited resource. So much so that regulatory organizations such as the ITU get involved in international orbital slot assignments. GEO represents the highest altitude orbit in which satellites are placed. The large distance between a GEO satellite and earth station translates into high attenuation and high propagation delay. Therefore, directional antennas, such as parabolic antennas, are used to maximize signal strength and distance. In addition, by using larger diameter antennas, especially at the earth station, more signal power density can be captured and transmitted. The propagation delay of the signal is determined by the speed of light within the vacuum of space and the atmosphere, and is approximately 270 ms from an earth station to the GEO satellite and back down to another earth station. This delay does not take into consideration the processing delays at the earth station or satellite, which when considered increases the overall propagation delay.

The modern satellite system has come a long way since the days of Sputnik. Today sophisticated phased array antennas and feeds are used along with more powerful digital processers installed onboard the satellites and into earth station facilities. The technologies and methods developed have also enabled deep space communications from earth to space probes such as *Voyager* and *Pioneer*, and to extraterrestrial vehicles such as the Mars rover.

4.5.3 Free Space Optics (FSO)

Standard operating wavelengths identified by ITU for both fiber optic cable and free space optics (FSO) are 850, 1300, 1310, and 1550 nm (10^{-9} m). The equivalent frequency ranges are 352.9, 230.7, 229.0, and 193.5 THz, respectively, which reside just below the visible light range, within the infrared range. At the THz (10^{12} Hz) frequency range, the signal beamwidth is very narrow and LOS becomes essential. This makes alignment between FSO transceivers and the avoidance of obstacles critical. The small wavelength of the optical signal also makes it extremely vulnerable to weather such as rain and fog. As such, free space optical links are typically limited to short distance communications, as would be found between buildings in an urban environment. FSO links are also used in high-capacity satellite cross links.

The benefits of using FSO is the high capacity it offers, its immunity from RFI, and the cost savings that can be realized, especially in an urban environment, by avoiding the need to lay communication cables underneath streets and sidewalks. Disadvantages include its high attenuation over distance, thus short transmission range, and its vulnerability to being easily blocked. While the narrow beamwidth improves physical security over other unguided methods, signal interception remains a threat since it operates within a shared medium that is accessible to anyone.

KEY TERMS

absorption
angle of incidence
angle of refraction
apogee
attenuation
AWG (American Wire Gauge)
AWGN (additive white Gaussian noise)
balanced configuration
beamwidth
chromatic dispersion
cladding
community antenna television (CATV)
coaxial cable
cochannel interference (CCI)
core
critical angle
cross link
crosstalk
Data Over Cable Service Interface Specification (DOCSIS)
delay distortion
delay skew
dense wavelength division multiplexing (DWDM)
dielectric

diffraction
direct LOS
fiber optic (FO)
free space optics (FSO)
fresnel zone
GEO
graded index
ground wave
guided Medium
Hartley's Law
HEO
impedance
impulse noise
insertion loss
intermodulation noise (IM)
ionosphere
laser diode (LD)
light emitting diode (LED)
link margin
LEO
MEO
microwave communications
modal dispersion
multimode fiber (MMF)
narrowband
noise floor
noise power (Pn)
Nyquist
on-off keying (OOK)

optical-electrical-optical (OEO)
perigee
reflection
refraction
refractive index (n, RI)
return loss
satellite communications
scattering
screen twisted pair (ScTP)
Shannon-Hartley theoretical capacity
shielded twisted pair (STP)
signal-to-noise ratio (SNR)
signal power (Ps)
single mode fiber (SMF)
skywave
Snell's Law
step index
thermal noise (N)
thermal noise density (No)
total internal refraction (TIR)
twisted pair (TP)
unbalanced configuration
unguided medium
unshielded twisted pair (UTP)
wavelength division multiplexing (WDM)
window

CHAPTER PROBLEMS

1. The signal-to-noise ratio (SNR or *S/N*) can be represented in decibel or nondecibel form. Select the correct decibel format where the use of brackets (i.e., [ ]) signifies dB values.
   a. [*N*]/[*S*]
   b. [*S*]/[*N*]
   c. [*S*] − [*N*]
   d. [*S*] + [*N*]

   Answer: c

2. What is the noise temperature for a receiver operating at room temperature ($T = 295°$ K) and frequency bandwidth of the receiver is $B = 3$ MHz?
   a. 1.22E−14 W or −139 dBW
   b. 4.07E−21 W or −204 dBW
   c. 1.22E+14 W or +139 dBW
   d. 4.07E+21 W or +204 dBW

   Answer: a

3. We can use thermal noise to estimate our noise floor, however other "wideband" noise sources should also be included in our noise floor calculation, when known, to improve our noise floor accuracy.
   a. True
   b. False

   Answer: a

4. Determine the SNR (dBs) for a received signal power, $Pr = -10$ dBm, and a receiver noise, $N = -203$ dBm?
   a. Pr(dBm)*N(dBm) = 2.03E3 dBm
   b. Pr(dBm)/N(dBm) = 49.26 dBm
   c. Pr(dBm)+N(dBm) = −213 dBm
   d. Pr(dBm)−N(dBm) = 193 dBm

   Answer: d

5. Describe the difference between *thermal noise* and *thermal noise density*.

6. Impulse noise only occurs as a result of natural phenomena such as a lightning storm.
   a. True
   b. False

   Answer: b

7. Intermodulation (IM) noise occurs when two or more frequency channels operating on adjacent center frequencies, create harmonic components that interfere with one another.
   a. True
   b. False

   Answer: a

8. Describe the difference between CCI and IM?

9. Signals on UTPs have a tendency to suffer from crosstalk.
   a. True
   b. False

Asnwer: a

10. Only transparent mediums such as air or water are associated with a material refractive index (n).
    a. True
    b. False

Answer: b

11. Wavelength division multiplexing (WDM) is used by optical systems to aggregate optical basebands.
    a. True
    b. False

Answer: a

12. For optical light sources, having a wider spectral width is preferred, since this equates to larger information carrying capability.
    a. True
    b. False

Answer: b

13. Optical amplifiers are more efficient than OEO repeaters; however, there still needs to be a conversion between optical to electrical and back, in order for the amplification process to work.
    a. True
    b. False

Answer: b

14. Describe the difference between *skywave* and *ground wave* propagation.

15. What impacts the transmitted RF beamwidth from a directed parabolic antenna?
    a. Frequency of the transmission
    b. Size (diameter) of the antenna
    c. Both a and b
    d. Neither a nor b have an effect on the beamwidth of the signal

Answer: c

16. The Shannon-Hartley equation gives us the *theoretical* maximum data rate capacity achievable.
    a. True
    b. False

Answer: a

17. What is the Shannon-Hartley theoretical maximum data rate capacity given a bandwidth, $B = 36$ MHz, and SNR $= 100$ (nondecibel ratio)?
    a. 36 Mbps
    b. 239 Mbps
    c. 239 kbps
    d. 36 MHz

Answer: b

18. Select the correct statements regarding propagation delay.
   a. Propagation delay is determined by the time it takes for a signal to travel through guided or unguided medium.
   b. Propagation delay includes the amount of signal processing time needed at each node along the path of the signal.
   c. a and b both are correct
   d. Neither a nor b are correct since propagation delay is experienced only by sound waves.

Answer: c

19. Select the correct statement(s):
   a. The greater the frequency bandwidth, the greater the information carrying capacity
   b. The higher the frequency, the greater the information carrying capacity
   c. The higher the frequency, the greater the attenuation of the signal over distance
   d. All of the above are correct

Answer: d

20. Guided UTP is configured as a balanced circuit.
   a. True
   b. False

Answer: a

21. Delay skew and crosstalk are only problems encountered when using coaxial cables for communications.
   a. True
   b. False

Answer: b

22. Which definition best describes *delay skew*?
   a. Delay skew causes light signals in different modes to reach the detector at slightly different times. This causes signal distortion.
   b. Delay skew is experienced with unguided medium in an urban environment where RF signals can take multiple paths from transmitter to receiver.
   c. Delay skew is inherent in UTP when more than one-wire pair is used to transmit data in parallel. Each wire pair has a different twist ratio, which equates to different wire pair lengths. This causes signal delay distortion.
   d. Delay skew is experienced on satellite communication channels, where the distances between earth terminal and satellite causes unacceptable delay.

Answer: c

23. A BER of 10E-5 tells you that there is a probability of having one bit error for every 1,000,000 bits sent.
   a. True
   b. False

Answer: b

24. Typically, two-wire pairs (one pair in the transmit and one pair in the receive directions) are used to enable full-duplex communications (FDX) when using UTP.
   a. True
   b. False

Answer: a

25. Signals on coaxial cables are unbalanced. When compared to UTP, coaxial medium has higher bandwidth and data rate carrying capability compared to UTP.
    a. True
    b. False

Answer: a

26. Coaxial cables have a smaller conductive core than UTP. The larger conductors used in UTP creates greater signal resistance resulting in signal attenuation. This is why coaxial cables can carry greater data capacity over longer distances.
    a. True
    b. False

Answer: b

27. Which satellite orbit revolves around the earth at the same rate as the earth's rotation (i.e., 24 h)?
    a. LEO
    b. MEO
    c. GEO
    d. HEO

Answer: c

28. Single mode fiber (SMF) can be categorized as either gradient or step-index depending upon the refractive index of the core.
    a. True
    b. False

Answer: b

29. Select the correct statement(s) regarding fiber optic medium.
    a. TIR is the principle that enables the propagation of light through a fiber optic cable
    b. MMF fiber can be *step-indexed* or *graded-index*
    c. SMF has a greater bandwidth and throughput capability over MMF
    d. ITU describes transmission windows associated with signal wavelength
    e. All of the above are correct

Answer: e

30. Regarding fiber optic transmission windows—*the higher transmission window, the lower the attenuation*
    a. True
    b. False

Answer: a

31. In order to ensure TIR in fiber optic cables, the core and cladding must have the same refractive index (n).
    a. True
    b. False

Answer: b

32. Given the following information, what is the power received (*Rx*) at the receiver? *Tx* = 33 dBm, FSL = −44 dB, given the equation: *Rx*(dBm) = *Tx*(dBm) + FSL(dBs)
   a. *Rx* = 78 dBW
   b. *Rx* = 78 dBm
   c. *Rx* = −11 dBm
   d. *Rx* = −11 dBW

Answer: c

33. Given the following information, what is the power received (*Rx*) at the receiver? *Tx* = 50 dBm, FSL = −50 dB, given the equation: *Rx*(dBm) = *Tx*(dBm) + FSL(dBs)
   a. *Rx* = 100 dBW
   b. *Rx* = 0 dBm
   c. *Rx* = −100 dBm
   d. *Rx* = 30 dBW

Answer: b

34. Given the following information, what is the power received (*Rx*) at the receiver? *Tx* = 23 dBm, FSL = −40 dB, given the equation: *Rx*(dBm) = *Tx*(dBm) + FSL(dBs)
   a. *Rx* = 63 dBW
   b. *Rx* = 63 dBm
   c. *Rx* = −17 dBW
   d. *Rx* = −17 dBm

Answer: d

35. Given the following information, what is the power received (*Rx*) at the receiver? *Tx* = 10 dBm, FSL = −90 dB, given the equation: *Rx*(dBm) = *Tx*(dBm) + FSL(dBs)
   a. *Rx* = 100 dBW
   b. *Rx* = 100 dBm
   c. *Rx* = −80 dBm
   d. *Rx* = −80 dBW

Answer: c

CHAPTER 5

RF Wireless Communications

5.1 INTRODUCTION

While optical fibers provide the high-capacity communications needed for today's multimedia environment, wireless communications give us mobility, free from wired connections, that is highly desired by today's typical subscriber. Our demand for mobile communications beyond the traditional voice call has increased exponentially; however, the available frequency spectrum needed to support such high bandwidth demand is limited. Wireless communications signals must also contend with natural and man-made *electromagnetic interference (EMI)*, and the varying weather and smog conditions existing within the atmosphere. In addressing these challenges, engineers have developed new techniques and methods designed to compensate for environmental changes, and to increase the efficiency of how we use the limited frequency spectrum that is available. In addition, industry partners have lobbied the government to release additional spectrum for mobile phone purposes. Through numerous efforts, today's wireless systems offer high-capacity multimedia capability to many users.

The technical innovations used in wireless communications typically centers around highly capable integrated chips (ICs), digital signal processors (DSPs), and efficient firmware and software designs that enable engineers to develop advanced and complex signal modulation techniques, as well as sophisticated antenna systems.

In this chapter, we go over the basic principles of antennas and the unique issues presented by multipath propagation of radio frequency (RF) signals. We introduce *link analysis*, which is a methodology in which we determine receive power based upon transmit power, signal attenuation or link losses, and antenna gain. In addition, we will discuss *spread spectrum* and *orthogonal frequency division multiplexing (OFDM)* techniques, and how these enable us to communicate in noisy radio frequency interference (RFI) environments.

5.2 ANTENNA BASICS

In chapter 1, we discussed how a current traveling through a conductive wire creates an electromagnetic (EM) wave that surrounds the wire. By using an antenna, the EM wave produced by the current flow can be transformed into an EM wave that can propagate outwardly in free space. When designing

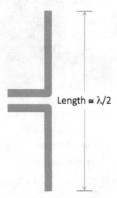

Length ≅ λ/2

FIGURE 5.1 Half-wave dipole antenna is a simple antenna with a length of λ/2. In the half-wave dipole, the signal conductor is connected to the middle of the antenna system.

an antenna for maximum signal power and efficiency, engineers will ensure that the antenna is ***resonant*** at the transmission frequency. Resonance occurs when the reactive[1] components of the antenna cancel one another out, leaving just the desirable resistive component that maximizes the RF power. ***Nonresonant*** antennas are also used for communications although they are not as sensitive or efficient as their resonant counterparts. Therefore, when using nonresonant antennas, receivers with greater sensitivity are typically required. Nonresonant antennas also have a wider frequency bandwidth in comparison to resonant antennas that operate within a narrow bandwidth near resonant frequency.

The physical dimensions of an antenna are closely related to the wavelength of the signal. As an example, a basic dipole antenna shown in fig. 5.1 has an antenna length that is one-half of the transmission wavelength. Knowing the relationship between wavelength and frequency (i.e., $f = c/\lambda$), we see that a wavelength of λ/2 equates to the second harmonic of the transmission frequency. In other words, an antenna length matching the transmission fundamental frequency or its harmonic component, will ensure resonance and transmission efficiency (i.e., efficient transfer of RF power from the antenna).

The ***Antenna Reciprocity Theorem*** further states that an antenna's RF properties will be identical whether it is transmitting or receiving. So the same antenna efficiency achieved while transmitting a signal will be the same efficiency realized when receiving a signal at the same frequency. The *Antenna Reciprocity Theorem* is an important concept that tells us that the *antenna gain* and *beamwidth* characteristics of an antenna are the same regardless of whether it is transmitting or receiving.

Regarding the half-wave dipole antenna length in fig. 5.1, we could have also selected a full wavelength (i.e., fundamental frequency vice a harmonic) as the length, however, depending upon the transmission frequency, this could lead to very long antennas that might be unacceptable for certain application. As an example, if we design a simple vertical full-wave antenna that resonates at 50 MHz, then the antenna length would be equal to the transmission wavelength, or:

$$\lambda = \frac{c}{f} = 3\text{E8 (m/s)} \div 50\text{E6 Hz} = \underline{6 \text{ m}}$$

---

[1] Recall from chapter 1 that reactance consists of both inductive and capacitive components.

Using a 6 m length antenna may be impractical for many situations; however, since we know that resonance will occur at fractions of the fundamental wavelength, we can also design an antenna with a much shorter length. As an example, we could have used $\frac{1}{2}\lambda$, or even $\frac{1}{4}\lambda$, which would have reduced the length of our antenna significantly.

$$\text{Ant. Length} = \frac{c}{2f} = 3\text{E8 (m/s)} \div 100\text{E6 (Hz)} = \underline{3 \text{ m}} \text{ (half-wave } (\lambda/2))$$

$$\text{Ant. Length} = \frac{c}{4f} = 3\text{E8 (m/s)} \div 200\text{E6 (Hz)} = \underline{1.5 \text{ m}} \text{ (quarter-wave } (\lambda/4))$$

When connecting an antenna to the signal cable, it is important to match the impedance of the cable to the impedance of the antenna. Impedance is comprised of both resistive and reactive components shown in equation (5.1), where Z is impedance, R is the resistive, and X the reactive components. (*Note: jX, is termed the imaginary reactive component of impedance where $j = (-1)^{1/2}$. The term jX gives us the phase angle information between signal voltage and current.*)

$$\text{Impedance, } Z = R + jX \tag{5.1}$$

As an explanation to what this means, consider an electric current flowing in a single direction (i.e., DC, direct current). The DC does not change direction so the impedance is considered purely resistive, and therefore impedance equals resistance, $Z = R$. However, if the electrical signal carries information, the current direction and voltage will vary, thus giving rise to additional reactive capacitive and inductive components. Both the antenna and the cable it attaches to are characterized by impedances, and it is important that these two impedances are identical in value in order to prevent destructive signal reflections from occurring. By matching impedance, we ensure maximum power transfer across the interface. While impedance values used today vary, two common values used for RF communications is 50 Ω and 75 Ω (ohms).

Antennas are designed to radiate transmitted power in different patterns depending upon their stated purpose. As an example, broadcast antennas need to radiate over large areas in all directions, while directional antennas are designed to radiate mostly in a single direction. The later is called antenna ***directionality***, and it describes the main direction, relative to the antenna, where the highest transmit or receive power is focused. As an example, a parabolic microwave antenna is *highly directional* because it maximizes power in a single direction toward the receive antenna.

Associated with directionality is ***antenna gain***, which describes the increase in power density (watts/m²) of a directional antenna when compared to an ***ideal isotropic antenna*** transmitting at the same power. To illustrate the concept of antenna gain, let's consider the *ideal isotropic antenna*, which is a theoretical antenna where transmit power radiates from a single point and the antenna pattern is represented by a perfect sphere (fig. 5.2a). Since the transmit power wave front spreads outwardly over the surface area of a sphere, the power density in watts per area decreases significantly with distance. However, if we direct the power from the antenna toward a certain desired direction, then we increase the power density in that direction, resulting in greater transmission distance. When comparing the power densities between the directional and ideal isotropic antennas (in the direction of the directional antenna), we see that greater power density is achieved with directional antenna. The ratio of directional antenna to ideal isotropic antenna is called *antenna gain*.

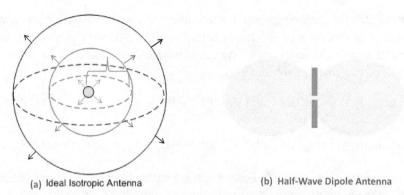

(a) Ideal Isotropic Antenna   (b) Half-Wave Dipole Antenna

FIGURE 5.2 Antenna propagation. (a) An ideal isotropic antenna is a theoretical antenna that propagates in a perfect spherical pattern from a single point. (b) Drawing shows a cross-section of the propagation pattern for a half-dipole antenna. The shape of propagation is the shape of a toroid where signal nulls appear at the ends of the antenna.

As another example, the half-wave dipole antenna in fig. 5.2b shows that maximum power radiation is concentrated around the sides of the antenna in a toroid or donut pattern. Since transmit power does not propagate in the areas above and below the dipole, more power density is available to propagate around the sides in a 360° pattern, thus higher power density is found in this area when compared to the isotropic antenna. The directionality of the dipole provides a **gain** of power density when compared to the isotopic antenna, and we typically use decibels to represent this gain. Equation (5.2) shows antenna gain in decibels as a comparison of the **power density (PD)** of a half-wave dipole relative to the PD of the ideal isotropic antenna. We use **dBi** to show that the antenna's gain is relative to that of the isotropic case. In this equation, we can replace the half-wave pole PD with any other type of directional antenna in order to determine antenna gain in dBi.

$$\text{Antenna Gain, } G(\text{dBi}) = 10\log_{10}\left(\frac{\text{PD}_{\text{half-dipole}}}{\text{PD}_{\text{isotopric}}}\right) \tag{5.2}$$

Antennas are designed to provide specific radiation patterns in order to meet particular applications. The *Antenna Reciprocity Theorem* tells us that the radiation pattern of an antenna is the same whether in transmit or receive mode. The design of the antenna also determines the EM polarity of the signal being transmitted and received. The next section discusses EM and antenna polarization.

5.2.1 Electromagnetic (EM) Wave and Antenna Polarization

EM polarization is defined by the direction of the *electric field*. In fig. 5.3, the **electric field (E-field)** is parallel to the y-axis and therefore the EM wave is considered **vertically polarized**. The **magnetic field (H-field)**, which lies along the x-axis, mirrors the E-field and is always perpendicular to it. Had the E-field been parallel to the x-axis instead, the EM wave would have been considered **horizontally polarized** with the magnetic field perpendicular along the y-axis. For terrestrial communications, *vertical antennas* are perpendicular to the earth's surface and they produce *vertically polarized* EM waves. *Horizontal antennas* are parallel to the earth's surface and produce *horizontally polarized* EM waves.

An EM wave can also be **circularly polarized** where the E-field rotates in either a clockwise or a counterclockwise manner. The rotation of a **right hand circular polarized (RHCP)** EM wave can

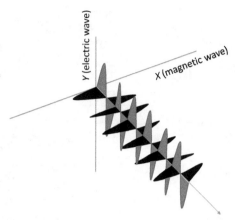

FIGURE 5.3 EM Wave. The E-field (red wave) is vertically polarized along the Y axis. The M-field (black wave) is perpendicular and proportional to the E-field.

be determined using the *"right hand rule"* where the thumb of the right hand points in the direction of propagation, and the fingers curl toward the rotation of the wave. In this case, RHCP waves appear to rotate in a clockwise direction when viewed from the antenna along the line of propagation. Likewise, the rotation of **left hand circular polarized (LHCP)** waves can be determined using the *"left hand rule"* in which the EM wave appears to rotate in a counterclockwise direction when viewed from the antenna along the propagation path.

To understand how a circularly polarized wave is created, we need to first understand the components that make up the E-field. For example, an E-field that is perfectly aligned with the vertical y-axis would only have an E_y component (i.e., wave only appearing along the y-axis). Similarly, an E-field perfectly aligned with the horizontal x-axis would only have the E_x component. However, if the E-field were not aligned with either y- or x-axis, then the E-field will have both E_y and E_x components with the absolute value of the E-field[2] being:

$$|E| = \sqrt{Ex^2 + Ey^2}$$

A circularly polarized wave can be produced by simultaneously transmitting the same signal on both the vertical and horizontal planes (i.e., E_x and E_y), but with one of the signals shifted by a phase angle of 90° or $\pi/2$ rad. By shifting the phase of either E_y or E_x, the combined *resultant* E-field, $|E|$, will rotate in either a clockwise or counterclockwise direction depending upon the direction of the phase shift.

In fig 5.4, we see that two identical signals create a **resultant wave** whose magnitude is $|E| = (E_Y^2 + E_X^2)^{1/2}$ at an angle of $\theta = \tan^{-1}(E_Y/E_X)$. In fig. 5.4(a), both E_Y and E_X signals are *in phase* and therefore the resultant wave lies within the same plane as E_Y and E_X, and therefore does not rotate (i.e., the resultant wave polarization lies inbetween the vertical and horizontal axes at an angle of $\theta°$. In fig. 5.4(b), we change the phase angle of the signal on E_Y by $+ \pi/2$ rad, to $E_Y = |E|\sin(2\pi ft + \pi/2)$, and leave $E_X = |E|\sin(2\pi ft)$ unmodified.[3] The phase shift in E_Y causes the

---

[2] This same concept applies to the magnetic field.

[3] E_Y leads E_X by $\pi/2$ rad.

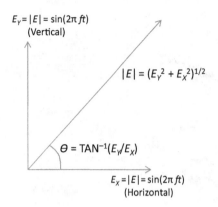

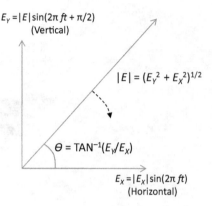

(a) Identical signals are placed on both the vertical and horizontal axis. Both have the same amplitude and phase angle. The Resultant E-field, $|E|$, remains at a constant angle of Θ.

(b) By shifting the phase of the vertical signal E_Y by +90° or $\pi/2$ rad, the resultant wave begins to rotate counterclockwise (LHCP) when viewed from the antenna.

FIGURE 5. 4 Circularly Polarized EM Wave. The propagation of the wave in (a) and (b) is outward from the page.

resultant wave to rotate in a counterclockwise direction (i.e., LHCP). We can similarly change the phase angle of either E_Y or E_X to cause a rotation in the opposite direction (i.e., RHCP). In practice, a quarter wave plate, which is designed to shift a signal plane phase by 90°, is one of the popular ways used to create circularly polarized waves.

In order to maximize the power transfer between transmit and receive antennas, the polarization of both antennas must be identical. Any variation between the two reduces the power transferred between antennas. This is true for linear polarized antennas (i.e., vertical and horizontal), as well as circularly polarized antennas (i.e., LHCP and RHCP). If the polarization of the EM wave changes during propagation from transmit to receive antennas, it is called ***depolarization***. The resulting misalignment between the EM wave and the receive antenna causes a weakening of the signal. The greater the misalignment, the weaker the signal power received. There are several causes of depolarization such as ice, snow, or an encounter with free electrons that are found within the ionosphere.[4]

To illustrate the concept of depolarization, consider a vertically polarized EM wave that is collected (i.e., received) by a vertically polarized antenna in fig. 5.5. We will assume that E_Y is a unit value equal to 1. Figure 5.5(a) shows the case where *no depolarization* of the EM wave has been experienced during propagation from the transmitter and, therefore all of the energy is found within the E_Y plane. In this case, maximum energy transfer[5] occurs between the EM wave and the receive antenna. In fig. 5.5(b), the EM wave encounters depolarization elements during propagation to the

---

[4] The ionosphere is the uppermost layer of earth's atmosphere. Satellite communications are particularly affected by this layer.

[5] Note: For this particular example, we are not considering attenuation, but are instead focusing on the power reduction cause by depolarization.

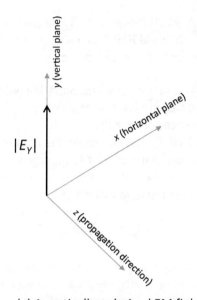

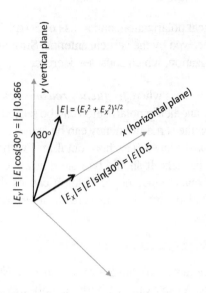

(a) A vertically polarized EM field with no cross-polarization element.

(b) A vertically polarized wave experiences a depolarization shift of 30°. The result is a co-polar element with a magnitude of $|E_Y| = 0.866|E|$, and a cross-polar element of $|E_X| = 0.5|E|$.

FIGURE 5.5 Effect of signal depolarization.

receiver, which in turn causes the EM wave to shift by 30°. This shift creates a resultant wave, $|E|$, that is comprised of a vertical **co-polar** component, E_Y, and a horizontal **cross-polar** component, E_X. The straight brackets around $|E|$ indicates the magnitude of the resultant wave, which in this case is $|E| = 1$. This is the same value as E_Y in the nondepolarized case. By applying basic trigonometry, we can determine the values of the *co-polar* and *cross-polar* components.

$$|E| = (E_X{}^2 + E_Y{}^2)^{1/2} = 1 \tag{5.3}$$

$$E_X = |E|\sin(\theta) = |E|(0.5) = 0.5$$

$$E_Y = |E|\cos(\theta) = |E|(0.866) = 0.866$$

From equations in (5.3), we find that the vertical (co-polar) component has decreased from 1 in the nondepolarized case, to 0.866 in the depolarized case. This means that depolarization has decreased the power transferred to the vertical antenna by $(1 - 0.86 = 0.14)$ 14%. In addition, a cross-polar component along the E_X plane has been created which could adversely impact signals operating in the horizontal plane.

As the depolarizing shift continues to increase, the signal power available to the receive vertical antenna decreases. At a maximum shift of 90°, the EM wave becomes horizontally polarized, or **orthogonal**[6]

---

[6] Orthogonal means opposite or perpendicular to. As an example, vertical polarization is orthogonal to horizontal polarization, and RHCP is orthogonal to LHCP.

to the vertical polarization, and a loss of 30 dB is experienced. A 30 dB loss essentially means that no power is received by the vertical antenna. Similarly, horizontal, LHCP and RHCP antennas are effected by depolarization, which causes a decrease in signal energy transfer to the receive antenna.

However, in cases where *frequency reuse* is desired, signals that are on the same frequency but orthogonal to one another in polarization can be reused. This means that the simultaneous transmission of two channels on the same frequency can be achieved without interference between the two when operating on orthogonal planes (i.e., horizontal and vertical, LHCP and RHCP), thus doubling the number of available channels. It should be noted, however, that depolarization in the case of frequency reuse is still problematic, since depolarization causes the formation of cross-polarization components in the orthogonal plane, which in turn creates interference to the signal operating in that plane.

5.2.2 Antenna Gain

All realistic antennas have a radiation pattern where power density is greater in some directions than others. As an example, with the half-wave dipole antenna in fig. 5.2(b) the greatest power density is found perpendicular to the antenna at the sides in a 360° pattern. The power density gradually decreases to zero toward the two tips of the antenna, making a three-dimensional toroid-shaped radiation pattern. When we compare this to the radiation pattern of the *ideal isotropic antenna* at the same power level, we see that the half-wave dipole has more power density perpendicular to the antenna than the ideal isotropic antenna. As discussed previously, we can describe this *antenna gain* in decibels referenced to the isotropic case in dBi.

Antenna gain is described by several variables which include *frequency, physical antenna dimensions*, and *antenna efficiency*. We will illustrate these variables by considering the case of a highly directional parabolic reflector antenna. *Parabolic reflector antennas* are typically circular in shape, although other rectangular or elliptical shapes are often used. The common characteristic of parabolic antennas is its reflector shape which creates a focal point for the collection or transmission of RF energy. When in receive mode, the reflector collects signal power density and reflects it toward a receiver feed which is located at the focal point of the parabola. When in transmit mode, power emanates from the transmit feed at the focal point and is reflected by the parabolic reflector toward the desired transmission direction.

Figure 5.6 depicts front and side views of a typical parabolic antenna. The main circular reflector is shaped into a *paraboloid* with a focal point located in front. The larger the area of the antenna is, the more power density it can collect during reception, and the greater the antenna gain. Likewise, per the *Antenna Reciprocity Theorem*, the transmit characteristics of the antenna are the same as for reception, therefore transmit antenna gain also increases as the area of the antenna increases. The physical area of the main reflector is simply the area of a circle, $A_{PHY} = \pi r^2$, where r is the radius. Since we know that the diameter of a circle is $D = 2r$, we can substitute D for r, see equation (5.4).

$$A_{PHY} = \pi r^2 = \pi \left(\frac{D}{2}\right)^2 = \frac{\pi D^2}{4} \tag{5.4}$$

However, not all of the antenna's physical area is useful in capturing the power density of the signal. The **effective aperture**, **Ae**, of the antenna is the useful receiving cross-section that actually

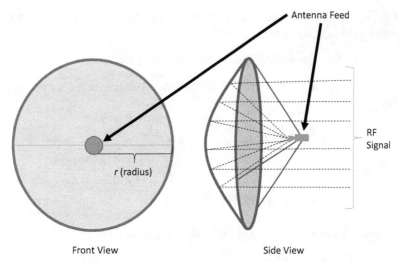

FIGURE 5.6 Parabolic Antenna.

captures the power density of the signal. Therefore, **antenna efficiency, η,** is the ratio of Ae over A_{PHY}[see equation (5.5)]. For a parabolic antenna, η can range from a low of 30% to a high of 70%. The typical value for parabolic antennas lies somewhere inbetween (e.g., 50%).

$$\eta = Ae/A_{PHY} \tag{5.5}$$

Example 5.1: A 3 m parabolic antenna has an antenna efficiency of $\eta = 55\%$. What is the area of the effective aperture Ae?

Answer: By using equations (5.4) and (5.5):

$$A_{PHY} = \frac{\pi D^2}{4} = \frac{\pi 3^2}{4} = \frac{9\pi}{4} = 7.0686 \text{ m}^2$$

$$Ae = \eta A_{PHY} = (0.55)(7.068 \text{ m}^2) = \underline{3.8877 \text{ m}^2}$$

The gain of a parabolic antenna is dependent upon the frequency of the signal, diameter of the antenna, and antenna efficiency as seen in equation (5.6), where λ is the signal's wavelength.[7] By substituting equation (5.4) into equation (5.6), we can derive a second equation (5.7) which has the antenna diameter, D, as a variable. Either equation (5.6) or (5.7) can be used to determine antenna gain.

$$G = (\eta \times A_{PHY})\left(\frac{4\pi}{\lambda^2}\right) \tag{5.6}$$

$$G = \eta\left(\frac{\pi D^2}{4}\right)\left(\frac{4\pi}{\lambda^2}\right) = \eta\left(\frac{\pi^2 D^2}{\lambda^2}\right) = \eta\left(\frac{\pi D}{\lambda}\right)^2 \tag{5.7}$$

---

[7] Frequency equals the speed of light in a vacuum divided by wavelength ($f = c/\lambda$ where $c = 3E8$ m/s)

Example 5.2: Given the effective antenna aperture in example 5.1, and an operating frequency of 14 GHz, what is the gain of the antenna in decibels?

Answer: We first determine the wavelength of the operating frequency,

$$\lambda = 3E8 \text{ (m/s)} \div 14E9 \text{ Hz} = 0.0214 \text{ m}$$

Using equation (5.6),

$$Ae = \eta A_{\text{PHY}} = 3.8877 \text{ m}^2$$

$$G = (\eta \times A_{\text{PHY}})\left(\frac{4\pi}{\lambda^2}\right) = (3.8877 \text{ m}^2)\left(\frac{4\pi}{4.5796 \text{ E} - 4 \text{ m}^2}\right) = 106{,}678$$

$$[G](\text{dBi}) = 10 \log_{10}(106{,}678) = \underline{50.28 \text{ dBi}}$$

Alternatively, we could have used equation (5.7), shown below.

$$D = 3 \text{ m}, \eta = 0.55$$

$$G = \eta\left(\frac{\pi D}{\lambda}\right)^2 = 0.55\left(\frac{3\pi}{0.0214 \text{ m}}\right)^2 = 106{,}678$$

$$[G](\text{dBi}) = 10\log_{10}(106{,}678) = \underline{50.28 \text{ dBi}}$$

When an antenna transmits, the power that emanates from the antenna is termed the ***effective isotropic radiated power (EIRP)*** which is the power entering the antenna from the power amplifier, P_T *(transmit power)*, combined with the gain of the antenna, G, [see equation (5.8)]. This value is typically shown in decibel form referenced[8] to 1 W(dBW) or 1 mW(dBm).

$$EIRP = P_T \times G \tag{5.8}$$

$$[EIRP]\text{dBW} = 10\log_{10}\left(\frac{P_T}{1 \text{ W}}\right) + 10\log_{10}G, \text{ with } P_T \text{ given in watts} \tag{5.9}$$

$$[EIRP]\text{dBm} = 10\log_{10}\left(\frac{P_T}{1 \text{ mW}}\right) + 10\log_{10}G, \text{ with } P_T \text{ given in milliwatts} \tag{5.10}$$

5.3 LINK ANALYSIS

In any communications system, whether guided or unguided, our goal is to ensure that enough power reaches the receiver so that the signal can be properly detected and demodulated. This requires an understanding of how much power is emitted by the transmit antenna (i.e., EIRP), the amount of path loss our signal may encounter during propagation, and how much power actually reaches the receiver itself. Each receiver will have a specification regarding ***receive sensitivity***, which tells us the minimum signal level required for that particular receiver to properly detect the signal for demodulation. As such, *receiver sensitivity* will vary depending upon the manufacturer of the receiver. Typically, receive sensitivity is given in values of minimum dBm that the receiver requires for proper signal detection. Determining the amount of receive power in our communications link by adding gains and subtracting losses is termed ***link analysis***.

---

[8] Other power references are used as well such as dBμW which is referenced to 1 μW.

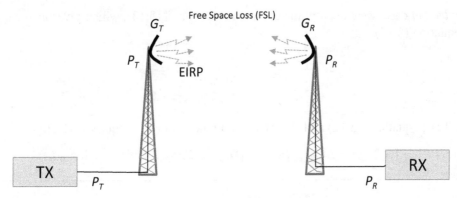

FIGURE 5.7 Simple microwave communications link.

Figure 5.7 shows a simple microwave communications link. We can perform link analysis using nondecibel or decibel values, although the later makes it mathematically much easier to perform especially if variables within the link, such as weather conditions causing attenuation, changes frequently.

With both decibel and nondecibel methods, we set P_R, the received power, to one side of the equation as seen in equation (5.11) for nondecibel and equation (5.12) for decibel methods.

Using the nondecibel method, we begin our analysis starting with P_T, transmit power. P_T is combined with the transmit antenna's gain, G_T, resulting in EIRP = $P_T G_T$. As the signal propagates from the transmit antenna to the receive antenna, the signal experiences attenuation due to signal spreading. This attenuation can be determined using the ***Friis free space loss*** equation (5.13), which is dependent upon transmission frequency, $f = c/\lambda$, and the distance between antennas, d, in meters. Finally, once the signal reaches the receive antenna, it is combined with the receive antenna's gain, G_R.

$$P_R = \frac{P_T G_T G_R}{FSL} = \frac{(EIRP) G_R}{FSL} \tag{5.11}$$

When performing the link analysis using decibels, we simplify our analysis considerably. First we convert all variables (P_T, G_T, G_R, FSL) into decibel values, and this enables us to simply add or subtract the variables in our link analysis. As an example, [EIRP] = [P_T] + [G_T], where EIRP, P_T and G_T have been converted to decibel values prior to addition.

$$[P_R] = [P_T] + [G_T] + [G_R] - [FSL] = [EIRP] + [G_R] - [FSL] \tag{5.12}$$

Friis free space loss (FSL) equation,

$$FSL = \left(\frac{4\pi d}{\lambda}\right)^2 \tag{5.13}$$

Friis FSL in decibel form,

$$[FSL](\text{dB}) = 20\log_{10}(4\pi d) - 20\log_{10}(\lambda) \tag{5.14}$$

In the *nondecibel* case, we can combine equations (5.11) and (5.13), which gives us the basic link analysis equation (5.15).

$$P_R = \frac{P_T G_T G_R}{\left(\frac{4\pi d}{\lambda}\right)^2} = \frac{P_T G_T G_R \lambda^2}{(4\pi d)^2} \qquad (5.15)$$

Using decibels, equations (5.12) and (5.14) are combined to give us equation (5.16).

$$[P_R] = [EIRP] + [G_R] - [FSL] = [EIRP] + [G_R] - (20\log_{10}(4\pi d) - 20\log_{10}(\lambda)) \qquad (5.16)$$

Note: The FSL equation can be rearranged as below:

$$-FSL = \left(\frac{\lambda}{4\pi d}\right)^2, \text{ which in decibel form gives you a negative value for FSL:}$$

$$[-FSL] = 20\log_{10}(\lambda) - 20\log_{10}(4\pi d)$$

Therefore, if using the above equation for FSL, you must add, vice subtract, FSL:

$$[P_R] = [EIRP] + [G_R] + [FSL] = [EIRP] + [G_R] + (20\log_{10}(\lambda) - 20\log_{10}(4\pi d))$$

Example 5.3: Determine the Friis FSL in decibels between transmitting antennas that are spaced 35 km from one another. The transmission frequency is 9 GHz.

Answer: First we determine the wavelength λ in meters as

$$\lambda = \frac{c}{f} = \frac{3E8 \text{ m/s}}{9E9 \text{ Hz}} = 0.03334 \text{ m}$$

Applying equation (5.13): *Note that we convert both frequency and distance to basic units of Hertz and meters. Doing this ensures that we do not inadvertently introduce large errors into our solution.*

$$FSL = \left(\frac{4\pi d}{\lambda}\right)^2 = \left(\frac{4\pi 35E3 \text{ m}}{0.034 \text{ m}}\right)^2 = 1.74E14$$

In decibels: $[FSL] = 10\log_{10}(1.74E14) = \underline{142.41 \text{ dB}}$

In all practical situations, there are other losses and gains that must be taken into consideration when determining the power at our receiver. The losses can come in the form of weather, signal obstacles such as a building or terrain features, as well as signal gains from amplifiers or digital repeaters. Let's consider fig. 5.8, where we've added signal amplifiers for gain, and coaxial runs which introduce attenuation losses.

We can analyze this link by breaking it into sections. Starting at the transmitter, P_T is amplified by Amp1. The amplified signal then suffers attenuation, L1, as it propagates through the coaxial cable up to the antenna. The resulting power P_1 enters the transmit antenna and is combined with the transmit antenna gain G_T, resulting in EIRP [equation (5.17)]. We can solve

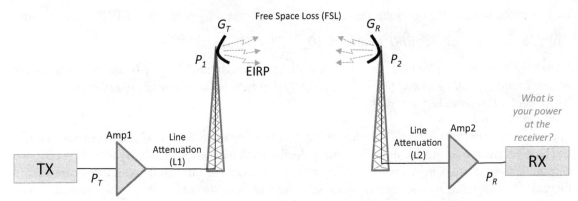

FIGURE 5.8 Link analysis of a microwave communications link where cable losses and signal amplifiers are part of the circuit.

EIRP using decibel notation, which reduces our equation to simple addition and subtraction [equation (5.18)].

$$EIRP = P_1 \times G_T = \frac{P_T * \text{Amp1} * G_T}{\text{L1}} \tag{5.17}$$

$$[EIRP] = [P_1] + [G_T] = [P_T] + [\text{Amp1}] + [G_T] - [\text{L1}] \tag{5.18}$$

Example 5.4: Given the communications link shown in fig. 5.8, determine the EIRP in decibels given the following: P_T = 10 W, Amp1 multiplies the signal $\times$ 10, L1 attenuates the signal by 2.2 db per 100 m, the coaxial cable length from Amp1 to the antenna is 100 m, G_T = 41 dBi.

Solution 1: Using the nondecibels, and equation (5.17),

[L1] = 2.2 dB

   or in nondecibel: L1 = $10^{(2.2/10)}$ = 1.659

[G_T] = 41 dBi, or in nondecibel form, G_T = $10^{(41/10)}$ = 12,589.254

$$P_1 = \frac{P_T \times \text{Amp1}}{\text{L1}} = \frac{10\ W \times 10}{1.659} = 60.277\ W$$

$EIRP = P_1 \times G_T = 60.277\ W \times 12,589.254 = \underline{758,842.463\ W}$

Solution 2: Using the decibels, and equation (5.18),

$$[P_T] = 10\log_{10}\left(\frac{10\ W}{1\ W}\right) = 10\ \text{dBW},$$

[L1] = 2.2 dB,

[G_T] = 41 dBi,

$$[\text{Amp1}] = 10\log_{10}\left(\frac{10}{1}\right) = 10\ \text{dB},$$

$[P_1] = [P_T] + [\text{Amp1}] - [\text{L1}] = 10\ \text{dBW} + 10\ \text{dB} - 2.2\ \text{dB} = 17.8\ \text{dBW}$

$[EIRP] = [P_1] + [G_T] = 17.8\ \text{dBW} + 41\ \text{dBi} = \underline{58.8\ \text{dBW}}$

We can check to see if the two solutions are the same by converting solution 2 [EIRP] back to watts.

$$EIRP \text{ (watts)} = 10^{(58.5/10)} = \underline{758,577.57 \text{ W}}$$

(Note: We see a slight difference in watts between solutions 1 and 2. This is due to rounding off errors. In this case, the two solutions, while slightly different, validate our use of either the nondecibel or decibel methods).

The next step in our link analysis is to determine the ***Friis free space loss (FSL)*** between our transmit and receive antennas using equation (5.13) or in decibels using equation (5.14). By including FSL, we determine the amount of signal power density reaching the receive antenna. This signal *power density (watts/m²)* is captured by the receive antenna's *effective aperture (Ae)* cross-sectional area in m², resulting in a signal power in watts entering the receive system. The receive antenna's gain, G_R, is applied to the receive signal resulting in signal power P_2 in watts. As the signal propagates through the coaxial cable, it suffers a power loss due to attenuation, L2, of the guided medium from the receive antenna to Amp2. Finally, the attenuated signal is amplified by Amp2, which results in P_R. By converting all variables in our link to decibel values, we can use simple addition and subtraction to determine the power P_R that we expect to see at the front of our receiver [see equation (5.19)].

$$[P_R] = [EIRP] - [FSL] + [G_R] - [L2] + [Amp2] \tag{5.19}$$

$$Where, [EIRP] = [P_T] + [Amp1] - [L1] + [G_T]$$

Example 5.5: Given the communications link shown in fig. 5.8, and the following information provided below, determine the received power, P_R.

Transmit system: P_T = 10 W, frequency 5 GHz, Amp1 × 10, L1 = 2 dB, G_T = 41 dBi.

Receiver system: G_R = 47 dBi, Amp1 × 2, L2 attenuates 1.5 dB.

Distance between antennas is d = 68 km

Solution: $\lambda = \dfrac{c}{f} = \dfrac{3E8 \text{ m/s}}{5E9 \text{ Hz}} = 0.06 \text{ m,}$

$[EIRP](\text{dBW}) = [P_T] + [Amp1] - [L1] + [G_T] = 10\log_{10}\left(\dfrac{10 \text{ W}}{1 \text{ W}}\right) + 10\log_{10}10 - 2 \text{ dB} + 41 \text{ dBi}$

$\qquad = 10 \text{ dBW} + 10 \text{ dB} - 2 \text{ dB} + 41 \text{ dBi} = \underline{59 \text{ dBW}}$

$[FSL](\text{dB}) = 20\log_{10}(4\pi d) - 20\log_{10}(\lambda) = 20\log_{10}(4\pi 68E3 \text{ m}) - 20\log_{10}(0.06 \text{ m})$

$\qquad = 118.64 \text{ dB} - (-24.44 \text{ dB}) = \underline{143 \text{ dB}}$

$[P_R](\text{dBW}) = [EIRP] - [FSL] + [G_R] - [L2] + [Amp2] = 59 \text{ dBW} - 143 \text{ dB} + 47 \text{ dBi}$
$\qquad - 1.5 \text{ dB} + 10\log_{10}(2)$

$\qquad = 59 \text{ dBW} - 143 \text{ dB} + 47 \text{ dBi} - 1.5 \text{ dB} + 3.01 \text{ dB} = \underline{-35.49 \text{ dBW}}$

Example 5.6: Given the P_R calculated in example 5.5, and a *receive sensitivity of −10 dBm*, will your link close—i.e., is there enough signal strength at the receiver to detect and demodulate the received signal P_R?

Solution: Convert $[P_R]$ from dBW to dBm: $-35.49 \text{ dBW} + 30 = \underline{-5.49 \text{ dBm}}$

Since the power reaching the receiver is greater than the receive sensitivity, the receiver is able to detect and demodulate the signal. The link margin is therefore,

[Link Margin] = $[P_R]$ − [Receive sensitivity] = −5.49 dBm − (−10 dBm) = <u>4.51 dBm</u>

5.3.1 Link Analysis—Determining Carrier-to-Noise Ratio (CNR)

Now that we have determined the level of power at the receiver, P_R, we need to consider the impacts that system and environmental noise has on our receiver. We do this by determining the noise contributors at the receiver which primarily include receive antenna and receive system noise.

Earlier we discussed the *signal-to-noise ratio (SNR)*, which we associated with a detected and demodulated signal found at the receiver's output. However, for our link analysis, we are more concerned with the signal, P_R, and noise, N, power (i.e., signal-to-noise ratio) at the input of the receiver, which we call the **carrier-to-noise ratio (CNR)**. CNR represents P_R measured over the noise environment at the input of the receiver, and as such, is independent of any receiver amplification or gain that appears at the output of the receiver. SNR and CNR are proportional to one another as can be seen in equation (5.20) where G_p represents the processing gain of the receiver.

$$\frac{S}{N} = \frac{C}{N} * G_p \qquad (5.20)$$

and in decibels: $[SNR] = [CNR] + [G_p]$

$$\frac{C}{N} = \frac{P_R}{N} \qquad (5.21)$$

In equation (5.21), we equate C *(carrier power)* to P_R. P_R represents the power at the receiver input after it has already experienced path attenuation. To determine noise, N, we need to focus on the contributing noise products within the receive environment. These contributing products include naturally occurring noises from the environment such as radiation, antenna noise, and noise generated from active and passive components that are part of the receive system such as the receiver, amplifiers, cables, connectors, etc. We measure noise as temperatures in Kelvin degrees, and we apply Boltzmann's constant and receive bandwidth to determine noise power in watts.

Equation (5.22) represents total receive system noise power, N_{System}, where k is the Boltzmann's constant (1.38E-23 J/K), T_{System} is the accumulated noise temperature in Kelvin degrees, and B is the bandwidth in Hz. Equation (5.23) represents **system noise power density** which represents noise power within a single Hz unit. Since all devices create a certain amount of noise, **system noise temperature**, T_{System}, is the summation of all noise sources. In equation (5.24), we show noise from two sources, the antenna, T_A, and receiver amplifier where Te stands for the *equivalent noise temperature* contributed by the receive amplifier. Later, we will discuss the addition of cascaded amplifiers and how we determine total system noise, T_{System}.

$$N_{System} = kT_{System}B \qquad (5.22)$$

$$No_{System} = kT_{System} \qquad (5.23)$$

$$T_{System} = T_A + Te \qquad (5.24)$$

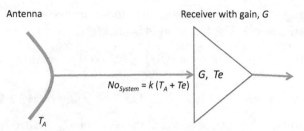

FIGURE 5.9 System noise density, *No*, measure at the output of the receiver amplifier.

Antenna noise, also called ***antenna noise temperature***, is represented by T_A. It represents several noise sources that include, (1) noise collected within the antenna's receive pattern, (2) the noise temperature of the antenna, and (3) the naturally occurring environmental or background radiation which is always present. T_A varies with frequency and antenna diameter. We determine the antenna noise power density in watts per Hz using equation (5.25).

$$No_A = kT_A \tag{5.25}$$

Once T_A has been determined, the noise produced by the receive amplifier is added. We reference the amplifier's noise contribution to the input of the amplifier prior to signal and noise amplification, see equation (5.26). We can then determine the system noise density value for this simple system using equation (5.27), which is represented by the system in fig. 5.9.

$$T_{System} = T_A + Te \tag{5.26}$$

$$No_{System} = kT_{System} = k(T_A + Te) \tag{5.27}$$

In more complex receive systems, there will be more than one amplifier connected in a cascaded fashion. Figure 5.10 shows the case of an antenna connected to three cascaded amplifiers. The basic idea applied in determining system noise for this complex system is to (1) note that the amplifier's noise contribution is referenced to the input of the amplifier, (2) the amplifier's noise gain is seen at the output of the amplifier, and therefore figured into the input of the next amplifier in line, and (3) the amplifier gain is applied to both signal power as well as noise power, and therefore, if we wish to just determine total noise temperature, we must compensate for the noise gain products of each cascaded amplifier.

Let's consider the three cascaded amplifiers in fig. 5.10(a). Each amplifier stage has an associated gain and output. The output of each stage is fed into the input of the following stage. We can treat this three-stage system as a single amplifier shown in fig. 5.10(b), the gain, G_{total} equals the cumulative effect of all three amplifiers and Te is the equivalent noise temperature from all three stages. Therefore, if we wish to calculate the total noise contribution, Te, of all three cascaded amplifiers, we will need to solve equation (5.28).

$$T_{out} = G_{total}(T_{in} + Te) \quad \text{or} \quad Te = \left(\frac{T_{out}}{G_{total}}\right) - T_{in} \tag{5.28}$$

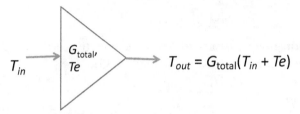

(a) Three-stage cascaded amplifiers

$$T_{out} = G_{total}(T_{in} + Te)$$

(b) Three cascaded amplifiers in (a) being represented as a single amplifier. T_A is removed from the equation to be added later. T_{in} represents the input to the first stage amplifier.

FIGURE 5.10 System noise temperature for the cascaded amplifier case.

Next, we analyze the noise temperature at each stage in fig. 5.10(a) to determine the output of each amplifier.

$$T_{out1} = G1(T_{in} + Te1)$$

$$T_{out2} = G2(T_{out1} + Te2)$$

$$T_{out3} = G3(T_{out2} + Te3)$$

By combining the above equations, we simplify the noise temperature T_{out3}.

$$T_{out3} = G3(G2(G1(T_{in} + Te1) + Te2) + Te3)$$

$$= G3(G2(G1T_{in} + G1Te1 + Te2) + Te3)$$

$$= G3(G1G2T_{in} + G1G2Te1 + G2Te2 + Te3)$$

$$= G1G2G3T_{in} + G1G2G3Te1 + G2G3Te2 + G3Te3$$

Since T_{out3} in fig. 5.10(a) equals T_{out} in fig. 5.10(b), we can substitute the above into equation (5.28), where $G_{total} = G1G2G3$.

$$Te = \frac{T_{out}}{G_{total}} - T_{in} = \frac{(G1G2G3T_{in} + G1G2G3Te1 + G2G3Te2 + G3Te3)}{G1G2G3} - T_{in}$$

$$= T_{in} + Te1 + \frac{Te2}{G1} + \frac{Te3}{G1G2} - T_{in}$$

$$Te = Te1 + \frac{Te2}{G1} + \frac{Te3}{G2G2}$$

Finally, when we add antenna noise T_A back into the above equation, we find our total system noise, equation (5.29).

$$T_{system} = T_A + Te1 + \frac{Te2}{G1} + \frac{Te3}{G1G2} \qquad (5.29)$$

Now that we know the system noise temperature, we can determine the system noise power, N_{System}, noise power density, No_{System}, shown in equations (5.30) and (5.31), respectively.

$$N_{System} = kT_{System}B \qquad (5.30)$$

$$No_{System} = kT_{System} \qquad (5.31)$$

We now have the information necessary to determine both the carrier over noise ratio (CNR) equation (5.32), and carrier over noise density, equation (5.33).

$$\frac{C}{N} = \frac{P_R}{N_{System}} \qquad (5.32)$$

$$\frac{C}{No} = \frac{P_R}{No_{System}} \qquad (5.33)$$

Next we can include C/N and C/No into our link equations (5.11) and (5.12). Here, we are using the basic equations without adding cable losses or amplifier gains. This is done to simplify the following explanation. As we discussed earlier, gains and losses can easily be applied in decibel form to the link calculation later.

We will derive the decibel and nondecibel equations for both C/N and C/No. For C/N, we take equation (5.11) and substitute P_R into equation (5.32) to derive the nondecibel case.

$$\frac{C}{N} = \frac{P_R}{N_{System}} = \frac{EIRP * G_R}{FSL * kT_{System}B} \qquad (5.34)$$

Converting equation (5.34) into decibel form we get equation (5.35).

$$\left[\frac{C}{N}\right] = [EIRP] + [G_R] - [FSL] - [k] - [T_{System}] - [B] \qquad (5.35)$$

Similarly, for C/No, we substitute equation (5.11) into equation (5.33) and get equations (5.36) and (5.37), the later in decibel form.

$$\frac{C}{No} = \frac{P_R}{No_{System}} = \frac{EIRP * G_R}{FSL * kT_{System}} \qquad (5.36)$$

$$\left[\frac{C}{No}\right] = [EIRP] + [G_R] - [FSL] - [k] - [T_{System}] \qquad (5.37)$$

Note, that it is much easier to subtract other losses (e.g., cables, connectors, etc.) and add in gains (e.g., amplifiers) by using the decibel formats in equations (5.35) and (5.37), where these modifications are simple additions and subtractions to our overall calculation.

Example 5.7: Determine the [C/N] and [C/No] in decibels given the following information:

Frequency: f = 12 GHz, B (bandwidth) = 36 MHz, d (distance between antennas) = 100 km

Transmit-side: P_T(Tx power) = 100 W, Parabolic Tx Ant. diameter D_T = 3 m, η_T (ant. Eff.) = 55%
Receive-side: Parabolic Rx Ant. Dia. D_R = 1.5 m, η_R = 45%, T_{System} = 185 K degrees

Solution: $\lambda = c/f$ = 3E8 (m/s)/12E 9 Hz = 0.025 m

We want to solve for *C/N* and *C/No* using equations (5.35) and (5.37) in decibel form.

$$\left[\frac{C}{N}\right] = [EIRP] + [G_R] - [FSL] - [k] - [T_{System}] - [B] \tag{5.35}$$

$$\left[\frac{C}{No}\right] = [EIRP] + [G_R] - [FSL] - [k] - [T_{System}] \tag{5.37}$$

Solve [EIRP] using equations (5.7) and (5.9),

$$G_T = \eta\left(\frac{\pi D}{\lambda}\right)^2 = (0.55)\left(\frac{3\pi}{0.025}\right)^2 = 78{,}167.27$$

$$[G_T] = 10\log_{10}(78{,}167.27) = 48.93 \text{ dBi}$$

$$[EIRP] = 10\log_{10}\left(\frac{100 \text{ W}}{1 \text{ W}}\right) + 48.93 \text{ dBi} = 20 \text{ dBW} + 48.93 \text{ dBi} = \underline{68.93 \text{ dBW}}$$

Solve [FSL] using equation (5.14),

$$[FSL](\text{dB}) = 20\log_{10}(4\pi d) - 20\log_{10}(\lambda) = 20\log_{10}(4\pi 100\text{E3 m}) - 20\log_{10}(0.025 \text{ m})$$
$$= 121.98 \text{ dB} - (-32.04 \text{ dB}) = \underline{154.02 \text{ dB}}$$

Solve [G_R] using equation (5.7),

$$G_R = \eta\left(\frac{\pi D}{\lambda}\right)^2 = (0.45)\left(\frac{1.5\pi}{0.025}\right)^2 = 15{,}988.76$$

$$[G_R] = 10\log_{10}(15{,}988.76) = \underline{42.04 \text{ dBi}}$$

With the information determined above, we can determine *C/N* and *C/No*,

$$\left[\frac{C}{N}\right] = [EIRP] + [G_R] - [FSL] - [k] - [T_{System}] - [B]$$
$$= 68.93 \text{ dBW} + 42.04 \text{ dBi} - 154.02 \text{ dB} - 10\log_{10}(1.38\text{E-23 J/K}) - 10\log_{10}(185 \text{ K})$$
$$- 10\log_{10}(36\text{E6 Hz})$$
$$= 68.93 \text{ dBW} + 42.04 \text{ dBi} - 154.02 \text{ dB} - (-228.60 \text{ dB}) - 22.67 - 75.56 \text{ dB} = \underline{87.32 \text{ dB}}$$

$$\left[\frac{C}{No}\right] = [EIRP] + [G_R] - [FSL] - [k] - [T_{System}]$$
$$= 68.93 \text{ dBW} + 42.04 \text{ dBi} - 154.02 \text{ dB} - 10\log_{10}(1.38\text{E-23 J/K}) - 10\log_{10}(185 \text{ K})$$
$$= 68.93 \text{ dBW} + 42.04 \text{ dBi} - 154.02 \text{ dB} - (-228.60 \text{ dB}) - 22.67 = \underline{162.88 \text{ dB}}$$

5.3.1.1 Noise Factor and Noise Figure

Besides using T_{System}, there are two additional ways we can describe system noise. ***Noise factor*** measures the ratio of input noise power to output noise power of an amplifier. To ensure consistency when comparing noise factors, we always measure noise factor at a temperature of T = 290 K. The equation for *noise factor*, F, using noise power densities is shown in equation (5.38) where N_{out}

is the output noise power density of the amplifier, N_{in} is the input noise density, G is amplifier gain, k is Boltzmann's constant (1.38E-23 J/K), and $T = 290$ K.

$$F = \frac{N_{out}}{N_{in}} = \frac{N_{out}}{GkT} \tag{5.38}$$

We can also express noise factor in terms of the ratio of SNR input to SNR output as shown in equation (5.39).

$$F = \frac{SNR_{in}}{SNR_{out}} \tag{5.39}$$

Noise figure, which is commonly used metric to determine the quality of an amplifier, is simply the decibel value of noise factor, see equation (5.40).

$$[F] = 10\log_{10}F \tag{5.40}$$

5.3.2 G/T, Receive System Figure-of-Merit

Receive antenna gain and total system noise contributed by receive system components play a critical role in determining the overall performance and efficiency of the communications link. As such we use the receive antenna gain over the total system noise as an important **figure-of-merit**, see equation (5.41).

$$\frac{G_R}{T_{System}}, \text{ or in decibels } [G_R] - [T_{System}] \text{ (dBK}^{-1}) \tag{5.41}$$

Since G/T is determined for a specific antenna and receive system, it is usually measured through testing once the system has been installed. *Characterizing* the antenna system involves taking G/T measurements and verifying these against calculated values. Because this characterization is dependent upon the specific receive system setup, it needs to be recharacterized each time a major component impacting antenna gain or receive system noise temperature changes.

Because G/T is a critical measure for understanding the noise present at our receive system, we want to include it as part of our link analysis. To do this, we need to modify the link equation (5.35) by first rearranging the variables. Working in decibel format simplifies our task.

$$\left[\frac{C}{N}\right] = [EIRP] + [G_R] - [FSL] - [k] - [T_{System}] - [B] \tag{5.35}$$

Rearrange equation (5.35) so that $[G_R]$ is next to $[T_{System}]$,

$$\left[\frac{C}{N}\right] = [EIRP] + [G_R] - [T_{System}] - [FSL] - [k] - [B]$$

Since we know that $[G/T] = [G_R] - [T_{System}]$, we can substitute $[G/T]$ into the equation

$$\left[\frac{C}{N}\right] = [EIRP] + \left[\frac{G}{T}\right] - [FSL] - [k] - [B] \tag{5.42}$$

Likewise, we can rearrange equation (5.37) to include $[G/T]$,

$$\left[\frac{C}{No}\right] = [EIRP] + [G_R] - [T_{System}] - [FSL] - [k]$$

$$\left[\frac{C}{No}\right] = [EIRP] + \left[\frac{G}{T}\right] - [FSL] - [k] \tag{5.43}$$

Once the receive antenna and system noise has been characterized in the form of G/T, we can determine changes in C/N or C/No, without the need to recalculate receive system noise each time. It provides a convenient metric for determining and comparing the quality of receive antenna systems.

Example 5.8: Given the previous example 5.7, determine the $\left[\dfrac{G}{T}\right]$ of the receive antenna.

Solution: $\left[\dfrac{G}{T}\right] = [G_R] - [T_{System}] = 42.04 \text{ dBi} - 22.67 \text{ dB} = \underline{19.37 \text{ dB/K}}$

5.4 DATA RATE CAPACITY

A primary goal for establishing a digital wireless link is to maximize resource efficiency, while achieving data rate maximization.[9] In order to maximize data capacity for a given situation, we need to consider the following.

- <u>Regulatory restraints on frequency and bandwidth assignments, as well as allowable transmit power.</u> Since RF communications share a common medium with other RF signals, as well as from other EM noise sources, RFI becomes an issue. Therefore, regulatory agencies such as the Federal Communications Commission (FCC) at the national level, and International Telecommunications Union (ITU) at the international level, oversee frequency, frequency bandwidth, and power level allocations. Even devices operating at the unlicensed *Industrial, Scientific and Medical (ISM)* frequencies must adhere to specifications approved by these agencies.

- <u>Bit error rate (BER) tolerances for a given application and the use of error control methods as needed.</u> A typical BER value for an unguided data link is 10^{-5}. However, this BER value may be worse depending upon the noise environment. As such, error control methods are used to reach an acceptable BER level. Any error control method used, whether error detection and retransmission, or error correction, adds additional bits to the link's overhead. This means that only a certain percentage of the data rate capacity transmitted will be true information. Therefore, if you were transmitting an uncompressed digitized voice grade signal of 64 kbps, you would need a higher capacity link that also includes error control bits.

- <u>Noise products within the communication channel or link, including receive system noise temperature.</u> This is closely related to BER tolerances. Depending upon the noise environment, an increase in noise causes a decrease in CNR, which translates into a lower achievable data rate capacity over the communications link.

- <u>Carrier power required at the receiver to enable signal detection.</u> The amount of carrier power over noise (CNR), determines the amount of carrier power available to the receiver. Depending upon the specific receiver's sensitivity there may, or may not, be enough power to allow for signal detection. As an example, a receiver used in a satellite communications link would require a very sensitive receiver in order to detect a very weak signal from a distant satellite. Therefore, considering applicable regulatory constraints, you would perform a link analysis to determine the expected receive power, and select the appropriate receiver for the application.

---

[9] The data rate capacity of a link includes the information rate (i.e., the actual information being conveyed) plus overhead bits which include framing and error control bits.

- Modulation scheme selected. M'ary modulation techniques increase the number of bits that a single symbol can represent. This means that for a given symbol rate, we can increase our data rate capacity; however, this increase requires greater equipment complexity as well as better transmission conditions. So a noisy channel would be forced to use simpler modulation schemes with lower M values, resulting in lower data rates.

- Application for the communications link. Understanding the intended use of the communications link is a key driver in establishing the requirements that feed the ultimate design of the communications system. Tolerances in BER and the use of reliable error control schemes have a greater significance when sending medical imagery, than for sharing compressed .jpeg images. Establishing simple push-to-talk (PTT) links require a less complex system compared to a satellite phone service. By understanding the use of the communication link, we can design a system built around key objectives, whether they include costs, reliability, responsiveness, bulk capacity, complexity, etc.

We want a large enough data rate capacity to support our applications, but we also want as low an error rate as possible. Through link analysis, *C/N* and *C/No* can be determined. If we also know the desired BER and modulation method to be used, we can determine the data rate capacity that can be supported. In equation (5.44), *C/N* equals **Eb/No (energy-bit per noise power density)** multiplied by **Rb (data rate)** divided by **BW (bandwidth)**. *Eb/No* stands for the energy per one bit, typically in units of Joules, over the noise power density in 1 Hz. Equations (5.44) and (5.46) represent *C/N* and *C/No*, respectively, as a function of *Eb/No and* data rate (*Rb*). The difference between *C/N* and *C/No* is the consideration of bandwidth for *C/N* calculations. Equations (5.45) and (5.47) represent these equations in decibel form.

$$\frac{C}{N} = \frac{Eb}{No} * \frac{Rb}{BW} \tag{5.44}$$

$$\left[\frac{C}{N}\right] = \left[\frac{Eb}{No}\right] + [Rb] - [BW] \tag{5.45}$$

$$\frac{C}{No} = \frac{Eb}{No} * Rb \tag{5.46}$$

$$\left[\frac{C}{No}\right] = \left[\frac{Eb}{No}\right] + [Rb] \tag{5.47}$$

Let's consider equation (5.45). If we know [*C/N*], [*Eb/No*], and [*BW*], then we can solve for [*Rb*],

$$[Rb] = \left[\frac{C}{N}\right] - \left[\frac{Eb}{No}\right] + [BW] \tag{5.48}$$

The value for *Eb/No* is typically derived from a graph such as the one in fig. 5.11. The curve represents BPSK modulation and associates BER with required [*Eb/No*] levels in decibels. Note that "*BER versus [Eb/No]*" graphs such as this will typically display several curves that represent numerous M'ary modulation and line coding methods. In fig. 5.11 we show a single curve representing BPSK (M = 2) modulation. If we wish to achieve a BER = 10^{-5} using BPSK modulation, then the required [*Eb/No*] needs to equal 9.7 dB as indicated on the [*Eb/No*] horizontal axis of the graph. If we also know the bandwidth of our signal, then we can determine the data rate using equation (5.48).

Example 5.9: Using equation (5.48) and the graph in fig. 5.11, determine the data rate capacity given the following. [*C/N*] = 40 dB, *BW* = 6 MHz, desired BER = 10^{-5}.

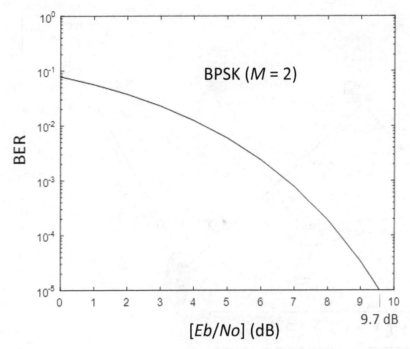

FIGURE 5.11 BER versus *Eb/No* plot showing that a BER = 10^{-5} using BPSK (*M* = 2) modulation can be achieved with an [*Eb/No*] = 9.7 dB.

Solution: With a desired BER of 10^{-5}, we determine a required [*Eb/No*] value of 9.7 dB. Using equation (5.48),

$$[Rb] = \left[\frac{C}{N}\right] - \left[\frac{Eb}{No}\right] + [BW] = 40 \text{ dB} - 9.7 \text{ dB} + 10\log_{10}(6\text{E6})$$

$$= 40 \text{ dB} - 9.7 \text{ dB} + 67.78 \text{ dB} = \underline{98.08 \text{ dB}}$$

We convert [*Rb*] from decibels to data rate,

$$Rb = 10^{(98.08/10)} = \underline{6.43 \text{ Gbps}}$$

5.5 MULTIPATH AND MIMO

Multipath propagation occurs in all unguided communications links. It is based upon the fact that electromagnetic waves within a given medium will travel at a constant speed of light. A transmitted RF signal will spread as it propagates in free space, which means that some paths of the signal may encounter signal impairments such as reflection (see fig. 4.17), while others may be direct line of sight (LOS) to the receive antenna. Since all signal paths propagate at the same velocity, path lengths will vary, thus causing copies of the same signal to reach the receiver at slightly different times resulting in signal distortion. Figure 5.12 shows the transmitted signal taking several different paths. L1 is the shortest distance, direct LOS path and therefore this signal will reach the receive antenna first. The other signals, L2 through L4, take different paths and are therefore subjected to different impairments such as reflection by one or more objects. This causes copies of the same signal to reach the receiver at slightly different times. The out-of-phase copies destructively combine together with one another, creating distortion of the original signal at the receiver which is termed ***multipath fading***.

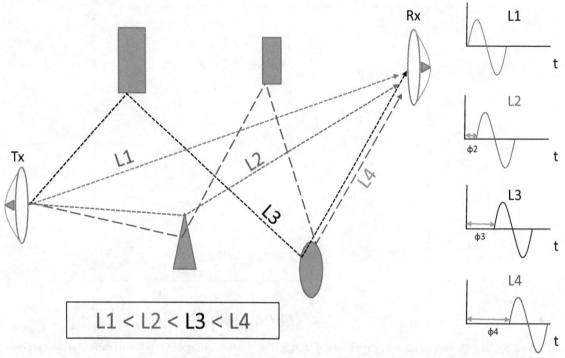

FIGURE 5.12 Multipath Propagation. A signal takes several different paths from the Tx antenna to the Rx antenna. Since all waves propagate at the same speed of light, the shorter distance, L1 reaches the Rx antenna first, followed by L2, L3, and L4. Multiple copies of the signal reaching the receiver at slightly different are destructively combined causing signal distortion.

One way to reduce the adverse effects of multipath is to buffer incoming signal copies during a specified sampling period, and then send these copies to a digital signal processor (DSP) that adjusts the phase angle of each copy received. Once the signal copies are adjusted to the same phase angle, they can be constructively combined to create an amplified receive signal.

While multipath propagation is typically undesirable between single transmit and receive antennas, it can be used to significantly improve data capacity when combined with multiple spatially diversified transmit and receive antennas and DSPs. This concept is termed ***multiple input, multiple output (MIMO)*** and it is a method used today in WLAN (wireless LAN, 802.11n), and 4G cellular standards such as LTE (Long Term Evolution) and WiMAX (802.11e).

Figure 5.13 represents a 2×2 MIMO system of four antennas,[10] two transmit and two receive. The two antennas located at either transmission ends are separated by approximately one-half wavelength or less. Tx antenna 1 has a direct LOS path to Rx antenna 1 (h_{11}), and an indirect path to Rx antenna 2 (h_{12}). Likewise, Tx antenna 2 has a direct LOS path to Rx antenna 2 (h_{22}), and an indirect path to Rx antenna 1 (h_{21}). The indirect paths, h_{12} and h_{21}, have longer distances to travel thus these signal will arrive later in time than the direct LOS signals h_{11} and h_{22}. In addition, these indirect paths may be reflected by objects within the environment, causing even greater signal delay. By using DSPs to adjust

---

[10] Any number of transmit or receive antennas can be used with the MIMO concept.

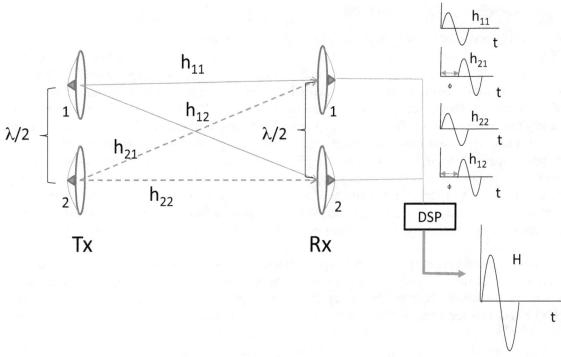

FIGURE 5.13 MIMO (2 × 2). Multiple signal paths can be combined constructively using DSPs to adjust signal phase angles resulting in a total receive signal with better SNR.

the timing (i.e., phase) of the direct and indirect signals from both receive antennas and then constructively combining them, we will realize a gain in the total signal power received. Per *Shannon-Hartley's Capacity Theorem, C(bps) = B × log₂(1 + SNR)*, increased SNR results in increased data throughput. Keep in mind that this gain is accomplished using the same operating frequency for each path, with the same power level used in the single transmit/receive antenna case. In other words, using the MIMO concept enables an increase in throughput without the need to increase power or add channel frequencies. Considering the limited frequency spectrum available and the market for higher data throughput, it is not surprising why cellular and WLAN technologies have embraced the MIMO concept.

MIMO can be classified into two broad categories.

- <u>Spatial Diversity</u>. The use of several spatially diversified antennas gives rise to multiple signal paths between the transmitter and receiver (i.e., multipath). As we saw above, these signals can be constructively combined using a DSP. In addition, since all signals propagate in different paths, they are not subjected to exactly the same propagation impairments. This increases the reliability to receive the signal compared to the single antenna pair model.

- <u>Spatial Multiplexing</u>. With spatial multiplexing, a signal or message is broken into several smaller parts. These parts are transmitted in parallel using different spatially diversified transmit antennas. Using this technique requires capable DSPs that can differentiate between parallel streams of signal data. As a result of spatial multiplexing, higher data throughput can be achieved compared to the single antenna pair model.

5.6 SPREAD SPECTRUM

The development of the first spread spectrum technology grew from a need to develop secure and reliable communications prior to World War II. Two unlikely inventors, Hedwig Maria Eva Kielser, who was a Hollywood actress going by the name of Hedy Lamarr, and George Anthiel, a musician, worked together on an invention that eventually led to today's *frequency hopping spread spectrum (FHSS)* concept. The device described in their 1942 patent involved a mechanical system that could rapidly change transmission frequencies during a communications session. Only the transmitter and intended receiver would know the correct sequence of frequency changes, therefore making eavesdropping nearly impossible. By rapidly changing the frequency during a communications session, the signal appeared to be spread over a large frequency bandwidth, making narrowband jamming extremely difficult. Although patented, the U.S. military did not take the patent seriously during the war. It was not until the 1950s, after electronic technologies had made numerous advances, that Lamarr's patent resurfaced to begin the era of development on spread spectrum communications.

The basic idea of spread spectrum is to spread narrowband signals into a much wider band, thus increasing spectral efficiency and improving communications security. Multiple communication sessions exist within the same frequency bandwidth, separated by unique *pseudorandom noise (PN) codes* that are only shared between communicating devices. The PN codes describes two aspects: (1) *"pseudorandom,"* which tells us that the code is not truly random, but deterministic, and (2), that *spreading* the signal in the frequency domain can be accomplished without adding additional signal power, thus making the signal appear more like *wideband noise* vice a signal. There are two main spread spectrum techniques used today,

- Direct Sequence Spread Spectrum (DSSS). With DSSS, an information data rate is combined with a PN code to produce a higher data rate which is termed the *chipping rate*. The higher chip rate causes the original nonspread signal to expand in bandwidth. This process will be discussed further in section 5.6.1.

- Frequency Hopping Spread Spectrum (FHSS). Similar to Lemarr's original 1942 patent, the concept behind FHSS is to rapidly change transmission frequencies during a communications session. Unlike Lamarr's version, FHSS is implemented on high-speed firmware chips used on both the transmit and receive systems. A shared *pseudorandom hop sequence* enables both transmitter and receiver to be on the same frequency to send and collect data. An example of FHSS in use today is IEEE 802.15 where Bluetooth devices operate at 1600 frequency hops per second over a 79 MHz bandwidth.

5.6.1 A Closer Look at DSSS

Direct sequence spread spectrum (DSSS) techniques have been used in 802.11 wireless local area networks (WLAN). In addition, code division multiple access (CDMA) is a form of DSSS used in 2G and 3G cellular phone networks. DSSS techniques have several advantages when compared to narrow band channels. The first is its survivability in an environment where interfering noise, to include intentional signal jamming,[11] is present. In the upper graph of fig. 5.14, we see how a narrow band interfering noise

---

[11] Most signal jammers are narrow band since it takes enormous amounts of power to jam a wideband signal.

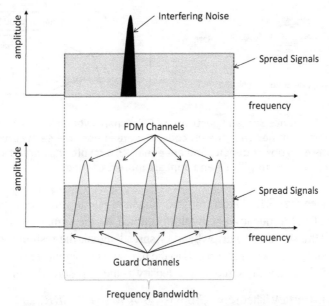

FIGURE 5.14 The upper plot shows a spread signal in the frequency domain with an interfering noise source identified. The noise source only affects a small portion of the spread signal, therefore most of the signal is not impacted by the noise and the signal can get through to the receiver. The lower plot shows a comparison between multiple narrowband channels that require separation by guard channels, compared to the spread spectrum signal which eliminate the need for guard channels and therefore increases spectral efficiency.

source will only disrupt part of a spread signal. Because most of the signal energy is left undisturbed, use of DSSS results in a more reliable communications link when operating in a noisy environment.

The second advantage when using DSSS is its spectral efficiency. In the lower graph of fig. 5.14, we have superimposed several narrow band FDM channels over spread signals for comparison. The FDM channels must be separated by guard channels in order to avoid interference between channels (i.e., intermodulation, IM, noise). Unfortunately, no information can be transmitted within these guard bands, therefore it represents unused frequency spectrum. When we consider the limited availability of frequency spectrum combined with today's desire for higher data throughput, the use of guard channels that carry no data becomes costly in terms of spectral efficiency. DSSS eliminates the need for guard channels since users occupy the entire frequency bandwidth and are separated by unique PN codes. By eliminating the need for guard channels, an increase in spectral efficiency is realized, which leads to increased data throughput.

A third benefit is that spread spectrum techniques provide greater security from data interception and eavesdropping. Since unique PN codes are required for each communicating pair, it is much more difficult to intercept and process user information without knowledge of the PN code being used. This enhances privacy to a much greater extent than FDM, where one only needs to know the frequency channel of interest to collect communication data.

In order to successfully implement DSSS, a unique set of *orthogonal* PN codes must be created. These codes are used by each communicating pair to increase the information data throughput to a much

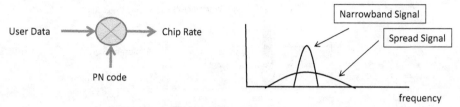

FIGURE 5.15 Direct Sequence Spread Spectrum (DSSS). A narrowband signal is spread over a wider bandwidth after being combined with the PN code. The area under the each curve, narrowband and spread signal, represents power density and are equal. As a result, the spread signal has a lower amplitude and appears more flattened.

higher *chipping rate* (see fig. 5.15). According to Shannon-Hartley theorem, increasing throughput results in an increase of the frequency bandwidth occupied by the signal. Since the same amount of power is used whether transmitting a narrowband or spread signal, the resulting spread signal appears flattened with a lower amplitude when compared to the narrowband signal. This is due to the fact that the pre-spread narrowband signal has the same power density as the post-spread signal as shown in fig. 5.15.

$$\text{Shannon-Hartley Theorem: } C(\text{bps}) = B \times \log_2(1 + SNR)$$

In order to explain how DSSS works, we will now go over a simple example. The first requirement is to identify a set of orthogonal PN codes for use. An N-bit codeword, at most, will have N number of orthogonal PN codes associated with it. As an example, let's say we decide to use a four-bit PN code ($N = 4$) which gives us $2^4 = 16$ permutations. However, only 4 of the 16 permutations will give us orthogonal PN codes. In order to be an orthogonal PN code, it must have zero correlation with any other PN codeword. This test for orthogonality is accomplished by determining the dot product between any two PN codewords in the set. Instead of using logical 1s and 0s as values in our PN code example, we will instead use voltage levels, either 1 V or −1 V. Therefore, our four orthogonal codes are represented by:

$$PN1 = (1 \text{ V}, 1 \text{ V}, 1 \text{ V}, 1 \text{ V})$$

$$PN2 = (1 \text{ V}, 1 \text{ V}, -1 \text{ V}, -1 \text{ V})$$

$$PN3 = (1 \text{ V}, -1 \text{ V}, 1 \text{ V}, -1 \text{ V})$$

$$PN4 = (1 \text{ V}, -1 \text{ V}, -1 \text{ V}, 1 \text{ V})$$

Any two PN codes are orthogonal provided their dot product equals zero. Therefore, we can test each combinations of PN codes in our set of four (note: the below dot products assume units of voltage). The resulting products confirm that the four PN codes represent an orthogonal code set.

$$PN1 \bullet PN2 = (1 * 1) + (1 * 1) + (1 * -1) + (1 * -1) = 1 + 1 + (-1) + (-1) = 0$$

$$PN2 \bullet PN3 = (1 * 1) + (1 * -1) + (-1 * 1) + (-1 * -1) = 1 + (-1) + (-1) + 1 = 0$$

$$PN3 \bullet PN4 = (1 * 1) + (-1 * -1) + (1 * -1) + (-1 * 1) = 1 + 1 + (-1) + (-1) = 0$$

$$PN4 \bullet PN1 = (1 * 1) + (-1 * 1) + (-1 * 1) + (1 * 1) = 1 + (-1) + (-1) + 1 = 0$$

With the four PN codes identified, we can now support four simultaneous user connections, with each transmitter and receiver pair sharing a single PN code. Table 5.1 shows a list of assigned PN codes for users 1 through 4, and the data each user wishes to send to the receiver.

TABLE 5.1 Direct sequence spread spectrum example—user assignment of PN codes and data to be transmitted.

User Tx/Rx Pair	Assigned PN Code	Data to be sent
User 1	$PN_1 = 1, 1, 1, 1$	$D_1 = 1, 1, 1$
User 2	$PN_2 = 1, 1, -1, -1$	$D_2 = 1, -1, -1$
User 3	$PN_3 = 1, -1, 1, -1$	$D_3 = -1, -1, 1$
User 4	$PN_4 = 1, -1, -1, 1$	$D_4 = -1, 1, -1$

TABLE 5.2 XOR logic table using voltage levels.

	1 V	−1 V
1 V	1 V	−1 V
−1 V	−1 V	1 V

The next step is to combine the user data with the PN code using an XOR logic gate in order to expand the data rate to the spread chipping rate. The XOR logic Table 5.2 is shown above which uses 1V and −1 V vice logical 0s and 1s.

Combining each user's PN code with the user's data using the XOR logic results in the below,

User 1: $PN_1 \oplus D_1 = $ 1 V, 1 V, 1 V, 1 V   1 V, 1 V, 1 V, 1 V   1 V, 1 V, 1 V, 1 V

User 2: $PN_2 \oplus D_2 = $ 1 V, 1 V, −1 V, −1 V   −1 V, −1 V, 1 V, 1 V   −1 V, −1 V, 1 V, 1 V

User 3: $PN_3 \oplus D_3 = $ −1 V, 1 V, −1 V, 1 V   −1 V, 1 V, −1 V, 1 V   1 V, −1 V, 1 V, −1 V

User 4: $PN_4 \oplus D_4 = $ −1 V, 1 V, 1 V, −1 V   1 V, −1 V, −1 V, 1 V   −1 V, 1 V, 1 V, −1 V

The sum of the four user voltages above represents the aggregate voltage signal that appears on the shared bandwidth.

Aggregate Total $= (PN_1 \oplus D_1) + (PN_2 \oplus D_2) + (PN_3 \oplus D_3) + (PN_4 \oplus D_4)$

User 1: $PN_1 \oplus D_1 = $ 1 V, 1 V, 1 V, 1 V   1 V, 1 V, 1 V, 1 V   1 V, 1 V, 1 V, 1 V

User 2: $PN_2 \oplus D_2 = $ 1 V, 1 V, −1 V, −1 V   −1 V, −1 V, 1 V, 1 V   −1 V, −1 V, 1 V, 1 V

User 3: $PN_3 \oplus D_3 = $ −1 V, 1 V, −1 V, 1 V   −1 V, 1 V, −1 V, 1 V   1 V, −1 V, 1 V, −1 V

User 4: $PN_4 \oplus D_4 = $ −1 V, 1 V, 1 V, −1 V   1 V, −1 V, −1 V, 1 V   −1 V, 1 V, 1 V, −1 V

*Aggregate Total = * 0, 4 V, 0,   0   0,   0,   0, 4 V   0,   0, 4 V, 0

The aggregate total voltage signal is seen by all users; however, unique PN codes separate the data for each user. As an example, if User 3 applies PN_3 code to the aggregate signal, then the data for User 3 will be revealed.

User 3 multiplies the aggregate signal with PN3:

PN_3:	1 V, −1 V, 1 V, −1 V	1 V, −1 V, 1 V, −1 V	1 V, −1 V, 1 V, −1 V
Aggregate Total:	0, 4 V, 0, 0	0, 0, 0, 4 V	0, 0, 4 V, 0
	0, −4 V, 0, 0	0, 0, 0, −4V	0, 0, 4 V, 0

Divide by 4 (4 PN codes) and the data becomes −1 V, −1 V, 1 V, which is User 3 D_3 per Table 5.1. It is left as an exercise for students to verify that Users 1, 2, and 4 data can be extracted from the aggregate signal.

5.7 ORTHOGONAL FREQUENCY DIVISION MULTIPLEXING (OFDM)

Orthogonal frequency division multiplexing (OFDM) is a multicarrier modulation concept in which user data is transmitted in parallel over several subcarriers. Figure 5.16(a) represents typical FDM channels that are separated by guard bands. In comparison, fig. 5.16(b) represents OFDM where the subcarriers overlap one another, thus increasing spectral efficiency and throughput. The spacing of the subcarriers is critical in order to enable overlapping; a situation that would cause intermodulation noise if traditional FDM were used instead. The subcarriers are orthogonal to one another, meaning that the subcarrier spacing equals one over the period of the symbol, or one over

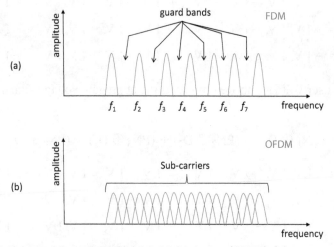

FIGURE 5.16 Orthogonal Frequency Division Multiplexing (OFDM). (a) represents typical FDM channels which are separated by a guard band. (b) represents OFDM subcarriers which can overlap, thus increasing spectra efficiency.

symbol-time, $1/T_{symbol}$. Doing this creates signal nulls from adjacent subcarriers. Essentially, this means that when we collect the center frequency of a subcarrier, the adjacent subcarriers present a null or zero signal at our center frequency. This leaves only the center frequency which is what we desire to collect.

Even though each subcarrier has a smaller bandwidth, transmitting data over several subcarriers in parallel increases data throughput when compared to DSSS and FDM. In addition, while it is not a spread spectrum technique, it has the benefit of transmitting a signal over a wider bandwidth using several subcarriers. As such, OFDM has greater resiliency from noise and fading similar to spread spectrum. OFDM has been implemented in many of today's communications standards such as 802.11n, 802.11ac, DSL (Digital Subscriber Line), WiMAX 802.16e, and LTE-Advanced.

A popular version of OFDM is *coded orthogonal frequency multiplexing (COFDM)* which incorporates an error correction capability.

Orthogonal frequency division multiple access (OFDMA) is an access scheme used by service providers that assigns several subcarriers to a user. Other examples of assigning resources to users are *frequency division multiple access (FDMA)*, *time division multiple access (TDMA)*, and *code division multiple access (CDMA)*.

KEY TERMS

antenna efficiency (η)	frequency hopping spread spectrum (FHSS)	orthogonal
antenna gain	frequency reuse	orthogonal frequency division multiplexing (OFDM)
antenna noise temperature	Friis free space loss	
antenna polarization	G/T	parabolic reflector
antenna reciprocity	horizontal polarization	power density
BER	ideal isotropic antenna	pseudorandom noise code
carrier-to-noise ratio (CNR)	impedance	reactive components
circular polarization	left hand circular polarization (LHCP)	receive sensitivity
co-polar	linear polarization	resistive components
cross-polar	link analysis	resultant wave
directionality	multiple input, multiple output (MIMO)	resonance
direct sequence spread spectrum (DSSS)	multipath	right hand circular polarization (RHCP)
Eb/No	noise factor	spatial diversity
effective aperture (Ae)	noise figure	spatial multiplexing
EIRP	nonresonant	system noise temperature
EM wave polarization		vertical polarization

CHAPTER PROBLEMS

1. The "Reciprocity Theorem for Antennas" states that the transmitting and receiving characteristics are the same for identical antennas operating at the same wavelength.
   a. True
   b. False

   Answer: a

2. An $\lambda/2$ dipole operating at a frequency of 900 MHz will have a length of _____ meters.

   Answer: $\lambda = c/2f = $ (3E8 m/s)/(2*900E6 Hz) = <u>0.167 m</u>

3. An "ideal isotropic antenna" is a hypothetical antenna that has an efficiency of 100%.
   a. True
   b. False

   Asnwer: a

4. When describing the antenna gain of directional antenna in decibels, we typically use an isotropic antenna as the reference (i.e., dBi).
   a. True
   b. False

   Answer: a

5. Antenna "gain" refers to the power density increase of a directional antenna in a given direction, over that of the ideal isotropic antenna. Gain is typically given in "dBi" which compares the ratio between a directional antenna and an ideal isotropic antenna.
   a. True
   b. False

   Answer: a

6. In an EM wave, the E-field defines the polarization of both the antenna and EM wave.
   a. True
   b. False

   Answer: a

7. Select the correct statement regarding antenna and EM wave polarization.
   a. A vertically polarized antenna can communicate with a horizontally polarized antenna
   b. A vertically polarized antenna can only communicate with another vertically polarized antenna
   c. An EM wave emitted from a vertically polarized antenna will be horizontally polarized
   d. All of the statements are correct

   Answer: b

8. A linearly polarized antenna (i.e., vertical or horizontal) will typically have components in both the horizontal and vertical poles (i.e., co-polar and cross-polar components).
   a. True
   b. False

   Answer: a

9. Depolarization of the EM wave causes polarization misalignment, which results in a weaker resultant wave and less power transfer from EM wave to antenna.
   a. True
   b. False

10. A RHCP antenna is orthogonal to a LHCP antenna.
    a. True
    b. False

11. An antenna can transmit two different signals on the same frequency by ensuring that both signals are orthogonally polarized (i.e., vertical and horizontal, or RHCP and LHCP). This is a method used for frequency reuse.
    a. True
    b. False

12. Select the correct statement regarding cross-polarization.
    a. Cross-polarization between two linear antennas can cause a 30 dB loss in signal
    b. Cross-polarization between two linear antennas can increase signal strength by 30 dB
    c. Cross-polarization is not a problem for earth terminals communicating with satellite in space
    d. both b and c are correct

13. What can cause cross-polarization?
    a. Ionosphere, radiation, meteors
    b. Ionosphere, ice crystals, rain
    c. Ionosphere, temperature, clouds
    d. Ionosphere, cosmic rays, x-rays,

14. Select the correct statement(s) regarding an antenna's "Effective Aperture."
    a. The effective aperture describes the physical dimensions of the antenna
    b. The effective aperture describes that part of the physical aperture that is actively involved in transmission and reception of power density
    c. The effective aperture is a theoretical antenna, similar to the ideal isotropic antenna but for directional antennas, that is not realistically achievable
    d. Both a and c are correct

15. Select the correct statement(s) regarding the gain of a parabolic antenna.
    a. Antenna gain increases as the diameter of the antenna increases
    b. Antenna gain increases as the transmit frequency increases
    c. Antenna gain increases as antenna efficiency increases
    d. All of the above are correct

16. EIRP (effective isotropic radiated power) decrease as antenna gain increases.
   a. True
   b. False

Answer: b

17. What is the effective antenna aperture, Ae, of a parabolic 3 m antenna where efficiency, η is 75%?
   ($Ae = \eta A$ and $A = \pi D^2/4$)
   a. 5.3 m^2
   b. 53 m^2
   c. 0.53 m^2
   d. 7.07 m^2

Answer: a

18. What is the gain, G, in decibels ($[G] = G(\text{dB})$), of a 9 m parabolic antenna aperture operating at a frequency of 12 GHz, with an antenna efficiency, η is 60%?
   a. $[G] = 68.85$ dBi
   b. $[G] = 48.85$ dBi
   c. $[G] = 58.85$ dBi
   d. $[G] = 38.85$ dBi

Answer: c

19. What is the thermal noise power given $T = 290$ K degrees, and BW = 40,000 Hz in watts and dBWs?
   a. 1.6E-23 W, −128 dBW
   b. 2E-16 W, −128 dBW
   c. 1.6E-16 W, −158 dBW
   d. 2E-23 W, 1.58E2 dBW

Answer: c

20. Determine thermal noise density ($No = kT$) in watts and dBs, at a receiver operating at a temperature of 295 K degrees.
   a. 4.1E-21, −203 dBW
   b. 4.1E21, 203 dBW
   c. 1.42E-16, −203 dBW
   d. −1.42E-21, 203 dBW

Answer: a

21. While a receiver provides gain to the signal and noise received at its input, it also contributes its own noise.
   a. True
   b. False

Answer: a

22. Select the correct statement(s) regarding SNR and CNR.
   a. SNR is measured at the input to the receiver
   b. CNR is measured at the input of the receiver
   c. CNR equals SNR plus receiver processing gain
   d. There is no difference between CNR and SNR

Answer: b

23. Determine the C/N in dB given the following: $Pr = -50$ dBm, $T = 290$ K degrees, B (bandwidth) $= 36$ MHz.
   a. $[N] = -158.41$ dBW, $[C/N] = 138.41$ dB
   b. $[N] = -158.41$ dBW, $[C/N] = 78.41$ dB
   c. $[N] = -128.41$ dBW, $[C/N] = 148.41$ dB
   d. $[N] = -128.41$ dBW, $[C/N] = 48.41$ dB

Answer: d

24. Determine the C/No required in decibels to support a 256 kbps link using BPSK modulation and a desired BER of 1E-4, using an $Eb/No = 8.5$ dB.
   a. $[C/No] = 62.6$ dB
   b. $[C/No] = 53.6$ dB
   c. $[C/No] = 256E3$ dB
   d. Insufficient information to complete calculation

Answer: a

25. The C/No at your receiver is 60 dB and you are attempting to push a data rate of 512 kbps. (a) What is your Eb/No, and BER from fig. 5.11. (2) What will be the performance of your link?
   a. $[Eb/No] = 117$ dB, your BER would be very high and the performance of your link will be excellent
   b. $[Eb/No] = 8.5$ dB, at a BER between 1E-1 and 1E-2, your link would be inadequate
   c. $[Eb/No] = 2.9$ dB, at a BER between 1E-1 and 1E-2, your link would be inadequate
   d. Insufficient information to complete calculation

Answer: c

26. Determine the power measured, Pr, at the receiver in decibels given the following:

Data rate $= 40$ kbps
$[Eb/No]$ for a desired BER of 1E-6 is: 10.4 dB
Noise temperature in Kelvin is 290°
Receive frequency bandwidth is 80 kHz
$(N = kTB, [C/N](dBs) = [Eb/No] + [Rb] - [BW], C = Pr)$

   a. $[N] = -185$ dBW, $[C/N] = 17.4$ dB, $C = Pr = -177$ dBW
   b. $[N] = -175$ dBW, $[C/N] = 4$ dB, $C = Pr = +147$ dBW
   c. $[N] = -155$ dBW, $[C/N] = 7.4$ dB, $C = Pr = -147$ dBW
   d. Insufficient information to complete calculation

Answer: c

27. Determine [FSL] in decibels given a distance between Tx and Rx of 10,000 km, and an operating frequency of 9 GHz.
    a. [FSL] = 191.53 dB
    b. [FSL] = 291.53 dB
    c. [FSL] = 91.53 dB
    d. [FSL] = 1915.3 dB

    Answer: a

28. Given the following information, what data rate (Rb) can be supported? C/No = 50 dBW, Eb/No = 8.4 dB
    a. 14,454 bps
    b. 41.6 bps
    c. 144 kbps
    d. Insufficient information available to determine maximum data rate

    Answer: a

29. Your earth station has a G/T of 20 dB/K. Given the following, what is the C/No at the receive earth station?

    Satellite EIRP = 35 dBW
    Losses = FSL + 2 dB additional losses
    Distance between satellite and earth station = 35,000 km
    Frequency = 9 GHz

    a. [C/No] = 179.2 dB
    b. [C/No] = 184.6 dB
    c. [C/No] = 79.2 dB
    d. [C/No] = 88.2 dB

    Answer: c

30. Select the correct statement(s) regarding multipath.
    a. Multipath results in several copies of a signal being received at slightly different times by the receiver, thus causing signal distortion
    b. Multipath is not a problem in urban environments where large buildings easily block multiple copies of a single signal
    c. Multipath is only a problem when transmitting analog signals (e.g., AM and FM radio)
    d. All of the above are correct

    Answer: a

31. CDMA (code division multiple access) is a form of DSSS (direct sequence spread spectrum) where users share the same frequency bandwidth, separated by unique PN (pseudorandom number) codes.
    a. True
    b. False

    Answer: a

32. Select the correct statement regarding signal propagation:
    a. The higher the frequency, the greater the attenuation
    b. The higher the frequency, the greater the need for line of site (LOS)
    c. The higher the frequency, the greater the capacity to carry information
    d. All of the above are correct

Answer: d

33. With orthogonal frequency division multiplexing (OFDM), a user is assigned a set of "sub-carriers" for parallel data transmission and reception. Using OFDM allows the service provider to more efficiently use valuable frequency allocations when compared with FDM.
    a. True
    b. False

Answer: a

CHAPTER 6

Local and Personal Area Networks

"The value of a telecommunications network is proportional to the square of the number of connected users of the system (n^2)."

Robert Metcalfe (https://planetechusa.com/
blog/23-tech-quotes-about-the-internet-and-information-technology/)

6.1 INTRODUCTION

Along with the revolution of the personal computers in the 1980's, came the desire to interconnect these computers together to facilitate communications and data sharing. ***Local area networks (LANs)*** are comprised of multiple PCs and servers interconnected to one another through guided and/or unguided mediums. The "*local*" in local area network (LAN), tells you that these networks are small, serving a single organization or location as opposed to ***wide area networks (WANs)*** which span greater distances and are commonly used to interconnect LANs together from different geographical locations. Organizations that initially adopted LAN configurations to support their business work flows realized additional efficiencies through the use of shared servers that enabled common access to peripheral devices, business applications, organizational data bases, and file storage. The LAN offered new ways for businesses to communicate within the organization through email, messaging, video, voice, and broadcasts to connected users.

As innovations of the integrated circuit (IC) brought more powerful microchips at reduced costs to the market place, the popularity of LANs grew, eventually extending out to the average residence. The desire for untethered network access led to the development of ***wireless LAN (WLAN)***, which allowed PCs to wirelessly connect to the network through ***access points (APs)***. Cables connecting peripheral devices such as a mouse, keyboard, printer, etc. eventually gave way to smaller ***wireless personal area networks (WPANs)*** which eliminated the need for such bothersome cables.

In this chapter, we will discuss the LAN, WLAN, and WPAN, and concentrate specifically on the most common standards: IEEE 802.3 (Ethernet), IEEE 802.11 (WLAN and Wi-Fi), and IEEE 802.15 (Bluetooth and ZigBee).

6.2 LOCAL AREA NETWORK ARCHITECTURE

In the 1980s, as less costly personal computers were made available to the public, the desire to organize PCs into computer networks gave rise to the creation of numerous LAN architectures. Some of these initial architectures include IEEE 802.3 Ethernet, IBM's Token Ring which conforms to IEEE 802.5, Datapoint's ARCnet, Novell, Banyan Vines, LANtastic by Artisoft, AT&T's Starlan which eventually conformed to IEEE 802.3 1Base5, and Appletalk which was developed to network Apple Macintosh computers together.

Physical networks are arranged in *mesh*, *star*, *bus*, and *ring*, as shown in fig. 6.1, as well as *hierarchical tree* architectures. The ***physical topology*** is selected to align with the specific LAN standard, the types of network devices available, and the ***logical topology*** of the network. The *logical topology* describes how connected computers are arranged to communicate with one another over the

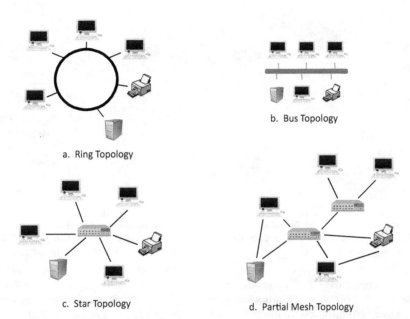

FIGURE 6.1 Local Area Network (LAN) Physical Topologies. The "Logical Topology" describes the order or method by which the computers communicate to one another. The physical topology may differ from the logical one.

Computer © My Portfolio/Shutterstock.com; Printer © owatta/Shutterstock.com; Server © Lineicons freebird/Shutterstock.com; Network switch © IconBunny/Shutterstock.com

physical topology. As an example, the *Token Ring (IEEE 802.5[1])* architecture was based upon the passing of a data frame called a *token* from one computer to the next in a circular round-robin fashion. The node that held the token frame was given exclusive access for transmitting on the shared medium. Doing this ensured that only one node would transmit data thus preventing data collisions. The use of a physical ring structure connecting computers [fig. 6.1 (a)] made the most sense since it allowed the logical passing of the token in a circular manner. In this example, both the physical and logical topologies are configured as a ring.

In another example, the 10Base-TX Ethernet LAN was configured in a *physical star topology* with all computers connected to a central device called a ***hub*** (see fig. 6.2). A hub is a broadcast device designed with several ports used to connect each computer on the LAN. As a signal enters one port, it is repeated or broadcast to all other ports, thus acting as the shared medium. As such, the manner in which computers communicate to one another is the same as a *logical bus topology*. Thus, we can say that this LAN is configured as a *physical star*, but operates as a *logical bus*. In essence, networks can have ***physical*** and ***logical configurations*** that differ.

LANs are built on ***peer-to-peer (P2P)*** or ***client-server*** concepts. In a P2P network, all computers connect directly to one another in order to share information. Since all computers

---

[1] IEEE 802.5, now an obsolete standard, described the Token Ring MAC access layer.

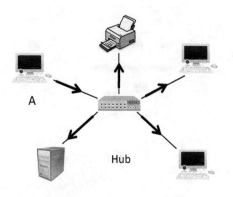
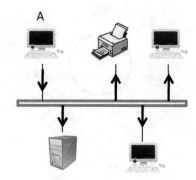

(a) Half-duplex Ethernet Star. Device A transmits data into the central hub. The hub broadcasts this data to all connected devices.

(b) Half-duplex Ethernet Bus. Device A transmits data onto the shared bus medium, which is received by all connected devices.

FIGURE 6.2 The hub in the center of (a) broadcasts data received from device A to all hub ports. Each device connected must inspect the address of the incoming frame to determine if it belongs to them. While the physical configuration is a star, it logically acts as if it were connected in a bus configuration. In figure (b), the LAN operates as a physical and logical bus over the shared medium.

Computer © My Portfolio/Shutterstock.com; Printer © owatta/Shutterstock.com; Server © Lineicons freebird/Shutterstock.com; Network switch © IconBunny/Shutterstock.com

participate equally, no central area to store shared files or applications exists. While this is a simple form of network that can be easily implemented, the lack of centralized authentication, storage of critical data and applications, and the possibility of multiple copies of data existing on several computers, makes this a poor choice for most organizations. In contrast, the *client-server* model provides dedicated highly capable network computers, called **servers**, that provide centralized services and data storage easily accessed by user computers called **clients**. Servers can be configured to provide numerous centralized services such as access to shared peripherals (e.g., printers, scanners, plotters, fax, etc.), access to other networks (e.g., gateways), access to applications and databases, email, storage of files, as well as to perform security functions (e.g., authentication, access, etc.). Unlike the clients that run on a computer **operating system (OS)**, servers run on a **network operating system (NOS)** designed specifically to operate in the client-server environment. Today, there are numerous professional NOS' available such as Window Server 2016, Red Hat Enterprise Linux (RHEL), Cumulus Networks Linux Network OS, Cisco NX-OS Software, etc., as well as NOS' developed specifically for the home office LAN.

6.2.1 Centralized and Decentralized Access Control

LAN devices communicate to one another on shared guided or unguided medium. On a shared medium, each device must take turns transmitting data in order to prevent data collisions from occurring. Therefore, for any set of linked nodes, rules for transmitting and receiving data must be in place at the physical and data link layers.

The physical layer specifications address signaling levels, the type of medium, communication modes (i.e., half-duplex, full-duplex), and the direction of data flows. The data link layer addresses the method of how each node accesses the medium to transmit and receive data, and whether this method involves centralized for distributed control.

Access to a shared medium is the responsibility of the ***medium access control (MAC)*** layer, which is the lowermost layer within the OSI reference model (RM) data link layer 2. MAC layer procedures can involve either a centralized or distributed control model.

Centralized access control approaches can involve the passing of a token or the use of polling by a master controller that grants transmit access to individual nodes on the network. ***Token ring*** is a centralized access control method that was developed by IBM and later adopted as an ***IEEE 802.5*** standard in 1988. This concept involves the passing of a *"token"* which is a special data frame containing no payload data. Only the node in possession of the token is allowed to transmit data onto the shared medium, and therefore data access and transmission is guaranteed. As such, centralized control leads to ***deterministic access***, which means that the node in possession of the token has sole access to the medium without fear of interference from other nodes. Once the node possessing the token has completed its transmission, it passes the token to the next node within LAN. Another centralized approach is through *polling*. A node within the network is designated as a master controller. The master controller polls each node in the network, one at a time, to determine if it has data ready for transmission. If it does, then the master controller gives the polled node permission to transmit. This type of centralized control is used on *IEEE 802.15 Bluetooth*, which is a *personal area network (PAN)* standard that will be discussed in a later section.

With a ***distributed access control*** approach, there is no centralized process. Instead, each node on the LAN is responsible for determining if it can access the shared medium. A big disadvantage to the distributed access control method is that data collisions on the shared medium can occur. As an example, *IEEE 802.3 shared[2] Ethernet* uses a protocol called ***carrier sense multiple access, collision detection (CSMA/CD)***. *"Carrier Sense Multiple Access"* tells you that all nodes on the LAN have access to the shared medium, and that each node must continuously listen and be aware of any data traffic or data collisions on the medium. *"Collision Detection"* means that each node is responsible for the detection of any data collisions that occur. As an example, two nodes that sense no traffic on the medium may transmit data simultaneously causing a data collision. The nearest node to the collision then sends out a *"jamming"* signal, which informs all other nodes that they must cease all transmissions. Each node executes different random *"wait"* periods before being allowed to transmit data. In this example, there were two nodes transmitting at the same time thus causing a collision; however, signal propagation delay can also create a situation where data collisions occur even in the absence of simultaneous transmissions. As an example, nodes A and B are

---

[2] With "shared Ethernet," all attached nodes must use CSMA/CD approaches since data collisions are possible. This is true for both shared HDX and FDX LANs. However, when "switched Ethernet" is used with FDX connections between the switch and each node, then collisions are completely eliminated. Therefore using the CSMA/CD approach is not necessary.

physically separated on a LAN by a distance of d meters. At time t_1, node A transmits data that propagates at the speed of light for that medium, v_m (m/s). It therefore takes $\Delta t = d/v_m$ for the signal to reach node B. During the time interval between t_1 and Δt, node B will not sense node A's traffic on the medium, and therefore begins transmitting its own data believing the medium to be clear resulting in a collision. This scenario tell us that data collisions can happen even if two nodes are not transmitting at exactly the same time (*i.e., due to propagation delays*), and that distance plays a role (*i.e., the further away two transmitting nodes are, the greater the Δt, and the longer the time in which a collision can occur*).

IEEE 802.11 is a standard for wireless LANs (WLANs) that uses a decentralized *distributed coordination function (DCF)* to enable access on shared air space. Similar to Ethernet, it supports CSMA where each wireless node is responsible for determining when it can transmit data. However, instead of detecting collisions, which is difficult to do in a radio frequency (RF) environment,[3] the transmitting node attempts to avoid them altogether. Therefore, the mechanism used for 802.11 is called *carrier sense multiple access collision avoidance (CSMA/CA)*. Similar to CSMA/CD, wireless nodes listen to the channel frequency for any traffic prior to sending frames. If the channel is clear of any traffic, the node wanting to transmit data will begin a handshaking process with the intended receiver. This handshaking process, which is heard by all nodes on the channel, informs them that a transmission will occur and that they should remain quiet.

There are two different handshaking protocols used with CA. The first is a *frame exchange protocol* where the transmitting node sends a data frame to the intended receiver and the receiver sends back an *acknowledgment (ACK)*. If an ACK is not received by the transmitter, then it is determined that the frame was lost or destroyed and is retransmitted. The second protocol is called the *four frame exchange* where the transmitter sends a *request-to-send (RTS)* frame to the receiver. The receiver responds with a *clear-to-send (CTS)* frame, and upon receipt, the transmitter begins sending data. After each successful data frame is received, the receiver sends an ACK back to the transmitter. During the data exchanges described above, wireless nodes not directly involved continue to remain silent until the data transaction has been completed therefore avoiding data collisions. Unfortunately, implementation of CSMA/CA adds additional overhead to WLAN communications.

6.2.2 DTE and DCE

The *data terminal equipment (DTE)* and *data communications equipment (DCE)* is a convention that helps to identify physical layer communication characteristics between devices in a network. As an example, DTEs are typically end devices such as terminals, computers, and servers, while DCEs typically describe network equipment such as modems. While the use of this convention leads to the categorization of equipment within a network, it is the direction of data flow and

---

[3] Collisions are determined by measuring power levels on the medium. This is straightforward when using guided 802.3 Ethernet mediums. However, measuring precise power levels that indicate that a collision has occurred over RF channels is much more difficult to accomplish. As a result, collision avoidance is used in wireless LANs instead.

signaling that are the most important aspects here. In fact, it is helpful to think of DTEs and DCEs as types of interfaces vice whole devices, especially considering that many of today's devices such as routers have both DTE and DCE interface ports.

Let's consider the physical interface standard, *EIA-568A* shown in fig. 6.3 and used extensively to connect devices to the network through eight-conductor (four twisted pairs) UTP such as Cat5e, 6, or 7. From an earlier chapter, we know that UTP is used in a *balanced* signaling configuration. Therefore, in its simplest form, one pair is used for transmit data, while another pair is used for receive data. The eight-conductor cable is terminated with RJ-45 8 pin connectors. Each pin is carefully numbered and coincides with the labels as seen in fig. 6.3. If your device has a DTE interface, then you know that the transmit data out of your device will appear on pins 1 and 2, labeled TX+ and TX−. You also know that data transmitted to your DTE device will appear on pins 3 and 6, RX+ and RX−. On the other hand, if your device has a DCE interface, you know you will receive data on pins 1 and 2, TX+ and TX− and transmit data on pins 3 and 6 labeled RX+ and RX−. One way to remember the direction of data flow is to say that the DTE is always correct in that it transmits on TX pairs and receives on RX pairs. Without this simple convention, you can imagine the confusion that would exist in properly separating data flow between networked devices.

However, when connecting devices together, there may be times when you want to connect a DTE interface on one device to a DTE interface on another device. This can easily be done through the use of a ***cross-over cable*** (see fig. 6.4), which essentially connects the TX+ and TX− lines on one end of the cable, to the RX+ and RX− pins on the other end. Using a cross-over cable is not limited to just DTE to DTE connections, but can also be used between two DCE interfaces.

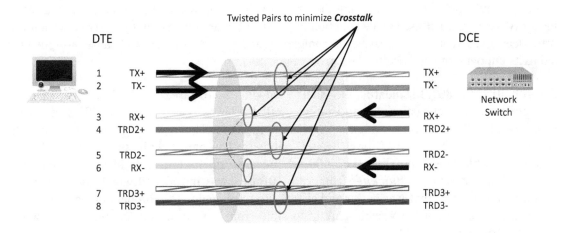

Note: pins 4, 5, 7, 8 are not used for slower 100BaseT Ethernet (i.e., only two pairs required). 1000BaseT requires four pairs.

FIGURE 6.3 EIA 568A over eight-conductor UTP.

Computer © My Portfolio/Shutterstock.com; Network switch © IconBunny/Shutterstock.com

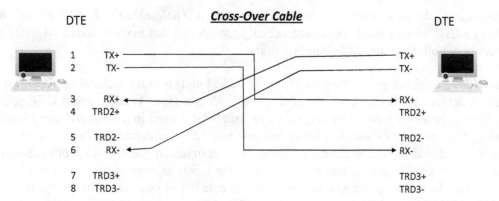

FIGURE 6.4 Cross-over cables used to connect two devices with similar interfaces (i.e., DTE-DTE or DCE-DCE).

Computer © My Portfolio/Shutterstock.com

6.3 IEEE 802.3 ETHERNET LAN

The IEEE 802.3 family of specifications describes both the physical layer (OSI layer 1) and the data link layer (OSI layer 2) and was developed in 1973 by Robert Metcalfe who was a Harvard Ph.D. working at the Xerox Palo Alto Center (PARC). The Ethernet concept was partially based upon the ALOHAnet developed earlier by Norman Abramson. Ethernet was patented in 1975 and was later approved as an IEEE 802.3 standard in 1983.

Early versions of 802.3 Ethernet (i.e., 10Base2 and 10Base5) used coaxial cables as the common shared medium. Using coaxial cable medium required *special connectors* and *terminators* that matched the impedance of the medium itself, thus preventing signal distortion caused by the reflection/bouncing of the signal along the coaxial cable. The medium and connectors needed to install 10Base2 and 10Base5 made adoption of physical bus architecture in fig. 6.1(b) a straightforward decision. Eventually, however, the complexity and cost of using coaxial cables as a medium led to its unpopularity and declined use over time.

As with all IEEE 802.3 standards, the labels used such as 10Base2 and 10Base5 describe certain physical characteristics. As an example, 10Base5 was one of the first 802.3 standards developed in 1983 for use on thick coaxial cable medium. The "10" in 10Base5 tells you the capacity of the LAN (i.e., 10 Mbps), "Base" stands for baseband,[4] while the "5" gives you the maximum cable length possible (i.e., 500 m). Because of the thickness of the coaxial cable used, this was known as *"thicknet."* In 1985, 10Base2 was introduced which used a cheaper thinner coaxial cable that was easier and cheaper to implement. The thinner coaxial cable used reduced the maximum LAN cable length possible from 500 m to 200 m, and was known as *"thinnet"* or *"cheapernet."*

---

[4] The broadband IEEE 802.3 LAN standard supported several baseband signals multiplexed together onto a shared medium. 10BROAD36 (1985) was the only broadband Ethernet standard approved and is now obsolete.

As devices such as network *hubs*[5] became available, the use of UTP (unshielded twisted pair) medium became popular due to its low costs and ease of installation. With the use of hubs, Ethernet LANs were implemented in physical star configurations as shown in fig. 6.1(c), with the hub acting as the central device connecting all computers together. In addition, multiple hub devices could be connected together in a partial mesh network as shown in fig. 6.1(d). In 1990, 10Base-TX, a standard for 10 Mbps baseband LANs over twisted pair (TP) became the popular choice. Like 10Base2 and 10Base5, it operated using half-duplex communications over a shared medium, which meant that only one computer or node could transmit at any given time thus requiring implementation of a data collision algorithm such as CSMA/CD.

As more capable and affordable Ethernet switches became available, physical configurations typically followed the mesh and/or star configurations, with each computer connected directly to the switch. Switches are intelligent devices that read source/destination addresses of each frame entering the switch, and then forwards the frame to the appropriate switch port coinciding with the frame's destination address. Therefore, other devices connected to the switch do not receive data unless it is specifically addressed to them. This differs from the ***shared Ethernet*** concept where all connected devices receive all transmitted data frames regardless of whether they are the intended recipient or not. This switching concept also has an effect on data collisions. We know that hubs act as a shared medium and data collisions will inevitably occur, thus requiring devices to take turns transmitting data. In contrast, ***switched Ethernet*** (see fig. 6.5) devices are connected to the switch through dedicated full-duplex (FDX) links (i.e., dedicated meaning that no other

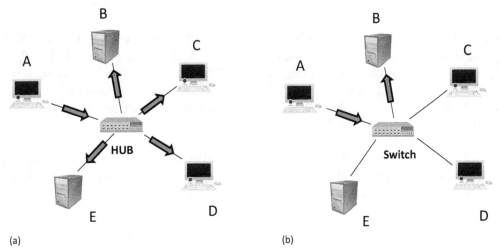

(a)   (b)

FIGURE 6.5 Shared and Switched Ethernet. In figure (a), devices are connected to a central hub device (i.e., shared medium). Device "A" sends data to "B," however, since the hub is a broadcast device, all attached devices receive the data intended for "B." Therefore, all devices must be able to read source and destination addresses to determine whether the data received is for them. In figure (b), devices are connected to a switch that reads the destination addresses. In this case, "A's" data is only forwarded to "B" and not to the other devices.

Server © Lineicons freebird/Shutterstock.com; Computer © My Portfolio/Shutterstock.com; Network switch © IconBunny/Shutterstock.com

---

[5] A hub is a broadcast device with several ports that connect to each computer on the LAN. The hub acts as a shared medium where data collisions are possible, thus requiring a collision handling protocol such as CSMA/CD.

TABLE 6.1 IEEE 802.3 specification examples

1983	10Base2 (Thicknet)
1985	10Base5 (Thinnet)
1985	10Broad36
1990	10Base-T
1995	100Base-TX, 100Base-FX (Fast Ethernet)
1999	1000Base-T (Gigabit Ethernet)
2002	10GBase-SR, 10GBase-LR, 10GBase-ER, 10GBase-SW, 10GBase-LW, 10GBase-EW
2003	(802.3af) Power over Ethernet
2006	10GBase-T

device shares the physical link, and FDX describing separate transmit and receive paths). Since the switch does not act as a shared medium and since each FDX connection is a dedicated link to each device, no data collisions can occur and the need for a collision detection algorithm such as CSMA/CD is not required.

The use of fiber optic cables as a LAN medium emerged in 1998 with 1000Base-FX. While fiber optic LANs required special optical connectors and optical-electrical-optical (OEO) signal conversion, it was quickly adopted because of the large data capacities inherent with the use of optical signals. Today, twisted pair and fiber optic cables remain popular 802.3 mediums. Some of the key 802.3 versions are shown in Table 6.1 with several of these versions discussed further in section 6.3.2 below.

Today, IEEE 802.3 Ethernet has emerged as the LAN standard of choice. Work to refine and upgrade Ethernet continues to this day with one of the latest versions being 10GBase-T, which describes a 10 Gbps, baseband specification over twisted pair guided medium.

6.3.1 IEEE 802.3 Physical and Data Link Layer

The Ethernet protocol can be aligned to the first two layers of the *OSI reference model (RM)*. At the data link layer, Ethernet is divided into the **logical link control (LLC)** and the **medium access control (MAC)** sub-layers. Figure 6.6 depicts the alignment of both Layers 1 and 2 with the OSI RM.

The Ethernet *physical layer* describes all mechanical and electrical specifications. It includes the type of medium used, such as twisted pair, coaxial or fiber optic cables, and their mechanical interfaces (e.g., RJ-45 for twisted pair, ST connectors for fiber optic cables, etc.). The electrical aspects of the specification include the type of line coding used (e.g., Manchester, NRZ, 4B5B, etc.), timing,

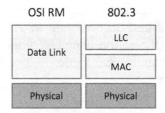

FIGURE 6.6 Comparison between the OSI reference model and IEEE 802.3 layers 1 and 2.

and voltage levels. The physical layer is responsible for attachment and removal of preambles[6] used for timing and synchronization, the line coding of logical data into electrical symbols, transmission and reception of signals, sensing traffic and collisions on the medium, and executing collision detection algorithms in the event of a data collision.

The *MAC sub-layer*, which is part of the data link layer, works closely with the physical layer below and the LLC data link sub-layer above. It is responsible for the generation of the preamble (*if used*), the creation of the Ethernet data frame (see fig. 6.7) which encapsulates data delivered from the upper LLC sub-layer, and the generation and attachment of a CRC (cyclic redundancy check) error detection field (frame check sequence, FCS) for the frame. To detect any bit errors experienced during transmission, the receiving node runs the same CRC algorithm to determine the validity of the data frame. If the data frame is found to contain bit errors, then the entire data frame is discarded.

The MAC sub-layer also inserts both the source (sender) and destination (receiver) 48-bit MAC addresses into the Ethernet data frame for transmission. This 48-bit MAC address is hard-coded

Number of Bytes	7	1	6	6	2	46 - 1500	4
Field	Preamble	Start frame delimiter	Destination address	Source address	Type	Data & Pad	FCS

- Preamble: alternating line coded 1's & 0's used for synchronization
- Start frame delimiter: indicates start of frame
- Destination address: 48 bit destination MAC address
- Source address: 48 bit source MAC address
- Type: identifies protocol inside frame (e.g., IPv4, IPv6)
- Data & Pad: data payload and padded data required to meet minimum length requirement
- FCS: frame check sequence

FIGURE 6.7 Ethernet Frame.

---

[6] In the Ethernet specification, preambles are 56 bit sequences consisting of alternating "1s" and "0s" used to synchronize receive timing. The preamble is not part of the Ethernet frame itself, but is appended to the front of the frame by the network interface card (NIC). Preambles are not used for more modern Ethernet specifications such as 100BASE-T, 1000BASE-T, or 10GBASE-T since constant signaling within the network is used, which eliminates the need for a preamble to be placed at the beginning of each transmission.

into the network interface card (NIC) and cannot be changed by the network operator.[7] This address can be traced back to the manufacturer of the NIC hardware. In addition to framing data, the MAC sub-layer is responsible for detecting traffic on the shared medium, and executing the CSMA/CD protocol which will be explained further in the next section. All of the functions of the MAC sub-layer are programmed into NIC firmware.

The LLC sub-layer manages the protocol interaction between the data link layer 2 and the network layer 3, and its specification is captured in the IEEE 802.2 standard. It is responsible for the interface between the MAC sub-layer and network layer protocols which include standards such as IP, IPX, ARP, etc. LLC prepares these packets for framing by the MAC sub-layer by multiplexing network layer 3 packets for transmission. Upon receipt of data from the MAC sub-layer, LLC performs the reverse process by demultiplexing data frames in preparation for transfer to the appropriate network layer protocol. LLC can provide two types of services, a *connectionless* or *connection-oriented* service. The LLC connection-oriented service provides reliability, flow control, and correct sequencing; however, this option is rarely used since the establishment of connection-oriented circuits are typically done at the *OSI RM transport layer 4* using protocols such as *transmission control protocol (TCP)*. Most instantiations of LLC are connectionless.

6.3.2 Ethernet 802.3 Selected Standards

The Ethernet LAN was initially developed as a contention-based LAN protocol over shared medium such as coaxial or copper twisted pair mediums. Over a shared medium, nodes communicated in either half-duplex (HDX) or full-duplex (FDX) modes. However, since the medium was shared by all connected nodes, data collisions occurred whenever two or more nodes attempted to communicate on the medium at or near the same time. As discussed previously, the ***carrier sense multiple access collision detection (CSMA/CD)*** method was developed as a way to handle collisions. *"Carrier Sense"* meant that all nodes continuously listened for traffic, as well as for data collisions, on the medium. If a node desires to transmit data, it would listen to the medium to ensure that no transmissions were occurring. If the medium was clear, then the node would place its data onto the medium. *"Multiple Access"* means that all nodes on the LAN access and share the same medium. If a data collision occurs, the *"Collision Detection"* algorithm is initiated by the closet node to the collision. This node sends out a *jamming signal* which informs all other nodes on the network to cease all transmit activity for a random period of time. Each node has a different wait period before it is allowed to transmit data, thus minimizing any chance of additional collisions after the waiting period.

Early 802.3 shared LANs were physically configured in a star configuration with a device called a ***hub*** in the center. The hub was connected to all LAN nodes, and it acted as a type of broadcast device where any signal entering one port was broadcast to all remaining hub ports. As such, it created a shared medium where data collision occurred, and where CSMA/CD was required. Eventually, hubs were replaced by ***Ethernet switches*** which enabled *FDX* connectivity from each node to a port on the switch itself. Unlike the hub, switches had the capability of inspecting data frame addresses. Therefore, when a

---

[7] While the MAC address which is hard coded into the NIC cannot be changed, it can be spoofed by the network operator by making changes in the operating system software. This is done for many legitimate reasons, but care must be taken to avoid network problems from occurring.

data frame entered the switch, the switch would read the *"to"* address and forward it to the port connected to the *"to"* node. Since no other connected nodes would receive a copy of the data frame, data collisions are completely eliminated. Eliminating collisions made Ethernet a viable protocol for larger ***metropolitan Ethernet networks (MEN)***, termed ***carrier Ethernet***, which is highly popular today.

6.3.2.1 10BASE-T

The 10BASE-T standard developed in 1990 enabled the use of unshielded twisted pair (UTP) in a balanced configuration as the LAN medium. Designed for Category 3 or 5, eight-conductor (four pair) cable and RJ-45 pin connectors, it used *Manchester* line coding to create the digital baseband signal. Initially configured to support half-duplex, it was eventually changed to support full-duplex over dedicated transmit and receive pairs. 10BASE-T is an older standard that supported 10Mbps Ethernet LANs, and today it is uncommon to find this standard in use.

6.3.2.2 100BASE-T (Fast Ethernet)

There are several standard versions associated with 100BASE-T (100BASE-TX, 100BASE-T4,[8] and 100BASE-T2). Used with Cat 3 and 5 UTP cabling, it provides 100 Mbps baseband connectivity in support of either half-duplex (HDX) or full-duplex (FDX) communications.

100BASE-TX operates over Cat 5e UTP cable in either the HDX or FDX mode. Since Cat5e cabling is thicker than Cat 3, it can support higher symbol rates (i.e., 125 Mbaud). In the FDX mode, two pairs are used, one pair for transmit and the other pair for receive. The encoding method used is 4B5B, which codes 4 bits of data into a 5-bit word. As such, only 4 out of 5 bits carries information, or a $4/5 = 80\%$ information rate, and $1/5 = 20\%$ overhead. The logical bit stream produced is line coded using NRZI (non-return to zero inverted), which codes one logical bit for each symbol sent. This means that each symbol can take on one of two values (e.g., $M = 2$, $+v$ for a logical "0", $-v$ for a logical "1"). Per Hartley's Law in this case, we know that baud rate equals data rate. Since each pair in a Cat5e cable can support 125 MBaud, we also know that each pair can support 125 Mbps. However, since 20% of our bit rate is overhead, the true information rate becomes $(80\%) \times (125E6 \text{ bps}) = 100$ Mbps. This, then, is why 100BASE-TX can support 100 Mbps.

Another version of the 100BASE-T family is ***100BASE-FX*** which uses a pair of fiber optic cables to support either HDX or FDX communications. Developed in 1993, this standard implemented 4B5B, NRZI over two pairs to support 100 Mbps Ethernet LANs. While the data capacity was the same as 100BASE-TX, the physical LAN length that could be supported doubled from 200 to 400 m.

6.3.2.3 1000BASE-T (GbE)

In 1999, as the demand for greater data rates to support multimedia applications grew, 1000BASE-T was developed. 1000BASE-T supports 1 Gbps data rates using all four pairs of Cat 5e cables in FDX mode. In addition, Trellis forward error correction (FEC), magnetic canceller transceiver, and PAM-5 (pulse amplitude modulation, $M = 5$) modulation were incorporated vice 4B5B and NRZI coding.

---

[8] For 100BASE-T4, the "T4" means that all four pairs of a Cat5e cable are used for transmit and receive paths.

Let's break down what the above information tells us about LAN capacity. First, 1000BASE-T was designed to work with Cat 5e cabling. However, we know that each cable pair only supports 125 MBaud each. Therefore, we need to use all four pairs (two pairs for transmits, two pairs for receive). Using two pairs for each direction only gives us 250 MBaud in each direction. If we adopt a new modulation scheme such as PAM-5, which translates to $M = 5$ or four values per symbol, with one value supporting FEC, then we can double our data rate according to Hartley's Law.

$$C(\text{bps}) = \text{Baud} \times \log_2 M = 250 \text{ MBaud} \times \log_2 4 = 250 \text{ MBaud} \times 2 = 500 \text{ Mbps per direction}$$

Now that we've managed to support 500 Mbps, we still need to somehow double this capacity to support 1 Gbps. We can do this by converting each wire pair from one-way transmit or receive (i.e., simplex) to FDX mode on each pair. However as we are aware, sending data on a shared medium at the same time causes data collisions, so we must use a device called a ***hybrid canceller transceiver***, which essentially cancels interfering data signals and enables FDX to operate on each wire pair. This doubles the capacity of our LAN to 2×500 Mbps $= 1$ Gbps (see fig. 6.8).

6.3.2.4 10GBASE-T

10GBase-T was adopted as an 802.3 standard in 2006. It defines a FDX-only Ethernet LAN that supports 10 Gbps rates over Cat 6 or Cat 7 twisted pair, as well as fiber optic cable pairs. Designed to work specifically with Ethernet switches in FDX mode, no data collisions can occur and therefore CSMA/CD and half-duplex (HDX) operations are not supported in this standard. In addition, a hybrid canceller transceiver is used to enable FDX on each of the four pairs within Cat 6 and Cat 7 cabling.

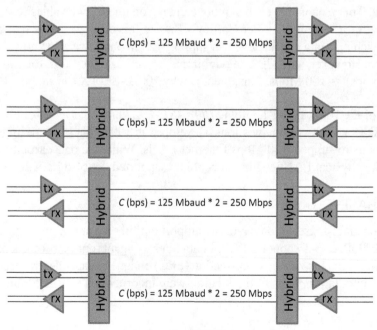

FIGURE 6.8 1000BASE-T

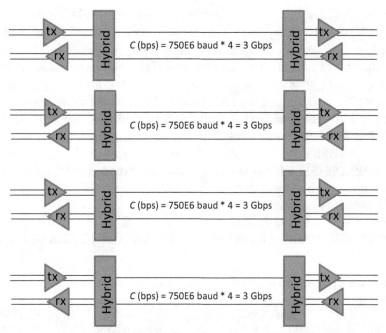

FIGURE 6.9 10GBASE-T using Cat 7 cabling

Cat 6 or Cat 7 medium enables higher signaling rates and lower signal resistance since these are thicker diameter copper wires than Cat 5e. As such, they can support 600 MBaud and 750 MBaud, respectively. Using hybrid canceller transceivers to enable FDX on each of the four cable pairs also double the cable capacity in terms of signal rates. PAM-16 (pulse amplitude modulation, $M = 16$) modulation is used, which enables us to support $N = \log_2 16 = 4$ bits/symbol. Therefore, considering thicker cabling, M'ary modulation and the use of FDX on each pair gives us the ability to meet 10 Gbps LAN capacity requirements (see fig. 6.9).

Cat 6: C(bps per FDX pair) = 600 MBaud $\times$ 4 bits/symbol = 2.4 Gbps
C(all four pairs, FDX) = 4 $\times$ 2.4 Gbps = 9.6 Gbps

Cat 7: C(bps per FDX pair) = 750 MBaud $\times$ 4 bits/symbol = 3 Gbps
C(all four pairs, FDX) = 4 $\times$ 3 Gbps = 12 Gbps

6.3.2.5 Ethernet and Fiber Optics

Today, the use of both *single mode fiber (SMF)* and *multimode fiber (MMF)* optic cables are very popular due to the decreasing costs of optical transceivers and fiber cables, and the advances made in connecting and splicing fibers together. The 802.3 standard includes several versions used with either SMF or MMF cables at varying capacities (see Table 6.2).

100BASE-FX: "FX" indicates that dedicated transmit and receive fiber optic cables are used for speeds up to 100 Mbs (*fast Ethernet over fiber*), baseband signaling in either half-duplex (HDX) or full-duplex (FDX) modes. Transceivers are required to perform the optical-electrical-optical (OEO) conversions between electrical devices (e.g., computers, repeaters, hubs, or switches) and the optical fiber cable. The 100BASE-FX topology is designed using a star configuration with a central hub or switch connecting to all network devices. With a hub acting as the central device, data collisions are possible and therefore CSMA/CD is required; however today switches are more often used in FDX mode rather than hubs, thus eliminating the need for a data collision algorithm. 100BASE-FX configured using MMF in FDX mode with a central switch enables a maximum distance between device and switch of 2 km, compared to the central hub configuration which limited the distance to approximately 412 m. Replacing MMF with SMF cables extends this distance to 10 km. Similar to 100BASE-TX, it uses 4B5B encoding and NRZI line coding methods. An alternative version of 100BASE-FX is 100BASE-SX, which uses a lower cost multimode fiber operating at a wavelength of 850 nanometer (nm) which reduces distances to 300 m.

1000BASE-SX and LX: IEEE 802.3z describes several 1 GbE (1 Gigabit Ethernet) standards including 1000BASE-SX, 1000BASE-LX, and 1000BASE-CX.[9] 1000BASE-SX operates at the

TABLE 6.2   Examples of Ethernet standards using fiber optic cabling.

Ethernet 803.3	Fiber Optic Cable	Throughput	Transmission Distances
100BASE-LX	SMF	100 Mbps	20 km
100BASE-FX	MMF	100 Mbps	2 km
100BASE-EX	SMF	100 Mbps	40 km
1000BASE-LX	SMF	1 Gbps	5 km
1000BASE-SX	MMF	1 Gbps	550 m
10GBASE-LR	SMF	10 Gbps	25 km
10GBASE-ER	SMF	10 Gbps	40 km
10GBASE-SR	MMF	10 Gbps	300 m
10GBASE-SW	MMF	10 Gbps	300 m
10GBASE-LW	SMF	10 Gbps	25 km
10GBASE-EW	SMF	10 Gbps	40 km
40GBASE-LR4	SMF	40 Gbps	10 km
40GBASE-SR4	MMF	40 Gbps	100 m
100GBASE-LR4	SMF	100 Gbps	10 km
100GBASE-ER4	SMF	100 Gbps	40 km
100GBASE-SR10	MMF	100 Gbps	150 m

[9] 1000BASE-CX uses a 9-pin shielded copper cable that has a maximum distance of 25 m.

770 to 860 nm wavelength in either HDX or FDX modes. Two thicknesses of MMF can be used, either 62.5 μm, which support distances up to 275 m, or 50 μm which support distances up to 316 m. The smaller wavelengths associated with SX makes this standard suitable for short distances (i.e., within a building) for high data rate requirements. The 1000BASE-LX standard also supports 62.5 and 50 μm MMF, as well as SMF. The use of SMF and longer wavelength signaling (i.e., less attenuation) enables LX to support distances up to 5 km. Like SX, LX can also operate in the HDX or FDX modes.

10GBASE-SR, 10GBASE-LR, 10GBASE-ER: Several 10 Gbps standards exist over fiber optic cables. 10GBASE-SR (*Short Reach*) operates in the 850 nm wavelength over MMF with a maximum distance of 400 m. 10GBASE-LR (*Long Reach*) operates at the 1310 nm wavelength, which experiences less attenuation than the SR operating wavelength and can therefore travel greater distances up to 10 km. 10GBASE-ER (*Extended Reach*) operating at the 1550 nm wavelength supports an even greater distance of 40 km over SMF.

6.4 IEEE 802.11 WIRELESS LAN

Our desire to connect to network resources while having maximum untethered mobility has led to numerous wireless innovations. IEEE 802.11 wireless local area network (WLAN) consists of a family of WLAN standards that have evolved over time to adopt new technologies as they become available. The IEEE 802.11 WLAN working group initiated its work in 1990 which led to its first approved standard in 1997, followed by two variants, 802.11a and 802.11b, released in 1999. WLAN frequencies within the 2.4 GHz band (2.4 GHz to 2.5 GHz) and 5 GHz band (5.725 GHz to 5.875 GHz), were selected because they were in the ISM (Industrial, Scientific, and Medical) unlicensed bands that required no licensing by the Federal Communications Commission (FCC). This was obviously an advantage since users weren't required to obtain operating licenses thus making it easier and more attractive for the standards adoption. However, operating in the shared unlicensed bands presented interference issues with other devices such as home security cameras, baby monitors, cordless phones, garage door openers, nearby microwave ovens, other WLAN networks, etc. Since the early days of 802.11, several technical innovations were introduced in subsequent versions making interference issues more manageable and throughput much higher. This has led to greater interest in the WLAN concept over time, and today it is an invaluable capability that connects the untethered users to wired LANs and the Internet.

6.4.1 IEEE 802.11 Physical Architecture

Today, the vast majority of *guided 802.3 Ethernet LANs* implement *full-duplex* connections using dedicated transmit and receive paths connected to an Ethernet switch, therefore eliminating data collisions and the need for CSMA/CD. This is in contrast to unguided wireless ***802.11 WLANs*** that operate in *half-duplex* mode over the unlicensed ISM band, thus requiring either a *centralized or distributed/decentralized* process for avoiding interference between WLAN stations operating on a shared channel.

Since all wireless workstations must be equipped with a transceiver, there are two main methods that can be used to create a wireless network. The first method is one in which workstations

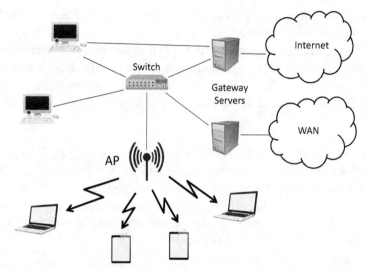

FIGURE 6.10 IEEE 802.11 Wireless LAN with Access Point (AP) interfacing the wireless access to the network backbone.

Server © Lineicons freebird/Shutterstock.com; Computer © My Portfolio/Shutterstock.com; Network switch © IconBunny/Shutterstock.com; Laptop © Igor Kyrlytsya/Shutterstock.com; Tablet © Andrey Mertsalov/Shutterstock.com; Antenna © Studio_G/Shutterstock.com

communicate with one another in a **peer-to-peer** or **ad hoc** fashion. No centralized node exists to control or provide access to the *wired network*. The second method involves a wireless **hub** or **access point**[10] **(AP)** which creates the wireless environment in which nodes can connect to one another, as well as to the *wired backbone network*, see fig. 6.10. The AP is the interface between the wireless workstations and the wired backbone network serving the WLAN. The wired portion of the WLAN consists of networking hardware such as switches, routers, servers, and wired workstations. It is through this backbone that wireless devices gain access to external networks such as the Internet, which enables access to multimedia rich content and services. It also enables connection to other geographically dispersed organizational LANs that either use **virtual private networks** **(VPNs)** that tunnel through the Internet, or uses established connections through a service provider's data link layer WAN.

The radio link between 802.11 devices operates on the 2.4 GHz and 5 GHz ISM unlicensed frequency bands. In figs. 6.11 and 6.12, we see that the 2.4 GHz channel bandwidths overlap, and that the 5 GHz channels are adjacent to each other. In order to avoid interference between adjacent coverage areas, care must be taken during implementation to ensure proper frequency separation.

Devices operating over the unlicensed frequency bands on shared wireless channels must contend with *radio frequency interference (RFI)* from outside devices operating near their operating frequency. To limit the impact of RFI, *direct sequence spread spectrum (DSSS)* and *orthogonal frequency division multiplexing (OFDM)* techniques were adopted. Both DSSS and OFDM,[11]

---

[10] Also termed "infrastructure mode."

[11] While OFDM has the same effect of spreading the signal across a wider frequency band, it is not considered a spread spectrum technology.

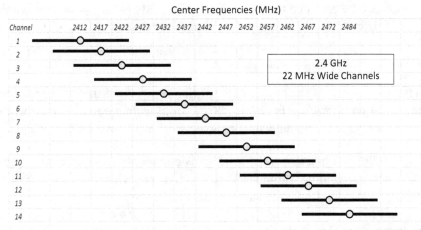

FIGURE 6.11 802.11 2.4 GHz frequency channel assignments. Since there is an overlap in channel assignments, care must be exercised when selecting channels used in adjacent coverage areas.

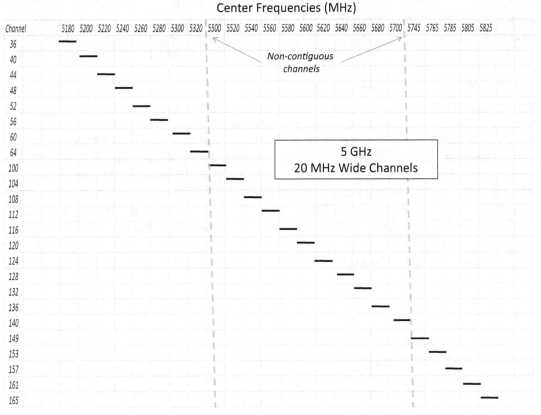

FIGURE 6.12 802.11 5 GHz frequency channel assignments.

discussed in chapter 5, essentially spread the signal across a wider frequency band, thus reducing the impact of any narrow band RFI. In addition, other techniques such as *multiple input and multiple output (MIMO)* are incorporated into later 802.11 versions to contend with multipath fading, and to improve signal strength and throughput.

These devices must also be prepared to deal with the possibility of data collisions within their own wireless network. This is discussed in further detail in the next section.

6.4.2 IEEE 802.11 Data Link Layer

There are two fundamental MAC techniques used with 802.11: the ***distributed coordination function (DCF)*** and ***point coordination function (PCF)***. Both techniques describe methods used by wireless devices to access and communicate on the network while avoiding interference.

The *distributed coordination function (DCF)*, which is commonly used on wireless networks, is a distributed access method, residing within the MAC layer, that provides contention-based algorithms such as CSMA/CA. With 802.11 DCF, all station transmissions are separated by a time gap called an ***interframe space (IFS)***. With the CSMA/CA *frame exchange protocol*, a station wishing to transmit data listens to the channel to determine if it is idle. If it is idle, and if the IFS time has passed, it can transmit. However, if the channel is busy with traffic, then all stations must wait until the transmission is over, after which time each station waits a random period of time before attempting any transmission. Each station has a different random wait time which prevents multiple stations from attempting to transmit simultaneously. All successful packet transmissions require the receiver to send ***acknowledgments (ACKs)*** (see fig. 6.13). If an ACK is not received by the transmitter, then the transmitter assumes that the information and/or the ACK was lost and a retransmission takes place.

The *frame exchange* scenario described above assumes that all stations within the WLAN are able to receive transmissions and ACKs from all other stations. However, if some stations within the WLAN are unable to detect another station's transmissions due to environmental or propagation characteristics, then a data collision could occur. This is called the ***hidden node*** problem in which two nodes at extreme ends of the network are not within reception range of one another. In fig. 6.14, node A and C are not within range of one another although they operate on the same WLAN. Node A begins to transmit data to B, but C does not hear the transmission. If C, believing that the medium is clear, also begins to transmit at the same time, a collision will occur at node B. Making this situation even more difficult is C's inability to detect a collision by simply monitoring for power level changes; especially when the station is transmitting. As a method to avoid the hidden node problem, the *four frame exchange* protocol using RTS and CTS frames have been proposed as an alternative method.

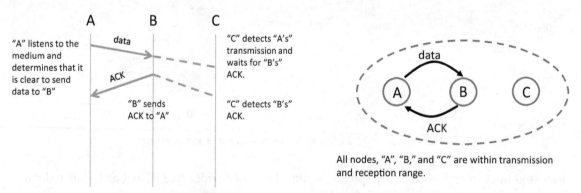

FIGURE 6.13 Frame Exchange Protocol. In this 802.11 network, nodes "A", "B," and "C" are within reception reach of one another. When data is transmitted by "A" to "B," node "C" remains silent until transmission had been completed and acknowledged.

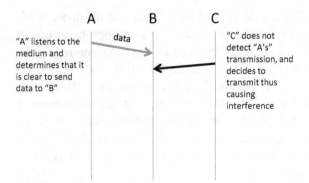

"A" listens to the medium and determines that it is clear to send data to "B"

"C" does not detect "A's" transmission, and decides to transmit thus causing interference

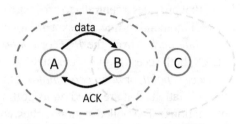

Node "A" is within transmit/reception range of "B", but not "C". "B" and "C" can communicate with one another. "C" is the *hidden node* in the scenario.

FIGURE 6.14 Hidden Node Problem using the Frame Exchange Protocol. In this 802.11 network, nodes "A" and "B," and "B" and "C" can communicate wirelessly; however, "A" and "C" are not within reception range of one another. "A" decides that the channel is clear, and sends data to "B". "C" does not hear "A's" transmission, and decides to transmit to "B" being unaware of "A's" transmission on the same channel. As a result, both transmissions interfere with one another at node "B".

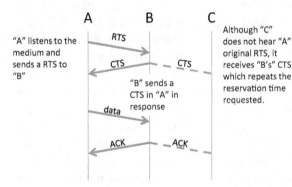

"A" listens to the medium and sends a RTS to "B"

"B" sends a CTS in "A" in response

Although "C" does not hear "A" original RTS, it receives "B's" CTS which repeats the reservation time requested.

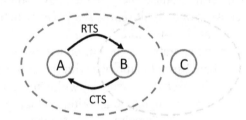

Node "A" is within transmit/reception range of "B", but not "C". "B" and "C" can communicate with one another. "C" is the *hidden node* in the scenario.

FIGURE 6.15 Four Frame Exchange Protocol. As in fig. 6.12, nodes "A" and "C" are not within reception range of one another. To solve the *hidden node* problem, "A" sends an RTS to "B" that contains a reservation time but no data. "B" responds with a CTS that repeats the reservation time request, that both "A" and "C" receive. Although "C" never received the "A's" original RTS, it does receive "B's" CTS, which lets "C" know that a transmission between "A" and "B" are about to occur.

The ***four frame exchange protocol*** depicted in fig. 6.15 is based upon the concept that a station can reserve channel time in order to access and send data. The station desiring to transmit sends an RTS frame that specifies the amount of transmission time needed (i.e., *reservation time frame*). All stations within reception range of the transmitting node then become aware of this request and waits. The receiving station responds with a CTS frame that repeats the time duration needed. By doing this, all stations within the receiving node's reception range, even if hidden from the transmitting node, hears the CTS request and waits until the reservation time has passed. With this method, all stations store the reservation time period in memory. By using the *four frame exchange* in our scenario, node A sends an RTS request to B. Although node C does not receive the RTS, it does receive node B's CTS response which contains the reservation time request. As such, node C waits until A and B exchange data even though it is out of node A's range. The *four frame exchange* protocol is an optional feature that can be invoked as needed, and serves to minimize collisions at the cost of increased complexity and overhead.

The ***Point coordination function (PCF)*** is an optional extension of DCF located in the upper MAC layer, that provides a centralized process for contention-free access. Both DCF contention-based access and PCF contention-free access work together, but are separated within a super frame that divides the *DCF time period* from the *PCF* or *contention-free (CF) period* in time. Therefore, within the same WLAN, both access models coexist. PCF requires the presence of a *base station* that acts as the *centralized access point*, or *point coordinator*. During the CF period of the super frame, the point coordinator polls all stations that are listed on its polling list (i.e., typically stations with higher priority than DCF-only stations). The polled station replies with either a data frame of a null frame (i.e., no data to send). Once the CF period of the super frame has passed, the DCF period resumes until the next CF period.

6.4.3 WLAN Security

Any method that uses a shared medium for communications also risks security compromise of its transmitted data. For WLANs, this is especially true since transmissions are in the ISM bands enabling any properly configured receiver to collect signal traffic. Considering this risk, the original 802.11 standard adopted ***wired equivalent privacy (WEP)*** in 1997 to encrypt communications between the AP and connected devices in the *infrastructure mode*. WEP uses the *RC4*[12] *(Rivest Cipher 4)* stream cipher to produce encrypted data by combining user data with an encryption key. A 64-bit WEP key consists of a 40-bit *shared secret key* which is manually configured into the devices, and a randomly generated 24-bit *Initialization Vector (IV)*. The IV is transmitted in plain text and its purpose is to ensure that traffic key repetition within the network is avoided. A 128-bit WEP key consists of a 104-bit shared secret combined with the 24-bit IV. The shared portion of the 64- and 128-bit keys is the same for each device and AP within the network. The concatenated *secret key* and *IV* bits go through the *RC4* cryptographic algorithm which produces a key stream. This key stream is then combined with user data though an XOR (exclusive-OR) logic process, resulting in the encrypted data stream. Thought to be secure for its time, researchers in 2001 soon discovered weaknesses in the WEP algorithm. These weaknesses involved the IV, which could not guarantee the uniqueness of the encryption key for each transmission, and was transmitted in plain text. Additional weaknesses were discovered in the RC4 algorithm which made it possible to uncover the WEP shared secret key over time by collecting numerous packet transmissions. Eventually, these weaknesses gave rise to a number of exploitation tools that could hack into WEP protected networks quickly.

In 2004, realizing weaknesses inherent in WEP, The Wi-Fi Alliance began work on two standards, ***WPA (Wi-Fi protected access)*** and ***WPA2*** which were based upon the IEEE 802.11i security standard. WPA was considered an intermediate solution that worked with older AP devices. WPA2 provided better security, but required hardware and firmware upgrades and would not work with most older APs used in networks.

WPA adopted the ***temporal key integrity protocol (TKIP)*** which improved confidentiality while maintaining backward compatibility with the older WEP capable devices. *TKIP* addressed issues associated with WEP's shared secret key. Using WEP, if IV failed to produce unique traffic keys,

---

[12] RC4 is a *symmetric encryption* technique used to encrypt and decrypt message data. Symmetric encryption means that both communicating nodes share a common key. This differs from *asymmetric encryption*, such as *public key encryption*, in which data is encrypted and decrypted using different keys.

the secret key could eventually be discovered and exploited by a hacker. Since WEP secret keys were rarely changed, the hacker would then have unauthorized network access for extended periods of time. To ensure backward compatibility, TKIP first used the shared key for authentication. Once authentication is complete, a *session key* is created between the AP and client devices. Since session keys change, and exposure of the secret key is limited, security was greatly enhanced.

Another security enhancement included the *message integrity code (MIC)*, which is an 8-byte hashed value that protects the integrity of the data packet. A hashing algorithm is applied to the entire data packet and its value is contained within 8 bytes that are appended to the payload. If a packet has been modified, the destination device will detect the modification by re-hashing the packet using the same algorithm and comparing the two hashed values. A difference in the values means that the data has been altered during transit.

There are two major versions of WPA and WPA2: (1) *802.1x* and (2) *PSK*. *WPA 802.1x* involves the use of network authentication servers that provide security services such as key distribution and credential authentication. Since an external authentication service is used, 802.1x, it is usually implemented on large organizational WLANs. For smaller WLANs, a common shared network key on each device is implemented. This is called *pre-shared key (PSK)*, and although it is similar to WEP, WPA's implementation of TKIP provides greater confidentiality.

6.4.4 Selected IEEE 802.11 WLAN Standards

The first IEEE 802.11 WLAN standard was introduced in 1997 and several prototypes soon followed to test and verify the wireless concept. After release and initial prototyping had been completed, two variants of the original standard, IEEE 802.11a and 802.11b, were developed and released in 1999.

6.4.4.1 IEEE 802.11a

IEEE 802.11a operated in the 5.8 GHz ISM band but was not widely accepted by manufacturers. At the time, chip sets operating at the 5.8 GHz band were not readily available, and developing these chip sets would delay release and increase overall development costs. This and other technical hurdles hindered development of 802.11a devices thus it failed to gain popular support. The specification provided up to 54 Mbps (theoretical signaling rate), using *coded orthogonal frequency division multiplexing (COFDM[13])*. The *OFDM subcarriers* used BPSK, QPSK, 16QAM, and 64QAM modulation techniques.

6.4.4.2 IEEE 802.11b

IEEE 802.11b, which was released during the same year, operated at the 2.4 GHz band and appealed to a larger audience since chip sets operating at this frequency were more readily available. Although the data throughput was theoretically 11 Mbps, much lower than 802.11a, the overall costs of

---

[13] Coded OFDM is a combination of FEC and OFDM. COFDM has greater immunity to multipath and impulse noise, and like OFDM, offers high spectral efficiency.

development made 802.11b development more attractive. Instead of using COFDM, 802.11b adopted a *direct sequence spread spectrum (DSSS)* technique called **complimentary code keying (CCK)**, along with two modulation techniques: **differential BPSK (DBPSK)** which provided a maximum throughput of 5.5 Mbps, and **differential QPSK (DQPSK)**, at a maximum of 11 Mbps. While this specification had a wider appeal, its full adoption was hampered by a daunting 400 page specification which was difficult for many manufacturers to comply with. This led to incompatibility issues between manufacturers across the industry. In response six manufacturers, Intersil, 3Com, Nokia, Aironet (now part of Cisco), Symbol, and Lucent decided to create the **Wireless Ethernet Compatibility Alliance (WECA)** in 1999 with the intent to create a simpler and more universal WLAN standard. Eventually, WECA was renamed the **Wi-Fi Alliance** which is now a trademark label. The same year that WECA was formed, Apple offered a Wi-Fi slot option as part of all Apple laptops. Soon after, numerous other PC companies followed by offering their own Wi-Fi interfaces.

6.4.4.3 IEEE 802.11g

IEEE 802.11g, which was released in 2003, incorporated the more popular technologies from both 802.11a and 802.11b. Work began on this standard in 2000, culminating in the release of 802.11g in 2003. The committee adopted the 2.4 GHz operating frequency from 802.11b, but selected the OFDM concept from 802.11a which used forty-eight 20 MHz wide subcarriers. This enabled higher data throughput compared to 802.11b. In addition, the committee voted to make this new standard backward compatible with 802.11b as this would facilitate seamless transition of devices during the upgrading process. This meant that the new standard needed to support both OFDM as well as 802.11b's CCK signal spreading technique. Today 802.11g is a widely used Wi-Fi standard that operates at the ISM 2.4 GHz band, providing data throughput from 6 Mbps to 54 Mbps.

6.4.4.4 IEEE 802.11n

IEEE 802.11n was released by the committee in 2009 as a way to meet ever growing user demands for higher throughput. In order to achieve this, the reintroduction of the 5.8 GHz operating frequency and modifications to the signal encoding, antenna architecture, and the MAC layer were required. Both the 2.4 GHz and 5 GHz frequency bands are used; however, for OFDM, the subcarrier bandwidth of 20 MHz was increased to 40 MHz. This had the effect of doubling the signaling rate and data throughput to a theoretical maximum of 300 Mbps. Since backward compatibility remained a requirement, the 802.11a and 802.11g 20 MHz subcarriers remained fully supported, as did the 802.11b DSSS CCK. The adoption of the multiple input multiple output (MIMO) spatially diversified antenna architecture was a major enhancement that enabled multiple parallel stream of data to be sent between antennas. The benefits of MIMO, discussed in an earlier chapter, provided 802.11n with greater data throughput, and superior handling of multipath fading and noise. Finally, at the data link MAC sub-layer, the ability to aggregate several MAC frames together allowed larger size data packets to be sent with less delay between frame transmissions.

6.4.4.5 IEEE 802.11ac

IEEE 802.11ac is the latest IEEE standard which was approved in 2013. It provides a 1 Gbps service that adopts 802.11n's MIMO antenna architecture operating primarily on the 5 GHz band.

TABLE 6.3   Other 802.11 standards.

802.1x	Port-based network access control (PNAC)—authentication mechanism
802.11i	Describes encryption, authentication, key dissemination, etc.
802.11ad	Uses 60 GHz spectrum to deliver up to 7 Gbps
802.11af	White-fi uses spacing between broadcast television channels for low data rate Wi-Fi requiring cognitive radio technology
802.11ah	Below 1 GHz range, intended for use by IoT
802.11ax	Successor to 802.11ac provides greater data rates and reduced interference between APs

In order to increase data throughput, the operating bandwidth was increased to 80 MHz, with an option to expand to 160 MHz per wireless station. This is a sizable increase from the 40 MHz bandwidth associated with 802.11n. In addition, M'ary modulation improved, thus enabling 256-QAM ($M = 256$ levels/symbol), which is in comparison to the 802.11n 64-QAM ($M = 64$). There are numerous specifications associated with the IEEE 802.11 family, some of which are listed in Table 6.3.

6.4.5 Simple 802.11 Link Analysis Example

The link analysis approach discussed in chapter 5 will be used to determine the power available to the receiver in a WLAN link. For simplicity of illustration, we will assume the following:

1. The noise floor equals thermal noise power for our example. Obviously, when operating in the ISM frequency bands, there will be numerous wireless devices that may interfere with the WLAN.

2. **Receive signal strength indicator (RSSI)** is defined as the power level measured at the receiver typically given in decibel value. **Receiver sensitivity** is the minimum receive power (typically given in mW) required for a given receiver to detect and demodulate a signal with an acceptable BER (bit error rate). For our example, we give receive sensitivity as a minimum required SNR.

3. In determining FSL, we will use:

$$-FSL = \left(\frac{\lambda}{4\pi d}\right)^2, \text{ which in decibel form is, } -[FSL] = 20log_{10}(\lambda) - 20log_{10}(4\pi d)$$

Therefore, the link equation in decibel form adds, vice subtracts, FSL:

$$[P_R] = [EIRP] + [G_R] + [FSL] = [EIRP] + [G_R] + (20log_{10}(\lambda) - 20log_{10}(4\pi d))$$

Example 6.1: Given the following information, determine if sufficient power will be received by the wireless station from the access point (AP):

AP transmit power: $Tx = 15$ dBm, with a transmit antenna gain, $G_t = 12$ dBi

Transmit frequency: $f = 2.4$ GHz

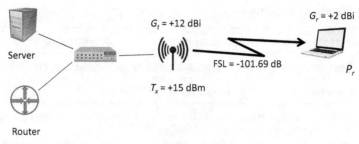

FIGURE 6.16

Server © Lineicons freebird/Shutterstock.com; Network switch © IconBunny/Shutterstock.com; Laptop
© Igor Kyrlytsya/Shutterstock.com; Antenna © Studio_G/Shutterstock.com

Free space loss: $FSL = -101.69$ dB

Receive antenna gain: $G_r = 2$ dBi

Receiver SNR required to detect/demodulate: $[SNR_{required}] = 8$ dB

Receiver noise temperature and bandwidth: 290 K degrees, 20 MHz

Solution: Through link analysis, determine the receiver power (P_R).

$$[P_R] = [Tx] + [G_t] + [G_r] + [FSL] = 15 \text{ dBm} + 12 \text{ dBi} + 2 \text{ dBi} + (-101.69 \text{ dB})$$
$$= \underline{-72.69 \text{ dBm}}$$

$$N \text{ (watts)} = kTB = (1.38 \times 10^{-23} \text{ J/K})(290 \text{ K})(20\text{E}6 \text{ Hz}) = 80.04 \times 10^{-15} \text{ W}$$
$$= 80.04 \times 10^{-12} \text{ mW}$$

$$[N] \text{ (dBm)} = 10\log_{10}(80.04 \times 10^{-12} \text{ mW/1 mW}) = \underline{-100.97 \text{ dBm}}$$

$$[SNR] = [P_R] - [N] = -72.69 \text{ dBm} - (-100.97 \text{ dBm}) = \underline{28.28 \text{ dB}}$$

$$\text{Link margin} = [SNR] - [SNR_{required}] = 28.28 \text{ dB} - 8 \text{ dB} = \underline{20.28 \text{ dB}},$$

therefore, sufficient power will be received

6.5 IEEE 802.15 PERSONAL AREA NETWORK (WPAN)

Similar to IEEE 802.11 WLAN, the IEEE 802.15 WPAN standard describes the physical and data link layers of the OSI RM. WLAN was intended to connect devices wirelessly within a local area such as a building, whereas WPAN serves a much smaller area, and is therefore characterized by the use of lower transmit power and shorter message sizes. While 802.11 connected users to a wired network infrastructure, WPAN was specifically designed to connect devices in a noninfrastructure manner. WPAN devices are often used to wirelessly connect earpieces to smartphones, peripheral devices to computers, or mp3 players to stereo head sets. 802.15 networks are *ad hoc* in nature and typically short in duration.

Released in 2002, 802.15 requirements consisted of three major goals: (1) providing solutions for short-range wireless real-time voice and data communications between devices, (2) enabling wireless connection to peripheral devices thus eliminating the need for wired cables, and (3) allowing devices to form ad hoc networks instantly when within the range of other 802.15 equipped devices. The lower transmit power over shorter distances combined with shorter messages are also an advantage for extending the battery life of WPAN devices. Along with the use of lower power and smaller message sizes, these devices can also operate in one of three low power modes to further extend battery life. In the *sniff* mode, a device operates in a power on-off duty cycle. In the *hold* mode, a device drops ACL[14] links and only responds to SCO time slots. Finally, in the *park* mode, the master node wakes the device when required.

The IEEE 802.15.1 standard (2005), known as *Bluetooth*, operates in the unlicensed ISM 2.4 GHz band frequency. A form of spread spectrum technology called *frequency hopping spread spectrum (FHSS)* was adopted to make the signal more immune from noise. With FHSS, all attached devices share a *pseudorandom hop sequence* that represents the sequence of frequencies to be used during transmission. This sequence is determined by the address of one of the communicating devices called the *master node*. The transmission bandwidth consists of 79, 1 MHz wide channels between 2.402 GHz and 2.480 GHz, that operates at a frequency hopping rate of 1600 hops/s. Data is modulated onto each 1 MHz wide channel using *Gaussian frequency shift keying (GFSK)*, which is a form of *frequency shift keying (FSK)* that is easily implemented onto Bluetooth devices.

An 802.15.1 network of connected devices operates in synchronization to a common clock and frequency hopping pattern over a common shared physical channel. The device initiating the connection is called the *master node*, and it provides the hop sequence and synchronization reference to a network of up to seven connected devices known as *slave nodes*. The role of the *master node* can be taken by any participating WPAN node, but is typically given to the initiating device. A total of eight connected devices (one master and seven slave devices) are termed a *piconet*. Within the piconet, the master node communicates with all slave devices; however, slave nodes can only communicate to the master node and not to each other.

Piconets can connect to other piconets in what is termed a *scatternet*. The node connecting two piconets together is called a *bridge* node. Unique *access codes* contained in the WPAN data frame (see fig. 6.17) defines each piconet. The *bridge* node which is a member of different piconets, serves to send data from one connected piconet to the other based upon the access code in the frame. Each node in a scatternet may take on different roles within each piconet. As an example, a master node in one piconet may act as a slave or bridge node in another piconet. Typically, when two or more piconets are connected in a scatternet, each piconet will operate on a unique physical channel, thus preventing data collisions. However, on rare instances, participating piconets may operate on the same channel where the possibility of data collisions can exist.

The physical channel is divided into time slots that contain data packets that are shared between the master and slave devices. By allocating time slots to and from the master device, full-duplex

---

[14] ACL (asynchronous connection-oriented logical) and SCO (synchronous connection-oriented) transports are described further in section 6.5.1.

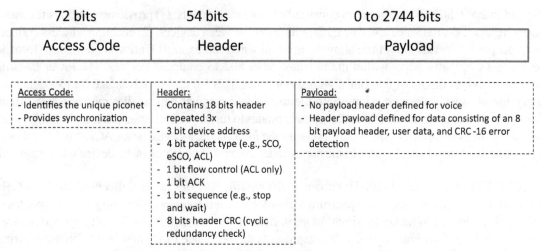

72 bits	54 bits	0 to 2744 bits
Access Code	Header	Payload

Access Code:
- Identifies the unique piconet
- Provides synchronization

Header:
- Contains 18 bits header repeated 3x
- 3 bit device address
- 4 bit packet type (e.g., SCO, eSCO, ACL)
- 1 bit flow control (ACL only)
- 1 bit ACK
- 1 bit sequence (e.g., stop and wait)
- 8 bits header CRC (cyclic redundancy check)

Payload:
- No payload header defined for voice
- Header payload defined for data consisting of an 8 bit payload header, user data, and CRC -16 error detection

FIGURE 6.17 IEEE 802.15.1 Bluetooth Data Frame.

communications is supported using a method called *time division duplexing (TDD)*. Within the packet frame format used for control and data exchange, the *access code* field assigned by the master node identifies the piconet and the data frames belonging to it. The piconet operates as a *centralized access network* where the master node polls each slave node to see if it has data to be transmitted. Since the piconet communicates over a single channel using TDD, simultaneous transmissions are not possible. Access by a node is accomplished using *time division multiple access (TDMA)*, and it is typical for Bluetooth methods to be described as *FH-TDD-TDMA (frequency hopping—time division duplex—time division multiple access)*. A physical channel can support one or more logical links by multiplexing these into specific time slot assignments.

The IEEE 802.15.2 (2003) standard describes the mechanism used to enable the coexistence of 802.11 WLAN and 802.15 WPAN devices in the same area, where both operate within the ISM unlicensed bands. The 802.15.3 (2016) standard offers high data rate WPANs operating within the 2.4 GHz and 60 GHz bands using low transmit power. The high power is well suited for multimedia music and video, and is ideal for home multimedia use.

As new WPAN standards such as 802.15.3 focused on higher data rates, another working group decided to go in the opposite directions toward less data rate and power. The *802.15.4 ZigBee* standard was developed by the *ZigBee Alliance* in 2002. The ZigBee Alliance includes a multinational membership comprised from governmental, private, and academic organizations. A major focus of this popular standard is to provide a family of simpler and reliable protocols intended for applications such as the *internet of things (IoT)*. As such, the ZigBee standard addresses very low power and data rate requirements for autonomous devices that could operate over a greatly extended periods of time.

6.5.1 802.15.1 Bluetooth Protocol Layers

The Bluetooth family of protocols was designed for application-specific uses and therefore contains both *core*, *adopted*, and *optional* capabilities that do not neatly align into the physical (PHY) or

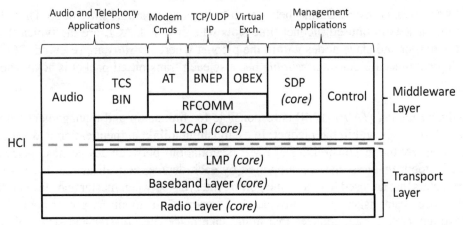

FIGURE 6.18 802.15.1 Bluetooth Protocol Stack.

medium access control (MAC) layers. Figure 6.18 shows the 802.15.1 Bluetooth protocol stack which is composed of mandatory core and optional protocols. The **Bluetooth Special Interest Group (SIG)**, which is the industry consortium that oversees Bluetooth standards development, intended to allow the optional portions of the protocol stack to enable the creation of application-specific *profiles*. These profiles serve to enable particular Bluetooth activities such as file transfers, streaming audio or telephony, modem command sets, etc., and are not mandatory for all devices.

The core capabilities consist of five protocols that are required for all Bluetooth devices. These layered protocols, described below, address the air link between devices, connection establishment, link management, the interface to upper layers, and node discovery. The **host controller interface (HCI)** is represented by a dashed line in fig. 6.18, and serves as the command interface where host software commands are implemented into device hardware by accessing the *Baseband* controller and *Link Manager* commands. Simply stated, HCI serves as the interface between software, firmware, and hardware within the protocol stack.

Below are descriptions of the core required protocols for Bluetooth operation.

Radio Layer: The radio layer is responsible for establishing the physical link within the piconet. It identifies the transmission power, frequency, modulation, and hopping sequence. The amount of power that can be transmitted is separated into three broadcast classification: **Class 1 (1 mW to 100 mW)**, Class **2 (0.25 mW to 2.5 mW)**, and **Class 3 (≤ 1 mW)**. Operating frequencies are within the ISM band between 2400 MHz and 2483.5 MHz, using FHSS over 79, 1 MHz channels.

Baseband Layer: The baseband layer is responsible for the formation of piconets and scatternets. It describes three different logical links that are supported: **synchronous connection-oriented (SCO)**, **enhanced SCO (eSCO)**, and **asynchronous connection-oriented logical (ACL)**. SCO links reserve channel bandwidth, typically in the size of a digitally uncompressed voice grade 64 kbps channel, for *symmetric*[15] communications between the master and a single slave node.

---

[15] "symmetric" indicates that the bandwidth allotted "to" and "from" the master node are equivalent.

eSCO links are *asymmetric* SCO links between the master and a single slave node. These links can also transmit packets in unused piconet time slots when needed. ACL are the typical links used between the master and slave nodes within the piconet where *no slots* are reserved. SCO, eSCO, and ACL logical links are consider *reliable* because each transmitted packet is acknowledged by the recipient.

Link Manager Protocol (LMP): LMP is responsible for link setup and management between the master and slave nodes within the piconet. In establishing a link, authentication and the setting of encryption flags are the responsibilities of LMP. Negotiations between devices take place to determine the Bluetooth features that are supported by each device, as well as the *quality-of-service (QoS)* parameters that are used to determine polling intervals between master and slave nodes. After the link has been established, LMP provides link supervision, monitors power control between devices, and any device state changes that might take place (i.e., master and slave role changes, devices entering or leaving the network, etc.).

Logical Link Control and Adaptation Protocol (L2CAP): L2CAP is a data link control protocol that enables three types of logical connections: (1) **connectionless** services consisting of simplex channel broadcasts from the master node to the slave nodes, (2) **connection-oriented** FDX services are established between master and slave nodes using TDD, (3) **signaling** service provide signaling messages between L2CAP devices. L2CAP depends upon the baseband layer for data flow and error control.

Service Discovery Protocol (SDP): SDP is responsible for the **discovery** of the types of services available on Bluetooth devices when ad hoc networks are formed. As devices learn what particular services are available from a communicating device, it caches these services for reference. While SDP discovers the services available, it does not execute them, instead leaving it to the appropriate application to execute.

Optional protocols are selected according to the application being supported. As an example, the **radio frequency communication (RFCOMM)** is a cable replacement protocol used with device serial ports. Traditional TCP/IP protocols are encapsulated using the **Bluetooth Network Encapsulation Protocol (BNEP)**, while telephony application use the **Telephony Control Specification Binary (TCS BIN)** protocol or the *AT (attention sequence)* modem protocols. The **Object Exchange (OBEX)** protocol operates at the session level to provide a mechanism for the exchange of objects similar to HTTP (hypertext transfer protocol). There are numerous profiles using optional protocols that are described in Bluetooth specifications.

The **adopted protocols** are those developed by other standards committees, such as TCP/IP, that are adopted into the Bluetooth protocol suite.

6.5.1.1 Bluetooth Security

Bluetooth uses three methods for secure communications: (1) authentication, (2) data encryption, and (3) generation of a session key. During the pairing process between two devices, a shared 4- to 16-byte secret code (PIN) combined with the device address and random generated number, produces a *link key* which is used for mutual authentication between the pairs through a challenge-response scheme.

Once authenticated, the current link key is combined with the master nodes address and clock, and random number to produce a 128-bit stream cipher. This stream cipher is then combined with user data through an XOR (eXclusive OR) process.

6.5.2 802.15.4 ZigBee

The IEEE 802.15.4 standard called **ZigBee**[16] was created by the **ZigBee Alliance** *of consortium companies*, which was established in 2002. As the 802.15.1 Bluetooth standard migrated towards higher data rates (i.e., 802.15.3), the 802.15.4 working group began development of a simpler standard designed to operate at lower data rates (20 kbps to 250 kbps) with less transmit power. The intent was to make ZigBee easier to implement and to extend device battery life. Both Bluetooth and ZigBee operate in the ISM 2.4 GHz band and both standards allow connected devices to *"sleep"* when not in use, thus helping to conserve overall battery life. However, the ZigBee standard calls for a much faster fast wake-up time on the order of 30 ms or less, compared to the slower Bluetooth standard which only requires devices to wake up within 3 s. In addition to the 2.4 GHz band that enables data rates up to 250 kbps, ZigBee uses the 868/915 MHz band to deliver data rates between 20 and 40 kbps. The lower power, lower data rate, and faster "wake-up" times makes ZigBee an ideal protocol for applications that support the *"Internet-of Things (IoT)."*

ZigBee supports numerous residential and commercial purposes such as home automation, industrial control, health care and fitness monitoring, commercial building automation, retail services, telecommunications services, and many more.

The ZigBee standard describes the automated formation of ad hoc networks by devices called the *coordinator*, *router* and *end device*. ZigBee 3.0, which was officially released in 2016 added enhanced developer tool kits, and introduced new security capabilities.

In order to establish a ZigBee WPAN, a device called the **coordinator** must initially scan and select an available RF channel. The *coordinator* then assigns a **PAN ID**, after ensuring that the ID is not being used by any other connected WPANs in the area. It then sends out a beacon invitation to other devices. The *coordinator* operates as a centralized node, and this role can be taken by any one ZigBee capable device. **Routers** are ZigBee devices that can pass data from one device to another, while **end devices** are only able to communicate to either a *router* or *coordinator*. Since the *end device* does not pass data along on behalf of other devices, it is allowed to spend much of its time in the sleep mode thus conserving battery life.

Once a WPAN has been formed, the coordinator can take on the duties of a router by relaying data on behalf of other connected nodes. Devices that wish to join a ZigBee network first scans for available networks within its reception range, and then determines if the scanned network's protocol stack is compatible with its own. If so, then it sends a join request to the network. Once the requesting device is allowed to join the network, it will operate on the same frequency as the network using the same PAN ID.

---

[16] ZigBee is a registered trademark of the ZigBee Alliance.

KEY TERMS

access point (AP)
acknowledgment (ACK)
adopted protocols
baseband layer
Bluetooth
bus topology
Carrier Ethernet
carrier sense multiple access
    collision avoidance
    (CSMA/CA)
carrier sense multiple access
    collision detection
    (CSMA/CD)
centralized access control
clear-to-send (CTS)
client-server
crossover cable
data communications
    equipment (DCE)
data terminal equipment
    (DTE)
decentralized
deterministic access
distributed access control
distributed coordination
    function (DCF)
Ethernet
four frame exchange

frame exchange protocol
hidden node
host controller interface
hub
interframe space (IFS)
link management
    protocol (LMP)
local area network (LAN)
logical link control and
    adaptation protocol
    (L2CAP)
logical link layer (LLC)
logical topology
medium access
    control (MAC)
message integrity
    code (MIC)
network operating
    system (NOS)
operating system
optional protocols
partial mesh topology
peer-to-peer
physical topology
piconet
point coordination
    function (PCF)
radio layer

receive signal strength
    indicator (RSSI)
request-to-send (RTS)
ring topology
scatternet
service discovery
    protocol (SDP)
session key
shared Ethernet
star topology
switched Ethernet
temporal key integrity
    protocol (TKIP)
time division duplexing
    (TDD)
token ring
virtual private
    network (VPN)
wide area network (WAN)
Wi-Fi Alliance
Wi-Fi Protected Access
    (WPA)
Wired Equivalent Privacy
    (WEP)
wireless LAN (WLAN)
Wireless Personal Area
    Network (WPAN)
ZigBee Alliance

CHAPTER PROBLEMS

1. The *physical* and *logical* topologies of a LAN must be identical.
    a. True
    b. False

Answer: b

2. IEEE 802.3 is a family of specifications that describe both the *physical* (OSI layer 1) and *data link* (OSI layer 2) layers of an Ethernet LAN.
    a. True
    b. False

Answer: a

3. Select the correct statement(s) regarding a *peer-to-peer (P2P)* configured LAN.
   a. In a P2P network, all computers participate equally
   b. There is no shared central database in a P2P network, therefore duplicate copies of a file can exist
   c. There is no centralized authentication mechanism
   d. All of the above are correct

Answer: d

4. In a *client-server* network, centralized authentication, data storage, and applications exist on a server that can be accessed by any computer on the network.
   a. True
   b. False

Answer: a

5. Network operating systems (NOS) are designed for use in a client-server network environment.
   a. True
   b. False

Answer: a

6. *Centralized control* methods, such as the use of polling or tokens, leads to *deterministic* medium access.
   a. True
   b. False

Answer: a

7. Ethernet is an example of _____
   a. Centralized control using a nondeterministic access method
   b. Decentralized control using a nondeterministic access method
   c. Centralized control using a deterministic access method
   d. Decentralized control using a deterministic access method

Answer: b

8. Select an example of *decentralized/nondeterministic* medium access control.
   a. Token passing
   b. Node polling
   c. CSMA/CD
   d. All of the above

Answer: c

9. Select the correct statement(s) regarding *shared Ethernet 802.3*.
   a. With shared Ethernet, all connected nodes share the same transmission medium
   b. CSMA/CD must be used as a decentralized/nondeterministic control and access method
   c. Data collisions are possible when two or more nodes transmit at the same time
   d. All of the above are correct

Answer: d

10. Select the correct statement(s) regarding full-duplex *switched Ethernet 802.3*.
   a. A OSI layer 2 switch is used to connect all nodes together
   b. CSMA/CD is not required, since no data collisions occur
   c. Both a and b are correct
   d. Neither a nor b are correct

Answer: c

11. IEEE 802.3 Ethernet must always use CSMA/CD whether in a switched or shared configuration.
   a. True
   b. False

Answer: b

12. IEEE 802.11 WLAN used a decentralized DCF access control, and requires CSMA/CA to avoid data collisions. However, data collisions can still occur.
   a. True
   b. False

Answer: a

13. CSMA/CA, which is used on IEEE 802.11 wireless LANs, requires the use of a *four frame exchange* protocol that includes RTS, CTS, and acknowledgments that help to avoid possible data collisions.
   a. True
   b. False

Answer: a

14. What is true regarding CSMA/CA?
   a. Enables a priority scheme between stations to be established
   b. Like CSMA/CD (collision detection), collisions can still occur
   c. Requires the use of an ACK to verify packet receipt
   d. All are true statements

Answer: d

15. A DTE device/interface can only interface to another DTE device/interface
   a. True
   b. False

Answer: b

16. Select the correct statement(s) regarding DTE and DCE.
   a. DTE and DCE interfaces tell you the direction of data flow between devices.
   b. DTE devices can be connected to other DTE devices by using a "straight-through" cable.
   c. DTE and DCE are device labels used to demarc (i.e., separate) service provider and user responsibilities for maintenance and operation purposes.
   d. All of the above are correct.

Answer: a

17. Cross-over cables are used to connect a DTE to a DTE, or a DCE to another DCE.
   a. True
   b. False

Answer: a

18. IEEE 802.3 is a *family* of Ethernet specifications that describes *physical* and *data link layers* attributes.
   a. True
   b. False

Answer: a

19. IEEE 802.3 logical link layer (LLC) is responsible for what?
    a. Placing data frames onto the physical medium
    b. Placing the MAC address into the data frame
    c. Providing communications between the data link layer and the network layer
    d. Framing data for placement onto the medium

Answer: c

20. IEEE 802.3 media access control layer (MAC) is responsible for what?
    a. Data encapsulation (framing, addressing, error detection)
    b. Placement of frames onto the physical medium
    c. Responsible for CSMA/CD process
    d. All of the above

Answer: d

21. The MAC sub-layer resides below the LLC sub-layer within the data link layer. The MAC sub-layer is responsible for CSMA/CD and CSMA/CA processes when required.
    a. True
    b. False

Answer: a

22. What is correct regarding 100Base-TX?
    a. By using 4B5B coding, only 80% of the logical data sent represents real information (i.e., 20% of the bits are considered overhead)
    b. Can operate in full or half-duplex modes.
    c. Operates over Cat 5e UTP which enables a signaling rate of 125,000 kBaud
    d. All are correct

Answer: d

23. 100Base-TX can be configured as either half-duplex or full-duplex. When operated in the full-duplex switched configuration, CSMA/CD is not required.
    a. True
    b. False

Answer: a

24. 100BaseTX Ethernet means what?
    a. 100 bps, baseband signaling, transmit only
    b. 100 m, baseband, twisted pair
    c. 100 Mbps, baseband, twisted pair
    d. 100 Mbps, baseband, transmit only

Answer: c

25. Cat 5e medium has a capacity of 125 MBaud. By applying 4B5B coding over two pairs of wires, full-duplex (FDX), what data rate capacity can you obtain.
    a. 125 Mbps
    b. 100 Mbps
    c. 250 Mbps
    d. 200 Mbps

Answer: b

26. What is correct regarding 1000BASE-T?
    a. Can only meet 1Gbps data rate capacity with Cat 6 or 7 UTP cable
    b. Requires fiber optic cables to support 1 Gbps
    c. Can only be supported using full-duplex pairs
    d. It is a broadband specification

Answer: c

27. In order to achieve 1 Gbps (1 GbE) over Cat5e cabling, what needs to be done?
    a. Use all four wire pairs in full-duplex
    b. Apply PAM-5 modulation to achieve $M = 4, N = 2$
    c. Use hybrids that enable full-duplex transmission over a single wire pair
    d. All of the above

Answer: d

28. 10GBaseT cannot be accomplished over Cat 5e.
    a. True
    b. False

Answer: a

29. In order to increase wired twisted pair medium LAN capacity, what things can be done?
    a. Decrease diameter of the conductor to reduce signal resistance
    b. Implement M'ary modulation or M'ary line coding techniques
    c. Operate in half-duplex mode in order to give transmit and receive signals access to the entire twisted pair medium
    d. All of the above

Answer: b

30. Which 802.3 specification is used with fiber optic medium?
    a. 10GBase-T
    b. 100Base-T
    c. 1000Base-SX
    d. None of the above

Answer: c

31. The IEEE 802.11 access point (AP) provides bridge and router functionality between the mobile user air interface and the wired network.
    a. True
    b. False

Answer: a

32. IEEE 802.11g and 802.11n are both backward compatible with 802.11b.
    a. True
    b. False

Answer: a

33. WLANs can be configured to operate in a peer-to-peer (P2P) mode or through a common *control module* or *access point*.
    a. True
    b. False

Answer: a

34. Since 802.11 WLANs implement DSSS and OFDM, there is no need for a collision avoidance mechanism.
a. True
b. False

Answer: b

35. All 802.11 WLAN operating frequencies must be licensed with the FCC.
a. True
b. False

Answer: b

36. 802.11 b incorporates Direct Sequence Spread Spectrum as a modulation technique. As such, modulation methods such as BPSK or QPSK are unnecessary.
a. True
b. False

Answer: b

37. For a WLAN system with a transmit power of $+10$ dBm, transmits antenna gain of 10 dBi, FSL $= -100$ dB, and receive antenna again of 1 dBi, what is the power received in dBm?
a. -79 dBm
b. 79 dBm
c. 121 dBm
d. -121 dBm

Answer: a

38. Describe the WLAN *hidden node* problem. Describe how this can be resolved.

39. The point coordination function (PCF) is an optional extension of DCF located in the upper MAC layer, that provides a centralized process for contention-free access.
a. True
b. False

Answer: a

40. Due to the weaknesses inherent in WEP, WPA (Wi-Fi protected access) and WPA2, which were based upon the IEEE 802.11i security standard, were developed as replacements.
a. True
b. False

Answer: a

41. Determine the noise power in dBm given the following: Boltzmann's constant $k = 1.38E-23$ (J/K), $T = 275$ K, $B = 5$ MHz.
a. $1.89E-14$ W
b. -137.23 dBm
c. -107.23 dBm
d. -137.23 dBW

Answer: c

42. Given a $[S] = -80$ dBm and $[N] = -130$ dBW, what is the [SNR]?
    a. 210 dB
    b. 50 dB
    c. 20 dB
    d. -210 dB

    Answer: b

43. Your receive sensitivity has an [SNR] = 30 dBm. Through link analysis, you find that you have an actual receive [SNR] = 10 dBm. What is your link margin and can you close the link?
    a. You have no link margin and cannot close the link
    b. -20 dBm, you can close the link
    c. 20 dBm, you cannot close the link
    d. 40 dBm, you can close the link

    Answer: a

44. Select the correct statement(s) regarding 802.15 Bluetooth.
    a. Bluetooth implements direct sequence spread spectrum and operates in the ISM frequency band
    b. Bluetooth implements frequency hopping spread spectrum and operates in the ISM frequency band
    c. Bluetooth implements OFDM and operates in the licensed frequency band
    d. Bluetooth implements frequency hopping spread spectrum and operates in the licensed frequency band

    Answer: b

45. What is the purpose of 802.15 Bluetooth?
    a. Provides data and voice access in real-time
    b. Eliminates the need for cable attachments/connections
    c. Enables ad hoc networking
    d. All of the above

    Answer: d

46. How many 802.15 Bluetooth devices make up a piconet?
    a. 6
    b. 7
    c. 8
    d. 9

    Answer: c

47. A 802.15 Bluetooth bridge device enables communications between two piconets within a scatternet.
    a. True
    b. False

    Answer: a

48. What is the 802.15 Bluetooth "access code"?
    a. It contains the MAC address of all piconet participating nodes
    b. It is the bridge device MAC address that enables intra-scatternet data exchanges
    c. Is defined by the master node and associates incoming packets to the piconet
    d. Performs error detection for each piconet payload

    Answer: c

49. For 802.15 Bluetooth what does FH-TDD-TDMA stand for?
   a.   Frequency Hopping Spread Spectrum, Time Division Duplex, Time Division Multiple Access
   b.   Full Header, Twisted Pair Duplex, Time Division Multiple Access
   c.   Full or Half Duplex, Time Delay Duplex, Time Division Multiple Access
   d.   None of the above

Answer: a

50. Select the correct statement(s) regarding 802.15 Bluetooth.
   a.   ZigBee is another term that describes Bluetooth
   b.   Bluetooth implements DSSS
   c.   Bluetooth operates as a TDD network
   d.   All of the above are correct

Answer: c

CHAPTER 7

Public Switched Telephone Network (PSTN) and Wide Area Networks (WANs)

"Great discoveries and improvements invariably involve the cooperation of many minds. I may be given credit for having blazed the trail, but when I look at the subsequent developments I feel the credit is due to others rather than to myself."

Alexander Graham Bell (https://www.brainyquote.com/search_results.html?q=alexander+bell)

7.1 INTRODUCTION

When we think about the ***public switched telephone network (PSTN)*** today, we often have images of an older, antiquated system whose time has come and gone. However, the modern PSTN, once referred to as the *plain old telephone system (POTS)*, has evolved into a modern digital data network that provides digital services to support ***wide area networks (WANs)***, the ***public data network (PDN)***, and the ***Internet***. These networks operated by numerous service providers consist of modern fiber optic, wireless broadband, and satellite communications technologies that operate predominantly in the lower layers of the OSI reference model.

From the PSTN's humble beginnings in 1876 to current times, it can be said that government regulatory actions and policies had as much influence on its evolution as did the technical innovations discovered. In fact, this can be said of the entire telecommunications industry, from Internet, to cellular, LANs, WANs, and satellites. The evolution of the telephone industry can be seen as a dramatic interaction between individual and public interests, and it is highly likely that this interaction of interests will continue to shape how the telecommunications industry will evolve well into the future. In order to better understand the influences that make change happen, we need to understand the history of this interaction.

7.1.1 A Brief History of the Telecommunications Industry

In 1876, a 29 year-old Alexander Graham Bell demonstrated the first telephone voice call to his assistant Thomas A. Watson with the phrase "Mr. Watson, come here, I need you." For many of us, we see this as the first momentous step toward the modern PSTN. However, at the time the future of the telephone, although demonstrated in the lab, was not so clear. During this period in history, the telegraph system had matured and was considered the principle long-distance means to send messages and to communicate. Even Bell's place in history was not guaranteed prior to being awarded the patent for the telephone, as other inventors worked on similar concepts for sending voice over wires in the form of an electrical signal. Elisha Gray,[1] an electrical engineer who founded

---

[1] In 1874, Elisha Gray retired from Western Electric Manufacturing Company, the company he had founded, and became a professor at Oberlin College. He passed away in 1901.

Western Electric Company's predecessor, Western Electric Manufacturing Company, also had a telephone apparatus that transmitted voice. Unfortunately for Gray, his patent was filed 3 hours behind Bell's, and after years of litigation, Bell's patent was upheld.

In 1876, the same year of Bell's famous demonstration, he attempted to sell the patent to Western Union for the small sum of $100,000. Western Union pulled together a team to evaluate the invention and the purchase, and a decision was made to decline the offer. The famous decision, found in an internal Western Union memo, is often quoted, *"The telephone has too many shortcomings to be seriously considered as a means of communications. The device is inherently of no value to us."* Unfortunately, the company's ineptness in not realizing the potential of the telephone is all too obvious from today's perspective. However, it should be noted that some modern-day historians question the validity of this memo, but in any case, despite the question of authenticity, there is no doubt that the company passed on one of the greatest bargains in modern history.

A year after the failed sale to Western Union, Alexander Graham Bell founded the *Bell Telephone Company*, which soon overshadowed *Western Union* as the lead telecommunications provider. The first telephone exchange opened in New Haven, Connecticut, with other exchange franchises opening in major cities across the country within a few years. The combination of these franchises across the country soon became known collectively as the Bell System. In 1885, **American Telephone and Telegraph (AT&T)** Company was formed as a subsidiary of the *American Bell Telephone Company*[2] to handle long-distance communications between cities.

When Bell's patent expired in 1894, numerous independent phone companies began springing up in towns and cities across the country. Understanding the threat to their market share that these independent phone companies posed, AT&T,[3] once the former subsidiary now turned parent company to American Bell, began an advertising campaign in 1908 with the motto *"One System, One Policy, Universal Service."* This motto addressed AT&T's belief that only a single telephone company, vice interconnected independent companies, could provide the quality of service desired. Soon after, AT&T began the acquisition of the majority of these independent phone companies. These acquisitions, along with its majority share holdings in Western Union, were in violation of the *Sherman Antitrust Act*, and the Wilson administration soon took notice. In order to avoid a long antitrust battle, AT&T chose to meet with the Justice Department officials to negotiate an amenable compromise. The compromise agreed to between AT&T and Wilson's Justice Department was known as the *"Kingsbury Agreement of 1913,"* named after the vice president of AT&T Nathan Kingsbury who sent the terms of the agreement in a memo to the then Attorney General. In the agreement, AT&T agreed to cease further acquisitions of independent phone companies unless approved by the *Interstate Commerce Commission (ICC)*, to divest itself from the majority holdings of Western Union shares, and to allow independent phone companies access to AT&T's long-distance networks between cities. Unfortunately, this agreement was also seen by many in the industry as permission for AT&T to act as a *regulated monopoly* free from competition. While independent local and long-distance telephone companies continued to exist, there was little doubt

---

[2] The Bell Telephone Company had changed its name to the American Bell Telephone Company.

[3] In 1899, the AT&T subsidiary became the parent of the American Bell Telephone Company.

that AT&T was the giant telecommunications company at the time. By 1924, the ICC had approved AT&T's purchase of 223 of the 234 independent phone companies.

As the desire for telephone service quickly spread across the country, the government realized the need for an organization specifically tasked to regulate and to set the nations communications policies. The ***Communications Act of 1934*** created the ***Federal Communications Commission (FCC)***, which took over many ICC oversight duties and was tasked with regulatory power over AT&Ts rate structure.

In 1956, the ***Hush-A-Phone*** company of New York mounted one of the first successful challenges to AT&T's monopolistic power. During the time, all personal and business telephones were rented from the phone company and could not be owned. Since it owned all telephone equipment, AT&T felt it could exercise its authority to determine what could be attached electrically or mechanically to the telephone itself. The Hush-A-Phone company manufactured a mechanically attached device called *"the phone silencer,"* that would block acoustic noise from entering the telephone's mouthpiece. Doing this helped to reduce ambient acoustic noise that often existed in busy office environments. However, AT&T objected to the sale of the phone silencer since it was specifically manufactured to attach to an AT&T telephone, which it claimed was a violation of the *Communications Act of 1934*. AT&T's suit was brought before the FCC in 1948, which agreed with AT&T at the time. However, unsatisfied with FCC's decision, Hush-A-Phone decided to appeal the decision to the U.S. Court of Appeals in DC, which reversed the decision in 1956, stating the following: *"To say that a telephone subscriber may produce the result in question by cupping his hands and speaking into it, but may not do so by using a device which leaves his hands free to write or do whatever else he wishes, is neither just nor reasonable."* (Hush-A-Phone Corporation v. United States, 1956)

While the Hush-A-Phone case allowed for the mechanical attachment of third-party devices on AT&T equipment, the landmark ***1968 Carterfone decision*** allowed non-AT&T devices to be connected electrically to the telephone network itself. The Carterfone decision opened competition and innovation for telephone devices such as facsimile machines, modems, answering machines, and telephones not manufactured exclusively by AT&T. Named for its inventor Thomas Carter, the Carterfone device connected two-way radios electrically to telephone lines. This made it possible for Texas oil drilling teams operating in remote areas to communicate with their home offices without having to leave the field. AT&T took the position that a foreign device, such as the Carterfone, would cause damage to the telephone network if connected electrically or by induction, and therefore decreed that anyone using the device would have their phone services terminated. In response Carter decided to file an antitrust suit against AT&T with the U.S. District Court in North Texas, who then referred it back to FCC for adjudication on the grounds that it fell within the FCC's jurisdiction. The FCC conducted numerous hearings and finally in 1968 made the surprise[4] decision that allowed third-party devices to be connected directly to the telephone network as long as AT&T telephone interface specifications were fully complied with.

---

[4] Most industry experts believed that the FCC would rule in AT&T's favor considering past legislative activity (e.g., Hush-A-Phone decision).

Along with the legal disputes that had been raised by individual companies such as Hush-A-Phone and Carterfone, the federal government also actively pursued antitrust litigation against AT&T. As early as 1949, the *Department of Justice (DOJ)* filed antitrust law suits against AT&T's manufacturing company, *Western Electric*, and in 1974 against AT&T as a whole. The 1974 charge claimed that AT&T companies conspired to monopolize the entire telecommunications industry. Thus began lengthy negotiations between DOJ and AT&T that were not concluded until January 7, 1982. The results of the negotiation and agreements were forwarded to Judge Harold Greene of the U.S. District Court for DC, who then modified the original agreement which became known as the *Modified Final Judgment (MFJ) of 1982*. In the MFJ, the 22 *Bell Operating Companies (BOCs)* were completely divested from the parent AT&T on January 1 of 1984, to become the seven *Regional Bell Holding Companies*[5] *(RBHCs) Ameritech, Bell Atlantic, Bell South, NYNEX, Pacific Telesis, Southwestern Bell and U.S. West*, which provided regional telephone service. AT&T no longer had control over the RBHCs, and was allowed to only provide long-distance services. Finally, after the long held monopolistic dominance over the telephone industry between 1885 and 1984, the AT&T giant was divided into independent companies and forced to compete in providing services. This represented a major win for the average consumer.

During the same year that AT&T divestiture began, Congress passed the *Cable Communications Policy Act of 1984* which amended[6] the previous *Communications Act of 1934*. The main purpose of this new legislation was to address the need for a national policy regarding the cable communications industry. Within the act were federal, state and local guidelines and franchise standard practices all aimed at encouraging greater competition within the relatively closed cable television market.

With the development of personal computers, computer networking, and the exponential growth of the Internet throughout the 1980's and 1990's, came a need to introduce new regulations and laws that would ensure continued competitiveness within the burgeoning field of digital communications. The original *Communications Act of 1934* had become severely outdated even with its amendment in 1984, and there was a need to address the unique challenges associated with the digital age. On February 8, 1996, President Clinton signed the *Telecommunications Act of 1996* into law. Seen as one of the most significant pieces of legislation during the digital era, the Act opened competition of voice and data services to local telephone companies, long-distance service providers, and cable companies. It allowed the seven original RHBCs to provide long-distance and information services in trade for allowing new entrants the use of their local telephone infrastructure at a reasonable price. Telephone companies were allowed to offer multimedia programming, and cable companies were allowed to provide voice services in hopes of increasing competition to the benefit of the consumer.

Another key objective was to bring broadband services to consumers at a competitive price. New entrants called *competitive local exchange carriers (CLECs)*[7] were created in mass numbers thus ushering in the *"dot-com"* era which addressed the increasing popularity of the Internet. During the *"dot-com bubble"* in the late 90's, numerous companies brought enormous wealth to investors,

---

[5] Also known as the "Regional Bell Operating Companies" (RBOCs), or "Baby Bells."

[6] Inserted "Title VI" into the Communications Act of 1934 to specifically address the cable industry.

[7] Incumbent local exchange carriers (iLECs) were the labels used to describe the original seven RBOCs or RHCPs.

only to be followed by the *"dot-com bust"* between 2000 and 2002, where investors began to lose fortunes due to the down turn in the market. While it has been over 20 years since the Act was signed into law, the discussion continues to this day whether the Act truly achieved what it was intended to do. Proponents point to the great success enjoyed by the telecommunications industry, while opponents point to the stock market crash that followed and the numerous scandals that eventually surfaced such as with *Worldcom*. However, one legacy that we all enjoy today is the massive infrastructure build that occurred in the late 90's. It provided today's telecommunications infrastructure with thousands of miles of fiber optic lines, innovative hardware, firmware and software, and new ways and expectations for how we communicate in the digital world.

7.2 PUBLIC SWITCHED TELEPHONE NETWORK (PSTN)

The *public switched telephone network (PSTN)*, also referred to as the *plain old telephone service (POTS)*, was originally comprised exclusively of the circuit switched analog voice telephone network. In contrast, the *public data networks (PDNs)* are specifically designed to support digital data networks and are often operated by the same organizations that provide PSTN service. However, modern-day PSTNs and PDNs have similar physical architectures that include digital broadband trunks consisting of copper, fiber optic, and coaxial guided mediums, as well as unguided mediums such as microwave and satellite links. Some might think of the PSTN as an outdated analog network; however, today's network uses modern digital technologies designed to increase the efficiency of the voice network. In fact, one of the only remnants of the old analog POTS network is the *local loop* that provides wired connectivity between the user premises and the network *central office (CO)*. Many of the capabilities between the PSTN and PDN have converged into today's modern digital network, and it is this modern network that provides the physical links which support numerous *wide area networks (WANs)* and the *Internet*.

7.2.1 The PSTN Architecture

Form follows function, and the function of the PSTN is to connect voice calls from any point within the network to any other point within the network. This obviously requires a large network whose nodes consist of switches interconnected by links. The user must have a convenient way to access the network, and must be able to tell the network which terminal node and telephone the call is to be placed to. This may sound simple, but to do so requires not only a complex fabric of switches, but also a numbering plan, control and signaling capability, and an ability to manage and operate the network to ensure reliability and availability.

Let's consider the typical analog voice call. The user's telephone is connected to the *central office (CO)* through a copper wire pair called the *local loop (LL)*. The LL is considered a dedicated link since no other telephones can connect to it. As soon as the user's phone goes "off-hook," the CO connects the LL to the *common channel signaling (CCS)* *and control network*, which is a completely separate network from the one used for actual voice traffic.

The CCS is an intelligent digital network comprised of computers and databases that have the responsibility for managing and operating the voice traffic network. It enables the *call setup and termination* processes. When the caller enters the destination phone number, the CCS network provides the signaling (i.e., ringing) to the called telephone, and then determines the best circuit switched path through the network for the voice call. Once the distant end answers the telephone and the connection is made, the CCS network makes the circuit switched path on the traffic network available for the voice call, and continues to monitor the call until termination.

An international standard for CCS networks based upon an *International Telecommunications Union (ITU)* recommendation is called **Signaling System 7 (SS7)**. Like CCS, SS7 is an **out-of-band** control and signaling system that describes the transmission of signaling information over a dedicated and separate network from the one used for actual voice traffic. This is in contrast to control and signaling functions occurring on the same network used for voice traffic, which is termed **in-band** control and signaling. An example of *in-band* control and signaling occurs on the local loop between the user and central office where control and signaling share the same physical medium as voice traffic.

The PSTN involves several types of switching centers. End-user LLs connect directly to switches located within a facility called the *central office (CO),* which provides user access to the telephone network within a given geographic area. Also known as **central office exchanges (COEs)**, these facilities are owned and operated by **local exchange carriers (LECs)** which are the service providing organizations within a given local area called the **local access and transport area (LATA)**. Switches within the CO aggregate multiple LLs together into *trunk lines* that are then connected to **tandem switches** located within provider's network switching centers. The tandem switches are connected to other tandem switches within the network, but do not connect directly to the end-user or subscriber. The telephone number tells the service provider (i.e., LEC), whether the *"called"* user resides within its own operating LATA. If so, then it is referred to as an **intraLATA** call. However, if the called number is outside of the current LATA, then it must go to an **Interexchange Carrier (IXC)** facility where different LECs exchange and connect **interLATA** phone calls. In some cases, the called number may reside outside of the caller's country and therefore the connection must go through an **International Gateway Facility (IGF)** which is where the switches of international carriers interface with one another.

The numerous switches that make up the global PSTN require a hierarchical structure based upon the telephone number. By routing a call in a hierarchical manner, the network can quickly provide the correct path through the switching network without having to perform exhaustive subscriber number look-ups within large databases. This hierarchical numbering plan is the responsibility of the ITU-T, who is responsible for the **Numbering Plan Administration (NPA)**, which is the telephone numbering standard used today. While this standard is considered voluntary according to ITU, it is closely followed by all countries wishing to ensure full global interoperability. The current *ITU-T E.164*(2010) recommendation consists of a hierarchically defined phone number that has a maximum of 15 digits as shown in fig. 7.1.

The **Country Code (CC)** which consists of one to three digits identifies the country that the number belongs to. So if calling a number in the United States from another country, you would use "011." Once the call reaches the United States, the **National Destination Code (NDC)**, which in this example is the three-digit *area code*, gets your call to the right local area within the United States. Finally, the seven-digit **subscriber number (SN)** connects you to the party you are calling.

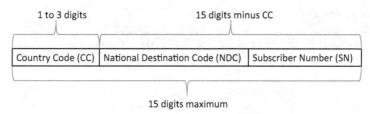

FIGURE 7.1   ITU-T E.164 International Telephone Numbering Plan.

Other countries have slight variations to this numbering plan. As an example, when calling the United Kingdom, you would use a *CC* of "00," combined with a two- to five-digit *NDC (area code)*, and a five- to eight-digit *SN*.

Prior to AT&T divestiture in 1984, telephones were the property and responsibility of telephone company. After divestiture, third-party manufacturers began selling telephones and other terminal devices to consumers, thereby making this equipment the responsibility of the user. Equipment attached to the PSTN, but owned by the user or organization is referred to as ***customer premises equipment (CPE)***. As long as the manufacturer of a CPE device complies with PSTN interface specifications, the service provider, in accordance with the MFJ of 1984, is required to allow the device to be electrically connected to the network. The point where the CPE connects to the PSTN is called the ***demarc***, and it represents the point where service provider operations and maintenance responsibilities begin and end. The demarc's physical interface is equipped with surge protectors that help to protect the network from excessive current coming from the CPE caused by malfunctioning equipment or by weather phenomena such as a lightning strike.

7.2.2 T-Carrier

In the early 90's when consumers were beginning to connect to the Internet, modems were used to send modulated digital signals over the analog PSTN. Over long distances, the analog modem signal would attenuate and noise would quickly become a limitation impacting data rate capacity. At its best, modems could provide data rate speeds of up to 56 kbps; however, as web pages became more complex, dial-up speeds became insufficient, and newer digital technologies were required to repeat and amplify digital signals in order to enable higher data rate transmissions over longer distances.

As early as the 1960's, the old analog PSTN was being upgraded with newer digital technologies that enabled greater efficiencies over trunk lines through the use of *time division multiplexing (TDM)* between tandem switches. *Pulse code modulation (PCM)* was used to convert 4-kHz-wide analog voice to uncompressed 64 kbps digital signals. Today, the local link remains one of the few parts of the network that still operates using analog signals. For voice calls transiting inside the network, the digitization process is transparent to users, as is the fact that the physical circuit switched path is now shared with other users virtually. Within the network, a single 64 kbps voice grade channel is termed a ***digital signal zero (DS0)***, which is a fundamental building block for digital voice. In this hierarchical scheme, a DS1 equals 24 DS0 channels as seen in Table 7.1. Likewise, a DS2 equals 96 DS0 voice channels and so on.

TABLE 7.1 T-Carrier and E-Carrier comparison.

T-Carrier	E-Carrier	DS Equivalent	No. DS0s Supported	Data Rate
-	-	DS0	1	64 kbps
T-1	-	DS1	24	1.544 Mbps
-	E-1	-	32	2.048 Mbps
T-2	-	DS2	96	6.312 Mbps
-	E-2	-	120	8.448 Mbps
-	E-3	-	480	34.368 Mbps
T-3	-	DS3	672	44.376 Mbps
-	E-4	-	1920	139.264 Mbps
T-4	-	DS4	4032	274.176 Mbps
T-5	-	DS5	5760	400.352 Mbps
-	E-5	-	7680	565.148 Mbps

In the 1960's and 70's as the desire to interconnect mainframe computers together across large geographic distances increased, AT&T began to offer digital services such as *Dataphone Digital Service (DDS)* and *Switched 56*, both of which are no longer available and therefore not discussed further. However, one of the earlier services that is still in use today by *Internet Service Providers (ISP)* is the ***T-Carrier***. Initially introduced in the 60's, the *T-Carrier* is a dedicated digital leased line service that is provided in either ***channelized*** or ***unchannelized*** forms. With *channelized T-carrier*, the physical circuit supports a number of DS0 voice channels depending upon the specific service selected. As an example, the basic service level is called the T-1, which supports 24 DS0 voice channels at an aggregate data rate of 1.544 Mbps (see Table 7.1). Similar to the hierarchical structure of the DS0s, a T-2 is equivalent to 96 DS0 voice channels, a T-3 is equivalent to 672 DS0 channels, up to a T-5 which is equivalent to 5760 DS0 channels.

In Table 7.1, you will also notice a column labeled *"E-Carrier."* Similar to the channelized T-Carrier adopted in North America, the channelized E-Carrier is based upon the 64 kbps DS0 voice channel building block. The standard was developed by the *European Conference of Postal and Telecommunications Administrations (CEPT)* to specifically satisfy European requirements for digital communications. One of the obvious differences is in the number of DS0s supported. As an example, T-1 supports 24 DS0s, while E-1 supports 32 DS0s. However, because they are based upon the DS0, there are many compatibilities between the two standards. Not shown in Table 7.1 is the J-carrier which is used in Japan and is also based upon the DS0. Since these standards are similar, the basic channelized framing concepts apply to all. Therefore, for the remainder of this section we will only discuss T-carrier.

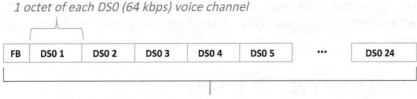

1 octet of each DS0 (64 kbps) voice channel

FB	DS0 1	DS0 2	DS0 3	DS0 4	DS0 5	...	DS0 24

T-1 Frame = 1 framing bit (FB) + 24 octets* = 193 bits/frame

* A T-1 frame supports just one 1 octet of each of the 24 DS0s. (1 octet = 1 byte = 8 bits)

DS0 = 1 (octet/frame) X 8 (bits/octet) X 8,000 (frames/second) = 64,000 bps

T-1 frame rate: **8,000 (frames/second)**

T-1 data rate: **8000 (frames/sec) x 193 (bits/frame) = 1.544 Mbps**

FIGURE 7.2 T-1 Data Frame Structure.

The T-Carrier has a TDM data framing structure based upon the 64 kbps DS0 voice channel. To understand the data frame structure, let's take a closer look at the T-1 frame in fig. 7.2. A T-1 carrier supports 24 DS0s; however, a T-1 frame only supports one octet, or 8 bits, from each of the 24 DS0s. In fig. 7.2, we see that a T-1 frame starts with a single *framing bit (FB)* at the beginning, followed by one octet from each of the 24 DS0s that are supported. Therefore, a single T-1 frame equals:

$$\text{Number of bits in a T-1 frame} = 1 \text{ FB} + (24 \tfrac{\text{DS0s}}{\text{frame}} * 8 \tfrac{\text{bits}}{\text{DS0}})$$

$$= 1 \text{ FB} + 192 \tfrac{\text{bits}}{\text{frame}} = \underline{193} \text{ total bits per T-1 frame}$$

If we consider that each DS0 must operate 64 kbps to achieve voice grade quality, and that only 8 bits of each DS0 is present within a single 193-bit T-1 frame, then we can determine that a frame rate of 8000 frames/s must be achieved to support each DS0.

$$\text{A single DS0} = 8 \tfrac{\text{bits}}{\text{frame}} * 8000 \tfrac{\text{frames}}{\text{second}} = 64 \text{ kbps}$$

To support 24 DS0s, with a frame rate of 8000 frames/s, then the total data rate of the T-1 needs to be:

$$\text{T-1 data rate} = 193 \tfrac{\text{bits}}{\text{frame}} * 8000 \tfrac{\text{frames}}{\text{second}} = 1.544 \text{ Mbps}$$

For the *unchannelized* version of the T-1, the frame is not divided by DS0s, but can be divided to support any sized data rate. Channelized T-Carrier is designed to support voice channels, while unchannelized T-Carrier is typically used to support data exchange between computers.

Today, the T-Carrier concept is used by businesses and organizations wishing to provide Internet access to workers or customers through Internet Service Providers (ISPs). Originally provisioned over four copper wires (two wire pairs, one pair for transmit and one pair for receive), fiber optic cables are now used thus providing much higher data speeds along with an ability to aggregate larger numbers of users.

7.3 PUBLIC DATA NETWORK (PDN)

As you have probably noticed so far, the story of the PSTN and public data network (PDN) is one of evolution. The progression from analog voice to digital multimedia is based upon regulatory efforts, innovation, and the convergence of multiple technologies such as digital networking, the Internet, and personal computer. Two major parts of this evolution involves the increased capacity and efficiency of the network itself, as well as the access technologies that enable users an entry point to this vast network. As an example, when users required greater data rate speeds for their mainframe computers and to access the Internet, digital access technologies, such as the T-Carrier, were developed to replace the much slower dial-up modem.

The basic concept of the PSTN is the circuit switching concept, where the caller retains the physical path through an analog network for the duration of the call. This means that no other users can use this physical path until the call has been terminated and the particular path released. Of course, as the PSTN modernized to include digital trunks between digitized switches, the physical path, or trunks, between switching centers could be shared with other users, thus making them virtual paths. In other words, physical network paths which once supported a single analog call, could now be shared amongst several calls through digital techniques such as TDM. The virtualization of the physical paths through the aggregation of digital calls were completely transparent to users, and helped to increase the efficiency of the overall network by increasing the number of calls that could be supported.

The PDN was initially designed to support digital communications between mainframe computers. As the PDN evolved, it expanded to support long-distance connectivity between LANs, WANs, virtual private networks (VPNs), digital voice and video teleconferencing, and access to the Internet and intranets. Similar in concept to the PSTN, the PDN supports both ***permanent virtual circuit (PVC)*** and ***switched virtual circuit (SVC)*** connections. PVC connections are similar to a *dedicated circuit*, in that the data frames or packets from a specified PVC user will always traverses the same switches, and therefore the same physical path. However, unlike the dedicated leased line in which the physical path is only used by the subscriber, PVC paths are virtual and shared with other users. SVC connections are similar to *switched circuit* calls, where the physical path through the network may change from call to call. Like the PVC method, the difference between the SVC and traditional circuit switched connection, is that the SVC path is shared with other users during the data exchange between source and destination.

As early as 1976, a packet switching standard called X.25 was introduced by *CCITT (International Telegraph and Telephone Consultative Committee)*, which was the predecessor organization to the current ITU-T. X.25 consisted of *packet-switching exchange (PSE)* nodes that were interconnected through the PSTN using dedicated leased lines that formed a *wide area network (WAN)*. As an international standard, X.25 represented an early form of packet switching on the PDN. Although the X.25 standard was published prior to the introduction of the *OSI reference model (RM)*, it introduced

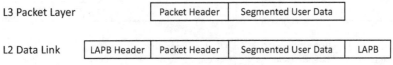

FIGURE 7.3 X.25 Packet and Data Link Layers.

a similar three-layer concept consisting of the *physical*, *data link,* and *packet layer* (see fig. 7.3). The physical layer used balanced and unbalanced digital signals such as *X.21, EIA-232,* and *EIA-449.* The data link layer used *LAPB (link access procedure balanced)* which is a subset of *HDLC (high-level data link control).* The packet layer was responsible for the segmentation of user data into packets. The X.25 standard is no longer used today, but it played an important role in advancing numerous data networking concepts that have evolved into today's modern digital network.

In the following sections, we will continue our discussion of the evolution of the PDN by first looking at the standards that make up the network itself, followed by Chapter 8, which discusses the standards used to gain broadband digital access into the PDN.

7.3.1 Frame Relay (FR)

With the X.25 standard, in-band control and signaling was used to set up and tear down virtual circuits. Aggregation of the virtual circuits occurred at the packet layer (layer 3), and flow and error control occurred in both the LAPB (layer 2) and packet (layer 3) layers. In an X.25 virtual circuit, at each link, the receiving node was required to acknowledge the received packets back to the sending node. This meant that each node within the circuit path had to retain information of all packets sent and received throughout the virtual connection. While this may be good for unreliable physical circuits, it added an enormous amount of overhead, and therefore slowed data throughput on more reliable physical circuits.

Frame Relay (FR) was developed as a replacement for X.25 during the 1990's by the ITU-T, and within the United States it became an *American National Standards Institute (ANSI)* standard. FR differed from X.25 in that out-of-band control and signaling was implemented on separate logical channels from the data traffic. Logical connections were aggregated at layer 2, vice layers 2 and 3 on X.25 links. In addition, X.25 acknowledgments between nodes (i.e., between hops) within a network were eliminated, with FR transferring flow control, as well as much of the error control functions to upper layer protocols above the FR layers 1 and 2. However, FR does perform simple *error detection* using the *cyclic redundancy check (CRC)* method, but does not perform *error correction.* As such, FR does not guarantee reliable delivery of packets. Finally, since each node in the network is not required to acknowledge packets on a hop-to-hop basis, nodes are not required to retain virtual circuit state information, thus making FR implementation simpler. All of these modifications meant that FR virtual connections had much less overhead resulting in greater throughput compared to X.25.

The Frame Relay standard is termed a *fast packet technology* that, like X.25, provides wide area network (WAN) services. More efficient than X.25 and cheaper than T-Carrier dedicated leased lines, the FR standard describes specifications at the *physical* and *data link* layers of the OSI RM.

Flag (7E)	Address	Data	FCS (CRC)	Flag (7E)

- Start
  Dilimeter
  (01111110)

- DLCI address (10 bits)
- Extended address
- FECN*, BECN**

- Payload up to 4096
  octets

- Frame
  Check
  Sequence
  (CRC)

- End
  Dilimiter
  (01111110)

*FECN (Forward Explicit Congestion Notification), 1 bit: *informs the end device if congestion was experienced from source to destination. FR only identifies congestion and leaves the flow control reaction to the upper layer or end device.*

** BECN (Backward Explicit Congestion Notification) 1 bit: *informs the end device upper layer if congestion was experienced in the opposite direction from destination to source.*

FIGURE 7.4 Frame Relay Packet Data Format.

While FR is not a reliable protocol, it is connection oriented, which means that a virtual (or logical) circuit is established through the network for each call. Each of these virtual circuits is identified by a *data link connection identifier (DLCI)*. Multiplexed links between FR nodes carry multiple virtual circuits throughout the packet switched network, and these virtual circuits can take the form of either a SVC or PVC. The FR packet shown in fig. 7.4, is variable in size, supporting a maximum data length of 4096 octets. The variable sized packet structure is well suited for the *"bursty"* nature of computer communication; however, it does not perform as well for real-time voice since the variable packet sizes leads to unpredictable delays.[8]

Frame Relay networks were either established by private organizations over leased dedicated digital links such as T-Carriers, or by service providers who developed public FR networks as a service to their subscribers. The public FR network switches were typically co-located with other switches within the traditional PSTN CO and switching centers. Today some service providers still offer FR services to ISPs and businesses; however, its popularity has declined significantly.

7.3.2 Asynchronous Transfer Mode (ATM)

Currently **asynchronous transfer mode (ATM)**, an ITU-T standard, is still offered by some service providers although support and use has declined due to the introduction of IP and *MPLS (multiprotocol label switching)* networks. However, ATM's unique *cell switching technology* and its ability to provide **quality-of-service (QoS)** to users made this standard especially popular in the 1990's as the need for broadband data transmission became evident. It was initially introduced as the technology to support *Broadband Integrated Services Digital Network (B-ISDN)*.

ATM is described as a *fast packet technology* that provides *connection-oriented, cell switched broadband services*. At the data link layer (layer 2) all ATM packets, also called *cells*, have a fixed length of 53 bytes. This is unique from the variable length packets used in FR, IP, and Ethernet.

---

[8] The frame relay Forum introduced FRF.11, Voice Over Frame Relay, which requires (1) a PVC between two communicating parties, and (2) the use of the same service provider between the parties.

ATM's fixed cell lengths allows it to easily accommodate any form of information including data, voice, and video. Since the cells have a fixed size, packet delays through the network are predictable as are the delays associated with cell switching. This is in contrast with variable sized packets where delays depend upon packet lengths and are more difficult to predict. In addition, fixed cells sizes allow ATM networks to quickly adjust to changing network conditions. However, since each cell is only 53 bytes long including header and payload, the overhead percentage on an ATM network is much greater compared to networks where the sizes of the packets are allowed to vary according to the amount and type of information transmitted. As a result, ATM is burdened with inefficiencies regarding bandwidth utilization; however, this is partially offset by the high switching speeds that are based upon fixed cell sizes.

The "*asynchronous*" part of ATM describes the manner in which the TDM time slots are allocated. In "*synchronous*" TDM, each circuit is allocated its own time slot regardless of the amount of data it may have to transmit. If the circuit has no data, the time slot is sent with no data, thus reducing overall bandwidth utilization. In contrast, ATM works like a statistical multiplexer, in that all time slots that are empty can be allocated to a circuit with data to transmit. Obviously, this later method is more efficient.

Like FR, ATM supports both SVC and PVC connections. There are three basic types of services offered by ATM. The first is the **constant bit rate (CBR)**, which supports applications, such as voice, that require a constant and guaranteed data rate. The second is the **variable bit rate (VBR)** service which supports "bursty" data traffic such as computer to computer communications. The third is the **available bit rate (ABR)** service, which provides time slots on an available basis and is a convenient method for LAN-to-LAN connectivity.

The ATM protocol consists of three basic layers as seen in figure 7.5. The **ATM physical layer** coincides with *layer 1* of the OSI RM. This layer is subdivided into the lower **physical media dependent (PMD) sublayer** and the upper **transmission convergence sublayer (TCS)**. The *PMD* sublayer is responsible for the line coding of logical data into a digital signal, placing this signal onto the medium, and providing bit timing. The physical medium used by ATM can be fiber optic cable, coaxial or twisted pair; however, it is typically paired with *SONET* fiber optic cables which will be discussed in section 7.4.1. The *TCS* prepares cell data for transmission over the physical medium and performs cell header error checking.

The **ATM layer** and the **ATM adaptation layer (AAL)** both operate at the *data link layer* of the OSI RM. The *ATM layer*, which is below AAL, multiplexes virtual circuits together, provides congestion

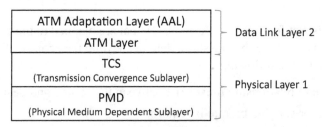

FIGURE 7.5 ATM Protocol Stack.

4 bits	8 bits	16 bits	3 bits	1 bit	8 bits	48 octets = 384 bits
GFC	VPI	VCI	PT	CLP	HEC	Payload

GFC – Appears at the user network interface (UNI) only. Provides congestion control

VPI – Identifies virtual path through the network

VCI – Identifies the user virtual circuit through the network

PT – Identifies user data from network service data

CLP – Identifies the priority of the cell

HEC – Cell error check/detection of the cell header only

FIGURE 7.6 ATM Cell Format.

control mechanisms, generates cell header, performs address translation, and provides sequential delivery of packets. Figure 7.6 shows the cell format. The description of the cell fields are presented below.

- Generic Flow Control (GFC). The GFC is a four-bit field used at the user interface to the network (i.e., UNI). This field is dropped within the core ATM network. GFC acts as a congestion control mechanism by flagging to end-user devices that data input into the network should be reduced.
- Virtual Path Identifier (VPI). VPI is an eight-bit field that identifies the *virtual path* through the network over the physical medium from input port to output port. As a virtual path, the physical medium is shared with other users.
- Virtual Channel Identifier (VCI). VCI is a sixteen-bit field that identifies the virtual channel, or virtual circuit, established for each user transmission.
- Payload-Type. PT is a three-bit field that identifies whether the payload contains user data traffic or network service information.
- Cell Loss Priority (CLP). CLP is a one-bit field that identifies a priority level for the transmitted cell. CLP is used during times of high congestion when lower priority cells must be dropped from the network.
- Header Error Control (HEC). HEC is an eight-bit field that provides error detection of the header but not the payload.

The *ATM adaptation layer (AAL)* resides above the *ATM layer* within the data link layer. The AAL consists of two sublayers: the **convergence sublayer (CS)** and the **segmentation and reassembly sublayer (SAR)**.

The *CS sublayer* consists of four classes (A, B, C, D), that are mapped to the services needed by the upper layer protocols. Describing the classes in detail is beyond the scope of this text, however, the classes are determined by the following:

- Whether a data timing relationship must exist between the source and destination.
- Whether a constant or variable bit rate is required.
- Whether the circuit is connection-oriented or connectionless.

The *SAR sublayer* takes user data and segments it into cell payloads for transmission. During reception, it performs the opposite function of removing the payloads and reassembling them back into user data for transfer to the upper layer protocols.

7.3.2.1 ATM Architecture

The ATM network is comprised of cell switches that are typically operated over optical fiber cable, although physical wired mediums can also be used. When operating over fiber optic cables, it is commonly paired with the *SONET* standard.

End-users access the network through **user network interfaces (UNIs)** which are in turn connected to layer 2 *ATM Edge Switches*. In fig. 7.7, we see that Ethernet LAN 1 is connected to a private ATM network through a *private* UNI. The Ethernet layer 2 protocol is exchanged for a layer 2 ATM cell at the UNI. ATM switches are connected to one another in both the private and public networks through the **network node interface (NNI)**, where both SVC and PVC circuits are supported. The *private* ATM network in this diagram is connected to a *public* ATM network, which is supported by a service provider, through a *public* UNI. Had both of the interfacing networks been public and operated by different service providers, the interface would be accomplished through a **network node interface-inter carrier interface (NNI-ICI)**. As the data in fig. 7.7 traverses the public ATM network, is finally reaches a *public* UNI that connects to Ethernet LAN 2, where data in cells are exchanged for Ethernet frames.

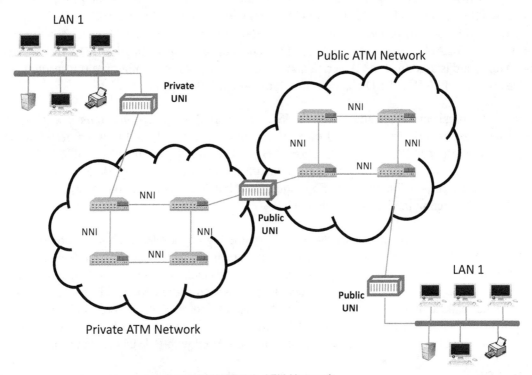

FIGURE 7.7 ATM Network.

7.3.3 Integrated Services Digital Network (ISDN)

The *Integrated Services Digital Network (ISDN)* is an ITU-T standard published in 1988 that described an evolutionary path from the analog voice PSTN to an all digital network capable of handling both voice and data traffic. It was a popular service in the 90's used by residential and businesses alike, especially in Europe. Today, its popularity has declined to the point that many service providers no longer offer ISDN services. However, we will briefly describe ISDN since it provides some insight regarding how digital telecommunications have matured over the years.

ISDN is a digital network where the end-user can gain access through the twisted pair local loop located at a business or residence. This enables users to gain direct digital access to the network at high data rates, and allows them to simultaneously conduct voice and data communications. *Narrowband ISDN(N-ISDN)* is considered the first generation offering a *digital circuit switching* approach. *Broadband ISDN (B-ISDN)* is the second generation that employs a *packet switching* approach based upon ATM technology. Outlined in an ITU-T recommendation, ISDN's requirements call for support of both PCM (pulse code modulation) digitized voice and data, as well as support for both circuit switched and packet switched approaches.

N-ISDN, which is based upon the PCM 64 kbps voice grade channel, consists mainly of two channel types, *B* and *D*. The B channel is 64 kbps used for PCM digital voice or a combination of other lower data rate traffic. The D channel, which is either 16 or 64 kbps, is used for either circuit switched control and signaling information, or packet switched data traffic. *Basic rate service* consists of two B channels and one D channel (2B + D) which is typically supported by existing two-wire pair local loops. The *primary rate service*, used by businesses that have higher capacity needs such as LAN-to-LAN connectivity, supports 23 B channels and 1 D channel for a total data rate of 1.544 Mbps, and is used in North America and Japan. Internationally in other regions, *primary rate service* consists of 30 B and 1 D channel for a total rate of 2.048 Mbps.

The user's terminal equipment attaches to the ISDN network through a *terminal adapter (TA)*. The TAs connect to network devices called *network termination 1 (NT1)* and *network termination 2 (NT2)*. NT1 is responsible for the aggregation of B and D channels, and the physical layer interface separating *customer premises equipment (CPE)* from service provider network devices. NT2 is an intelligent device responsible for switching functions at the data link and network layers. Typically, NT1 and NT2 are combined into a single device.

B-ISDN was the next evolution of ISDN, addressing the high data rate requirements that were not satisfied by N-ISDN. B-ISDN supports a channel data rate of 150 Mbps, and an overall aggregate rate of 600 Mbps. Because of the high aggregate data rates, it was felt at the time that B-ISDN could not be properly supported by two or four wire local loop lines, and many experts felt that full capability could not be realized until fiber optic loops into businesses and residences were in place. To ensure backward compatibility with N-ISDN, B-ISDN supports circuit switched and packet switched data, and D channel control and signaling. The ATM standard is used with B-ISDN packet switching.

While ISDN became popular in Europe, it did not receive as much attention in the United States mainly due to popularity of *Digital Subscriber Line (DSL)* at the time. Today, *Passive Optical Network (PON)* technology is quickly replacing traditional UTP wire local loops with a fiber optic cable. Compared to both DSL and B-ISDN, PON technology provides greater data capacity and is currently the choice for many service providers such as *Verizon FIOS*.

7.3.4 Carrier Ethernet

As we reviewed in chapter 6, switched full-duplex Ethernet essentially eliminates data collisions when used in a star or partial-mesh LAN configuration. The ability to easily expand and reconfigure Ethernet LANs has led to cheaper hardware costs and greater acceptance. Ethernet is the accepted standard for LANs; however, with the elimination of data collisions, many within the industry began looking at Ethernet as a potential solution for both metropolitan area networks (MANs) and WANs. Service providers have long understood how Ethernet MANs and WANs could be supported through the *Carrier Ethernet (CE)* standard, but there were still a few issues that needed to be addressed.

One of the major concerns in advancing Ethernet to carrier status was the network topology itself. Most Ethernet LANs use the *IEEE 802.1D Spanning Tree Protocol (STP)* to avoid loops, or circular connections, within the network. This may not always be possible or desirable when implementing a flexible MAN or WAN, and in fact causes inefficient use of available network bandwidth (i.e., poor network utilization). Let's look at why the spanning tree algorithm is needed, and how it works, by first looking at a simple four switch logical network example where spanning tree is not used. In fig. 7.8, each switch has two paths that allow them to reach all other switches

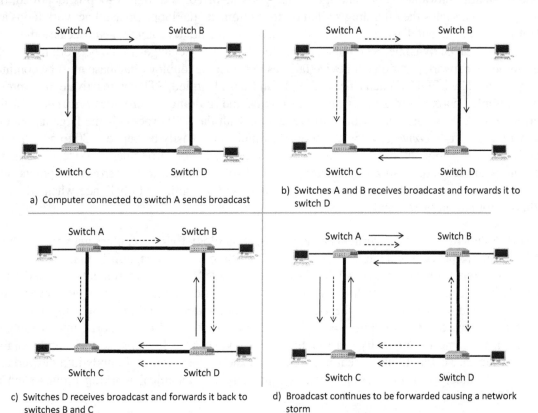

a) Computer connected to switch A sends broadcast

b) Switches A and B receives broadcast and forwards it to switch D

c) Switches D receives broadcast and forwards it back to switches B and C

d) Broadcast continues to be forwarded causing a network storm

FIGURE 7.8 Example of how a loop in switching network causes a network storm.

Computer © My Portfolio/Shutterstock.com; Network switch © IconBunny/Shutterstock.com in the network. Typically this would be done to ensure availability in the event of a network partition or device failure. The computer connected to switch A transmits a broadcast. Switch A repeats this broadcast through all connected ports, and eventually it reaches switches B and C. Upon receipt, switches B and C forwards the broadcast to switch D. Switch D receives the same broadcast from both of its network connections, and then forwards B's broadcast to C, and C's broadcast to B, essentially sending it in the opposite direction. Switches B and C sends the broadcast out of all of it ports, eventually reaching A. A then forwards the broadcast received from B and C, and the transmit loop continues infinitely resulting in a network storm. This same situation could happen with routine data traffic provided the routing tables are not up-to-date causing network congestion and duplicate message receipts.

So it's obvious from this simple example, that a mechanism is needed to prevent network loops from occurring. The *Spanning Tree Protocol (STP)*, which is implemented on network switches, provides a mechanism that prevents *logical* loops from occurring even if they are present on the *physical* topology. In order to eliminate network loops, network switches need to communicate with one another. Port information between switches are exchanged at the data link layer (layer 2) using special ***bridge protocol data units (BPDUs)***. This information is entered into a topology database, and a reference switch, known as a ***root bridge*** or ***root switch***, is then selected[9]. The *root bridge/switch* provides the central reference point for the mapping of the logical network which is done to identify unwanted loops and the switch ports involved. If a logical loop is identified, the STP protocol disables the offending switch ports to eliminate the loop. Once all network loops are identified and eliminated using this method, the network is said to be ***converged***. Because the logical network can be dynamic, STP must be able to adjust to any changes in the network that might be caused by network partitions or device failures. As such the topology database must be continuously updated by BPDUs. When a network link failure is identified, STP can reactivate those previously disabled ports in order to restore connectivity, and in doing so, provides *protection* for the entire network. However, one of the major concerns with the STP process is the large amount of time it takes to fully *converge* a logical network, which could easily be between 30 to 50 s (Hogg, 2009) depending upon the size and complexity of the network. For carrier class service, this amount of time is unacceptable, especially for large networks that connect to numerous end points over long distances. As such it presents service providers with a significant challenge when adopting Ethernet for use on MANs and WANs.

Despite STP's limitations, Ethernet is an attractive technology for carrier class networks because of its ability to provide scalable and flexible bandwidth to users. A capability that FR and ATM does not offer. With FR and ATM, bandwidth is provided in fixed increments or fixed-sized circuits. So if a user requires additional bandwidth, fixed circuits are *bonded* together even if the user only requires a fraction of the added circuit bandwidth. Bonding circuits together (i.e., combining ports together) requires additional equipment attached to the ports, thus leading to greater management complexity. Carrier Ethernet provides both low cost services and scalable service interfaces, which means that users pay for exactly the amount of bandwidth desired and not more. Therefore, a motivation exists within numerous technical working groups such as

---

[9] Any switch within the network can be selected as the root bridge (root switch).

IEEE, ITU, and the ***Metropolitan Ethernet Forum (MEF)***, to overcome the limitations posed by STP and to ensure *protection*[10] for *carrier* Ethernet networks at the MAN or WAN levels.

IEEE 802.1w introduced a faster version of STP called ***Rapid STP (RSTP)*** that performs network convergence after a failure in a matter of seconds compared to the 30 to 50 s required by STP. A ***Multiple STP (MSTP)*** defined by IEEE 802.1Q supports multiple virtual LANs (VLANs) by implementing separate RSTPs for each VLAN. Further details regarding RSTP and MSTP are beyond the scope of this textbook.

Another technology that enables the use of Ethernet at the MAN-level is ***IEEE 802.17 Resilient Packet Ring (RPR)*** which is a data link layer (layer 2) protocol designed for use over fiber optic cables which are arranged in a physical dual-ring configuration. Physical ring topologies are commonly used by service provides in metropolitan networks partly due to the efficiency of interconnecting numerous users to a shared high bandwidth fiber optic ring, vice providing separate and more costly point-to-point connections. In addition, metropolitan fiber ring topologies have been in existence for many years (e.g., FDDI, SONET), so applying Ethernet on existing ring topologies makes sense economically. The biggest hurdle, however, is the convergence time required by STP to map the logical topology, and then to disable ports that result in transmission loops. RPR is a data link layer protocol that is an alternative to STP, that provides faster network convergence and protection times.

Based upon Ethernet, RPR provides packet transmission over dual counter-rotating fiber optic rings that typically operate using the SONET[11] standard at the lower layers. The dual fiber rings provide network protection in the case of a link or node failure, while a modified data link MAC layer enables faster network convergence times. Implementing a dual-ring topology enables the ring network to quickly restore services in case of a failure. Often termed a "self-healing" network, service restoration can be achieved in a matter of milliseconds vice the seconds required by STP.

To better understand the modifications made at the MAC layer, we first consider how traditional Ethernet works over a shared medium. Since a centralized switch is not involved, as a packet transits the medium each node must process the packet to determine if it belongs to them by inspecting the destination address. If not, it passes the packet to the next node, which must also inspect and process the packet similarly. While this is adequate for a LAN, it causes delays, choke points, and possible data collisions on larger networks. This would be a big problem for a MAN architecture considering the greater number of nodes that can exist. With RPR, the MAC protocol is modified to control each nodes access to the shared ring by use of buffers or queues. Only those packets destined for the node will be queued and processed by the node, while all other packets pass through without queuing or processing. In addition, since the destination node removes the packet from the ring,[12] and because data traverses in both directions of the optical ring pair, greater data throughput rates are realized.

---

[10] Protection is the term used to ensure that a network can continue to operate when a link or node outage is experienced. With STP, this is done by restoring ports that were blocked during network convergence.

[11] Synchronous Optical Network (SONET) is discussed in section 7.4.

[12] In other ring topologies such as FDDI, it is the source node that removes the packet, and therefore even though the packet has reached its destination, it remains in the network taking up valuable network space.

Other benefits of RPR include quality-of-service support for service level agreements (SLAs), categorized into three basic classes, A, B, and C, which are based upon data latency and jitter[13] metrics, and a *fairness algorithm* which ensures that all nodes on the ring have equal bandwidth based upon their SLA class. In addition, since RPR is independent of the physical layer, it can be implemented over other physical mediums or standards such as WDM.[14] Unfortunately, RPR's modified MAC header is not compatible with the traditional Ethernet 802.3 LAN protocol, thus causing an increase to the complexity of the interface between the two.

ITU-T G.8032 Ethernet ring protection switching (ERPS), also known as ***ring automatic protection switching (R-APS)***, is another technology intended to provide carrier Ethernet capability using a ring protection method called the *automatic protection switching (APS) mechanism,* which can quickly detect and recover from network failures (i.e. in the order of milliseconds). Similar to RPR, ERP is independent of the physical medium, thus SONET or WDM can be used at the physical layer. It operates over several VPNs that operate within the MAN or WAN ring topology.

In order to prevent logical loops from occurring, the ERPS algorithm identifies a ***Ring Protection Link (RPL)*** between two nodes that are designated as the *"RPL owner"* and *"RPL neighbor"* (see fig. 7.9). During normal operations, the *RPL owner* and *neighbor* nodes block their RPL ports to ensure no loops exist in the network. Doing this breaks the continuity of the logical ring and

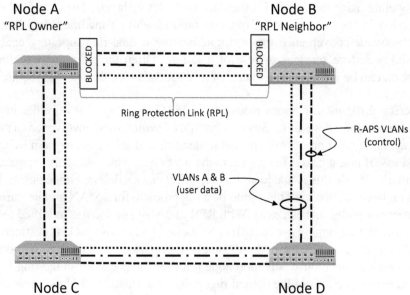

FIGURE 7.9 ITU-T G.8032 Ethernet Ring Protection (ERP).

Network switch © IconBunny/Shutterstock.com

---

[13] "Jitter" within a network defines the variation in time delay between received packets experienced at the destination often caused by network congestion.

[14] Wavelength division multiplexing (WDM) is discussed in section 7.5.

prevents a network loop from naturally occurring. In addition to the RPL, one of the virtual networks on the ring is designated as the ***R-APS VLAN*** which is used only for control and management of the ERPS, and not for data traffic. Each node connected to the ring operates an instance of the ERPS application which allows them to receive control *R-APS messages* from the *R-APS VLAN*. In order to keep all nodes apprised of the current logical network, a *forwarding database (FDB)* on the ERPS ring is used which contains packet forwarding information. The FDB uses the *Address Resolution Protocol (ARP)*[15] to map Ethernet MAC addresses to IP addresses.

In the event of a network failure, the node that detects the failure generates an R-APS message which is transmitted over the R-APS VLAN indicating to all nodes that a failure has occurred. The node then blocks its port and begins a "flush" process which updates the FDB database and initiates the *protection sequence*. The R-APS message indicating the failure is received by every node, including the nodes designated as the *RPL owner* and *RPL neighbor* nodes. The RPL owner and neighbor then restore connectivity to the impacted nodes by removing the blocks originally placed on the RPL link. By opening this link, the network can continue to transmit data despite the network failure, thus protecting the ring. Once the network failure is resolved, R-APS messages are sent to all nodes, the FDB is updated, and the RPL owner and neighbor nodes once again place blocks on the respective RPL ports.

7.3.4.1 Metropolitan Ethernet Forum, Carrier Ethernet (CE)

Today, carrier Ethernet (CE) solutions are quickly becoming the most popular methods for connecting LAN systems over a large geographic area. Continued technological developments enable better and more cost-effective solutions that are of great interest to both service providers and consumers alike. However, as we saw in the previous section, there are many ways CE can be provided and this can cause confusion regarding *quality-of-service (QoS)* and *service level agreements (SLAs)* between service providers, as well as increased complexity of the physical and service interfaces between provider networks. Several standards organizations have been principally involved in CE such as *ITU*, whose focus is on international standardization, the *Internet Engineering Task Force (IETF)* which deals with the IT aspects of supporting Internet standards, and *IEEE* whose responsibilities involve the 802.3 Ethernet protocol.

In 2001, the ***Metro Ethernet Forum (MEF)*** was formed with the focus of creating a CE framework that would help ensure interoperability across provider networks. Today, MEF membership consists of international service providers, software developers, and equipment manufacturers, all of whom share the common vision of advancing CE solutions through an Ethernet services defined framework. As such, an initial goal of MEF was to define the services framework that would enable the Ethernet protocol to operate over any reliable physical layer standard such as T-carrier, Frame Relay, ATM, SONET/SDH, WDM, MPLS, and others. As part of this effort, the standardization of *quality-of-service (QoS)* and *service level agreements (SLAs)* were also included to ensure consistency across provider networks. All of these efforts led to the development of several *MEF certification* processes specifically designed for services, manufacturing and professional competencies.

---

[15] Address Resolution Protocol (ARP) is used to map Ethernet MAC to IP addresses. ARP will be discussed in a following chapter.

The first MEF certification process designed for industry partners was ***CE 1.0***, and it required the successful completion of a set of rigorous tests designed to demonstrate framework compliance. In 2015 CE 1.0 testing was phased out and fully replaced by ***CE 2.0*** certification which was initially introduced two years earlier in 2013. Similar to CE 1.0, organizations achieving CE 2.0 certification successfully complete a number of test cases intended to demonstrate their compliance with the MEF requirements for the interoperability of both services and interfaces.

As part of the CE 2.0 certification, MEF introduced three new services, ***E-Tree, E-Access,*** and ***E-Transit***, which were added to the original CE 1.0 services that included ***E-Line*** and E-***LAN***. To better understand these services, we need to take a closer look at the example CE network in fig. 7.10. Subscribers interface to the ***metropolitan Ethernet network (MEN)*** through an interface provided by the network service provider called the ***user network interface (UNI)***. In fig. 7.10, we see that *subscriber 1* is an individual computer and *subscriber 2* is an organizational LAN. *Subscriber 1* connects to service provider *MEN 1*, while *subscriber 2* connects to *MEN 2*. Switches which make up the MEN are connected to one another through the ***internal network-to-network***

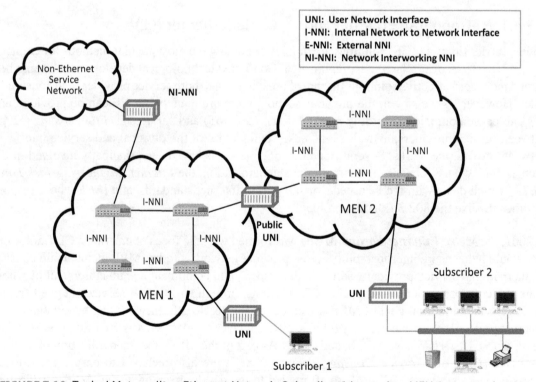

FIGURE 7.10 Typical Metropolitan Ethernet Network. Subscriber 1 located on MEN 1 communicates to subscriber 2 on MEN 2. Subscribers connect to their respective MENs through an UNI. Switches within the MEN connect with one another through the I-NNI. Two autonomous MENs connect together through an E-NNI, while other non-Ethernet networks can connect through a NI-NNI.

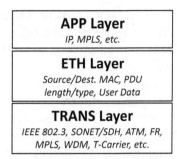

FIGURE 7.11 MEN Layered Network Model.

interface (I-NNI). Separate autonomous[16] MENs provided by different service providers connect their MENs together through an *external NNI (E-NNI)*. Finally, other networks such as ATM, FR, or MPLS, can interface to the MEN through a *networking interworking NNI (NI-NNI)*.

The MEN layered model (see fig. 7.11) consists of the *Ethernet services layer (ETH layer)*, *transport services layer (TRAN layer)* and an optional *applications services layer (APP layer)*. The network layer model is based upon client-server interaction, with each layer also containing *data*, *control*, and *management planes*.

The *ETH layer* is responsible for carrier Ethernet connection services across the MEN and the exchange of service frames that are used to support operations, administration, maintenance, and service provisioning. As the connection layer, it ensures that all internal and external interfaces are in compliance with the framework. Essentially, the ETH layer makes CE transport services possible in a service-aware manner that supports QoS and SLAs. It is this layer that is used to implement the various CE services (E-Line, E-LAN, E-Tree, E-Access, E-Transit).

The *TRAN layer* enables various network protocols at the lower OSI RM layers to be supported such as SONET/SDH, MPLS, IEEE 802.3, and others mentioned previously. These "other" networks interface to the MEN through the *NI-NNI*.

The *APP layer* supports user network protocols and applications such as IP, MPLS, etc., that are carried over the ETH layer.

Within each of the MEN layers exists three operational planes. These planes can be thought of as enabling different aspects of the MEN. The *Data Plane* is responsible for data *PDUs (Protocol Data Unit)* and ensuring that subscriber traffic reaches its destination. The *control plane* basically supports management functions that support signaling and control. The *management plane* is responsible for administrative functions such as accounting, performance, security, and maintenance. Obviously, for a service provided CE network, these planes are essential to ensure that the various subscriber SLAs are met, and that there is efficient provisioning of services to all subscribers.

---

[16] An autonomous network is one that is managed and operated by a single service provider. Nonautonomous networks are managed and operated by different owners or service providers. While nonautonomous networks may operate on the same standards and protocols, each organization configures their routers and switches according to their own organizational policies.

MEN leverages protocols developed by other standards committees, and establishes the framework from which Ethernet connectivity services are defined and offered. The services are delivered over **Ethernet virtual circuits (EVCs)** between subscriber UNIs. The attributes associated with the EVC are dependent upon the Ethernet service type, which under CE 2.0 consists of five types described below.

E-Line. This is a point-to-point EVC service provided between two subscriber UNIs as depicted in fig. 7.12. In its basic form, E-Line provides a *symmetric* connection on a *best effort*[17] basis. However, *asymmetric* connections can also be supported. In addition, high performance SLAs can be provisioned to subscribers requiring lower packet delays, lower data losses, and improved network availability, for a higher service cost.

E-LAN. This service depicted in fig. 7.13, provides a multipoint-to-multipoint EVC service used to connect multiple subscriber UNIs.

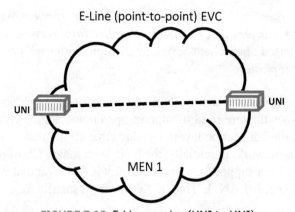

FIGURE 7.12 E-Line service (UNI to UNI).

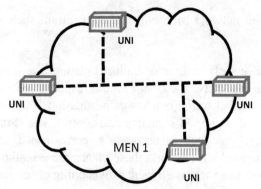

FIGURE 7.13 E-LAN service (multiple UNIs interconnected over the MEN).

---

[17] PDU delivery is not guaranteed. This is similar to IP which is a best effort protocol.

E-Tree (root-to-leaf) EVC

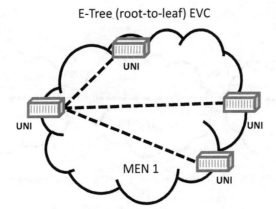

FIGURE 7.14 E-Tree service (root and leaf EVC).

E-Access EVC

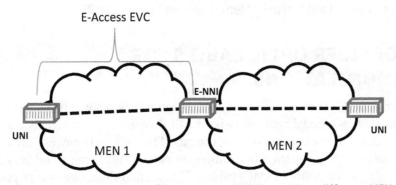

FIGURE 7.15 E-Access service (EVC between UNIs located on different MENs).

E-Tree. The E-Tree service, shown in fig. 7.14, has a single "root" UNI which branches out to several "leaf" UNIs. The "leaf" UNIs can only exchange data frames with the "root" UNI. E-Tree services are used for such requirements as Internet access and multicast or broadcast packet transmissions. More sophisticated services allow leaf UNIs to communicate with two or more root UNIs. Doing this enables redundant root designs.

E-Access. E-Access (see fig. 7.15) is used by service providers to help establish connectivity between UNIs on different MENs. Essentially, if a subscriber on one MEN connects to another subscriber on a different MEN, the virtual connection travels through the E-NNI. An E-Access service provides the connection and services from the UNI to the E-NNI, and for the service provider, it is more efficient, has higher throughput, and lower costs.

E-Transit. This service, depicted in fig. 7.16, addresses the case where an EVC between two UNIs traverses several MENs. An intermediate MEN that does not contain a user end point (i.e., UNI), provides transit through its MEN to support the EVC connection. This means that the EVC simply passes through this MEN, and is classified an E-Transit service between E-NNIs.

This section only served to introduce basic concepts associated with CE and the MEF. Significant work is planned for the MEF framework to include *"Third Network Services"* which will be focused

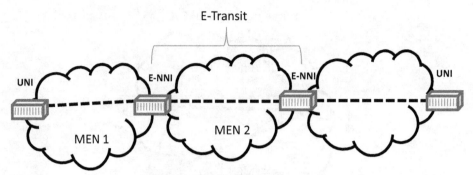

FIGURE 7.16 E-Transit service (E-NNI to E-NNI connection).

on expanding CE 2.0 to include a new orchestrated layer 1 to 3 connectivity service, as well as an orchestrated layer 4 to 7 cloud service. (Metro Ethernet Forum, 2017)

7.4 USE OF FIBER OPTIC CABLES FOR TELECOMMUNICATIONS

The use of fiber optic (FO) cables for telecommunication has many advantages over traditional guided mediums such as coaxial cable or twisted pair. Because optical signals operate at a much higher frequency than RF or electrical signals, (i.e., the THz vice GHz ranges), optical signals have a much greater data carrying capacity. In addition, an optical signal can travel very long distances when used with single mode fiber (SMF) cables. This section discusses two physical layer standards that are commonly used today—SONET/SDH and WDM/DWDM.

7.4.1 Synchronous Optical Network (SONET) and Synchronous Digital Hierarchy (SDH)

Synchronous Optical Network (SONET) is a North American OSI physical layer standard defined by the *American National Standards Institute (ANSI)* in 1988 for optical communications over fiber optic cables. ITU-T adopted the SONET concept and developed an international version called the *Synchronous Digital Hierarchy (SDH)*, which is very similar to SONET, with a few minor exceptions regarding the service bit rates that are offered. Today, SONET and SDH are still used globally; however, its popularity has declined since the introduction of *wavelength division multiplexing (WDM)* and *dense wavelength division multiplexing (DWDM)*.

Although based upon the transmission of an optical signal over fiber optic cables, SONET and SDH standards address both electrical and optical segments. This is because conversions between electrical and optical signals are required at communicating end points, and by OEO (optical-electrical-optical) repeaters that are used to boost optical signal strength over long distances. In order to distinguish between the two signals, different labels are used to describe raw bit rates. *Synchronous transport signal (STS)* is used to describe the SONET electrical signal. A SONET *STS-1* defines a raw data rate of 51.84 Mbps. The equivalent *optical* signal is labeled as an *optical carrier (OC)*, and an *OC-1*

TABLE 7.2 SONET/SDH Hierarchy of Raw Bit Rates.

Optical	SONET (electrical)	SDH (electrical)	Raw Bit Rate	No. DS0 supported
OC-1	STS-1	NA	51.84 Mbps	627
OC-3	STS-3	STM-1	155.52 Mbps	1344
OC-12	STS-12	STM-4	622.08 Mbps	8064
OC-24	STS-24	STM-8	1.24416 Gbps	16,128
OC-48	STS-48	STM-16	2.48832 Gbps	32,256
OC-192	STS-192	STM-64	9.953 Gbps	129,024
OC-768	STS-768	STM-256	39.813 Gbps	516,096
OC-3072	STS-3072	STM-1024	159.252 Gbps	2,064,384

optical signal bit rate is equivalent to an STS-1, with a raw bit rate of 51.84 Mbps. OC and STS services are hierarchical, so an STS-3 is equivalent to an OC-3 at a raw bit rate of 155.52 Mbps, and so on (see Table 7.2).

The *ITU-T SDH* version of the standard has a slightly different hierarchy in raw bit rate services; although the basic data frame format is the same. The electrical signal for SDH is called the *Synchronous Transport Module (STM)*, which starts at an *STM-1* rate of 155.52 Mbps. STM-1 is equivalent to STS-3 and OC-3 in raw bit rates. While these rates differ slightly in nomenclature, they are compatible. Table 7.2 lists some of the SONET/SDH service rates commonly used.

Although considered a physical layer standard, elements of what we could consider layer 2 functionality such as line coding and logical data framing, are part of the SONET format. This means that both SONET and SDH provide specific data formats. The SONET[18] data frame, shown in fig. 7.17, is based upon the fundamental DS0 64 kbps uncompressed voice grade channel. Similar to T-Carrier, each SONET/SDH frame supports only one byte of each DS0. As an example, an STS-1 can support 672 DS0s; however only one byte of each DS0 is in a single SONET STS-1 frame. Therefore, a frame rate of 8000 frames/s is required to provide sufficient data transfer to support multiple DS0s (i.e., 1 byte $\times$ 8 bits/byte $\times$ 8000 frames/s = 64 kbps = 1 DS0).

The SONET data frame in fig.7.17 is for an STS-1, 51.84 Mbps service; however, the formats for higher bit rate services are similar. Depicted as 90 bytes per row with 9 rows, each STS-1 row

---

[18] The SONET data frame in fig. 7.17 is for a STS-1 service which has a bit rate of 51.84 Mbps. Other SONET rates such as STS-3, have similar data frame formats but with greater payload lengths.

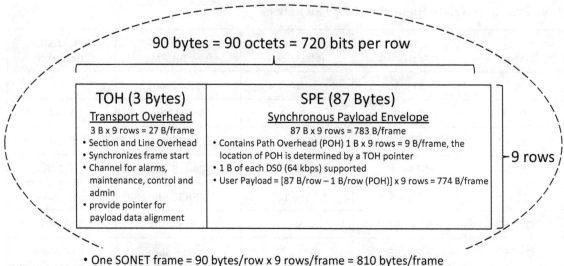

- One SONET frame = 90 bytes/row x 9 rows/frame = 810 bytes/frame
- Frame rate = 8000 frames/s
- STS-1 total bit rate = 810 B/frame x 8000 frames/s x 8 bits/B = 51.84 Mbps
- STS-1 Payload supported = 774 B/frame x 8000 frame/s x 8 bits/B = 49.536 Mbps

FIGURE 7.17 STS-1 SONET Frame.

contains three bytes called the ***transport overhead (TOH)***, that are dedicated for ***section*** and ***line*** overhead information. A *section* is responsible for proper data formatting during the OEO conversion process between network elements such as routers, optical repeaters and multiplexers [see fig. 7.18(b)]. The *line* consists of one or more *sections* and is responsible for synchronization and multiplexing of SONET frames. The remainder of the bytes in each row (90 bytes minus 3 bytes, or 87 bytes) is termed the ***synchronous payload envelope (SPE)*** which contains ***path overhead (POH)*** and payload data. *POH* is one byte of information used to map SONET data to non-SONET interfaces, and is responsible for end-to-end connectivity. The STS-1 format is essentially the same for STM and other STS service rates with the exception of minor changes in row length. For example, an STS-3 or STM-1 would have a total row length of three times that of an STS-1, or 3×90 bytes/row = 270 bytes per row for a STS-3.

SONET/SDH depends on accurate timing references in order to provide accurate high data rate framing. Use of a *Stratum 1 primary reference source (PRS)*, as defined by the ANSI/T1.101 standard, provides SONET/SDH *synchronous network timing*. The ANSI standard identifies four basic ***Stratum*** levels that essentially categorize clock accuracy by estimating the length of time between frame slips caused specifically by clock inaccuracies. For example, the time between slips for Stratum 1 is estimated at 72 days, for Stratum 2, 7 days, and for Stratum 3, 6 to 7 hours.

With synchronous network timing, network clocks are constrained within specified frequency and phase limits by a hierarchical timing network in which the master source is a Stratum 1 clock. The hierarchical structure starts with a master Stratum 1 PRS that provides a reference source for less accurate Stratum 2 clocks located within the network. Stratum 2 clocks, in turn,

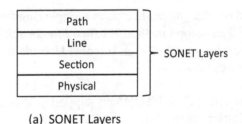

(a) SONET Layers

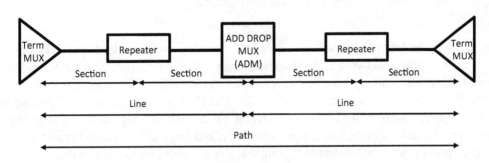

(b) SONET Architecture

FIGURE 7.18 SONET Architecture.

distribute the timing reference to lower level clocks (i.e., Stratum 3 and 4 timing sources). This master-slave arrangement helps to ensure that accurate data framing takes place. Today, synchronous network timing is a popular method used in many high-speed networks.

The SONET protocol layered structure is shown in fig. 7.18(a) and the physical architecture is shown in fig. 7.18(b). As described above, the *section layer* converts electrical signals to optical signals and back. This process exists between terminal multiplexers, repeaters, and ***add drop multiplexers (ADMs)***. The *ADM* is an optical multiplexer that combines several optical signals of different wavelengths together, and is a key piece of equipment for any optical telecommunications service. The *line layer* connects ***line terminating equipment (LTE)***, such as the ADM and terminal multiplexer shown in fig. 7.18(b). A *line* consists of one or more *sections*, and is responsible for the synchronization and multiplexing of SONET frames. Finally, the *path layer* ensures an end-to-end data path through SONET and provides the interface to end-user systems or other networks. The device that is located at each of the path end points is called a ***Path Terminating Equipment (PTE)***.

The SONET architecture can be implemented in any physical topology. For high reliability communications that can survive network failures, a *dual fiber optic ring* topology is typically used. Similar to other ring topologies, a network failure experienced on one of the rings can initiate the ***automatic protection switching (APS)*** procedure which is a self-healing process invoked to reestablish network connectivity. Two different APS protection mechanisms can be implemented. The ***path-switched*** method involves data traffic on each of the dual rings moving in opposite directions. During normal operations, each node inspects the traffic on both rings and selects the better of the two signals. There would be little impact in case of a single ring failure since traffic from both rings is received continuously. The second method is called *line-switching, or line-switched,* where one of the dual rings is active, and the other is on standby. Upon failure of the active ring, the standby ring is activated and resumes traffic flow.

As a physical layer standard, SONET/SDH can support just about any data link layer protocol including ATM, FR, T-Carrier, carrier Ethernet, etc.

7.4.2 Wavelength Division Multiplexing (WDM) and Dense Wavelength Division Multiplexing (DWDM)

The popularity of the Internet and the thirst for ever-increasing network speeds pushed many service providers towards optical network technologies. Thanks to the *dot.com* era which followed the signing of the *Telecommunications Act of 1996*, a robust fiber optic cable infrastructure was laid across the United States and overseas in the late 90's. SONET/SDH became the answer for many service providers; however, SONET/SDH presented several issues such as a high costs for implementation and operations, complexity inherent in the technology, and large data overhead requirements. As a consequence providers within the industry sought better and more economical solutions.

Fortunately, *wavelength division multiplexing (WDM),* a concept that had been proven in the laboratory in the 1980s, became a viable option. Operating over existing fiber optic cables, WDM supports multiple optical channels on a single fiber cable by separating each channel by wavelength, or commonly termed *"colors of light,"* and multiplexing them together into a single aggregate for transmission (see fig.7.19). This is similar to frequency division multiplexing for RF channels, in which each channel is modulated over a different carrier frequency and then aggregated together into a broadband signal. For WDM, since higher optical frequencies are used instead of RF, channels are described in terms of wavelength vice frequency (recall the relationship between frequency

and wavelength: $\text{frequency} = \dfrac{\text{speed-of-light (vacuum)}}{\text{wavelength } (\lambda)}$).

In chapter one, it was mentioned that the ITU-T organized optical transmission wavelengths into windows for use in telecommunications. The organization of ITU designated windows was

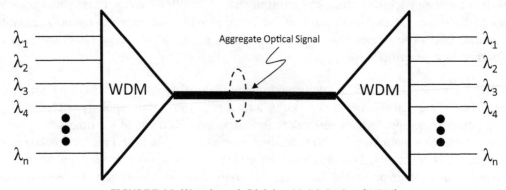

FIGURE 7.19 Wavelength Division Multiplexing (WDM).

shown in Table 1.2 and is repeated below. WDM primarily operates at the 1310 nm (O-Band) and 1550 nm (C-Band) wavelengths and can support a number of channels[19] over long distances using SMF (single mode fiber) optical cables, or shorter distances using MMF (multi-mode fiber) optical cables. Originally expensive and complex to implement, advances in light sources, detectors and optical amplifier technologies have made WDM an attractive alternative to SONET.

A significant advantage of WDM over SONET are the costs associated with network capacity expansion. Increasing capacity over a SONET network leads to high costs since equipment must specifically be replaced to support the higher rates. In contrast, WDM capacity can be increased by simply adding a wavelength channel to the multiplexer. This solution does not require replacement of equipment, only a modification to the multiplexer. Although SONET and WDM are physical layer technologies, SONET can be implemented as one of the WDM wavelength channels. Therefore, both can be supported over the same fiber infrastructure.

There are three basic versions of WDM: *wavelength division multiplexing (WDM)*, *dense wavelength division multiplexing (DWDM)*, and *coarse wavelength division multiplexing (CWDM)*. As the name describes, *"dense"* WDM can accommodate between 40 and 80 channels over a single FO cable depending upon the spacing allocated between the channels (i.e., 100 GHz spacing between channels to support 40 channels, 50 GHz spacing to support 80 channels). DWDM operates in the optical C-Band window (1530 nm to 1565 nm), and has benefitted from technical advances in optical amplification (i.e., Raman and EDFA optical amplifiers). DWDM is commonly used for long distance telecommunications over SMF optical cables. CWDM operates over the

TABLE 7.3 ITU-T Optical Transmission Bands (Window)

	Wavelength (nm)		Frequency (THz)	
Band	From	To	From	To
850 Band	810	890	370.37	337.08
O (Original Band)	1260	1360	238.10	220.59
E (Extended Band)	1360	1460	220.59	205.48
S (Short Wavelength Band)	1460	1530	205.48	196.08
C (Conventional Band)	1530	1565	196.08	191.69
L (Long Wavelength Band)	1565	1625	191.69	184.62
U (Ultra long Wavelength Band)	1625	1675	184.62	179.10

---

[19] Initially only two channels were supported by WDM. Improvements in optical technologies have improved this number dramatically.

same original WDM 1550 nm and 1310 nm bands. CWDM supports approximately 16 channels over a FO cable, but allows for wider spacing between adjacent channels in order to accommodate cheaper, and therefore less capable, source and detector equipment.

Today, the WDM physical layer, to include DWDM and CWDM, can support numerous protocols. As examples, SONET, Internet Protocol (IP), and ATM can all be directly implemented onto a WDM channel. This gives service providers significant flexibility in supporting a wide range of user requirements.

7.5 VOICE TECHNOLOGY SYSTEMS FOR BUSINESSES AND ORGANIZATIONS

With the advent of the PSTN into businesses and organizations, efficiencies were quickly realized as better communications contributed to improved work flows, thus resulting in increased productivity. No longer did businesses have to rely upon face-to-face meetings or telegrams with suppliers and manufacturers. The PSTN gave organizations an ability to communicate in real time.

However, when it came to internal organizational calls within the same building, or to organizational offices separated geographically, it didn't make sense to always use PSTN switches. Large organizations realized the need to own their own switches to enable calls within their organization without involving the PSTN central office (CO). As an example, consider a hotel that has 100 rooms, each room equipped with a telephone. Guests need to be able to connect to the outside world, as well as to other rooms and services within the hotel itself. It would be impractical for a hotel of this size to have 100 dedicated local loop lines connected physically to the PSTN CO, and it would be just as impractical to require a connection to a CO switch when a guest is simply calling down to the hotel's front desk. By owning its own switch called a *Private Branch eXchange (PBX)*, the hotel can easily connect guests to other guest rooms or to hotel services without having to involve the PSTN. If a caller needs an outside line, then the PBX accommodates by providing a local loop line connected to the PSTN CO. By doing this, fewer dedicated phone lines are required between the hotel and the CO, thus reducing PSTN costs. However, since the PBX is owned exclusively by the organization, the PSTN would not be responsible for its upkeep. So although the hotel saves on PSTN costs, it must procure PBX hardware and software, and hire experts who are trained to handle all aspects of PBX operations and maintenance.

Like the PSTN switch, the early PBX performed only analog voice circuit switching. Today, the PBX is a sophisticated computerized switching system that connects digital voice and data, in addition to traditional analog voice calls. Organizational equipment such as analog telephones, IP phones, LANs, and standalone servers connect to the PBX through *line cards*, which are specific to the type of device or network being connected. The *trunk* side of the PBX connects to an enterprise WAN, PDN, PSTN, or the Internet. Large organizations that have presence in different geographical areas will typically network their PBX systems together through trunk lines leased from service providers, thus providing an efficient way to communicate internally.

However, the complexity of maintaining and operating these systems can grow quickly, thus resulting in the need for organizational IT departments, which represents significant costs to the organization.

While PBX systems are equally beneficial to small- and medium-sized businesses, the costs associated with staffing IT departments are typically out-of-reach for these organizations. Fortunately, service providers offer a similar, more cost effective service called **Central Exchange (CENTREX)**. Offered by service providers at a monthly cost, *CENTREX* offers many of the same features of a PBX but without the need to own, maintain, or operate any of the switching equipment. CENTREX equipment resides at the CO with connections to the organization made through multiplexed fiber optic or copper lines, or through the existing local loop wiring. While costs to the organization are less than if owning a PBX, flexibility in customization and in adding desired features are limited with CENTREX since the service provider must cater configurations to the general market.

Today, the use of **automatic call distributors (ACDs)** are widely used especially in the services industry. Similar to the PBX, ACDs are switches owned by the organization that can accept consumer calls in a *non-blocking* manner. *Non-blocking* means that arriving calls are placed in queue in the order that they arrive. This is in contrast to *blocking*, which means that incoming calls are *blocked* if no open lines are available. With the older blocking method, consumers attempting to call during peak periods would receive a busy signal, forcing them to redial until they gained access to an open line. Today with non-blocking systems, the call is placed in queue without requiring the caller to redial even if an open line is not available.

ACDs are typically equipped with an **interactive voice response (IVR)** system where the caller is asked several questions from an automated source. The intent of the questions and caller responses are to help direct the call automatically to the correct department within the organization. Since IVR does not require an operator to direct the call, significant cost savings can be realized by the organization.

In addition ACDs, like PBXs, can be networked over a large geographic area. This means that organizational departments are not required to reside within the same building or region. Large service organizations will typically disperse departments such as call centers to locations where labor may be cheaper. To the caller, the ACD behaves as if all of the departments were collocated. In reality however, the entire organization may be widely scattered across the globe, to even include employees working from their homes.

KEY TERMS

American National Standards Institute (ANSI)	automatic protection switching (APS)	Cable Communications Policy Act of 1984
asynchronous transfer mode (ATM)	Bell Operating Companies (BOCs)	carrier ethernet (CE)
		Carterfone

coarse wavelength division multiplexing (CWDM)
country code (CC)
central office (CO)
central office exchange (COE)
channelized service
common channel signaling (CCS)
Communications Act of 1934
competitive local exchange carriers (CLECs)
customer premises equipment (CPE)
demarc
dense wavelength division multiplexing (DWDM)
digital signal zero (DS0)
E-Access
E-LAN
E-Line
E-Transit
E-Tree
Ethernet ring protection switching (ERPS)
Ethernet virtual circuits (EVCs)
Federal Communications Commission (FCC)
frame relay (FR)
Hush-A-Phone
in-band signaling

interexchange carrier (IXC)
international gateway facility (IGF)
Internet
Interstate Commerce Commission (ICC)
interLATA
intraLATA
integrated services digital network (ISDN)
Kingsbury Agreement of 1913
local access and transport area (LATA)
local exchange carriers (LECs)
local loop
Metropolitan Ethernet Forum (MEF)
Modified Final Judgment (MFJ) of 1982
national destination code (NDC)
network node interface (NNI)
numbering plan administration (NPS)
optical carrier (OC)
out-of-band signaling
permanent virtual circuit (PVC)
plain old telephone service (POTS)

public data network (PDN)
public switched telephone system (PSTN)
quality-of-service (QoS)
Regional Bell Holding Companies (RBHCs)
resilient packet ring (RPR)
ring automatic protection switching (R-APS)
ring protection link (RPL)
signaling system 7 (SS7)
spanning tree protocol (STP)
subscriber number (SN)
switch virtual circuit (SVC)
synchronous digital hierarchy (SDH)
synchronous transport mode (STM)
synchronous transport signal (STS)
synchronous optical network (SONET)
T-Carrier
Telecommunications Act of 1996
terminal adapter (TA)
unchannelized service
user network interface (UNI)
wavelength division multiplexing (WDM)
wide area network (WAN)

CHAPTER PROBLEMS

1. Which act or decision created the Federal Communications Commission (FCC) to oversee telecommunications in the United States?
   a. The Kingsbury Agreement
   b. Communications Act of 1934
   c. The Modified Final Judgment (MFJ)
   d. Telecommunications Act of 1996

Answer: b

2. Which act or decision led to the divestiture of AT&T?
   a. The Kingsbury Agreement
   b. Communications Act of 1934
   c. The Modified Final Judgment (MFJ)
   d. Telecommunications Act of 1996

Answer: c

3. Which act or decision allowed new entrants to enter the telecommunications market (known as the *"dot com boom"*)?
   a. The Kingsbury Agreement
   b. Communications Act of 1934
   c. The Modified Final Judgment (MFJ)
   d. Telecommunications Act of 1996

Answer: d

4. The Kingsbury Agreement essentially re-affirmed the idea that AT&T could continue to operate as a regulated monopoly free from competition.
   a. True
   b. False

Answer: a

5. Describe how *"Hush-A-Phone"* and *"Cartefone"* helped to change regulatory policy regarding AT&T.

6. What was the significance of the 1982 MFJ?
   a. It was interpreted as a government stance to allow AT&T to function as a regulated monopoly
   b. It was a Supreme Court ruling that allowed devices not manufactured by AT&T to be attached to AT&T telephones
   c. It was a judgment that led to the divestiture of AT&T
   d. It allowed new telecommunications companies to compete fairly with AT&T

Answer: c

7. What did the *"Cable Communications Policy Act of 1984"* do?

8. What was the significance of the *Telecommunications Act of 1996*?

9. What is the importance of NPA?
   a. It provides a standard telephone numbering scheme that enables call connection at the international level
   b. It provides specifications for international IP addressing
   c. It was an attempt to standardize international telephone numbering; however it never caught on
   d. It was the first standards organization which led to the creation of ANSI and OSI

Answer: a

10. What is the difference between an *intraLATA* and *interLATA* call?

11. IXCs are used to connect *interLATA* calls.
   a. True
   b. False

Answer: a

12. Today the PSTN UTP local loop still supports analog voice signals.
    a. True
    b. False

Answer: a

13. The PSTN local loop is a *dedicated* user link connecting the office or residence to the PSTN central office (CO).
    a. True
    b. False

Answer: a

14. Channelized T-1 carrier is a dedicated digital link that consists of _____ DS0s, _____ bps per DS0, _____ bits per frame, _____ frames per second.
    a. 64 DS0s, 64 bps/DS0, 192 bits/frame, 1000 frames/s
    b. 48 DS0s, 64 bps/DS0, 192 bits/frame, 1000 frames/s
    c. 24 DS0s, 64 kbps/DS0, 193 bits/frame, 8000 frames/s
    d. 12 DS0s, 64 kbps/DS0, 193 bits/frame, 8000 frames/s

Answer: c

15. A channelized T-1 frame must have a frame rate of 8000 frames/s in order to support 24 DS0 channels.
    a. True
    b. False

Answer: a

16. A DS0 is a basic 64 kbps building block for T-1 and SONET standards.
    a. True
    b. False

Answer: a

17. A DS0 has a data rate of 64 kbps. Why?
    a. A DS0 is equivalent to a single voice grade channel with a bandwidth of 4 kHz. Using PCM, the equivalent uncompressed data rate is therefore 64 kbps
    b. A DS0 is equivalent to 16, 4 kHz voice grade channels
    c. A DS0 is equivalent to 8, 4 kHz voice grade channels traveling at 8000 frames/s
    d. A DS0 rate of 64 kbps was randomly selected

Answer: a

18. The unchannelized T-1 is not divided into 24 DS0s, and therefore can support data applications that do not neatly fall into 64 kbps channels.
    a. True
    b. False

Answer: a

19. Both T-1 and E-1 carriers operate at a data rate capacity of 1.544 Mbps.
    a. True
    b. False

Answer: b

20. Select the correct statement(s) regarding Synchronous Optical Network (SONET).
    a. STS and STM both represent electrical signaling bit rates
    b. SONET and SDH are both based-upon OC optical carriers
    c. SONET and SDH both implement a synchronous timing scheme to ensure accurate data clocks
    d. All of the above are correct

Answer: d

21. A SONET frame must have a frame rate of 8000 frames/s in order to support 672 DS0 channels.
    a. True
    b. False

Answer: a

22. With SONET, the optical building block is termed an OC-1, and its electrical counterpart is STS-1. Both OC-1 and STS-1 equates to a capacity of 51.84 Mbps.
    a. True
    b. False

Answer: a

23. A SONET or SDH link can be implemented on a WDM channel.
    a. True
    b. False

Answer: a

24. A SONET frame consists of _____ bytes per frames, _____ frames per second, which support _____ DS0s.
    a. 410 bytes/frames, 64,000 frames/s, 672 DS0s/frame
    b. 410 bytes/frames, 64,000 frames/s, 572 DS0s/frame
    c. 810 bytes/frames, 8000 frames/s, 372 DS0s/frame
    d. 810 bytes/frames, 8000 frames/s, 672 DS0s/frame

Answer: d

25. What is a true statement regarding WDM?
    a. WDM is another name for SONET.
    b. SONET can be implemented onto one of the wavelengths in a DWDM multiplexer.
    c. Since WDM and SONET are competing optical signal standards, they cannot be used together on the same fiber optic cable.
    d. There are no true statements above.

Answer: b

26. What is true regarding the comparisons between asynchronous transfer mode (ATM) and Frame Relay (FR)?
    a. FR has predictable data delays compared to ATM where delays are variable
    b. ATM cannot easily support real-time voice, whereas FR readily supports real-time voice
    c. FR consists of variable sized data frames, whereas ATM is comprised of fixed cell sizes
    d. Neither ATM nor FR are connection-oriented protocols

Answer: c

27. Select the correct statements regarding asynchronous transfer mode (ATM):
    a. ATM is a fixed-length cell standard that supports voice, video and data
    b. ATM is connection-oriented
    c. ATM offers predictability regarding latency; therefore ATM can offer quality-of-service (QoS) to users
    d. All of the above are correct

Answer: d

28. Frame Relay (FR) is a fixed-length protocol that is best used for *"bursty-type"* traffic between local area networks (LANs). FR is a connectionless protocol at the data link layer.
    a. True
    b. False

Answer: b

29. Describe the *Spanning Tree Protocol (STP)* and why it is needed on Ethernet LANs.

30. Both ERPS and RPR describe the same technology standard.
    a. True
    b. False

Answer: b

31. *Carrier Ethernet*, describes the use of the Ethernet protocol for MAN and WAN connectivity at the OSI RM Layer 2. With CE 1.0, E-Line, E-LAN and E-Tree services are offered.
    a. True
    b. False

Answer: a

32. What are the differences between WDM, DWDM, and SONET?

33. The demarcation point separates the CPE from the service provider (carrier) network. It also separates network responsibilities between the customer and the network provider.
    a. True
    b. False

Answer: a

34. The PSTN local loop is implemented on which physical layer mediums?
    a. Fiber Optic
    b. UTP
    c. Wireless
    d. All of the above

Answer: d

35. Common channel signaling (CCS) is a dedicated signaling network that is separate from the actual voice and data traffic networks.
    a. True
    b. False

Answer: a

36. The Common channel signaling (CCS) is a separate *"in-band"* signaling network used by the PSTN to provide signaling, connection and control functions to users on the network.
    a. True
    b. False

Answer: b

37. The PSTN makes use of both *in-band* and *out-of-band* signaling and control.
    a. True
    b. False

Answer: a

38. Select the correct statement(s) regarding the PBX.
    a. Organizations using PBXs must have technical expertise on their staffs to operate and maintain them
    b. A PBX can support both analog and digital communications
    c. Numerous PBXs can be configured as a distributed network to support organizational requirements
    d. All are correct

Answer: d

39. Select the correct statement(s) regarding CENTREX.
    a. CENTREX systems reside at the service providers central office, however, the operations and maintenance are still the responsibility of the user organization
    b. CENTREX systems reside at the service providers central office, and the operations and maintenance responsibilities belong to the service provider
    c. CENTREX systems offer greater flexibility of services and customization to users than the PBX
    d. All are correct

Answer: b

40. ACDs are typically equipped with an IVR system.
    a. True
    b. False

Answer: a

CHAPTER 8

Broadband Access

> *"Broadband access is the great equalizer, leveling the playing field so that every willing and able person, no matter their station in life, has access to the information and tools necessary to achieve the American Dream." Michael K. Powell, former chairman of the Federal Communications Commission.*
>
> (https://www.brainyquote.com/search_results.html?q=broadband+access)

8.1 INTRODUCTION

High-speed digital networks have revolutionized just about every aspect of our daily lives. Large organizations were the first to enjoy the benefits of high speed digital networks in areas such as airline reservation systems, automated supply chain, inventory management, and business-to-business (B2B) ecommerce. These organizations could afford broadband access through dedicated T-Carriers, fiber optic cables, B-ISDN, or satellite system. However, as the popularity of the Internet grew, so did the desire of individuals and small businesses to gain similar broadband access. Initially in the 90's, access was achieved through low data rate dial-up modems, but this method soon proved inadequate as the Internet itself grew into a rich multimedia environment. Fortunately, the dial-up modem gave way to newer technologies that offered a host of broadband access solutions over the same PSTN twisted pair local loops, as well as over affordable fiber optical cables, broadband wireless local loops, and residential access to satellite systems.

8.2 DIGITAL SUBSCRIBER LINE (DSL)

Digital Subscriber Line (DSL) is an ITU, *physical layer (OSI RM layer 1)* broadband technology that is provisioned over ordinary copper twisted pair local loop wires. It consists of a family of specifications such as *Asymmetric DSL (ADSL)*, *Very-High-Data-Rate DSL (VDSL)*, *Single Pair High-Speed DSL (SHDSL)*, and *Symmetric DSL (SDSL)*. Prior to the development of DSL, narrowband ISDN provided broadband access over two pairs (four wire) copper local loops. Although ISDN enjoyed popularity in Europe, DSL proved to be a more cost-effective solution and soon became predominant over ISDN in the United States. Still used today, its popularity is decreasing due to other technologies, such as the distribution of passive optical networks (PONs) to residential and small business locations.

Prior to establishing a DSL capability to a resident or business office, the service provider must first carefully inspect each local loop to ensure that DSL implementation is possible. Implementation on an existing copper local loop requires the following:

- That the local loop distance should be no more than 18,000 feet from the subscriber location to the CO. This is necessary because the typical local loop wire is either 24 or 26 gauge, and subject to large attenuation over distance.

- Removal of *loading coils* from the local loop is required. For analog voice transmission, loading coils were installed on each local loop pair to counteract naturally occurring line capacitance which exists between wires in a pair. Without the added inductance introduced by the loading coils, the analog voice signal would suffer significant attenuation caused by the capacitance between wires. Unfortunately, the combination of inductance from the loading coils combined with the capacitance between wires results in the creation of a low pass filter that eliminates all frequencies above the 4 kHz voice signal. Since DSL depends upon these higher frequencies in order to provide high bit rate performance, it is necessary to remove the loading coils so that higher frequencies and larger bandwidths can be used.

- The local loop itself must be inspected for splices and the addition of any electronic equipment such as amplifiers, that might prevent DSL operation. On older local loops, there may be numerous line repairs that have been done over the years. Fixing a broken line requires the splicing of wire for repair, however, splices if done poorly will cause signal attenuation. In addition, if mixed gauge wires are used in a repair, the impedance at the splice's interface will differ, thus causing signal reflection and distortion. Added electronics can have similar detrimental effects on a DSL digital signal. As such, the overall condition of the local loop must be determined.

- *Radio frequency interference (RFI)* within the local loop environment also plays an important factor. Since *unshielded twisted pair (UTP)* is commonly used, it is susceptible to the surrounding EM noise environment. While RFI may be tolerated at the lower analog voice frequencies, the DSL spectrum is much wider and includes higher frequencies that may suffer greater impact from noise sources.

Depending upon the application, there are several DSL specifications that can be implemented based upon data rate, whether communications symmetry is required (i.e., asymmetric vs. symmetric), and whether analog voice needs to be supported. In this section, we will only discuss *Asymmetric Digital Subscriber Line (ADSL)* since this is the specification most often applied to residential local loops. Other forms of DSL will not be presented here; however, our discussion of ADSL will provide insight on how these other forms can be implemented. The reader is encouraged to research the other forms of DSL which are listed in Table 8.1 along with brief descriptions.

8.2.1 Asymmetric Digital Subscriber Line (ADSL), ADSL2, and ADSL2+

Typical home users and small businesses download much more data from the Internet than they upload to the Internet. Because of this, it makes more sense to provide greater bandwidth for downloads than uploads, hence the label *Asymmetric DSL*, or *ADSL*. Being able to provide an asymmetric connection is especially critical considering the limited overall data capacity of typical UTP wiring found on most local loop lines.

As mentioned, analog voice requires the placement of several *loading coils* along the local loop line to counteract the signal attenuation caused by the capacitance between the wire conductors in a pair. This enables 4 kHz analog voice transmission to travel further; however, it also inhibits the transmission of the higher frequency signals that ADSL depends upon to provide higher data capacity. As such, the service provider must remove every loading coil along the local loop, which may exist every 3000 to 4000 feet. Another issue found typically in older neighborhoods is the number

TABLE 8.1   xDSL, ITU-T G.99x-series Forms (International Telecommunication Union, 2011).

DSL Form	Rates	Remarks
Asymmetric DSL (ADSL)	Downstream: 8–10 Mbps Upstream: 1 Mbps	Used for Internet access where downloads from web are higher than uploads; ideal for residential access; spectral partition supports analog voice
ADSL (G.lite)	Downstream: 1.5 Mbps Upstream: 512 kbps	Speeds are slower than ADSL, but signal extends further (5.4 km); physical splitter to separate analog from digital not required; enables "plug and play" installations
ADSL2	ADSL2 8–12 Mbps	Improves ADSL data rate and extends distance by 300 m; uses filter vice splitters at both communicating end points
ADSL2+	ADSL+ 16 Mbps	Improves upon ADSL2 by increasing bandwidth on the line
Symmetrical DSL (SDSL)	Symmetric 160 kbps (over 7 km) to 1.5 Mbps (over 3 km)	Download and upload speeds equivalent; no support for analog voice; higher data rates offered by combining TPs; ideal for business file/information exchanges
Very-High-Data-Rate DSL (VDSL)	Symmetric or Asymmetric 52 Mbps for short distances	Supports both symmetric and asymmetric exchanges over short distances
Single Pair High-Speed DSL (SHDSL)	Symmetric 2.3 Mbps over single pair, 4.6 Mbps over two pairs	Analog voice not supported; ideal for business file exchanges

of repairs that local loops have undergone over time. Since the number of repairs and associated splices may be high, signal strength may be limited thus limiting data throughput. Therefore, in addition to the removal of loading coils, the local loop must be tested to ensure that proper SNR exists to enable ADSL service.

Several challenges exist for any high data rate circuit, such as ADSL, xDSL,[1] and ISDN, when implementation involves use of UTP lines. First, since adjacent UTP cables are susceptible to crosstalk, the service provider must monitor the ***attenuation-to-crosstalk ratio (ACR)*** to ensure that an interfering wire pair does not overwhelm adjacent pairs with noise. Secondly, unlike analog

---

[1] "x" in xDSL signifying different versions of DSL.

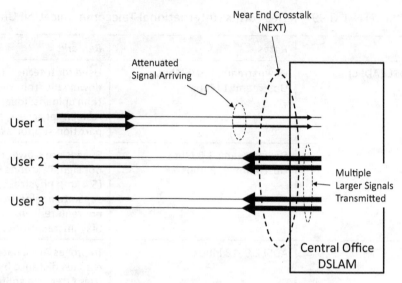

DSLAM – Digital Subscriber Line Access Multiplexer

FIGURE 8.1 Near-End Crosstalk (NEXT) measured at the CO.

signals, full-duplex digital communications over a single wire pair requires *frequency division duplexing (FDD)* which separates transmit and receive signals by frequency so that digital data is not distorted. Finally, UTP is not an ideal medium to send high-speed data over long distances because of the typical wire gauges used and its vulnerability to RFI.

In communications, two types of crosstalk are defined, *Near-End Crosstalk (NEXT)* and *Far-End Crosstalk (FEXT)*. The easiest way to remember the difference between these two types of crosstalk modes is to associate the line end where the crosstalk occurs in relation to the noise source itself. So with NEXT, *"near"* tells you that the crosstalk occurs at the same end of the wire pairs from where the noise is transmitted. In fig. 8.1, three local loops terminate at a device called the *Digital Subscriber Line Access Multiplexer (DSLAM)* located at the CO. User 1's transmitted signal is attenuated after having traversed the length of the local loop. At the same time, the CO sends signals out to users 2 and 3.[2] Since the CO's signal has not yet been attenuated, it has much greater strength than user 1's incoming signal. As a consequence, the signal transmitted from the CO causes *near-end crosstalk* interference to occur on user 1's wire pairs. To avoid degraded service to user 1, the service provider must ensure that a proper ratio of the *attenuated signal to the crosstalk strength* is maintained, i.e., the *attenuation-to-crosstalk ratio (ACR)*. This ratio is often given in a decibel value, see equation (8.1).

$$[\text{ACR}](\text{dBs}) = 10 \log_{10}\left(\frac{\text{attenuated signal strength}}{\text{crosstalk strength}}\right) \tag{8.1}$$

---

[2] Note that the numbers of incoming local loops at the CO in real situations are significantly larger than in this simple example.

While NEXT can be a significant issue on the CO's side of the line, it is not considered an issue at the user's end since most residences only have one or two local loop lines active, and because the asymmetry means that the amount of data being sent to the network is smaller than the attenuated signal data being received from the CO.

FEXT is defined as the crosstalk that occurs at the other end, or *"far"*, from the interfering noise source. So in fig. 8.1, instead of measuring crosstalk nearest the noise source, the crosstalk would be measured at user 1's location. Since multiple users do not typically reside at the same residential or business locations, the outgoing signals from the network (i.e., CO) would be split to numerous other locations, and would therefore not cause a problem for user 1. In addition, even if some user local loops were co-located, the noise interference itself would have suffered attenuation. Therefore, proper ACR is more easily attained and FEXT would not be considered a significant problem in this particular case.

Finally, the use of FDD (frequency division duplex) not only enables the use of greater bandwidth over the local loop, but also dramatically reduces NEXT problems. In essence, with FDD, transmit and receive signals reside in separate frequency bands therefore avoiding the coupling of same frequency transmit and receive signals from occurring.

In the typical case where residential analog phones are supported by an ADSL installation, the frequency spectrum is divided into separate analog and digital sections. The analog section coincides with the traditional analog voice grade frequency band of 300 to 4000 Hz. The frequency band above 4000 Hz is used for digital communications where the transmit and receive channels are separated. A device called a *splitter* is used to separate analog from digital signals, and can be installed near the analog device (i.e., modular device), at the CPE demarc, or at the CO end of the local loop. Along with the splitter, *low-pass microfilters* are placed in-between each analog device (e.g., phone or facsimile machine) and the phone line connected to the CPE demarc. The *microfilter* prevents high-frequency noise from entering the analog device. If analog devices are not supported, then the entire bandwidth is used for digital data.

ADSL is based upon the *Discrete MultiTone (DMT)* modulation technique which incorporates OFDM as discussed in chapter 5. *Orthogonal frequency division multiplexing (OFDM)* is a technique in which the operating spectrum is divided into multiple *orthogonal* subcarriers. These *orthogonal* carriers are allowed to overlap with one another without creating interference between adjacent subcarriers. Messages are segmented and transmitted in parallel fashion over several subcarriers at once. By using OFDM, major benefits are achieved such as greater spectral efficiency and better immunity from narrow-band noise products.

Of course each OFDM subcarrier must be modulated and this is done using *quadrature amplitude modulation (QAM)* which was discussed in chapter 3. Considering the susceptibility of UTP wiring to the surrounding noise environment, smart *ADSL modems* are used. These modems monitor and detect changes in subcarrier signal strength, identify impaired subcarriers and reassign signals to nonimpaired subcarriers as needed. In addition, these modems are developed to be *dynamically rate adaptive*, which means they can automatically adjust the *"M"* (number of signaling levels assigned per symbol) in *M'ary QAM* modulation to either increase or decrease data rate throughput.

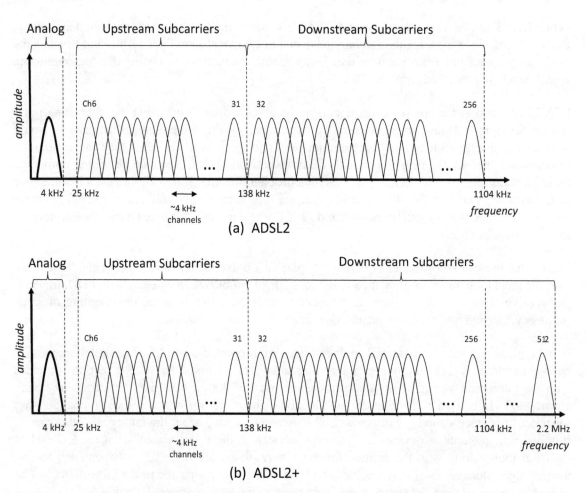

FIGURE 8.2 ADSL2 and ADSL2+ frequency structure in the frequency domain.

ADSL, ADSL2, and *ADSL2+* are all similar in that they use DMT, OFDM, and QAM. The differences reside in throughput capacity. ADSL initially covered a frequency spectrum up to 552 kHz. ADSL2 expanded the spectrum out to 1.1 MHz, while ADSL2+ expanded further to 2.2 MHz. By expanding the occupied frequency spectrum, greater data rates were achieved. Figure 8.2 depicts ADSL2 and ADSL2+ spectral structures. In both fig. 8.2(a) and 8.2(b), analog voice is supported in the lower 4 kHz band, and *upstream*[3] 4 kHz subcarrier data channels (6 through 31) resides between 25 kHz and 138 kHz. The major difference between ADSL2 and ADSL2+ is in the capacity of the downstream[4] data from the network. ADSL2 supports *downstream* data between 138 kHz and 1104 kHz or subcarrier channels 32 to 256. In comparison, the enhanced ADSL2+ extends the upper spectral limit to 2.2 MHz, which enables it to support additional subcarrier channels for a total of 512. So while the upstream throughput did not change with ADSL2+, the extended downstream

---

[3] Upstream describes data uploads to the Internet.

[4] Downstream describes data downloads from the Internet.

bandwidth offered greater download speeds in support of higher quality multimedia reception. It should be noted that if analog voice was not supported, the lower voice bandwidth would be occupied by OFDM subcarrier channels 1 through 5.

There are several ways that a service provider can provision an ADSL local loop. However, common to all are the following: (1) modems must be used to ensure separation of downstream and upstream digital transmission (DMT), (2) a device called a splitter is needed to separate analog voice and digital data at the CO and/or CPE end points, (3) at the CO, PSTN analog voice and PDN digital data must be combined and separated, since both signal types are present on the local loop, and (4) numerous ADSL local loop lines must be multiplexed together for transport over the PDN.

Figure 8.3 depicts three methods used to provide ADSL capability. At the CO, the **DSL Access Multiplexer (DSLAM)** aggregates upstream digital data from users, and demultiplexes downstream traffic intended for users. Each local loop is associated with an **ADSL Transmission Unit— Centralized (ATU-C)** modem which is typically in the form of a line card that is plugged into the DSLAM. This modem can dynamically change bit rates according to line conditions as described above. Prior to the signal leaving the CO in the downstream direction, voice signals from the PSTN are added onto the local loop. Therefore, if voice is supported, the modem must ensure no digital data is transmitted below 4 kHz. For the upstream traffic from the user, a splitter at the CO must separate the data traffic from the analog voice, sending the voice traffic to the PSTN. The signal is

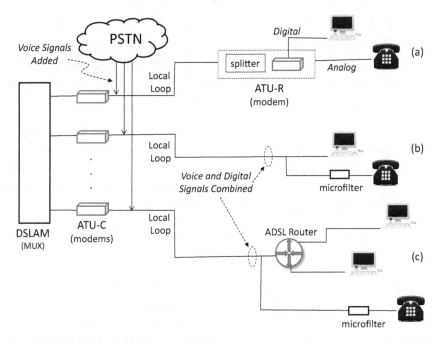

FIGURE 8.3 Typical ADSL Implementations. (a) ATU-R modem and splitter installed by the service provider, (b) spliterless ADSL where analog and digital signals remain on the CPE UTP wiring thus requiring microfilters on all analog devices, (c) no splitter installed at user site, router enables connection of more than one digital device, microfilters required on all analog devices.

then demodulated by the ATU-C, and then multiplexed with other ADSL signals for transport to the data network.

At the user side of the local loop, there can be variations regarding how ADSL signals are handled. In fig. 8.3(a), the combined analog and digital signal transmitted on the local loop line is processed by the ***ADSL Transmission Unit—Remote (ATU-R)*** modem which splits voice from data and then demodulates the digital signal. These were the first types of installation methods used, however it required a visit from a technician to install the ATU-R and eventually became too costly for the service provider. To alleviate the costs of technician visits, service providers began offering self-install kits to customers. In fig. 8.3(b), ***G.lite*** which is an *ITU-T G.992.2* extension of ADSL, provided a *splitterless* installation option that did not require technician support. With *G.lite*, UTP lines associated with the user's premises contains both analog and digital signals. An ADSL modem is required to be connected to the user's computer, and microfilters are placed on each analog device to filter out frequencies above 4 kHz. This was a popular installation method capable of providing downstream speeds of up to 1.544 Mbps and upstream speeds of up to 512 kbps. Finally, in fig. 8.3(c), since most users have a need to connect several digital devices, an ADSL modem/router is provided to users which can be connected to multiple computers within the premises. Similar to 8.3(b), microfilters are required for each connected analog device.

8.3 CABLE TELEVISION, CABLE ANTENNA TELEVISION (CATV)

The use of coaxial cable medium to send information dates back to the turn of the 20th century, with the most publicized instance occurring during the 1936 Olympics in Nazi Germany where live events were transmitted through coaxial cables to special reviewing rooms equipped with large screens.

While images over coaxial cables had been experimented with in both the United States and Europe in the late 1920's, the first evolutionary steps in the United States occurred in the late 1940's at a time when over-the-air television broadcasts were becoming very popular. Unfortunately, many rural, mountainous or valley communities could not reliably receive RF broadcast transmissions due to *line-of-sight (LOS)* limitations from the broadcast towers.

In 1948, John Walson, a store owner who sold television sets in such an area, decided to distribute coaxial cables to television owners who could not receive RF broadcasts. By distributing the signal from the broadcast tower to users through coaxial cables, signal reception improved dramatically. This concept worked so well, that the idea of setting up coaxial cable networks to improve signal quality soon expanded to numerous neighborhoods both with and without RF LOS limitations. Soon cable television companies began installing cable networks in residential communities across the country. However, these new cable companies were seen as being similar to, and competing with, the local broadcast stations who fell under the jurisdiction of the Federal Communications Commission (FCC). As such, the FCC expanded its regulatory authority over cable networks and limited them to distributing only local programming. This regulatory policy over the cable industry existed through the early part of the 1970's, but gradually lessened until the ***Cable Communications Policy Act*** *of 1984* was enacted. The 1984 Act removed the restrictive regulations placed on the cable industry and ushered in a period of strong industry growth.

Prior to the *Telecommunications Act of 1996*, local telephone companies, long-distance telephone companies, and cable networks were restricted from entering each other's markets. However, during the early 1990's, with growing access to the Internet and advances in digital communications technologies, the time for *universal services*[5] and an update to the nation's regulatory policies were needed. *The Telecommunications Act of 1996* allowed local and long distance telephone and cable companies to compete with one another. It also paved the way for new start-up companies to enter the communications services industry by requiring local telephone companies to provide access to their local infrastructures. This major change to the long-standing communications regulatory policies created a swell of new entrants fueled by eager investors, and it led to a heighten period of mergers and acquisitions within the industry. The *"dot.com"* era made many individuals wealthy, but eventually ended with the *"dot.com bust."* Despite the failure of many start-up firms, the act forever changed the telecommunications landscape, and helped to usher in the new digital era.

The 1996 Telecommunications Act also allowed the cable industry to enter the telephony and Internet access markets. However, since cable networks were originally designed for broadcast distribution and not for two-way communications, the industry was not fully prepared to take advantage of the opportunities enabled by the Act. In addition, most cable equipment was proprietary and specific to the cable provider, thus an overarching standard for cable equipment was nonexistent.

In response to the lack of cable modem standardization, *CableLabs* along with organizations such as *3Com, Cisco, Intel, Motorola, Netgear, Texas Instruments, Time Warner Cable,* and many others, came together to develop *DOCSIS 1.0 (Data Over Cable Interface Specification)* which provided manufacturers with a specification for the design and development of two-way interoperable cable modems. DOCSIS addressed the standardization needs and allowed the industry to offer alternative Internet access, other than ADSL, to consumers. The original publication of DOCSIS 1.0 in March 1997 was followed by DOCSIS 1.1 (April 1999), DOCSIS 2.0 (December 2001), DOCSIS 3.0 (August 2006), and DOCSIS 3.1 (October 2013), and full-duplex DOCSIS 3.1 (February 2016). DOCSIS was approved by ITU-T[6] as an international standard in 1998 and in Europe it is referred to as *EuroDOCSIS*.

The DOCSIS standard describes the physical (layer 1) and data link (layer 2) layers of the OSI RM. The cable service provider operates a *Cable Modem Termination System (CMTS)* located within its facilities *(or head-end[7])*, which is connected to each of the subscriber's DOCSIS compliant *cable modem (CM)* in a *one-to-many* arrangement. To provide two-way transmission, the cable spectrum is separated by frequencies into downstream (CMTS to CM) and upstream (CM to CMTS) bandwidths. The downstream transmission band begins at 50 MHz and can be higher than 1 GHz depending upon the specific system configuration. Channel size in North America is 6 MHz using

---

[5] Universal services describe the availability of basic communications services to the public at fair and competitive rates.

[6] ITU-T Recommendation J.112.

[7] "head-end" refers to the suite of equipment located at the provider's distribution center which connects and provides services to cable modem subscribers.

M'ary (M = 63 to 256) Quadrature Amplitude Modulation (QAM) techniques, while the international version of DOCSIS uses a channel width of 8 MHz and the *Digital Video Broadcasting for Cable Systems (DVB-C)*[8] modulation standard. For upstream transmission, DOCSIS versions 1.0 and 1.1 define channel widths between 200 kHz and 3.2 MHz, and DOCSIS 2.0, which is backward compatible with the earlier versions, define a channel width of 6.4 MHz. Depending upon the specific version of DOCSIS used, upstream channel modulation can include QPSK, or *M* = 8 to *M* = 4096 QAM. Below is a brief description of the DOCSIS versions follows.

DOCSIS 1.0 (March 1997) offered two-way transmissions over cable at a downstream rate of 42.88 Mbps and upstream rates of 10.24 Mbps.

DOCSIS 1.1 (April 1999) added Quality of Service (QoS), which enabled cable providers to prioritize VoIP traffic in order to compete with the telephone companies (telcos). It did not increase upstream or downstream throughput.

DOCSIS 2.0 (December 2001) maintained the downstream rate of 42.88 Mbps, but tripled the upstream rate to 30.72 Mbps. While this upstream speed was an impressive increase, actual rates depended upon the number of subscribers uploading information to the Internet.

DOCSIS 3.0 (August 2006) dramatically increased downstream rates to 1372.16 Mbps and upstream rates to 245.76 Mbps by enabling the binding of several channels together in order to increase throughput.

DOCSIS 3.1 (October 2013) was yet another dramatic improvement in throughput that advertised downstream rates up to 10 Gbps and upstream rates up to 2 Gbps. To achieve these increases, the previous version's channel specifications were replaced with orthogonal frequency division multiplexing (OFDM) using multiple subcarriers that could send and receive data in parallel.

Full-Duplex DOCSIS 3.1 (February 2016) is currently a project to improve DOCSIS 3.1 to enable gigabit symmetric services in both the downstream and upstream directions.

While we often think of the cable networks as being exclusively composed of coaxial cables, today's cable networks are a hybrid mix of both fiber optic and coaxial cable links between the CMTS and CM (see fig. 8.4). Called **hybrid fiber coaxial (HFC)**, optical signals are distributed from the cable provider's head-end to *optical nodes* located near each cable service area. Optical nodes located within each service area convert the optical signals to electrical signals that can then be transmitted over shared coaxial links to each user CM. The use of fiber optic cables allows providers to increase capacity, which in turn enables them to better compete with traditional telephone service providers that currently offer high-speed fiber-to-the-premises (FTTP) connections. Although HFC helps to increase throughput to the neighborhoods, cable providers must still deal with the possibility of their users experiencing congestion and slower speeds during peak usage hours. This is the result of multiple users being connected through a shared coaxial segment that has

---

[8] DVB-C is a family of open international standards for digital broadcasting over cable networks. DVB-C uses MPEG-2, MPEG-4, and QAM modulation techniques.

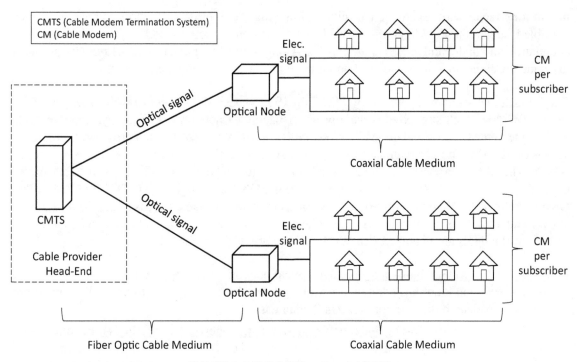

FIGURE 8.4 Hybrid Fiber Coaxial (HFC).

limited bandwidth capacity. As user demands for higher bandwidth programming grows, these congestion issues will be further exasperated. By locating optical nodes closer to the subscriber, and thus minimizing the number of subscribers on a given coaxial segment, the impact of congestion to users during peak hours can be reduced.

8.4 PASSIVE OPTICAL NETWORKS (PONS)

Throughout the 90's, major advances in personal computers and the Internet, combined with greater competition and a more friendly regulatory environment, incentivized telephone companies towards seeking new ways to increase bandwidth capacity to end users. DSL over UTP wire-pairs (in North America), and ISDN over copper wires (overseas), were popular but technically limited. With the desire for higher upload and download Internet speeds, and high definition (HD) premium television over local loop lines, local service providers turned to fiber optic solutions to help meet exponentially growing demands for capacity.

Passive optical network (PON) technologies had advanced sufficiently to make the cost of installing fiber optic cables to neighborhoods and to homes affordable. PON systems do not require active components such as repeaters or optical amplifiers to be placed between the CO and end user. This translates into lower maintenance costs for the service provider even though optical fibers must be installed up to the home (*FTTP*,[9] *fiber-to-the-premises*), to the curb side (*FTTC, fiber-to-the curb*), or to the neighborhood (*FTTN, fiber-to-the-neighborhood*). Since UTP local loops are typically

---

[9] FTTP is also called FTTH, *fiber-to-the-home*.

the limiting factor with regards to capacity, terminating the fiber cable as close to the end user as possible is ideal. Single *SMF (single mode fiber)* is used throughout the PON system due to its low attenuation and high bandwidth characteristics. Along with SMF, **passive optical splitters** are used to divide the signal in a *one-to-many* fashion from the CO to numerous end users.

The initial PON standard approved by ITU-T in 1998 was G.983 ***Asynchronous Transfer Mode PON (APON)***, which supported service provider backbone networks. Eventually, improvements were made to the G.983 standard leading to ***Broadband PON (BPON)*** which provided asymmetric speeds of 622 Mbps downstream and 155 Mbps upstream, and maintained the fixed sized frames of APON. The BPON standard is popular in the United States and deployed widely by Verizon (Altera Corporation, 2012). In 2008, further improvements in PON technologies led to ITU-T G.984, called ***Gigabit PON (GPON)***, which improved spectral efficiencies to enable speeds of 2.488 Gbps downstream and 1.244 Gbps upstream. As the anticipation for greater bandwidth demands continues, follow-on standards are planned by the ITU-T, some of which are cited below.

- (ITU-T G.984.5) Gigabit-capable passive optical networks (G-PON): Enhancement band. This recommendation identifies additional wavelength windows and ranges to be applied for future WDM (wavelength division multiplexing) channels.
- (ITU-T G.987 series) 10-Gigabit-capable passive optical networks (XG-PON). Recommendation addresses requirements to support the physical and convergence layers of the 10 Gbps PON systems, to include user network interfaces (UNIs), service node interfaces (SNIs), and deployment configurations.
- (ITU-T G.989 series) 40-Gigabit-capable passive optical networks (NG-PON). NG-PON supports multiple WDM channels and the flexibility that enables the addition of channels to support future 100 Gbps capacity.

IEEE (Institute of Electrical and Electronics Engineers) developed a PON standard based upon 802.3. called ***Ethernet PON (EPON)*** which was mostly adopted in Japan and China. Unlike BPON and GPON where data frames are fixed lengths, EPON adopted the concept of variable sized Ethernet frames. 10G-EPON was ratified as an IEEE 802.3av standard in 2009 and is designed to enable downstream speeds of 10 Gbps, with upstream speeds of 1 Gbps or 10 Gbps.

Figure 8.5 depicts a typical PON architecture. At the service provider facility, an ***Optical Line Terminal (OLT)*** acts as the terminal point for the PON network. It transmits downstream and receives upstream optical signals to and from subscribers. The OLT interfaces with the Internet, PSTN, and television programming networks either electrically or optically depending upon the specific network. Several SMF fiber optic cables span out from the OLT arranged in a single or dual fiber configuration applying BPON or GPON. While the ITU-T allows for dual fiber runs, typical implementations such as FTTP, use single fiber runs with downstream and upstream signals separated by different wavelength windows, 1490 nm and 1310 nm, respectively.

Traditional PON systems can operate as high as 2.5 Gbps; however, an increase to XG-PON speeds, requires transmission window increases of 1577 nm downstream and 1270 nm upstream, thus enabling speeds up to 10 Gbps. To achieve ITU-T G.989 NG-PON 40 Gbps speeds, *wavelength division multiplexing (WDM)* is applied over several wavelength windows.

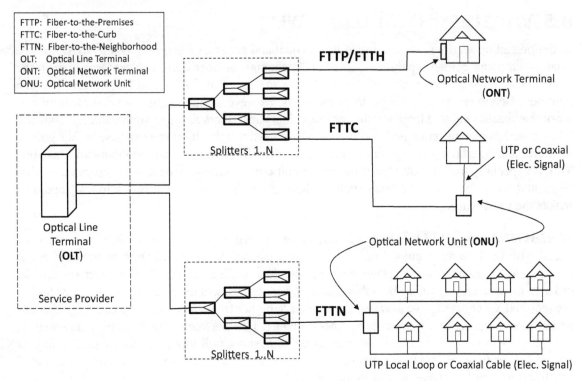

FTTP: Fiber-to-the-Premises
FTTC: Fiber-to-the-Curb
FTTN: Fiber-to-the-Neighborhood
OLT: Optical Line Terminal
ONT: Optical Network Terminal
ONU: Optical Network Unit

FTTP/FTTH

Optical Network Terminal
(ONT)

FTTC

UTP or Coaxial
(Elec. Signal)

Splitters 1..N

Optical Line
Terminal
(OLT)

Service Provider

Optical Network Unit (**ONU**)

FTTN

Splitters 1..N

UTP Local Loop or Coaxial Cable (Elec. Signal)

FIGURE 8.5 Passive Optical Network (PON) System.

In order to distribute the light signal from the OLT, the fiber cable is connected to several *optical splitters*, which are connected in a cascading fashion. Each splitter divides the incoming light into two halves (i.e., 1:2 ratio). Since these splitters are passive, each split causes the signal strength to be reduced by half, or 3 dB, and this loss is termed *insertion loss*. Therefore, the number of splitters used and the strength of the incoming signal dictate the practical distance of the total fiber run to the subscriber, as well as the data capacity that can be supported. In the case of fig. 8.5, an optical signal reaching the cascaded splitters will experience a total insertion loss of 3 dB + 3 dB + 3 dB = 9 dB.

From the splitters, the fiber cable can terminate in several ways depending upon the service provided. With FTTP/FTTH, fiber cable extends to an *Optical Network Terminal (ONT)*, which is located at the demarc between the service provider network and CPE. The ONT converts optical into electrical signals and back, and is connected to the subscriber's system which typically consists of coaxial cables. With the FTTC and FTTN scenarios, SMF fibers are connected to an *Optical Network Unit (ONU)*, which provides a more centralized location for optical to electrical signal conversion. The ONU can connect to the traditional UTP local loops or CATV coaxial networks either at curbside or central neighborhood location. A single fiber typically supports up to 32 ONUs.

Both the CATV and telephone service providers have benefitted greatly from PON technologies. ITU-T and IEEE continue to adopt and standardize future PON technologies that will help to meet the ever-increasing demands for data capacities.

8.5 WIRELESS LOCAL LOOP (WLL)

In the preceding sections, we discussed how broadband access, or *last mile connectivity*, can be established using guided mediums such as UTP, coaxial, or fiber optic cables. Over time in the United States and in many parts of the world, the existence of CATV and PONS have become commonplace to residential and business locations. However, establishing a guided medium network that reaches out to a large number of individual subscribers requires significant material and labor costs. For many poor nations, the costs associated with digging trenches, laying guided medium, and interfacing equipment to each individual household, is not economically feasible. This is especially true if individuals and communities are widely dispersed or separated by distance and terrain features. In cases such as these, providing access through wireless mediums makes the most sense.

Wireless local loops (WLL), or *fixed wireless access*, provide an alternative to the high costs associated with implementing guided medium access networks. Since the digging of trenches is not required, WLL access can be established quickly, thus leading to significant project savings. In order to provide high-capacity broadband access, carrier frequencies in the GHz ranges or higher are required. Of course, as we discussed in chapter 5, higher frequencies suffer greater signal attenuation over distance, and require more line-of-sight (LOS) between communicating antennas as compared to lower frequency carriers. In addition, rain, snow, pollution, etc., have a greater impact on the higher frequencies, thus causing an increase in signal attenuation. Therefore, the use of amplifiers and repeaters over distances are required.

Another disadvantage for wireless systems is RF interference (RFI) and electromagnetic interference (EMI). Interference can occur naturally (solar flares, cosmic interference, weather, etc.) or can be manmade (machinery, etc.). Implementing a successful WLL requires frequency licensing and regulation by an authority such as the FCC (Federal Communications Commission) in order to minimize transmission interference and intermodulation (IM) noise from occurring. However, even with strict regulatory policing, environmental noise sources still impact transmission and reception, thus close link monitoring by the service provider is required.

WLLs can consist of either optical or RF subscriber links. Obviously, with optical links, attenuation, LOS, weather, and pollution are of greater concern compared to RF links. The use of *free space optics (FSOs)* between buildings in an urban area is especially attractive since it avoids expensive trenching costs underneath city streets and sidewalks. However, while the optical carriers provide the greatest capacity, it is much more vulnerable to pollution and weather conditions. For the remainder of our discussion on WLL, we will concentrate on IEEE 802.16 WiMAX.

8.5.1 IEEE 802.16 Worldwide Interoperability for Microwave Access (WiMAX), Broadband Wireless Access (BWA)

Today when we think about WiMAX, we often think about mobile WiMAX 4G cellular capability and its competition with the mobile LTE cellular standard. However, WiMAX started out as a standard covering *point-to-multipoint (PMP)* data links in support of wireless metropolitan *area networks (MANs)*, and as a wireless alternative to DSL and CATV. The first 802.16 standard approved in December 2001, described PMP links in the 10 to 66 GHz frequency range. The first set of standards recommended by the *IEEE 802.16*[10] working group and the WiMAX forum,[11] suffered from high implementation costs, poor system reliability, and other performance issues that were exasperated by LOS restrictions. As a consequence, this initial standard did not garner full support.

IEEE 802.16 was followed by *802.16a* in 2003, which supported both point-to-point and PMP configurations, and operated in a lower 2 to 11 GHz range thus eliminating the strict LOS requirements. A major performance improvement with 802.16a was the adoption of OFDM which improved spectral efficiency and helped to reduce the effects of noise within the environment. *Quality-of-Service (QoS)* was introduced with *802.16b* also in 2003. *802.16c* covered operations in the 10 to 66 GHz range. Today, 802.16, 802.16a, 802.16b, and 802.16c are no longer in use. IEEE 802.16d and e, discussed below, were converged into the 802.16 (2012) standard, so while the d/e specifications have been superseded, the information contained still remains, for the most part, relevant.

The separation of *fixed* and *mobile* WiMAX standards occurred with the approval of *802.16d* (2004) and *802.16e* (2005). 802.16e[12] provided enhancements in support of mobile use within the 2 to 6 GHz range, and was considered a 4G cellular option to 4G LTE (Long Term Evolution). 802.16d, operating in the 2 to 11 GHz range, described the *fixed* WiMAX standard known as *Broadband Wireless Access (BWA)* which provides a WLL capability.

The *BWA 802.16d (2004)* standard defines the *physical layer 1 (PHY)* and *data link layer 2, medium access control (MAC)* of the OSI RM.

Within the PHY layer, the RF interface, or *"air link"*, operates at transmission frequencies below 11 GHz and can support point-to-point and point-to-multipoint topologies. By operating within this lower frequency range, *non-LOS (NLOS)* between the service provider's *base station (BS)* and subscriber antenna is possible, and distances up to 30 km can be supported.

The air link is configured using *orthogonal frequency division multiplexing (OFDM)* with *256 FFT (fast Fourier transform)*. So you're probably asking what this means. First, let's consider OFDM which we discussed in an earlier chapter. OFDM is a method that divides an operational frequency spectrum into *N* number of subcarriers. Information is divided and transmitted over several assigned subcarriers in parallel fashion. Unlike FDM, each of the subcarriers are "orthogonal," which means that adjacent subcarriers can overlap without interfering with one another. Doing this gives us several benefits including greater spectral efficiency, greater immunity to both RFI and multipath fading. A *fast Fourier transform (FFT)* is an algorithm that, in simple terms, mathematically converts signals

---

[10] European Telecommunications Standards Institute (ETSI) HiperMAN standard and 802.16 are aligned and based upon one another.

[11] The WiMAX Forum is a special interest group formed in 2001, comprised of manufacturers, service providers, and industry consultants.

[12] 802.16e Mobile WiMAX will be discussed further in chapter 10.

between the time and frequency domains. This is useful in OFDM because it allows us to separate, modulate, and transmit information across several subcarriers. At the receiver, FFT allows us to quickly demodulate and recombine these subcarriers into the original information transmitted. Achieving signal conversion for high-capacity information requires speed, therefore the FFT algorithms are implemented in hardware/firmware integrated chips called *FPGA (field programmable gate array)*. In essence, the *FFT* and *IFFT (inverse FFT)* processes enables us to perform OFDM quickly. The *"256 FFT"* represents the number of subcarriers, or $N = 256$; however, only 192 subcarriers transmit user data. Of the remaining 256 minus 192 or 64 subcarriers, 8 are used as *pilot* subcarriers for synchronization, and the remaining 56 subcarriers are used as guard bands. Subcarrier modulation techniques include BPSK, QPSK, 4-QAM, 16-QAM, and 64-QAM. The *forward error correction (FEC)* techniques used include Reed-Solomon combined with convolutional error correcting codes. Subscriber data rates of 4 to 70 Mbps can be supported, although the actual rates are dependent upon RF conditions, environmental noise, modulation techniques, transmission distances, and terrain.

IEEE 802.16 (2012)[13] is an enhanced version of WiMAX, describing both previous standards for fixed and mobile broadband wireless access. This standard describes *WirelessMAN-SC (wireless metropolitan area network—single carrier)*, *WirelessMAN-OFDM*, and *WirelessMAN-OFDMA (OFDM access)*. The operational frequency band between 2 and 11 GHz is used for non-line-of-sight (NLOS), while the 10 to 66 GHz band is used for line-of-sight (LOS) transmissions.

WirelessMAN-SC (wireless metropolitan area network—single carrier) is a PHY specification for fixed LOS transmissions operating in the 10 to 66 GHz frequency band. Unlike OFDM, single carrier is more susceptible to multipath fading; however, since LOS is required for WirelessMAN-SC, it does not present a significant issue. A key advantage of implementing SC is the great amount of flexibility given to the service provider in assigning frequency spectrum to subscribers. Either *time division duplex (TDD*[14]*)* or *frequency division duplex (FDD*[15]*)* can be implemented, with channel bandwidths of 25 MHz or 28 MHz being common. A similar version of WirelessMAN-SC is called *WirelessMAN-SCa*, which addresses the lower 2 to 11 GHz frequency range and incorporates *time division multiple access (TDMA)* and *time division multiplexing (TDM)*. The ability to control spectral use helps service providers optimize cell planning, subscriber services, and enables flexibility in assigning user capacity.

WirelessMAN-OFDM is the PHY specification that describes fixed 802.16d NLOS transmissions that fall between 2 and 11 GHz. Either TDD or FDD can be implemented and common channel bandwidths are 3.5 MHz and 7 MHz.

WirelessMAN-OFDMA (OFDM access), which is based upon OFDM, can be applied to both fixed and mobile WiMAX at frequency bands below 11 GHz. Recall that OFDMA (OFDM access)

---

[13] 802.16 (2012) supersedes 802.16d/e, but retains the same concepts of both previous standards.

[14] Recall that TDD (time division duplex) describes a single frequency channel that is shared between communicating users. Each user sends and receives according to assigned time slots.

[15] FDD (frequency division duplex) describes the use of two separate frequency channels used for full-duplex communications between users.

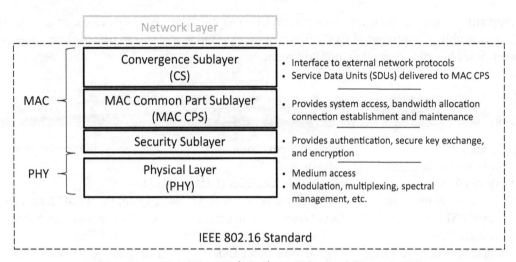

FIGURE 8.6 WiMAX 802.16 (2012) Layer One and Two Standard.

assigns different sets of subcarriers to support subscriber communications. FFT sizes of 2048, 1024, 512, 256,[16] and 128 can be supported.

Above the PHY layer is the MAC layer that is comprised of three sublayers as shown in fig. 8.6. At the uppermost MAC sublayer resides the ***convergence sublayer (CS)***, which acts as the interface to other network protocols such as ATM, Ethernet, IP, etc. You will note that other protocols such as Ethernet will define layers 1 and 2 of the OSI RM. However, as we have seen with some of the other standards discussed in this textbook, Ethernet layer 2 frames can be encapsulated into WiMAX layer 2 MAC frames. For many situations, this is the preferred method since the disassembly and reframing of data link frames between different networks is not required. Doing this presents a more expedient way to process messages, especially if the message is only passing through the network.

The CS sublayer receives the data from the upper layer protocol and places this data into ***service data units (SDUs)***. The SDUs are then mapped to the external network and protocol by appending a ***Service Flow Identifier (SFID)*** and ***Connection Identifier (CID)*** that identifies the external network and connection. The WiMAX standard identifies multiple CS specifications that are used to interface with different network protocols. Once this is completed, the SDUs are delivered to the ***MAC common part sublayer (MAC CPS)***. The MAC CPS is responsible for quality-of-service (QoS), system access, bandwidth allocation, connection establishment and maintenance. The ***security sublayer*** represents the lowest MAC layer, and is responsible for providing authentication, secure key exchange, and encryption.

The evolution of the 802.16 family of standards continues, with 802.16m addressing future air link requirements including 100 Mbps throughput for mobile users and 1 Gbps rates for fixed users. While mobile cellular WiMAX may have lost market share to rival LTE, the WiMAX BWA

---

[16] Compatible with 802.16d 256 FFT OFDM.

standard still remains a viable alternative for WLL "last mile" connectivity, for use as a broadband backhaul capability in support of LTE cellular networks, and as a means to provide interconnection between WiFi hotspots thus allowing WiFi roaming.

KEY TERMS

ADSL Splitter
ADSL Transmission Unit
  Central (ATU-C)
ADSL Transmission Unit
  Remote (ATU-R)
Asymmetric Digital
  Subscriber Loop (ADSL)
Asynchronous Transfer Mode
  PON (APON)
attenuation-to-crosstalk ratio
  (ACR)
Broadband PON (BPON)
broadband wireless access
  (BWA)
cable antenna television
  (CATV)
Cable Communications
  Policy Act of 1984
cable modem (CM)

cable modem termination
  system (CMTS)
connection identifier (CID)
convergence sublayer (CS)
Data Over Cable Interface
  Specification (DOCSIS)
Digital Subscriber Line
  (DSL)
Digital Subscriber Line
  Access Multiplexer
  (DSLAM)
Discrete MultiTone (DMT)
Ethernet PON (EPON)
far-end crosstalk (FEXT)
fiber-to-the-curb (FTTC)
fiber-to-the-neighborhood
  (FTTH)
fiber-to-the-premises (FTTP)
fixed wireless access

frequency division duplex
  (FDD)
G.lite
Gigabit PON (GPON)
MAC Common Part Sublayer
  (MAC CPS)
near-end crosstalk (NEXT)
optical line terminal (OLT)
optical network terminal
  (ONT)
optical network unit (OPU)
optical splitters
passive optical network (PON)
passive optical splitters
Security Sublayer
Service Data Unit (SDU)
time division duplex (TDD)
universal services
wireless local loop (WLL)

CHAPTER PROBLEMS

1. ADSL is used over PSTN UTP local loops to provide support for both traditional analog voice communications as well as high-speed digital data.
   a. True
   b. False

Answer: a

2. In order to provide ADSL services to a traditional PSTN UTP local loop, what must be considered?
   a. The total local loop distance between the CPE and CO must be less than 18,000 feet.
   b. Loading coils used to counter the capacitance within the wire pair must be removed from each local loop.
   c. The length of the local loop must be inspected for splices, mixed gauge wiring, and added active or passive devices used for analog voice transmission. Problems encountered must be fixed or removed prior to implementing ADSL.
   d. All of the above.

Answer: d

3. Select the correct statement(s) regarding ADSL implemented over wired local loops.
   a. ADSL uses a wider frequency bandwidth compared to analog voice. Signal attenuation at the higher frequencies is greater than at the lower analog frequencies.
   b. ADSL digitizes the entire local loop line, therefore all analog devices at the CPE must be replaced by digital devices.
   c. Due to the vulnerability of noise on UTP local loops, ADSL data rate speeds are less than the data rates achievable using traditional dial-up modems over analog local loops.
   d. All of the statements are correct.

Answer: a

4. Select the correct description of a *DSL Splitter*.
   a. The DSL Splitter separates the CPE from network devices
   b. The DSL Splitter splits the optical signal passively
   c. The DSL Splitter separates the analog signal from the digital signal
   d. The DSL Splitter enable asymmetric communications by separating downstream data from upstream data transmissions

Answer: c

5. "Asymmetric" in ADSL means that more bandwidth is provided for data coming from the network compared to the bandwidth going to the network.
   a. True
   b. False

Answer: a

6. ADSL implements discrete multi-tone (DMT) modulation. Select the correct statement.
   a. DMT uses FDM which requires the use of guard channels to separate subcarriers in order to avoid interchannel interference
   b. DMT uses spread spectrum technologies which require shared PN codes per communicating entities
   c. DMT uses OFDM with 256 overlapping subcarriers of 4 kHz bandwidth each
   d. DMT uses OFDM which is considered a orthogonal spread spectrum technology

Answer: c

7. FEXT is considered more problematic than NEXT on ADSL connections. As long as proper ACR ratios are observed, the probability of successful data exchange will be high.
   a. True
   b. False

Answer: b

8. NEXT is considered more problematic than FEXT on ADSL connections. As long as proper ACR ratios are observed, the probability of successful data exchange will be high.
   a. True
   b. False

Answer: a

9. Each OFDM subcarrier used on an ADSL DMT link must be modulated.
   a. True
   b. False

Answer: a

10. The *DSL Access Multiplexer (DSLAM)* aggregates upstream digital data from users, and demultiplexes downstream traffic intended for users. Each local loop is associated with an *ADSL Transmission Unit—Centralized (ATU-C)*modem which is typically in the form if a line card that is plugged into the DSLAM.
    a. True
    b. False

    Answer: a

11. *ADSL Transmission Unit—Remote (ATU-R)* modem is located at the CPE. The ATU-R splits voice from data and then demodulates the digital signal.
    a. True
    b. False

    Answer: a

12. Select the correct statements regarding the comparison between *ADSL2* and *ADSL2+*.
    a. ADSL2 and ADSL2+ support the same 4 kHz analog signal bandwidth
    b. Upstream subcarriers are the same between ADSL2 and ADSL2+
    c. ADSL2+ downstream bandwidth increases at the upper most frequency from 1.104 MHz to 2.2 MHz
    d. All are correct statements

    Answer: d

13. The *G.lite* extension of *ADSL*, provides a splitterless installation option that does not require technician support.
    a. True
    b. False

    Answer: a

14. ADSL modems are capable of detecting problems and adjusting the selection of subcarriers sets, as well as the M'ary modulation method used, in order to ensure unimpaired data transmission.
    a. True
    b. False

    Answer: a

15. *DOCSIS 1.0 (Data Over Cable Interface Specification)* provided manufacturers with a specification to design and develop two-way interoperable cable modems. It addressed the need for cable industry standardization, and provided an alternative means to access the Internet other than ADSL.
    a. True
    b. False

    Answer: a

16. DOCSIS standard describes the physical (layer1) and data link (layer 2). DOCSIS 3.1 introduced the use of OFDM to increase downstream rates.
    a. True
    b. False

    Answer: a

17. PONS implements SONET optical frames and central timing. As such, data capacity is high thus enabling the transmission of numerous HD channels as well as high-speed access to the Internet.
    a. True
    b. False

    Answer: b

18. Which of the following is part of the passive optical network (PON) architecture?
    a. Optical Splitters
    b. WDM
    c. Optical Line Terminal
    d. All of the above

Answer: d

19. Which PON standard supports ATM implementation on backbone networks?
    a. APON
    b. BPON
    c. GPON
    d. XG-PON
    e. NG-PON

Answer: a

20. EPON is a PON standard based upon IEEE 802.3 Ethernet.
    a. True
    b. False

Answer: a

21. In a PON system, the OLT interfaces with the Internet, PSTN, and television programming networks either electrically or optically depending upon the specific network.
    a. True
    b. False

Answer: a

22. Identify the group of devices that support PONS.
    a. NEXT, FEXT, ACR
    b. DOCSIS, DSLAM, HFX
    c. OLT, ONU, ONT
    d. WDM, optical splitters, BWA

Answer: c

23. Wireless local loops (WLLs) only describe unguided communications operating in the RF frequency spectrum. Therefore, optical free space optics (FSOs) are not considered a WLL capability.
    a. True
    b. False

Answer: b

24. *WiMAX BWA* is a standard used to describe both *fixed* and *mobile* WiMAX standards.
    a. True
    b. False

Answer: b

25. Describe the difference between *WirelessMAN-SC* and *WirelessMAN-OFDM*.

26. The 802.16d(2004) convergence sublayer (CS) resides at the top of the MAC sublayer and is responsible for interfacing to other network protocols such as ATM, Ethernet, IP, etc.
    a. True
    b. False

Answer: a

CHAPTER 9

The Internet

"The Internet didn't get invented on its own. Government research created the Internet so that all companies could make money off the Internet. The point is, is that when we succeed, we succeed because of our individual initiative, but also because we do things together."

Barrack Obama (https://www.brainyquote.com/search_results.html?q=internet)

9.1 INTRODUCTION AND BRIEF HISTORY

The genesis of the Internet is a fascinating story based upon numerous technological threads, global politics, and the desire for entrepreneurship. To say that the Internet was purposefully conceived to what it is today would be misleading. In fact, key scientists, engineers, agencies, and organizations would never have thought that the Internet would be the revolutionary game changer that it is today, and thoughts of where the next evolutions of the Internet will take us only guesses at best.

While there were many technological breakthroughs that marked the beginnings of the Internet, the former Soviet Union's launch of the unmanned *Sputnik I* satellite on October 4, 1957 is typically considered the milestone that started the revolution. In order to understand the significance of this experimental launch, we need to understand the global climate that existed immediately after World War II. Democratic ideals led by the western countries collided with socialist philosophies led by the Soviet Union and China, during an era we called the "Cold War." This Cold War officially ended when the Soviet Union was dissolved in 1991 and was renamed the Russian Federation. During the Cold War era, tensions between the west and east were exasperated by the development and existence of nuclear weapons on both sides of the philosophical conflict. Atomic bombs had been used by the United States to end the war with the empire of Japan, so the devastation that this new generation of weapons could deliver was well known. Therefore, the fear caused by the success of Sputnik I was understandable. If a satellite with a beacon can revolve around the earth in space, it can also carry a nuclear payload in space above its target. A nuclear warhead tumbling directly onto its target from outer space would be virtually unstoppable, and would destroy cities with very little warning from ground-based sensors. This fear spurred on the "race to space," and the creation of the Department of Defense's *Advanced Research Projects Agency (ARPA)* in 1958, whose priority was to accelerate U.S. presence in space. As vulnerabilities to national security were reviewed, it was thought that an attack against the national telecommunications system would lead to a loss of command and control communications as well as an inability to maintain contact with critical strategic commands across the country and the globe. In response, ARPA developed the precursor to the Internet called ARPAnet in 1969 which was based upon the idea of a packet switching network that was invented by Paul Baran of the Rand Corporation in 1962. The packet network would break down messages into separate packets that could be transmitted over different paths to its destination, and then reassembled back into its original message. By doing this, a single network segmentation or outage would not deter the message from reaching its destination (i.e., survivable communications). The first ARPAnet packet network was established between mainframe computers located at UCLA and Stanford universities. Eventually, this small network expanded to include the University of Hawaii and London University.

In order for information to be transmitted and received over a digital packet network, sophisticated computers capable of coding/decoding (codec) signals between analog and digital forms, with the ability to assemble and disassemble this data into packets, were required to be both fast and accurate. The first computers during the post World War II era were typically comprised of large vacuum tubes that acted as simple logic switches used for computational purposes. The vacuum tubes not only took up a lot of room, but also used significant amounts of energy which created enormous amounts of heat. The large components, enormous energy requirements, and slow computational speeds obviously limited these early computers to only the simplest of computations (e.g., missile trajectories, etc.).

To enable a dramatic increase in computational speeds, two major goals needed to be satisfied. The first was to increase the number of logic switches within a given area. The greater the number of logic switches, the more powerful the computational capability of the computer. The second goal was to reduce the signal propagation time between components within the computer, which meant reducing the distance between components.

Research into the development of much smaller solid-state transistor switches to replace the vacuum tubes had actually been studied as early as the 1925 by Julius Edgar Lilienfeld, but much of the research was ahead of its time and went ignored for many years. Bell Labs continued research into solid-state transistors during WWII, which led to the first working transistor in 1956 invented by John Bardeen, Walter Brattain, and William Shockley, all of whom later received the Nobel Prize in Physics for their work. While the solid-state transistor reduced the size of WWII era computers, it still remained a capability only accessible to universities, governments, and large organizations.

In 1958, Jack Kilby, an engineer working at Texas Instruments, invented the first integrated circuit (IC), which essentially revolutionized the electronics industry. The silicon IC is essentially a small chip containing numerous switches or transistors. Shrinking and then increasing the number of switch devices within a given area not only decreased the size of the computer, but also minimized the distance between switches. Since electrical signals are limited to the speed of light within the medium, reducing the distance between components reduced the propagation time of the signal between switches, thus increasing overall computational speed. The smaller dimensions and much higher device concentrations of the IC made data processing both fast and powerful. For his work on the IC, Jack Kilby received the Nobel Prize in Physics in 2000.

Since the initial IC, the numbers of devices (e.g., transistors) on a chip have steadily increased at a remarkable rate, thus resulting in greater computational capability in smaller packages. In 1965, Gordon Moore, co-founder of Intel, made an astounding prediction which stated that the number of devices that could be placed onto a silicon chip would double every 18 months.[1] At the time of Moore's statement, only 60 devices existed on a single chip, however, since this time, the growth in numbers of devices per chip have closely paralleled his prediction. Staying true to *Moore's Law*, as his prediction is now known as, IBM announced in June 2017 that it was working on a new chip that would contain 30 billion devices, and that manufacturing would begin in the 2020 time frame.

During the 1970's, multiple research milestones were achieved on both the computer and digital networking fronts. On the networking front in 1973, Vinton Cerf of Stanford University and Robert Kahn of the now renamed *Defense Advanced Research Projects Agency*[2] *(DARPA)*, invented the *Transmission Control Protocol/Internet Protocol (TCP/IP)*, which are the backbone protocols used on today's Internet residing at the OSI RM layers 4 and 3, respectively. During the same year, Robert Metcalf invented the Ethernet protocol which eventually became known as the IEEE 802.3 standard for common data link networks. Ethernet enabled local connection of computer devices in a LAN configuration, while TCP/IP enabled connection between devices across different common networks and over large geographic distances. Computer networking was quickly advancing, and the stage was set for the introduction and rise of the interconnected personal computer (PC).

The PC's first milestone occurred as an article entitled *"World's First Minicomputer Kit to Rival Commercial Models . . . 'ALTAIR 8800'"* written by Ed Roberts (Micro Instrumentation and Telemetry Systems, MITS), in the January 1975 edition of the *Popular Electronics* magazine. At this period in time, small computer chips such as the Motorola 6800 and Intel 8080 existed, as did a few smaller computers; however, it was still viewed by the general public as being something of interest only to academics or researchers. Fortunately, groups of mostly college students had a great desire to own their own computer, and the Altair just happened to be within their reach. Small clubs of enthusiast such as the *Homebrew Computer Club* at Stanford University began to assemble around the Altair. The Altair, although equipped with an Intel 8080 computer chip, was quite primitive, having only toggle switches for programming input and LEDs for display outputs. Still, the possibilities of what it could become drove many to test and experiment with the Altair. In 1976, Stephen Wozniak demonstrated a prototype of a PC named the Apple I at one of the Homebrew Computer Club meetings. Although the Apple I prototype was simply an experiment to see what could be done, he gained the attention of a high school friend, Steve Jobs, who he eventually partnered with to develop and market the first generations of the Apple I and II personal computers. Many in the computer industry took notice of the success of these initial Apple PC sales; however, it was still thought to be in a niche market catering to high-tech hobbyists vice mainstream business professionals.

The "killer app" that accelerated the Apple PC into business prominence was a spread sheet application called *Visicalc*, developed by Dan Bricklin and Bob Frankston of the Harvard Business School. As the first electronic spread sheet, it made accounting and financial "what if" analysis much easier to perform, especially when compared to the labor intensive and

---

[1] Moore later revised this estimate to every 24 months.

[2] Formerly ARPA.

human-error prone analysis typically conducted by hand at the time. The *"What if"* analysis is a strategic tool that allows businesses to consider changes in present and future values over time, thus enabling them to make critical decisions based upon known or unknown market conditions. The importance of being able to perform this analysis quickly and accurately is fundamental for strategic business success. Visicalc, which began sales in 1979 on Apple II PCs, allowed accountants and financial officers to run "what-if" queries from their desks, without the delays inherent in queuing job requests through a mainframe computer, and without the human errors associated with hand calculations. The combination of the Apple II and Visicalc turned the PC into a legitimate tool for management decision making, and sales to business organizations began to increase dramatically.

Of course, the largest computer manufacturer of business computers at the time soon took notice of Apple's success and challenge to its long held business dominance. The company was IBM (*International Business Machines*), and their product line only included large expensive mainframe computers. The lack of having a PC of their own to rival the fledgling but very popular Apple PC created an immediate need to develop and market their own personal computer quickly.

The origins of IBM date back to 1911 when it was called the *Computing Tabulating Recording Company*, which changed to IBM in 1924. Over many decades *"Big Blue"* as it was nicknamed, had become the iconic symbol for the development, manufacture, and sales of large sophisticated computers to business organizations around the world. Well established and set in its own proven development processes, the company was ill equipped to quickly perform the rapid technology innovation needed to develop an IBM PC that could challenge the Apple's growing popularity.

In 1980, IBM management wisely decided that a new PC should be developed separately from the traditional, and somewhat inflexible, IBM development process. Instead, the new IBM PC would be developed under its own special project called *SCAMP (Special Computer APL Machine Portable)*. Bill Lowe, who was placed at the head of the SCAMP project, promised that the new IBM PC would be developed in one year. Although this time frame must have pleased IBM executives, it required compromises which included the use of *commercial-of-the-shelf (COTS)* components, vice the development of proprietary hardware and firmware. Even though these COTS components were available to any PC manufacturer, the schematics for how it was assembled and integrated (hardware, firmware, and software) were IBM proprietary. Eventually, however, numerous manufacturers would *"reverse engineer"* the IBM PC, giving rise to numerous *"IBM-clones"* that operated very much like the IBM PC, but at a much lower cost. While the IBM clone presented a loss of market share for IBM, the competition between PC manufacturers kept PC prices low to the benefit of consumers.

A key component needed to complete the first IBM PC was the operating system (OS). Bill Gates (*Microsoft*), who IBM had approached to develop a BASIC interpreter, did not have an operating system at the time, so he referred them to Gary Kildall of the *Digital Research, Inc. (DRI)*. Gary had an operating system called *CP/M* that worked with the Intel 8008 and 8080 processing chips. However, due to issues regarding IBM's desire for DRI to sign nondisclosure agreements, as well as Gary's absence from the meeting, negotiations for CP/M were never concluded. IBM had no choice but to go back to Microsoft with the news, and Bill Gates, who understood the potential of the PC market, seized upon the opportunity and promised to deliver his own, yet-to-be developed OS, which eventually became known as PC DOS.[3] In PC lore, Gary Kildall faced criticism for having turned down a deal that would have made DRI, and not Microsoft, the giant within the software world. However, the true facts of what occurred and the intentions of the individuals behind the decisions may never be known for certain. In any case, the legendary partnership between IBM and Microsoft began after the fateful meeting in 1980.

From these opportunistic and sometimes accidental beginnings, the stage was now set for competition to ensue between the Apple, IBM PC, and IBM-clone developers.

By the 1980's, ARPAnet had grown quickly from its humble beginnings in 1969 to an expanded network funded by the National Science Foundation (NSF) in 1981. The TCP/IP protocol was adopted by DARPA[4] (Defense Advanced Research Projects Agency) a year later. Eventually ARPAnet became known as NSFNET from 1985 to 1995, connecting several supercomputers across the nation in San Diego, Boulder Colorado, Champaign Illinois, Pittsburgh, Ithaca NY, and Princeton. In 1988, NSFNET partnered with another computer network called MERIT (Michigan Educational Research Information Triad), established much earlier in 1966, that connected the University of Michigan, Michigan State University, and Wayne State University. In 1995, MERIT took over management of the Internet from NSFNET.

During the period prior to the introduction of the PC, the Internet mainly provided connectivity between large mainframe and supercomputers located at research institutions. As the PC became more popular, so did the idea of interconnecting them together into local area networks (LANs). LANs enabled the sharing of data and peripheral equipment between connected PCs, which in turn led to better workplace communications and data sharing. Soon, large organizations dispersed in separate locations desired a way to interconnect their LAN systems together. As a consequence, this desire led to the development of metropolitan area networks (MANs) and wide area networks (WANs). The idea of the globally interconnected organization flourished, and numerous MAN and WAN standards and services were offered by service providers. However, many of the more popular WAN standards (e.g., ATM, frame relay) were configured as provider-specific common networks (OSI layer 2), therefore interface differences between the different service provider networks existed. Considering the difference between WAN operators, their selected protocol standard and the network parameters they selected, protocol conversion was typically required. Fortunately, OSI layer 3 network protocols provided an end-to-end solution from source to destination addresses, regardless of the common network (data link layer protocol) underneath. The *Internet Protocol (IP)* is the best known of the OSI layer 3 protocols, and is the network protocol used on the Internet. IP allows us to connect from any client over any common network, to any server over any other common network. Today, the Internet is a critical capability for organizations wishing to establish virtual networks across disparate geographic locations.

---

[3] It had been seen by many in the fledgling industry, including to DRI, that PC DOS looked very much like CP/M.

[4] ARPA had changed its name to Defense Advanced Research Projects Agency (DARPA) in 1971.

TABLE 9.1 Internet Timeline. Some highlights, but definitely not the whole story!

Date	
1957	Soviet Union successfully launches Sputnik I into space
1958	ARPA (Advanced Research Projects Agency) created
1964	Paul Baran of the Rand Corp. writes a paper "On Distributed Communications" which describes survival packet networking[1]
1964	IBM releases the first modern computer architecture with the introduction of the Model 360 computer
1969	ARPAnet created initially connecting computers at Stanford University and UCLA
1970	First packet network called "Alohanet" become operational at the University of Hawaii
1973	Vinton Cerf (Stanford University) and Robert Kahn (DARPA) develop TCP/IP
1973	ARPAnet reaches overseas to University College of London and NORSAR, Norway
1973	Robert Metcalfe invents Ethernet based upon the Aloha Net protocol
1975	Article written by Ed Roberts (MITS, NM) appears in Popular Electronics describing the first microcomputer kit based upon the Intel 8080 chip
1976	Stephen Wozniak demonstrated his prototype Apple I computer at the Homebrew Computer Club. He then joins forces with Steve Jobs to form the "Apple company".
1977	Apple II is released for sale
1978	Bill Gates and Paul Allen form Microsoft
1979	Visicalc (the killer application for Apple computers) is developed by Dan Bricklin and Bob Frankston of the Harvard Business School
1980	Bill Lowe (IBM) is placed in charge of the IBM's SCAMP program tasked with developing the first IBM PC
1983	Domain Name System (DNS) introduced on the Internet by Jon Postel, Paul Mockapetris, and Craig Partridge
1984	Apple Macintosh PC released with new GUI/mouse pointing system
1987	Internet breaks 10,000 hosts
1988	First Internet virus "Morris Worm" introduced by Robert Morris (then Cornell University student) infects 10% of the Internet. Morris receives 3 years probation, 400 hours of community service and a $10,000 fine under the "1986 Computer Fraud and Abuse Act".
1989	Internet breaks 100,000 hosts
1990	The first Internet search engine created called "Archie" by McGill University
1990	Tim Berners-Lee creates the World Wide Web
1992	Windows 3.1 released

Date	
1993	First Internet browser, Mosaic, developed by Marc Andreesen at the University if Illinois
1994	Pizza Hut creates the first Internet ordering system.
1996	Microsoft release Window 95
1996	"Telecommunications Act of 1996" opens competition to new entrants into the telecommunication markets. First Internet Service Providers (ISPs) appear (e.g., MCI, Sprint)
1998	Google is launched (Larry Page, Sergey Brin)
1999	Wi-Fi IEEE 802.11b released
2004	Facebook is launched (Mark Zuckerberg, Dustin Moskovitz, Eduardo Saverin, Andrew McCollum, Chris Hughes)
2004	First email computer worm "Mydoom" introduced
2005	YouTube.com is released (Chad Hurley, Jawed Karim, Steve Chen)
2006	Twitter is launched (Jack Dorsey, Evan Williams, Noah Glass, Biz Stone)
2011	Snapchat released (Evan Spiegel, Bobby Murphy, Reggie Brown)

[1] Donald Davies (National Physical Laboratory, UK) came up with a similar concept. It was Davies who used the term "packet". Baran also acknowledged Davies' use of the term "packet."

Thanks to the Cold War, Sputnik, the integrated chip, the PC, and many more technical innovations, the Internet's growth around the globe has been exponential and dramatic to say the least. Boosted by regulatory policies such as the *Telecommunications Act of 1996*, which opened competition to newcomers into the industry, the Internet today can be considered one of the most important inventions of the modern world. It represented a disruptive technology that could not have been foretold by even the most intelligent individuals or futurists; and its future remains just as unpredictable. In 2016, the United Nation's *Universal Declaration of Human Rights* was appended to declare that access to the Internet was a human right that should not be disrupted by governments.

9.2 INTERNET ARCHITECTURE

Early ARPAnet and MERIT connectivity between computers were mostly provisioned by PSTN service providers through dedicated links. This limited the number of users to those few who had access to large computers located within the interconnected research facilities. As digital technologies advanced, so did the PDN, which could connect individual computers, LANs, mainframes, and supercomputers to and from any location within the service area.

The physical layer included many different guided (UTP, coaxial cables, fiber optics, etc.) and unguided (microwave, satellite, etc.) mediums. Each service provider would operate their own physical and data link layer protocols in a *common network* configuration. As an example, let's say that a service provider operates an ATM network. Nodes within this ATM network can freely communicate

ICANN AND IANA

The Internet Corporation for Assigned Names and Numbers (ICANN) is a nonprofit international non-governmental organization (NGO) that was founded in September of 1998 in California. ICANN is responsible for Internet domain names, DNS root registries, and IP addresses through its Internet Assigned Numbers Authority (IANA) organization. Previous to 1998, these functions were the responsibility of the U.S. Department of Commerce, who quickly realized that the global nature of the task required administration at an international level between peer partners in both the public and private sectors. On October 1, 2016, ICANN, which was under contract with the U.S. Department of Commerce, was officially transferred to the private sector.

with one another and this is considered a *common network*.[5] However, let's say the same, or different provider, also operates a Carrier Ethernet (CE) network, which is also considered a *common network*. Nodes on the ATM network can communicate within their common network, but not with nodes on the CE network, and vice versa. Therefore, use of the network layer (OSI layer 3) above the data link layer is required to enable connectivity between these different common networks.

Luckily, the Internet has the **Internet Protocol (IP)**, which is the network layer specification that enables data to be exchanged across different common networks. The IP addresses that are used by communicating nodes are managed internationally by the **Internet Corporation for Assigned Names and Numbers (ICANN)**, which is a nonprofit organization founded in 1998. Blocks of IP addresses are assigned to five specific regions of the world: RIPE NCC (*Réseaux IP Européens Network Coordination Centre*), ARIN (*American Registry for Internet Numbers*), APNIC (*Asia Pacific Network Information Centre*), LACNIC (*Latin American and Caribbean IP address Regional Registry*), and AfriNIC (*African Regional Registry for Internet Number Resources*). These regional allocation and registration services then distribute blocks of IP addresses to *ISPs (Internet Service Providers)*, for use by individuals and organizations. The IP address is similar to telephone numbers in that they are assigned by controlling agencies to support user connections. By controlling IP addressing, the Internet achieves a logical stability over how nodes are connected, which then enables users to connect to any desired node regardless of the underlying service provider common networks involved. More will be said later about how IP addressing works.

In order to facilitate the exchange of IP traffic between various service provider networks, **Internet exchange points (IXPs)**, also known by their previous name as **network access points (NAPs)**, were created across the globe. An IXP is a data switching facility operating at the physical, data link, and network layers of the OSI RM. Similar to layer 2 common networks, each service provider operates their own layer 3 IP network. These independent layer 3 networks are termed an **autonomous system**[6] **(AS)** or **autonomous networks (AN)**, because the day-to-day management and operations

---

[5] Common networks at the data link layer (OSI RM layer 2) are typically under the administration and control of a single service provider or organization.

[6] AS can be thought of as a single Internet Service Provider (ISP); however, some large ISPs may operate several autonomous systems or networks.

are administered by a single service provider, and therefore router and device configurations are the responsibility of the service organization. Since network parameters can differ between AS', IXPs provide the mechanisms required to interface and pass IP packets between separate AS'.

The IXP acts as an interface between autonomous systems at both the national and international levels, thus enabling the global flow of IP traffic between service providers. Each AS is associated with a unique number assigned by the ***Internet Assigned Numbers Authority (IANA)***, which operates under *ICANN*. This unique number helps to identify the routing of packets between and through multiple AS'.

Initially, service providers attempted to perform an accounting of all data passing through their networks; however, this soon proved to be an unmanageable task that resulted in costly overhead accounting. The additional processing at the AS interfaces also created throughput choke points that negatively impacted overall Internet speeds. To deal with this issue, service providers met to eliminate the unnecessary accounting practices and to allow the free flow of IP packets across AS boundaries. Known as ***peering agreements***, service providers benefited by eliminating the costly overhead, which in turn enabled the Internet to experience greater overall throughput speeds.

Considering that separate service provider networks come together at the IXP, a method to provide routing information between autonomous systems is needed since each AS controls its own routing configurations. This is accomplished using the ***Border Gateway Protocol (BGP)***[7] that operates over gateway servers and routers, and are specifically designed to enable the exchange of packet routing information and cost metrics. Cost metrics, in the case of AS network routing, is defined as measurements (e.g., time, hops, distance, etc.) based upon some algorithm that determines the most efficient path through a network. AS service providers also establish internal routing policies for their network that are taken into consideration when determining routing paths.

BGP gateways communicate routing information with one another using the ***Transmission Control Protocol (TCP)***, typically on port 179. The information received through BGP is entered into a ***Routing Information Base (RIB)***, which is used to determine external packet routing. Unlike the standard IP routing tables, BGP RIB tables do not require periodic updates. These tables are updated when an event causing a change to the network path has been identified and reported.

The following terms and definitions are associated with BGP and are commonly used.

BGP Speaker. This is the router that executes BGP within an AS. The "speaker" sets up a TCP connection to send *UPDATE* messages to inform peers that the routing remains the same, has been updated, or is no longer in service.

Routing Information Base[8] *(RIB).* The RIB is the database that resides with the BGP speaker. This information contains routing received from other connected AS', information received internally from IGP protocols, and routes learned by BGP itself.

---

[7] BGP replaced the Exterior Gateway Protocol (EGP) which was used in the NSFNET backbone network.

[8] Also known simply as a routing table; however, the BGP RIB is specific to BGP routing functions. A BGP speaker that also acts as a basic router will have two routing tables. One for BGP external routing and another for internal basic routing.

BGP Peer (BGP Neighbor).   Peer or neighbor, describes the routers that have formed a BGP connection using TCP.

Internal BGP (IBGP).   BGP connection between internal peer routers within the same AS.

External BGP (EBGP).   BGP connection between external peer BGP routers located on two different AS'.

The BGP message that traverses the TCP connection has a maximum size of 4096 octets, and must be received in its entirety prior to being processed.

BGP is categorized as an **Exterior Gateway Protocol (EGP)** used to share routing information between AS' as discussed above. There are also **Interior Gateway Protocols (IGPs)** that enable the sharing of routing information within the same AS. Examples[9] of IGPs are **Routing Information Protocol (RIP)** and **Open Shortest Path First (OSPF)**. These IGPs work closely with BGP and are described in the next section.

9.2.1 Gateway Protocols

The *OSI network layer 3* is responsible for providing end-to-end connectivity independent of the underlying *OSI data link layer 2* common networks underneath. This makes it possible for LANs to interconnect to one another over WANs despite the different *data link* protocols involved. In an IP network, intelligent devices called **routers** are used to interface *common* networks together at the network layer. Each device on the network has an IP address that identifies the specific network it resides in (i.e., *network identification number*) and its specific device address. This enables each router to build a **routing table** that is used to forward datagrams on a *router-to-router* basis through the network. The routing tables are kept in data files and copies are maintained in the routers RAM (random access memory). The tables contain information regarding the *network ID* of connected IP networks, *network masks,* the IP address of the *next hop*, cost/quality metrics, etc. The routing tables are classified as either *static* or *dynamic*. The difference between the two is quite simple. A **static routing table** is created and maintained manually by a system administrator, while a **dynamic routing table** is updated and maintained automatically (i.e., no human intervention needed) using a protocol such as *RIP, OSPF,* or *EIGRP.*

As mentioned in the previous section, *OSPF (open shortest path first)* is an IGP defined by the *Internet Engineering Task Force (IETF)* RFC 2328, and used specifically with IP networks. OSPF is classified as a **link-state routing protocol**, which means that each router maintains the topology of the AS within its routing tables. In contrast, RIP is classified a **distance vector protocol** where routing tables are based upon *reachability* information.

OSPF has essentially replaced the older *Routing Information Protocol (RIP)* because the later has slower convergence times and poor scalability; however, RIP is still used for smaller IP

---

[9] Another major IGP is the Cisco proprietary Enhanced Interior Gateway Routing Protocol (EIGRP), which students are encouraged to research and study. However, it is considered beyond the scope of this textbook.

networks. RIP uses a *hop count* methodology that limits the number of hops a packet can take as it traverses[10] the network. This helps to prevent unwanted network loops[11] from occurring. When RIP is implemented on each IP network router, full table updates are broadcast every 30 s using a *OSI Transport layer 4* protocol called **UDP (User Datagram Protocol)**. These broadcasts, unfortunately contribute to overall network congestion, especially in larger networks where tables may be lengthy. Therefore, IGP protocols such as OSPF have been preferred over RIP.

OSPF, which is based upon Dijkstra's algorithm, differs from RIP in several ways.

- OSPF incorporates a *link-state protocol*, vice RIP's *distance vector protocol*. This means that each OSPF router in the AS constructs its own network topology, and then applies Dijkstra's algorithm to determine best routes through the network.

- At the beginning of the process, all OSPF routers exchange link state information with one another using *flooding*.[12] This allows each router to create a topology of the network. Updates are sent only when the network experiences a change, vice broadcasting information at 30 s intervals like RIP. This means that OSPF uses less network overhead than RIP; however, more processing power per router is required since new network topologies must be created when updates are received.

- In determining best routes through the network, RIP uses a simple hop count. However, OSPF can compute the costs of routes using metrics such as packet delay, data rate, actual dollar amounts, or other metrics that are configured by the user.

- OSPF does not use a transport layer protocol to send messages to other routers as does BGP and RIP. Instead, it encapsulates table updates within IP packets.

- OSPF is better suited for larger and more complex networks than RIP.

OSPF uses IP multicast to send routing updates, and provides a mechanism for authenticating the received updates. Once updates are received, each router running OSPF creates a network topology and calculates best paths based upon the selected metric (i.e., distance, hop, data rate, etc.). The convergence time to develop loop-free routes is much shorter than RIP, and therefore the network impact much less.

All routers in the AS maintain identical topology databases; however, the routing tables are based upon their location within the AS itself. The routing tables identify other routers, networks, and gateways that the router is directly connected to. For large networks, OSPF allows network devices to be grouped together in what is termed *"areas."* An area can be thought of as a separate network isolated from the other network areas within the AS. As such, sending traffic from one area to another requires a gateway router called an **Area Border Router (ABR)**. Since only the routers within the same area share the same topology databases, routing updates are only sent within the

---

[10] Typically a hop count of 16 is considered "unreachable."

[11] If the number of network hops is unbounded, then it is very difficult to prevent network loops from occurring.

[12] Flooding is a way that routers can distribute routing information and updates quickly to other routers within a network.

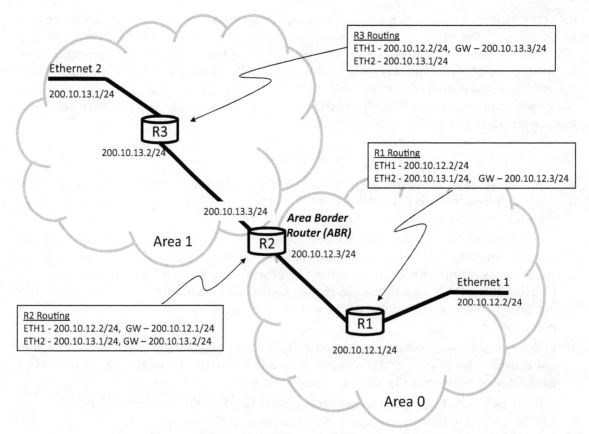

R3 Routing
ETH1 - 200.10.12.2/24, GW – 200.10.13.3/24
ETH2 - 200.10.13.1/24

Ethernet 2

200.10.13.1/24

R3

200.10.13.2/24

R1 Routing
ETH1 - 200.10.12.2/24
ETH2 - 200.10.13.1/24, GW – 200.10.12.3/24

200.10.13.3/24

Area Border Router (ABR)

Area 1

R2

200.10.12.3/24

Ethernet 1

200.10.12.2/24

R2 Routing
ETH1 - 200.10.12.2/24, GW – 200.10.12.1/24
ETH2 - 200.10.13.1/24, GW – 200.10.13.2/24

R1

200.10.12.1/24

Area 0

FIGURE 9.1 Simple OSPF Example with two areas designated.

area itself. This is advantageous for a couple of reasons. First, since updates are only sent within an area, the routing update traffic across the entire AS is significantly reduced. Second, since areas are isolated from one another, bad update information is limited to the area, thus protecting other areas from this erroneous data.

Whenever more than one area is configured, OSPF requires that one of the areas be designated a *backbone area* (i.e., typically designated *Area 0*). All other areas created within the AS must be connected to this backbone area.[13] This means that the backbone area interfaces with all ABR border routers within the AS. As such, the backbone is responsible for distributing routing information between nonbackbone areas.

Let's take a look at a simple IP network using OSPF in fig. 9.1. The AS consists of three routers (R1, R2, R3) and two connected Ethernet networks (Ethernet 1, Ethernet 2). The network is divided into two areas; Area 0 which is the backbone area and Area 1. R2 is the ABR gateway that interfaces

---

[13] In special cases where an area does not interface physically with the backbone (Area 0), a virtual link can be configured to Area 0.

between Area 0 and Area 1. Each device is associated with an IPv4 address which will be discussed further in the next section. Each router captures information about its neighbor in its routing table. The information in the boxes next to each router shows some of the information that appears in a routing table.[14] R1 (IP addr.: 200.10.12.1) is directly connected to Ethernet 1 (IP addr.: 200.10.12.2) and R2 (IP addr.: 200.10.12.3). R2 is the ABR gateway which is directly connected to R1 and R3 (IP addr.: 200.10.13.2). Finally, R3 is connected directly to R2 (IP addr.: 200.10.13.3) and Ethernet 2 (IP addr.: 200.10.13.1). You'll note that R2 can be reached using two IP addresses which are associated with the two areas.

In our example, a computer located in Area 0 on Ethernet 1 wishes to communicate to a computer on Ethernet 2 located in Area 1. Ethernet 1 sends the packet to R1. R1 then determines that in order to get the packet to Ethernet 2, it must send it to the ABR R2. The packet reaches R2 and based upon its routing table, realizes that the packet must be forwarded to R3, which acts as the gateway to Ethernet 2. Once the packet reaches R3, the packet is sent through a direct connection to Ethernet 2.

In this simple network, the use of metrics to determine the best path is meaningless. However, for networks containing many more routers and links, multiple routes will exist and the use of OSPF algorithms to determine the best path to a destination will appear as next hop entries within the routing tables. As network conditions change and routing updates sent out, each OSPF router will create new topologies that are void of harmful network loops. The amount of time is takes to develop new topologies and routing tables is called *convergence time*.

9.3 INTERNET PROTOCOL (IP)

The Internet Protocol (IP) operates as a packet switched network where data from the transport layer (OSI Layer 4) are divided into packets, or datagrams, for transmission across the network. IP is considered a ***connectionless*** protocol, which means that IP does not establish a connection between source and destination nodes prior to the exchange of data. Therefore, each ***datagram***, which is also termed an IP *packet*, must contain both a ***source*** and ***destination*** address. This enables each datagram to independently traverse the network in different paths based upon network conditions.

Without an established connection between communicating nodes, several detrimental consequences can occur. First, as mentioned above, the packets may take different paths through the network. Since different path lengths cause variations in propagation delay, packets may not arrive in sequential order. This means that the destination must buffer incoming datagrams in order to resequence them. Second, the absence of a connection means no *flow control* will occur between source and destination. This can cause receive buffer overflow if the buffer size cannot sufficiently store the rate of incoming packets arriving. As a result, data loss will occur. Finally, no connection means no assurance of packet delivery, therefore IP communications can be characterized as a "***best effort***" only protocol.

---

[14] It should be noted that not all of the information that typically appears on a routing table is shown.

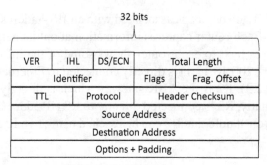

FIGURE 9.2 IPv4 Datagram.

The IP protocol leaves the job of establishing reliable communications to upper layer protocols such as the *Transport Control Protocol (TCP)* when needed (i.e., in some cases, *connection-oriented* communications is not required, making the selection of the *connectionless* User Datagram Protocol, UDP, appropriate).

Figure 9.2 shows the format of the IPv4 datagram. The following describes the elements of the datagram.

VER (4 bits): Version of the IP protocol (e.g., IPv4)

IHL (4 bits): Internet Header Length—number of total bits included in the IP header. The size of the IPv4 header is variable depending upon the options selected.

DS or DSCP (6 bits): Differentiated Services Code Point, formerly called "Type of Service." Supports real-time streaming data applications such as VoIP (Voice over IP).

ECN (2 bits): Explicit Congestion Notification, which carries information regarding network congestion. Optional feature that must be invoked by communicating nodes.

Total Length (16 bits): Indicates the entire length of the datagram in bits.

Identification (16 bits): Field used for identifying fragments of a single IP datagram. This is used if a datagram, during transmission, is fragmented. Fragmented pieces carry the same identification number.

Flags (3 bits): If the datagram in transit is large, then this field tells the network device whether it can be fragmented or not. Of the three bits, the first bit is reserved, the second bit means "don't fragment" (DF), and the third bit means "more fragments" (MF). For fragmented datagram, all fragments are set to MF (3rd bit) except the final datagram.

Fragment Offset (13 bits): Identifies the offset in bits of fragment relative to the beginning of the datagram.

TTL (Time-to-Live, 8 bits): Identifies the maximum life the datagram can stay alive on the network; typically by in maximum hop counts. This ensures that the datagram will not remain in the network indefinitely, thus helping to avoid network loops.

Protocol (8 bits): Identifies the next layer protocol that the datagram belongs to (e.g., TCP, UDP, ICMP).

Headers Checksum (16 bits): Checksum field is used for error detection of the IPv4 header only.

Source Address (32 bits): Source address.

Destination Address (32 bits): Destination address.

Options and Padding: Options are rarely used and therefore not discussed here. Padding is used to ensure that the header ends at the 32-bit boundary (i.e., header divided by 32 bits should give you a whole number. If it does not, then padding bits are inserted).

Note: The *"Total Length"* field is 16 bits long; therefore, the maximum number that the field can represent is (2^{16}) or 1 through 65,535. Keep in mind that this is simply a counter representing the number of bytes in the datagram. Therefore, the maximum length of an IPv4 datagram is 65,535 bytes.

9.3.1 IP Addressing

Every device on an IP network has an associated IP address that is used to establish connections between source and destination devices. An IP address is comprised of a network identification number (*Net ID*), and a host or device address. This combination gives network routers valuable information regarding a specific host's address and the IP subnetwork that the host resides on. This enables the router to send packets to just the gateway routers serving the destination subnetwork without having to search the entire network for the host.

There are currently two versions of IP that are in use on the Internet today. IPv4 was developed in the 1980s with an address space of 32 bits. The total number IPv4 addresses is equal to $2^{32} = 4.29$ billion possible addresses; however only 3.7 billion are assigned to hosts with the remainder being used for special protocols such as multicasting. At the time of its release, 3.7 billion available IP addresses appeared to be sufficient considering that the number of Internet users were less than 100,000 during the 1980s. However, the dramatic numbers of users and devices on the Internet has grown exponentially to over 3.7 billion as of March 31, 2017 (Internet World Stats, 2017), and therefore it is apparent that IPv4 addressing alone cannot keep up with the large demand.

In response to the alarming growth of the Internet, IPv6 was standardized in 1996, with first production releases provided to ISPs in 1999. IPv6's address space is 128 bits long, providing $2^{128} = 340 \times 10^{36}$ addresses, which is considered more than sufficient to meet future growth. Unfortunately, IPv6 is not backward compatible with IPv4, although methods have been developed to interface IPv4 and IPv6 networks.

9.3.1.1 IPv4 Addressing

To understand how IP addressing works, we turn to the smaller IPv4 address for simplicity. Since 32 binary 1 s and 0 s are difficult to work with, the IPv4 address is turned into an equivalent decimal dot address. To come up with this address, the 32-bit binary address shown in fig. 9.3 is divided into

Each "x" represents a binary number ('0' or '1')

XXXXXXXX . XXXXXXXX . XXXXXXXX . XXXXXXXX

8 bits	8 bits	8 bits	8 bits
$2^8 = 256$	$2^8 = 256$	$2^8 = 256$	$2^8 = 256$
or (0-255)	or (0-255)	or (0-255)	or (0-255)

(0-255) . (0-255) . (0-255) . (0-255)

FIGURE 9.3 IPv4 Address.

four sections of 8 bits each separated by a "dot." Each 8-bit section is then converted from a binary to decimal number. From 8 binary bits, you get $2^8 = 256$ possible decimal values. Since 0 is considered one of the possible decimal values, 8 binary bits will give you a decimal range from 0 to 255. Therefore, an IPv4 address is represented by four decimal segments separated by a dot, with values no greater than 255 per segment.

Example 9.1: Given the IPv4 binary address shown in fig. 9.4, determine the dot decimal IPv4 address.

Answer: Each binary segment is treated separately. Like decimal values, the most significant valued bit is on the far left, to the least significant bit on the far right (see values for each binary bit placement in the first segment). For each binary "1" that appears in the binary address, there is an associated decimal value. Therefore, we can easily add the decimal values for each binary "1" as shown in the figure.

Therefore, the binary address of 11000000.10101000.00001010.00001010 is equivalent to the decimal address 192.168.10.10, which is much easier work with.

There are five classes (A through E) of IPv4 addresses. Class A, B, and C addresses are associated with the size of the IP network, while class D is used for multicast addressing and class E reserved for future use.

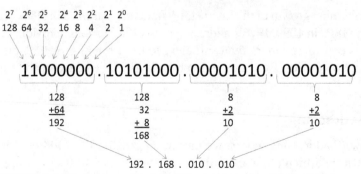

FIGURE 9.4 IPv4 conversion from binary to decimal dotted address.

Class A addresses are used by large networks because it gives the ISP the greatest number of IPv4 addresses that can be allocated to hosts. As I mentioned earlier, the IP address is divided into network and host IDs. For Class A networks, a "0" is placed at the most significant binary bit of the first segment. This identifies an IPv4 address as belonging to a class A network. The remainder of the bits in the first segment represents the specific network ID. However, Class A network IDs 127 (loopback testing) and 0 are reserved and not used. So valid class A network IDs range from 00000001 to 01111110, or in decimal form, 1 to 126. This means that there are a total of 126 IPv4 Class A networks possible using IPv4. The remaining three segments totaling 24 bits are allocated for host IDs, or $(2^{24} - 2) = 16,777,214$ possible host addresses. Note that within each Class A network, two network addresses are reserved for special purposes—i.e., the lowest valued address is the **network number, or network ID,** which represents the entire network and is used by routers to forward packets to the network. The highest address is reserved for **network broadcasts**. A subnet mask helps to distinctly identify network from host IDs. For a Class A, the subnet mask is 255.0.0.0 and is used by routers to quickly determine which network the IP address belongs to.

Let's look a bit closer at how many hosts a particular Class A network supports by using an example. If you were assigned a Class A network number of 124, then your valid IPv4 address range would be from 124.0.0.0 to 124.255.255.255. However, two of the addresses are reserved. The lowest network address, 124.0.0.0 in this case is reserved as the *network number* and is used by routers to direct packets to your network. The highest network address, 124.255.255.255 is reserved for network broadcasts. Therefore, instead of having (2^{24}) available addresses that you can use for hosts, you only have $(2^{24} - 2)$ host addresses available. The valid range of your host address is from 124.0.0.1 to 124.255.255.254, which is still a significant number, i.e., 16,777,214 possible host addresses.

An alternative way to identify the network ID contained within the IPv4 address is by using the **Classless Interdomain Routing (CIDR)** format which was introduced by IETF in 1993. The CIDR identifies how many of the most significant bit positions represent the network ID. As an example, the address 125.10.20.1/8 is in CIDR format, where the /8 tells you how many of the most significant bits represent the network ID. In this example, the network number is 125.0.0.0. By using CIDR, networks and subnetworks can be constructed without the need to classify them as an A, B, or C network. More will be said regarding CIDR notation below.

Class B addresses are assigned to medium sized networks and can be identified by a binary "10" in the two most significant bit positions within the address. The first two address segments provide the network ID, and the last two segments identify the host. Therefore, the number of host addresses that can be support by a single Class B network is $(2^{16} - 2) = 65,534$. Once again, the lowest host address is reserved as the network number, and the highest host address reserved for broadcasts. The valid range of Class B network numbers that can be assigned to a service provider is from 128 to 191. The subnet mask is 255.255.0.0, which identifies the first two segments as the network ID. The CIDR form can be used with a "/16" appended at the end of the address identifying the most significant 16 bits as the network ID. As an example, the address 130.34.12.5/16 tells you that the network ID is 130.34.0.0 with the host address being 130.34.12.5.

Class C addresses are used for small networks and can be identified with the binary bits "110" in the three most significant bit positions of the IP address. The first three segments represent the network

ID, and the remaining segment is used for host addresses. There are $(2^8 - 2) = 254$ host addresses available in a class C network. Like Class A and B networks, the lowest host address is reserved for the network number, and the highest reserved for network broadcasts. The valid range of Class C network numbers is from 192 to 223. The subnet mask for Class C networks is 255.255.255.0. Using CIDR, an IP address of 195.10.10.10/24 tells you that the most significant 24 bits of the 32-bit address is the network ID (195.10.10), with the remaining segment of 8 bits identifying the host.

Considering that the Class A, B, and C networks are fixed in both the number of networks and hosts they can support, CIDR was introduced to allow network operators the flexibility to further subdivide their class networks into smaller subnetworks. This process of subdividing Class A, B, or C networks is called *subnetting*. Subnetting an IP network helps to simplify packet routing within the network and reduces network congestion. As an example, if a service provider were given a Class C network, then there would be 254 hosts within the same network. There would be no hierarchical method for finding a specific destination IP address, since all hosts belong to the same Net ID, thus a search of the entire network would be required. Obviously, doing this causes an increase in network traffic. However, if we subdivided the Class C network into several subnets, then the subnet ID associated with the destination address would be used to limit the search to this destination subnet, thus avoiding a network-wide search. This reduces the number of nodes involved in the search to only the nodes belonging to the destination subnet ID, and as a result reduces overall network congestion.

Let's take a look at how this is done through some simple examples.

Example 9.2: You are given the IPv4 address 192.20.210.62/27. Determine the subnet ID that the address belongs to and subnet mask.

Answer: There are several things that can be immediately determined just by looking at the address (see fig. 9.5). First, the "192" in the first segment tells you that the address belongs to a Class C

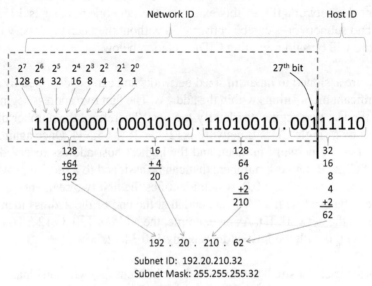

FIGURE 9.5 Subnetting example 9.2.

TABLE 9.2 IPv4 Class Addressing Ranges

Class	Bit Identifier (most significant bit)	Binary Network ID Range (first segment)	Decimal Network ID Range (first segment)	Number of Hosts Supported
A	0	00000001 to 01111110	1 to 126	$(2^{24} - 2) = 16,777,214$
B	10	10000000 to 10111111	128 to 191	$(2^{16} - 2) = 65,534$
C	110	11000000 to 11011111	192 to 223	$(2^{8} - 2) = 254$

Note 1: Class A network numbers, 0 and 127, are reserved and not used.

Note 2: Each network reserves the lowest host address as the network number which represents the entire network, while the lowest host address is reserved for network broadcasts.

Note 3: Class D (224-239) is reserved for multicast and Class E (240-255) is reserved (i.e., experimental).

network (see Table 9.2), therefore, the first three segments of the subnet mask will equal "255." In addition, the "/27" tells you that the first 27 most significant bits represents the subnetwork ID. This means that the first three segments (24 bits total) plus the *first three bits in the fourth segment* represents the subnet ID for a total subnet ID that is 27 bits long from right to left (i.e., 27 most significant bits in the IPv4 address). The first three bit positions of the fourth segment are associated with the values 128, 64, and 32 (see fig. 9.6). In this example IPv4 address, the fourth segment decimal value is determined to be "62" which equates to a binary "00111110," where the first three bits are "001," which equates to a decimal value of "32." Therefore, the subnet ID is 192.29.210.32, and subnet mask 255.255.255.32.

In example 9.2, you were given a Class C address and wished to create subnets using the first three bits of the host ID (i.e., first three bits in the fourth segment). So the question becomes: *given a Class C network address, by borrowing the first three bit of the host ID for subnetting ("/27"), how many subnets can be created, what are the subnet IDs, and what are the host ID address ranges?*

Table 9.3 shows the subnetting of our Class C network 192.20.219.0/27. Since three of the most significant bits are used to subdivide our network, we know that $2^3 = 8$ subnetworks can be created. The first column shows each of the eight possible subnets in binary, while the second column shows the entire subnet ID in decimal form. Note that the values of the three most significant bits equal 128, 64, and 32, respectively. In other words, a subnet ID of 011 equals $0 + 64 + 32 = 96$ in decimal form, hence, in the third row, our subnet ID is 192.20.219.96. The remaining

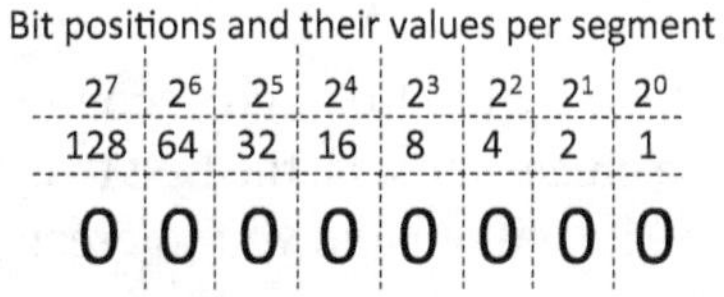

Bit positions and their values per segment

2^7	2^6	2^5	2^4	2^3	2^2	2^1	2^0
128	64	32	16	8	4	2	1

0 0 0 0 0 0 0 0

FIGURE 9.6 Eight bit segment—most significant bits from right to left.

TABLE 9.3 Example IPv4 Subnetting, 192.20.219.0/27. The newly created subnets using the first three most significant bits gives you the following subnetwork IDs.

Subnet ID[1] (binary)	Subnet ID (decimal)	Subnet Mask	Host ID Range[2] (binary)	Host ID Range (decimal)
000	192.20.219.0	255.255.255.224	00001-11110	192.20.219.1–192.20.219.30
001	192.20.219.32	255.255.255.224	00001-11110	192.20.219.33–192.20.219.62
010	192.20.219.64	255.255.255.224	00001-11110	192.20.219.65–192.20.219.94
011	192.20.219.96	255.255.255.224	00001-11110	192.20.219.97–192.20.219.126
100	192.20.219.128	255.255.255.224	00001-11110	192.20.219.129–192.20.219.158
101	192.20.219.160	255.255.255.224	00001-11110	192.20.219.161–192.20.219.190
110	192.20.210.192	255.255.255.224	00001-11110	192.20.219.193–192.20.219.222
111	192.20.210.224	255.255.255.224	00001-11110	192.20.219.225–192.20.219.254

[1] First three bit position of the fourth segment in the binary.
[2] Last five positions of the fourth segment in binary.

five bits of our fourth segment have values of 16, 8, 4, 2, and 1. So the number of hosts per newly created subnet is $(2^5 - 2) = 30$ hosts (note that the first and last host IDs are reserved and used for the subnetwork ID and broadcasts). The last column shows the host ID range. As an example, in the last row, the subnet ID is 111, or 224. The host ID range is from 11100001 to 11111110, or 225 to 254.

Example 9.3: You are given a Class B network ID of 130.21.0.0, and wish to subnet. You select "/18" to perform subnetting. Answer the following questions:

(a) How many subnets are created?

(b) What are the subnet IDs?

(c) What are the subnet masks associated with each subnet?

(d) How many hosts per subnet can be supported?

Answer: 130.21.0.0 in decimal is equal to 10000010.00010101.00000000.00000000 in binary

(a) The Class B network ID is defined by the first and second segments of the address (i.e., first 16 bits). Since you are using "/18" to create subnets, the first two bits of the third segment are being used for subnetting. These first two bits will enable you to create $2^2 = 4$ total subnets (00, 01, 10, and 11).

(b) The first two segments are given: 130.21, and the first two bits of the third segment gives you "00" = 0, "01" = 64, "10" = 128, and "11" = 192. Keeping in mind that you are using the most significant two bits of the third segment. Therefore, the subnet IDs are:

Subnet ID #1: 10000010.00010101.**00**000000.00000000 or <u>130.21.0.0</u>
Subnet ID #2: 10000010.00010101.**01**000000.00000000 or <u>130.21.64.0</u>
Subnet ID #3: 10000010.00010101.**10**000000.00000000 or <u>130.21.128.0</u>
Subnet ID #4: 10000010.00010101.**11**000000.00000000 or <u>130.21.192.0</u>

(c) The first two segments of the Class B address are given, therefore the subnet mask begins with 255.255; however, you used the first two bits of the third segment which gives you a subnet mask of 192. Therefore, your subnet mask for "/18" is:

Subnet Mask: <u>11111111.11111111.11000000.00000000 or 255.255.192.0</u>

(d) Since the remaining $32 - 18 = 14$ bits are used for host IDs, the total number of hosts per subnet is given below.

$(2^{14} - 2) = $ <u>16,382 host IDs per subnet</u>

9.3.2 Address Resolution Protocol (ARP)

We discussed how IPv4 operates at the network layer providing an end-to-end communications protocol over different common networks operating at the datalink layer. The ***Address Resolution Protocol (ARP)*** works specifically with both the network and data link protocols to create an address mapping between these layers. Separate ARP standards exist depending upon the data link layer protocol used (e.g., Ethernet, ATM, Frame Relay, etc.). With Ethernet LANs, ARP maps IP addresses to Ethernet MAC addresses. It is the MAC address on the LAN that is used to deliver the IP datagram to the correct station, while the principle job of IP is to get the datagram to the correct IP network associated with the common network.

Recall in our discussion of LANs that the *Ethernet medium access control (MAC)* layer is where the 48-bit MAC address operates. The MAC address is programmed into firmware which resides on the *Network Interface Card (NIC)* of each device connected to the LAN. If the intention was to only allow internal communications between LAN devices, then the MAC address and Ethernet protocol would be more than sufficient. However, today LAN devices typically communicate externally beyond the common network, and therefore implementation of a network layer protocol, such as IP, is required. This means that an IP address must be associated with each externally communicating device on the LAN. Depending upon the method used by a particular network, distribution of IP addresses can be accomplished in several ways. The simplest method is to assign each device its own IP address; however, considering the limitations of IPv4, it is common practice for a device wishing to communicate on the Internet to borrow an IP address from a pool of shared addresses. The *Dynamic Host Configuration Protocol (DHCP)* is used by many Internet Service Providers (ISPs) to assign IPv4 addresses to users seeking to communicate on the Internet. More will be said about DHCP in a later section.

For the purposes of discussing ARP in this section, we will assume that each device on the LAN has been assigned its own IPv4 address as shown in fig. 9.7(a). The LAN on the left of the figure has the network ID 192.160.13.0 and a subnet mask of 255.255.255.0. Therefore, we know that this is a Class C network. The five stations, A through E, are directly connected on the same common network; therefore, if station E wishes to connect to station C as shown, it can do so without requiring ARP or the IP network layer.

However, what happens if station E wishes to connect to station X which is located on a different common network [fig. 9.7(b)]? In this case ARP, the IP network, and a gateway are all required. Station E transmits an Ethernet frame which envelopes an IP packet that contains both IP source and destination addresses. The network ID portion of the destination IP address, which belongs to station X (192.160.15.0), identifies a network that is external to the common network E is on. Therefore, the Ethernet frame is delivered to a gateway (192.160.13.6), which is connected to both IP networks. Upon arriving at the destination IP network, ARP searches the cache that holds the IP to MAC address table to see if a MAC address is currently mapped to the destination IP address. If it is, then X's MAC address is attached to an Ethernet frame enveloping the datagram, and the frame is delivered. If, on the other hand, no mapping between X's IP and MAC addresses exist, then ARP broadcasts a special frame to all stations on the common network in hopes that a station will claim the IP address. Once claimed, a mapping between the IP and MAC addresses is created within the ARP cache.

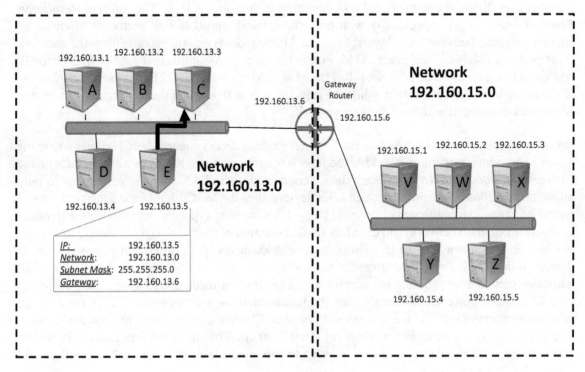

(a) "E" communicates to "C" on the same common network.

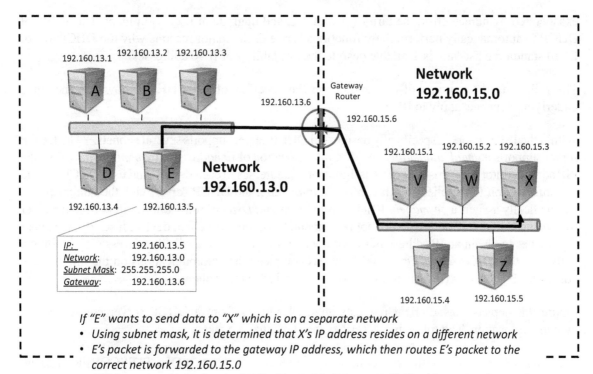

If "E" wants to send data to "X" which is on a separate network
- Using subnet mask, it is determined that X's IP address resides on a different network
- E's packet is forwarded to the gateway IP address, which then routes E's packet to the correct network 192.160.15.0
- ARP is used to determine the MAC address that belongs to X's IP address, then forwards the packet to X's MAC address

(b) "E" communicates to "X," which is located on a different common network.

FIGURE 9.7 Address Resolution Protocol (ARP) Example.
Server © Lineicons freebird/Shutterstock.com

9.3.3 Dynamic Host Configuration Protocol (DHCP)

The *Dynamic Host Configuration Protocol (DHCP)*, defined by IETF RFC 2131 published in 1997, is a client-server protocol that dynamically, or permanently, assigns IPv4 addresses to hosts when requested. DHCP operates over a connectionless *UDP (User Datagram Protocol)/IP* model. DHCPv6 supports IPv6 addresses and is covered by RFCs 3315,3633, and 3736. DHCP is based upon the *BOOTP (Bootstrap Protocol)* that operated over UDP to enable diskless[15] network terminals to discover its own IP address.

For ISPs who are allocated IPv4 address blocks, use of DHCP helps to extend the pool of addresses available to users by dynamically assigning them on an "as needed" basis. In addition, network parameters such as network IDs and subnet masks are sent automatically to clients. Without DHCP, ISP administrators would be required to manually configure each user IP address and associated network parameters. Depending upon the size of the network, this could become a laborious task,

---

[15] "diskless" refers to a network workstation, or "dumb" terminal, that does not have persistent memory such as a hard drive.

exasperated by human error, the turn-over of users, and upgrade of user equipment. The ability of DHCP to automatically perform these functions is one of the major reasons why the DHCPv6 (for IPv6) standard exists and is available despite the availability of IPv6 addresses.

The following discussion will concentrate on the specifics of IPv4 DHCP; however, the same underlying concepts apply to IPv6.

Within the ISP network, a specifically designated DHCP server supports several subnets.[16] The DHCP server supports *manual*, *automatic*, and *dynamic* allocation of IP addresses. In *manual allocation*, the ISP administrator performs the actual assignment of addresses to each device, and uses DHCP to send this information to the client. With *automatic allocation*, the DHCP server, vice the administrator, automatically assigns a *permanent* IP address to the client. *Dynamic allocation* differs from the other two methods in that IP addresses are not permanently assigned to a client device. Instead, each client that wishes to obtain an IP address must borrow one from a pool of available addresses by sending a request to the DHCP server. Once the client has completed its communications on the Internet, the borrowed IP address is returned to the pool for allocation to other clients.

Figure 9.8 depicts how a client requests an IPv4 address from a DHCP server configured for dynamic allocation. The following describes the steps that are taken.

Step 1. The client wishing to obtain an IP address broadcasts a DHCPDISCOVER message within its local subnetwork. The DHCPDISCOVER message may contain an optional field that identifies the amount of time during which the address is required. This is termed the "lease duration."

Step 2. One or more DHCP servers may receive the client request, and each will respond with a DCHPOFFER message that includes an IP address and configuration parameters.

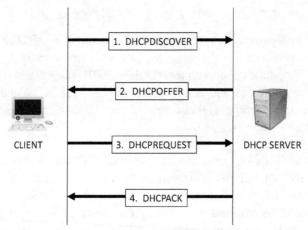

FIGURE 9.8 Dynamic Host Configuration Protocol (DHCP) address request.
Server © Lineicons freebird/Shutterstock.com; Computer © My Portfolio/Shutterstock.com

---

[16] A single DHCP server can support several subnets. This differs from BOOTP which requires a server for each subnet.

Step 3. Upon receipt of one or more DHCPOFFER messages, the client selects one of the offers based upon network parameters, and broadcasts a DHCPREQUEST containing the identification of the server that has been selected.

Step 4. All DHCP servers receive the DHCPREQUEST message containing the select server's identification. As such, all servers are notified which server's offer has been accepted. The selected server sends a DHCPACK message back to the client thus binding the server to provide persistent storage to the client throughout the duration of the connection.

9.3.4 Network Address Translation (NAT)

Private networks, or **intranets**, are popular with large organizations that wish to interconnect their internal common networks together using IP. Intranets use their own private IP addressing blocks that provide network administrators full control over the creation of subnets and allocation of addresses. Private networks also enjoy better security from external attacks since they are isolated by gateway routers and firewalls. However, the ability for intranet computers to reach the Internet is still required by most organization for the purposes of ecommerce, research, and data exchange.

The **Network Address Translation**[17] **(NAT)** operates on a gateway router inbetween the internal private network and the Internet. Computers that wish to communicate externally require an IP address that is recognized by the Internet. The NAT gateway maps the computer's internal network address to a valid Internet address, thus allowing the exchange of datagrams with the Internet. Since only a fraction of the intranet computers communicate externally at the same time, valid IPv4 addresses assigned to the organization can be shared. This helps to extend the limited number of IPv4 addresses available.

While one of the goals of the NAT RFC was to conserve the limited IPv4 addressing space, introduction of IPv6 does not mean the end of NAT gateways. NATs will continue to be used on private networks for several of the following reasons.

- A NAT gateway reduces exposure and helps to isolate the internal network from external threats. In addition, it can force incoming traffic to go through an authentication process.

- IPv6 is currently deployed, however private networks not wishing to upgrade their intranets to the new protocol immediately can use NAT to translate between IPv4 and IPv6 addresses.

- In the absence of a NAT capability, each private network device wishing to communicate externally would need to either have an assigned permanent IPv6 address, or go through a DHCPv6 process to obtain one. Doing this increases the intranet's exposure to the external environment.

- For the network administrator, assigning a valid IPv6 address to each internal device would be laborious. In the event that the organization switches ISPs, new IP addresses would need to be configured for each intranet device. By implementing a private IP address block for the intranet, these changes would only affect gateway servers and not the entire private network.

---

[17] Also known as "Network Address Translator."

There are also drawbacks regarding NATs which stem from the concept that communications between two devices are not truly end-to-end, but must undergo a change in IP addresses at the NAT gateway. The idea that source and destination IP addresses must change impacts some protocols such as *IPSec*, which is briefly discussed below. In addition, NAT gateways introduce network choke points, which can act as a *single-point-of-failure (SPF)* for external communications.

IPSec (IP Security) is an IETF suite of security protocols used to *authenticate* and *encrypt* datagrams traversing an IP network. IPSec supports a *"transport"* operational mode where only the payload is encrypted, and not the IP header. IPSec also supports a *"tunnel"* mode where both the IP header and payload are encrypted. Either modes can use the **Authentication Header (AH)** and **Encapsulating Security Payload (ESP)** protocols either in conjunction with one another or separately.

AH provides a data integrity[18] check using a *hashing algorithm* that is applied to the datagram. The results of the hash is appended to the datagram and sent. Upon receipt, another hash is performed on the datagram using the same algorithm, and the results are compared to one another. If the results are identical, then data integrity is verified. It should be kept in mind that AH only verifies data integrity, and does not provide confidentiality of the datagram itself. Because NAT changes the source and destination IP addresses at the gateway between the intranet and Internet, the hashing algorithm will produce a result that is different from the hashing result appended by the transmitter. This causes the datagram to be rejected.

IPSec ESP in the **transport** mode encrypts the payload, but not the original IP header. The ESP header is appended after the IP header so the IP header is not altered. As such, NAT can swap IP addresses. However, since the entire payload, which includes the transport layer segment, is encrypted, transport layer port assignments may be impacted; especially if the *Port Address Translation*[19] *(PAT)* protocol had been implemented. Therefore the transport mode of ESP can be unreliable depending upon its implementation.

IPSec ESP used in the **tunnel** mode differs in that the entire datagram, including the original IP header, is encrypted with authentication typically implemented. Like AH, the swapping of IP addresses would cause an integrity issue to be flagged, and the datagram would be discarded.

There are advantages and disadvantages with NAT gateways, but the drive to improve the NAT standard continues because it is seen by many as an essential tool in securing private IP networks.

---

[18] Data integrity does not provide privacy from eavesdropping, but ensures that the data has not been tampered with during transit. This is accomplished by applying a hashing algorithm, such as MD5 or SHA-1, and appending the results to the datagram itself. Upon receipt, the same hashing algorithm is executed on the received datagram and the results compared to the results originally appended by the transmitter. If the two results are identical, then data integrity has been verified.

[19] Note: PAT is an extension of NAT used to allow more than one device to operate using a single IP address with the intent of conserving IP addressing space. Further discussion of PAT is beyond the scope of this text.

9.3.5 Domain Name System (DNS)

IPv4 addresses are key to establishing communications across the network layer, but when using a browser or email application, most of us do not keep a list of those addresses we wish to communicate with. Instead, we use a ***Uniform Resource Locator***[20] ***(URL)*** such as *www.gmu.edu*, which is much easier to remember than the IP address *129.174.1.59*. With IPv6 128-bit addresses, is becomes even more difficult to remember IP addresses.

To describe the usefulness of the DNS system, let's compare it to the standard telephone book. When searching for a specific telephone number, we simply look up the name of the individual or business to find the associated telephone number. Over time the telephone numbers of people and businesses may change, thus requiring the phone companies to reissue updated telephone books. Even though the telephone numbers may have changed, the owners name have not, therefore still enabling telephone contact by simply looking up the individual or business names and updated telephone numbers. DNS works like an automated online book linking URLs to IP addresses. As users change ISPs and therefore IP addresses, the DNS server is updated. So despite a change in IP address, the URL through the DNS process will connect you to the correct location. The process of taking an URL and translating it to an IP address is called ***DNS name resolution***.

DNS has a decentralized hierarchical structure based upon the URL. At the top of this hierarchy in fig. 9.9 is the ***root domain*** (also termed the ***root zone***) which is the responsibility of the

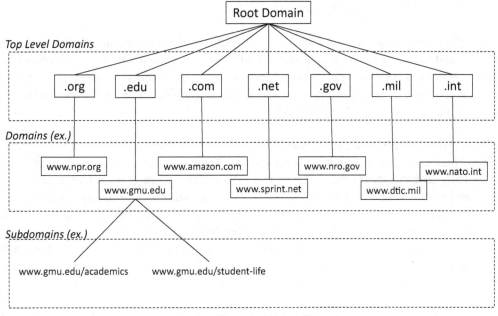

FIGURE 9.9 Domain Name Hierarchy.

---

[20] A URL provides a location of the resource and is a subset of a URI (Uniform Resource Identifier), which describes the resource itself.

TABLE 9.4   *Just a Few* Top-Level Domains and Sponsoring Organizations.

Domain	Sponsoring Organization
.arpa	Internet Architecture Board (IAB)
.bbc	British Broadcasting Corporation
.cisco	Cisco Technology Inc.
.com	VeriSign Global Registry Services
.edu	EDUCAUSE
.gov	General Services Administration
.int	IANA
.mil	DoD Network Information Center
.net	Verisign Global Registry Services
.org	Public Interest Registry (PIR)

Internet Assigned Numbers Authority (IANA). As the root zone manager, IANA assigns the responsibility of the ***top-level domains (TLD)*** to various operators. Table 9.4 shows a few of the numerous TLDs and the responsible operators.

Below the TLDs are the domains which represent individual organizations. So for *gmu.edu*, the TLD is *.edu*, and the domain which identifies the organization is *gmu*. Of course, a domain such as *gmu.edu* is almost always associated with numerous other ***subdomains***, representing suborganizations or subtopics within the main organization. In our example, sub-domains include *www.gmu. edu/academics* and *www.gmu.edu/student-life*.

Let's look at an example of how the DNS process works. You open your browser and enter the URL for *George Mason University*, which is *www.gmu.edu*. If you are connected to the Internet, the URL is automatically sent to a local DNS resolver as a *DNS query*. The resolver, which exists on a DNS server located within your ISP, first checks its own cache and internal host database to see if the URL and IP address are present there. If the local server finds the IP address, it returns this information to your computer. If it does not find the associated IP address, then it begins a query process to other DNS servers. Keep in mind that a vast network of distributed DNS servers exists globally for this purpose. If the local server successfully finds the IP address, it passes it to your computer and temporarily caches this information for any future queries.

Finally, there are two major classifications of a DNS query. A ***recursive query*** is one in which the DNS server essentially does all of the work in resolving the domain name to an IP address. The example above uses this type of query. While in a ***non-recursive query***, the DNS server does not perform all of the work, but instead provides information back suggesting other DNS servers that should be queried in order to resolve the domain name.

9.3.6 Internet Control Message Protocol (ICMP)

IP is a connectionless "*best effort*" protocol that is considered "*unreliable*" because it does not guarantee datagram delivery. IP relies upon the upper layer protocols to deal with the delivery, error control, and resequencing of datagrams. However, it is still important to inform the source node when a datagram has encountered problems during transit. This is the job of the ***Internet Control Message Protocol (ICMP)***.

ICMP, which is described in *IETF RFC 4884,*[21] operates at the network layer and is used by networks to help identify any issues that might be impacting the network. As an example, if a datagram's *time-to-live (TTL)* has expired, this may indicate network congestion or the existence of a network partition; information that is useful for making routing decisions. Other situations where ICMP is used is when a datagram cannot reach its destination for any reason, when a gateway router has a buffering issue and cannot accept additional datagrams, and to provide information regarding better routing information through the network. ICMP keeps network routers and their operators apprised of the condition of the network; however, it should be noted that it does not make IP reliable.

ICMP datagrams follow the normal IP header format and are identified as ICMP messages in the 8-bit "*protocol*" field of the header. Additional information specific to the error being reported is provided at the beginning of the "*payload*" field. Also included after the ICMP header in the *payload* field is the IP header of the impacted datagram. Figure 9.10 depicts IPv4 ICMP format using the standard IP header. *Note: IPv6 is supported by ICMPv6, and the message formats are similar.*

The *type* of ICMP message depends upon the problem encountered. Examples would be "*destination unreachable*" or "*time exceeded,*" plus others. Most *types* have several codes that help to further define the problem. Table 9.5 provides details regarding the ICMPv4 message in fig. 9.10.

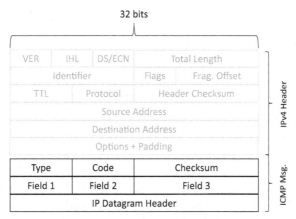

FIGURE 9.10 ICMP Message

---

[21] RFC 4884 redefines previous IPv4 RFC 792 and IPv6 RFC 4443.

TABLE 9.5 ICMPv4 message types and codes (IETF RFC 792 and 4884)

Type	Code	Extended Fields[1]	Remarks
0: Echo Reply			
3: Destination Unreachable	0: net unreachable 1: host unreachable 2: protocol unreachable 3: port unreachable 4: fragmentation needed 5: source rote failed	Field 1 - unused Field 2 - length of original datagram Field 3 - unused	Destination address unreachable
4: Source Quench			Gateway buffer exceeded and datagram discarded
5: Redirect	0: redirect for the network 1: redirect for the host		Gateway redirects datagram
8: Echo			
11: Time Exceeded	0: time to live exceeded 1: fragment reassembly time exceeded		TTL is determined to be zero
12: Parameter Problem	0: pointer indicates error	Field 1 - pointer Field 2 - length of original datagram Field 3 - unused	Gateway discovers problem with header
13: Timestamp			
14: Timestamp Reply			
15: Info. Request			
16: Info. Reply			

Note1: fields extended by RFC 4884.

9.3.7 IPv6

Primarily in response to the unanticipated growth of the Internet and the need for more addressing space, IETF developed IPv6 RFC 1883 in 1995, which was updated by RFC 2460 in 1998. A key feature of IPv6 is its expanded 128-bit address field which provides $2^{128} = 340 \times 10^{36}$ addresses, and is considered more than sufficient into the foreseeable future. Unfortunately, IPv6 is not backward compatible with IPv4, thus necessitating a translation process to enable these protocols to interact with one another. The major improvements from IPv4 to IPv6 are described in the following subsection.

9.3.7.1 Expanded Addressing Field

The 128-bit address is segmented into eight groups of 16 bits. Each 16-bit segment is represented by hexadecimal digits (0 through 9, A, B, C, D, F) and separated by a colon. *So why use the hexadecimal (Base 16) numbering system vice the IPv4 decimal system which seems easier for us humans to comprehend?* The answer to this is two-fold.

First, if we used the same IPv4 decimal representation on a 128 binary bit address by organizing them into eight bit groups, we would have 16 segments total. Each segment would be represented by three decimal numbers, which means that our total address in decimal form would be 48 decimal digits long. This is too large a number for most of us to work with efficiently. Using hexadecimal the number of digits is reduced to 32. While this might not appear to be a large difference, the hexadecimal address is a bit friendlier.

The second reason is probably more important. All computers operate in binary, and translators must eventually convert either decimal or hexadecimal numbers into binary digits for processor computations. However, hexadecimal numbers are much easier to translate and compile into binary than decimal and thus processing efficiencies can be gained. Table 9.6 presents a comparison of these numbering systems. As an example, a four-digit binary number gives you $2^4 = 16$ different

TABLE 9.6   Comparison of numbering systems.

Binary	Octal (Base-8)	Hexadecimal (Base-16)	Decimal (Base-10)
0000	0	0	0
0001	1	1	1
0010	2	2	2
0011	3	3	3
0100	4	4	4
0101	5	5	5
0110	6	6	6
0111	7	7	7
1000	0	8	8
1001	1	9	9
1010	2	A	10
1011	3	B	11
1100	4	C	12
1101	5	D	13
1110	6	E	14
1111	7	F	15

values, which equate to a single hexadecimal digit. So a binary "1111" equals a hexadecimal "F." An eight-bit binary number gives you $2^8 = 256$ values, which equate to a two-digit hexadecimal number (e.g., "11111111" = "FF"). Both binary and hexadecimal numbers are based upon the powers of 2, so there is a natural correlation between the two numbering systems. This is also true for the octal (0 through 7) numbering system. This makes computational algorithms more efficient. It is one of the reasons why MAC addresses are hexadecimal, and why computer data is typically described in octal or hexadecimal terms vice decimal numbers.

IPv6 addresses can support one of three modes: unicast, anycast, and multicast. In *Unicast* mode, two nodes essentially exchange data with one another, each having addresses associated with their interfaces to the network. Like IPv4 addresses, IPv6 unicast addresses can be used with CIDR to perform subnetting.

Anycast addresses are probably the least understood of the three addressing modes. An IPv6 anycast address is allocated from the unicast addressing space and is assigned to more than one nodal interface with the condition that the datagram sent to the anycast address results into shortest or least-cost metric. Anycast addresses can be used to identify a set of routers belonging to a subnet or organization, or in situations where finding the nearest service (e.g., DNS server) is desired. In essence, communications is set up with only one of many nodes that share the same anycast address, and this node will be selected based upon the cost metric used.

IPv6 *Multicast* replaced *IPv4 broadcasts*. With IPv4, broadcasts are sent to every node in the subnet causing inefficiencies especially for those nodes not wishing to receive it. With IPv6 multicasts, only a select group of nodes receive the multicast. Broadcasts can be considered a subset or a multicast. IPv6 enables the selection of interfaces that the multicast is sent to. This is useful for IoT (Internet-of-Things) devices that remain in "sleep-mode" to conserve battery power until a multicast message is specifically received. In this same scenario, if an IPv4 broadcast were used, it would wake up every device within the network regardless, thus unnecessarily expending battery power.

Similar to the IPv4 address structure, the IPv6 address is comprised of a subnet prefix (subnet) and interface ID (host). Below is an example of an IPv6 address:

FEDC:BA98:3210:1080:0:0:8:200C

Colons separate the 16 segments and as you can see leading zeros are not necessary at the beginning of each segment. The use of double colons "::" indicates that one or more segments consist of all zeros. "::" can only be used once. Therefore, our example address can appear as follows:

FEDC:BA98:3210:1080::8:200C

The CIDR notation can be used to identify the subnet prefix. As an example below, the first 60 binary bits represents the subnet number.

FEDC:BA98:3210:1080::8:200C/60

Similar to IPv4, there are also special addresses such as 0:0:0:0:0:0:0:0 which is an unspecified address that is never used, and 0:0:0:0:0:0:0:1 which is a loopback address. Other special addresses exist but for the purposes of this description are considered beyond the scope of this section.

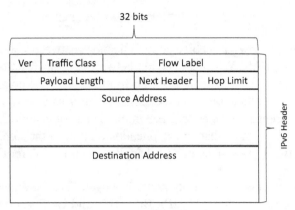

FIGURE 9.11 IPv6 Header.

9.3.7.2 Header Format Simplification

In the IPv6 header, several of the IPv4 fields were dropped or made optional to enable more efficient datagram processing.

Figure 9.11 depicts the IPv6 header which includes the following fields:

- Version (4 bits): IPv6
- Traffic Class (8 bits): Use to identify different classes or priorities of IPv6 packets.
- Flow Label (20 bits): Indicates the sequence of packets from a specific source to a destination, either unicast or multicast.
- Payload Length (16 bits): Length of the IPv6 payload in octets.
- Next Header (8 bits): Identifies the header following the IPv6 header. This is similar to the IPv4 "protocol" field.
- Hop Limit (8 bits): Hop limit for packet (replaces IPv4 TTL).
- Source Address (128 bits)
- Destination Address (128 bits)

9.3.7.3 Support for Extensions, Options, Flow Labeling, and Security

IPv6 provides support for *optional extension* headers to be identified in the "next header" field (e.g., to identify TCP, UDP, or an enveloped IPv4 header). In most cases, these extension headers are not seen by intermediary routers, but are examined for the first time at the destination node. The exception to this is the "hop-by-hop" options header that must be examined by every router along the path. *Options* are carried over from IPv4, and are used to provide additional information regarding how a packet should be processed. New to IPv6 is a *flow labeling* capability. This allows packets to be identified with particular traffic flows which require special handling such as real-time services. Finally, extensions to support authentication, data integrity, and confidentiality have been added to IPv6.

9.4 TRANSPORT LAYER 4 (TCP AND UDP)

We discussed that the *data link layer 2* enabled communications between stations residing on the same common network, such as a LAN. When connection between stations residing on different common networks is required, we depend upon the *network layer 3* to provide the connectivity. However once the IP packet has reached the destination node, there must be information available to direct the packet to the correct application running on the node. Keep in mind that computers and servers are multitasking and therefore typically have more than one application running at the same time. Making sure the data received from the network goes to the intended application is the job for the ***transport layer 4***.

The two transport layer protocols that commonly work above IP are the ***Transport Control Protocol (TCP)*** and the ***User Datagram Protocol (UDP)***. Both TCP and UDP segments contain source and destination ***port*** assignments. A *port assignment* identifies the appropriate computer/server application that the data is intended for. Table 9.7 identifies some of the more popular port assignments.

TABLE 9.7 Some Popular Transport Layer Port Assignments.

Port Number	Assignment
20,21	File Transfer Protocol (FTP)
22	Secure Shell (SSH)
23	Telnet
25	Simple Mail Transfer (SMTP)
53	Domain Name Server (DNS)
80	Hypertext Transfer (HTTP)
88	Kerberos
110	Postal Office Protocol 3 (POP3)
119	Network News Transfer Protocol (NNTP)
123	Network Time Protocol
161	Simple Network Management (SNMP)
179	Border Gateway (BGP)
443	Hypertext Transfer Protocol Secure (HTTPS)
546	Dynamic Host Configuration (DHCPv6)
554	Real Time Streaming Protocol (RTSP)
614	Secure Socket Layer (SSL) Shell
989, 990	FTP over TLS/SSL
992	Telnet over TLS/SSL
993	IMAP4 over TLS/SSL
995	POP3 over TLS/SSL
Etc.	. . .

As an example, a computer may be running a web browser (port 80) and using an email program (port 110) at the same time. IP packets arriving at the computer will then be inspected at the transport layer for destination port assignments in order to segregate browser data from email traffic.

TCP is a *connection-oriented* protocol, which means that a connection between source and destination ports is established using a *three-way handshake*. Establishing a connection ensures that all TCP segments arrives reliably and in the proper sequence. In contrast, UDP is a *connectionless* protocol similar to IP. As such, UDP does not guarantee delivery or proper sequencing; however, it has a much simpler header that enables faster processing. UDP is often used for delay sensitive real-time streaming applications (e.g., Voice-over-IP or VoIP), thus leaving the task of ensuring reliability to upper level protocols.

9.4.1 Transport Control Protocol (TCP)

Operating at OSI layer 4, TCP takes the data from the upper layers, divides this data into smaller more manageable groupings as needed, and then appends a header to form a **TCP segment**. Each TCP segment header (see fig. 9.12) contains source and destination *port assignments* that identify the application the data is to be delivered to. The TCP segment is then delivered to the network layer (OSI layer 3) where it is assembled into packets (i.e., *packetized*), with each packet affixed with an IP header containing the source and destination network addresses. Once completed, the IP packets are delivered to the data link layer (OSI layer 2), and a data link protocol such as Ethernet is used to frame the entire packet with its own information. Note that all of the above encapsulation is performed prior to any actual transmission over the physical network medium. The data link MAC (medium access control) layer, works closely with the physical layer (OSI layer 1), and together the binary bits are converted into an electrical, electromagnetic, or optical signal which is then transmitted. At the destination end, the reverse of the process takes place (see fig. 9.13).

- Source Port (16 bits): port number associated with the process located at the source end.
- Destination Port (16 bits): port number associated with the intended process at the destination end.
- Sequence Number (32 bits): sequence number associated with each byte/octet, that is incremented to enable the sequential tracking of data transmissions.
- Acknowledgment Number (32 bits): acknowledgments sent and incremented per sequence number received.

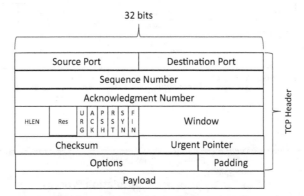

FIGURE 9.12 TCP Segment, which includes a header and payload.

- Data Offset (4 bits): specifies the number of 32 bit words are used in the TCP header, and indicates the beginning of the payload data.
- Reserved (6 bits): future use.
- Control Bits (1 bit each for total of 6 bits):
  - ○ URG: "1" indicates a priority data transfer. Used in conjunction with the "Urgent Point field."
  - ○ ACK: "1" indicates that the segment carries an ACK.
  - ○ PSH: push bit (PSH) feature invoked requesting that the data be immediately pushed to the application.
  - ○ RST: sender encountered a problem and the connection must be reset.
  - ○ SYN: SYN bits represent a request to reset synchronization sequence numbers and to establish a connection.
  - ○ FIN: sent when the connection is requested to be closed.
- Window (16 bits): indicates the number of octets to be sent in a window at one time.
- Checksum (16 bits): applied to the total TCP segment.
- Urgent Pointer (16 bits): contains the sequence number of the last byte of urgent data. Used in conjunction with the "URG" control bit.
- Options (variable bit length): mechanism to address sets of optional data.
- Padding (variable bit length): bits added to ensure 32-bit blocks.
- Payload (variable bit length)

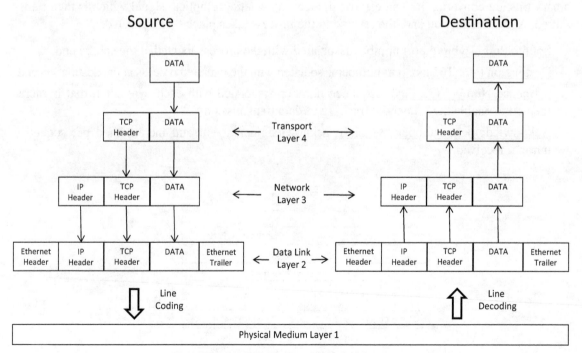

FIGURE 9.13 TCP/IP Encapsulation Process.

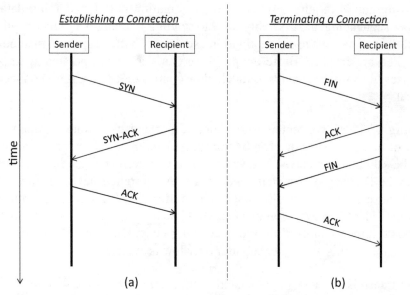

FIGURE 9.14 (a) TCP Three-way Handshake and (b) Connection Termination.

By establishing a connection at the transport layer using a ***three-way handshake***, TCP makes the communications between source and destination reliable. The three-way handshake in fig. 9.14(a), starts with the sender transmitting a "SYN" (synchronize) segment to the recipient. In the TCP header of the "SYN" request, the SYN bit is set to "1" and a proposed start number appears in the sequence number field.[22] If the recipient is ready to accept a connection, it replies with a "SYN-ACK" segment in which both SYN and ACK bits are set within the header. Upon receiving the "SYN-ACK" the sender returns with an "ACK", which formally establishes the connection.

The TCP termination sequence begins when one of the nodes wishing to terminate the connection, sends a "FIN" segment, with the FIN bit within the header set. Unlike connection setup, both nodes must agree to the termination, and therefore both must send and acknowledge "FIN" requests. Upon receipt of a "FIN" request, the receiving nodes send out an "ACK" which acknowledges the receipt of the request. If the receiving nodes also wishes to terminate the connection, it sends a "FIN" request . Once this second "FIN" request has been acknowledged with an "ACK," the connection is formally closed.

Once a TCP connection has been established, acknowledgments for all data received is required so that the proper sequencing of segments can be attained and any missing data can be flagged for retransmission. To facilitate data sequencing and retransmission, buffer storage is required at both source and destination nodes. At the source buffer, transmission data is temporarily stored

---

[22] The sequence number field in the TCP header is used to track the sequence of bytes between source and destination ports. The acknowledgment number tracks the sequence of "ACKS" between source and destination. This enables the proper sequencing of all data between the two nodes, and also helps to identify any lost data segments.

in case retransmission is required. While at the destination buffer, incoming data is stored to allow for proper sequencing and assembly prior to sending it to an upper layer application. However, if the delivery of packets to the destination exceeds its buffer capacity, then buffer overflow occurs and packets are dropped. Buffering problems can also be exasperated by network congestion which causes transmission delays. As such, flow control mechanisms for connection-oriented data are critical.

TCP uses *sliding window*[23] concept as a flow control mechanism. A transmission *window* consist of the number of octets or bytes that can be transmitted and received before an acknowledgment, "ACK," must be sent by the receiver. The *window size* in bytes/octets is represented by the 16-bit *window* field in the TCP header, which is negotiated between source and destination devices during the three-way handshake; typically reflecting receive buffer size. The source transmits no more than the amount of data identified by the window size, and then waits until it receives an "ACK," along with an "acknowledgment number" from the receiving node. Once the "ACK" is received, it can resume transmission. In this way, receive buffer overflow is avoided.

Every window transmission is also associated with a *time-out period* within which an "ACK" must be received by the source. The time-out period prevents the source from immediately retransmitting data and causing duplicates to be received. However, if the time-out period has expired with no "ACK" received, the source assumes that data was lost and begins to retransmit unacknowledged data.

To better understand the sliding window concept, let's take a look at a very simple example in fig. 9.15, where our window size equals 100 octets, which means that an "ACK" is required after each successful receipt of 100 octets[24]. In this example, each TCP segment carries 50 octets of data, therefore two segments, or 100 octets total, are delivered before an "ACK" is required. The first 50 octets are sent with a *sequence number (Seq)* of "1" in the TCP header representing the first of the 50 octets (1 through 50) sent. The next 50 octets are sent with a Seq number equal to "51," representing the first of the next 50 octets (51 through 100) sent. Once the 100 octets have been successfully received, an "ACK" along with the next expected *acknowledgment number*, in this case "101," is sent back to the source.

However, what happens when data is lost while enroute to the destination? In fig. 9.16(a), Seq "1" (octets 1 through 50) is sent successfully reaching its destination. However, the next segment Seq "51" never makes it to the destination, and therefore ACK "101" is never sent. The sender waits until the timeout period is expired, at which time it assume that either Seq "51," or both Seq "51" and "1" never reached the destination. Since it does not know which segments were successfully received since the last ACK was sent, the sender sends both Seq "1" and "51" again. Once the destination receives both segments, it sends back an ACK "101" identifying to the sender the next expected sequence number.

---

[23] "Sliding Window" is also known as "windowing".

[24] Window sizes can be as large as $2^{16} = 65,536$ octets; however, this would depend upon network traffic and congestion.

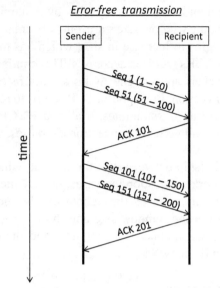

FIGURE 9.15 TCP Sliding Window Exchange.

For the sender, a "lost ACK" in transit is essentially treated the same way [see fig. 9.16(b)]. No ACK is received so the sender does not know whether the cause is due to lost data or a lost ACK. In either case, the timeout period expires and the sender retransmits all segments since the receipt of the last good ACK.

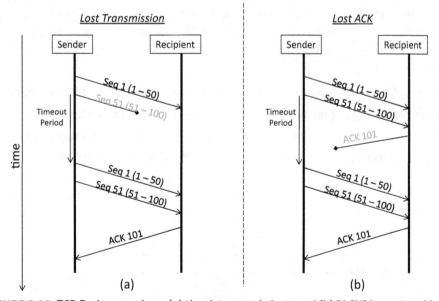

FIGURE 9.16 TCP Exchange where (a) the data sent is lost, and (b) "ACK" is sent and lost.

TCP flow control also helps to avoid network congestion by dynamically controlling the window size. Upon connection initiation, the window size starts out very small. With each successful receipt of an ACK, the window size begins to increase in size, which has the effect of increasing overall throughput since the number of ACKs required decreases. This continues until a maximum window size is reached. However, if packets are lost and ACKs are not received, then TCP assumes that failure is caused by network congestion. In response, TCP begins to reduce the size of the windows, which effectively decreases data transmission rates. If all active TCP sessions on the network follow the same procedure, then overall network congestion decreases.

Equation (9.1) provides a relationship between data throughput, window size, and latency caused by network congestion. As network congestion increases, latency increases, causing data throughput to decrease. By increasing window size, throughput can be increased; however, if network congestion is an issue, then increasing window size and throughput only exasperates congestion seen on the network. Instead, TCP reduces window size, and therefore data throughput, in an attempt to reduce congestion on the network.

$$\text{Maximum Throughput} = \frac{\text{TCP window in Bytes}}{\text{Data latency in seconds}} \qquad \textbf{(9.1)}$$

9.4.2 User Datagram Protocol (UDP)

Unlike TCP, UDP is connectionless, unreliable, does not guarantee sequencing, and does not have built in flow control or internal retransmission mechanisms. However, the minimal header length, shown in fig. 9.17, enables UDP to be a much faster protocol, which is useful for real-time communications or for applications that do not require the exchange of large amounts of data. Essentially, UDP performs transport layer functions very quickly.

Some of the applications that use UDP at layer 4 are Domain Name System (DNS), Simple Network Management Protocol (SNMP), Dynamic Host Configuration Protocol (DHCP), Routing Information Protocol (RIP), Voice over IP (VoIP), video teleconferencing, and gaming. For those applications such as VoIP, that require greater reliability, the upper layers above UDP are tasked with the responsibility.

- Source Port (16 bits): port number associated with the process located at the source end.
- Destination Port (16 bits): port number associated with the intended process at the destination end.
- Length (16 bits): length of the entire UDP segment including header and payload.
- Checksum (16 bits): optional checksum computed over the entire USP segment.

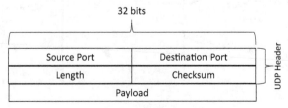

FIGURE 9.17 UDP Header and Payload.

9.5 MULTIPROTOCOL LABEL SWITCHING (MPLS)

Connectionless protocols such as IPv4 lack the ability to differentiate and prioritize packets through a network. This means that every packet is treated exactly the same preventing service providers from being able to offer scalable[25] networking solutions and quality-of-service (QoS) features. This becomes a greater challenge as organizations strive for global reach with multimedia connections that require a mix of real-time and non-real time communications.

Multiprotocol Label Switching (MPLS) used in conjunction with IPv4 provides the connection-oriented services that enable service providers to meet a wide variety of user requirements. While MPLS is commonly used for IP networks, it is applicable to any network protocol. As an example, MPLS versions exist to support *connection-oriented* protocols such as *Frame Relay* and *ATM*.

In a typical IP network, routers make their routing decisions based upon the addresses appearing in the packet's header. The idea behind MPLS is to affix a label in front of the packet which is used to make routing decisions (see fig. 9.18). Each entering packet is associated with a specific ***forwarding equivalence class (FEC),***[26] which defines the "next-hop" routing through the entire MPLS network. This is unlike conventional IP networks where each router makes a "next-hop" decision. Since the ***MPLS label*** is only recognized by other routing switches within the MPLS common network, it has sometimes been argued that it should be considered a layer 2 vice layer 3 protocol.[27] Despite the classification, however, labels enable IP packets to move quickly through an MPLS network because inspection of the IP header itself is not required and because the FEC, which is associated with a particular group of packets, is assigned only once to identify the ***label switched path (LSP)*** through the network.

Figure 9.19 depicts a simple MPLS network. A packet entering the network first arrives at a ***Label edge router (LER)*** which serves as the MPLS network entry and exit points. Upon entry, the *LER* determines which FEC that the packet belongs to and appends the appropriate label to the packet. The FEC assigned to the packet identifies the routing needed through the network in order to comply with associated QoS and prioritization. With the label affixed, the packet tunnels though the

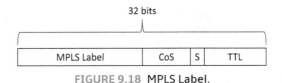

FIGURE 9.18 MPLS Label.

---

[25] As organizational networks grow in size and complexity, network management becomes a greater task for many service providers. Being able to offer scalable solutions makes it possible for these service providers to offer quality-of-service (QoS) in order to meet service level agreements (SLAs).

[26] FEC is a term used with conventional IP routers and it determines the packets next hop. In a standard IP network, FEC is determined by each router that the packet transits. In a MPLS network, FEC determination for a packet is done only once when it enters the MPLS network through a LER.

[27] However, there is no definitive argument that classifies it as one or the other.

network guided by ***label switched routers (LSRs)*** that need only read the label itself and not the original IP header. Upon determining the next hop, the LSR exchanges the old label for a new one and passes the packet to the next LSR. This enables fast switching through the network. Finally, once through the MPLS network, the packet arrives at an exit LER which removes the label and forwards the IP packet to the next network or destination.

- <u>MPLS Label (20 bits):</u> label identification
- <u>CoS (3 bits):</u> "class-of-service"
- <u>S (1 bit):</u> "stack," supports hierarchical label stacking
- <u>TTL (8 bits):</u> "time-to-live," similar to IPv4, determine the number of maximum hops

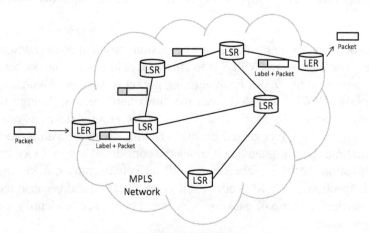

FIGURE 9.19 Simplified MPLS Network.

KEY TERMS

address resolution protocol (ARP)
Advanced Research Projects Agency (ARPA)
area border router (ABR)
ARPAnet
autonomous network (AN)
autonomous system (AS)
border gateway protocol (BGP)
classless Interdomain Routing (CIDR)
connection-oriented
connectionless
datagram

destination
distance vector protocol
domain name system (DNS)
dynamic host configuration protocol (DHCP)
dynamic routing table
exterior gateway protocol (EGP)
external BGP (EBGP)
gateway
interior gateway protocol (IGP)
internal BGP (IBGP)
Internet
Internet Assigned Numbers Authority (IANA)

internet control message protocol (ICMP)
Internet Corporation for Assigned Names and Numbers (ICANN)
Internet Exchange Point (IXP)
Internet Protocol (IP)
intranet
IP security (IPsec)
IPv4
IPv6
link-state routing protocol
multiprotocol label switching (MPLS)

network access point (NAP)	routing information protocol	three-way handshake
network address translation (NAT)	(RIP)	top level domain (TLD)
	sliding window	transport control protocol
open shortest path first (OSPF)	source	(TCP)
peering agreement	static routing table	uniform resource locator
port	subnet mask	(URL)
routing information base (RIB)	subnetwork	user datagram protocol
	subnetting	(UDP)

CHAPTER PROBLEMS

1. Which organization is responsible for the management of IP addresses across the world?
   a. ISO
   b. IETF
   c. ICANN
   d. ARPANET

   Answer: c

2. _____ facilitates the exchange of IP traffic between service providers.
   a. IXP
   b. IANA
   c. BGP
   d. ICANN

   Answer: a

3. What is an Internet Exchange Point (IXP)?
   a. An Internet web portal where html and xml data are exchanged between ISPs
   b. A physical location where standards committees get together to discuss Internet specifications
   c. A physical infrastructure that enables ISPs to exchange Internet traffic between networks through peering agreements
   d. None of the above

   Answer: c

4. _____ is a protocol that is used to communicate routing information within an autonomous network.
   a. IGP
   b. BGP
   c. DNS
   d. NAT

   Answer: a

5. *Peering agreements* between AS' enable the free flow of IP data between networks without regard to compensation or throughput charges.
   a. True
   b. False

   Answer: a

6. Select the correct statement(s) regarding the *Border Gateway Protocol (BGP).*
   a. BGP exchanges information with other BGP gateways through *IP datagrams*
   b. BGP provides the protocol that enables route sharing between separate AS'
   c. *BGP speaker* is another name for *Routing Information Base (RIB)*
   d. All of the above are correct

Answer: b

7. A *dynamic* routing table is updated and maintained automatically (i.e., no human intervention needed) by a protocol such as RIP, OSPF, or EIGRP.
   a. True
   b. False

Answer: a

8. OSPF incorporates a *distance vector protocol*, vice RIP's *link-state protocol*.
   a. True
   b. False

Answer: b

9. What is true regarding OSPF?
   a. OSPF uses less network overhead than RIP
   b. OSPF can compute the costs of routes using metrics such as packet delay, data rate, actual dollar amounts, or other factors that can be configured by the user
   c. OSPF is better suited for larger and more complex networks than RIP
   d. All are true

Answer: d

10. In an OSPF network divided into several areas, one area must be designated as the backbone area which interfaces with all ABR border routers within the AS. The backbone is responsible for distributing routing information between non-backbone areas.
    a. True
    b. False

Answer: a

11. Select the correct statement(s) regarding the IP protocol.
    a. IP is a connection-oriented protocol
    b. IP guarantees delivery of IP datagrams to the destination
    c. IP is a best effort protocol and does not address the correct sequencing of packets
    d. All of the above are correct

Answer: c

12. Since the IP is an end-to-end protocol, it must establish a connection prior to sending packets from source to destination node.
    a. True
    b. False

Answer: b

13. The Internet Protocol (IP) must guarantee packet delivery since it was designed to serve as a survival network.
    a. True
    b. False

Answer: b

14. The IP address 192.256.181.300 is a legal IPv4 address. If not, why not?
    a. True
    b. False

Answer: b

15. The IPv4 subnet mask 255.255.0.0, belongs to a Class B network.
    a. True
    b. False

Answer: a

16. Which IPv4 subnet mask belongs to a Class C network?
    a. 255.0.0.0
    b. 255.255.0.0
    c. 255.255.255.0
    d. 255.255.255.255

Answer: c

17. Your IPv4 address is 192.23.8.64 and you want to send a message to 192.23.9.32. Your subnet mask is 255.255.0.0. Select the correct statement.
    a. Source and destination are located on non-autonomous networks, therefore the message datagrams will need to be sent to a gateway router.
    b. Both source and destination nodes are on the same autonomous IP network.
    c. Source and destination addresses are class A addresses thus datagrams can be delivered directly.
    d. No statement is correct.

Answer: b

18. *Classless Interdomain Routing (CIDR)* format identifies how many of the most significant bit positions represent the network ID.
    a. True
    b. False

Answer: a

19. CIDR was introduced to allow networks the flexibility to further subdivide their class networks into smaller subnetworks. This process of subdividing Class A, B, or C networks is called subnetting.
    a. True
    b. False

Answer: a

20. What is the function of the IPv4 *ARP* protocol?
    a. Maps IP addresses to the common network MAC address
    b. Automatically assigns an IPv4 address from an available pool of addresses
    c. Replaces internal IPv4 addresses within an intranet, with an external Internet IPv4 address
    d. An error reporting protocol used by routers to send messages regarding delivery problems

Answer: a

21. ARP is a protocol only used with IPv4 and Ethernet.
    a. True
    b. False

Answer: b

22. What is the function of the IPv4 *DHCP* protocol?
    a. Maps IP addresses to the common network MAC address
    b. Automatically assigns an IPv4 address from an available pool of addresses
    c. Replaces internal IPv4 addresses within an intranet, with an external Internet IPv4 address
    d. An error reporting protocol used by routers to send messages regarding delivery problems

Answer: b

23. *DHCP* servers supports *manual*, *automatic*, and *dynamic* allocation of IP addresses. With *automatic* allocation, . . .
    a. the ISP administrator performs the actual assignment of addresses to each device
    b. the DHCP server, vice the administrator, automatically assigns a permanent IP address to the client
    c. the DHCP server allocates an available IPv4 address from a pool of shared addresses

Answer: b

24. *DHCP* servers supports *manual*, *automatic*, and *dynamic* allocation of IP addresses. With *dynamic* allocation, . . .
    a. the ISP administrator performs the actual assignment of addresses to each device
    b. the DHCP server, vice the administrator, automatically assigns a permanent IP address to the client
    c. the DHCP server allocates an available IPv4 address from a pool of shared addresses

Answer: c

25. Describe the process involved when a client requests an IPv4 address from a DHCP server.

26. What is the function of the IPv4 *NAT* protocol?
    a. Maps IP addresses to the common network MAC address
    b. Automatically assigns an IPv4 address from an available pool of addresses
    c. Replaces internal IPv4 addresses within an *intranet*, with an external *Internet* IP address
    d. An error reporting protocol used by routers to send messages regarding delivery problems

Answer: c

27. Identify the benefit(s) of using a *NAT*.
    a. Reduces exposure and helps to isolate the internal network from external threats
    b. Private networks not wishing to upgrade their *intranets* to a new protocol or ISP can use NAT to translate between intranet and Internet
    c. Helps to conserve limited IPv4 addressing space
    d. All of the above are benefits

Answer: d

28. A NAT adversely impacts the use of certain protocols that are sensitive to the changes in source and destination addresses (e.g., IPSec).
   a. True
   b. False

Answer: a

29. DNS is a decentralized system used for translating IP addresses to URLs and domain names.
   a. True
   b. False

Answer: a

30. Select the correct statement(s) regarding DNS.
   a. *DNS* services translates domain names (URLs) to an IP address
   b. No translation from URL to IP address is required
   c. DNS is responsible for translating private IP addresses to public IP addresses
   d. All are correct

Answer: a

31. *URL* root domains are the responsibility of _____
   a. IETF
   b. ISO
   c. IEEE
   d. IANA

Answer: d

32. The process of taking an URL and translating it to an IP address is called *DNS name resolution*.
   a. True
   b. False

Answer: a

33. What is the function of the IPv4 ICMP protocol?
   a. Maps IP addresses to the common network MAC address
   b. Automatically assigns an IPv4 address from an available pool of addresses
   c. Replaces internal IPv4 addresses within an intranet, with an external Internet IPv4 address
   d. An error reporting protocol used by routers to send messages regarding delivery problems

Answer: d

34. *ICMP* is an error reporting protocol only, and does not improve the reliability of the IP network.
   a. True
   b. False

Answer: a

35. *ICMP* messages are sent using IP datagrams.
   a. True
   b. False

Answer: a

36. IPv6 brings which of the following enhancements?
   a. Expanded Addressing Field
   b. Header Format Simplification
   c. Multicast and Anycast
   d. All of the above

Answer: d

37. UDP is a connection-oriented OSI Layer 4 protocol.
   a. True
   b. False

Answer: b

38. TCP is a connection-oriented protocol that implements a three-way handshake in order to establish a connection between source and destination nodes.
   a. True
   b. False

Answer: a

39. What is the purpose of the *timeout period* within the TCP protocol?
   a. Is the period of time in which a connection must be established before reinitiating the three-way handshaking sequence
   b. Is the period of time that source and destination nodes must wait after a data collision has occurred
   c. Is the time period in which an ACK must be received before retransmission in order to prevent duplicate packets from being sent
   d. None of the above

Answer: c

40. TCP handles congestion control by varying the size of transmission windows.
   a. True
   b. False

Answer: a

41. UDP is an OSI Level 4 protocol that is unreliable and connectionless.
   a. True
   b. False

Answer: a

42. Both TCP and UDP protocols must contain source and destination addresses.
   a. True
   b. False

Answer: b

43. Select the correct statement(s) regarding TCP.
   a.   The TCP port identifies the specific physical layer interface on the communicating device
   b.   TCP three-way handshakes are only used when determining window sizes
   c.   A TCP window size can change depending upon network conditions
   d.   All are correct

Answer: c

44. Like TCP, UDP segments are delivered in sequence. The only difference is the number of bits within the segment header.
    a. True
    b. False

Answer: b

45. Describe the *TCP sliding window* process and why it is important.

46. Similar to the *TCP three-way handshake* used to establish a connection, there is a formal TCP connection termination process.
    a. True
    b. False

Answer: a

47. The combination of a _____ and _____ is called a "socket."
    a. eye, skull
    b. light bulb, lamp
    c. IP address, port
    d. IP address, application

Answer: c

48. Select the protocol that provides network quality-of service (QoS) by appending an FEC (Forwarding Equivalence Class) to each datagram.
    a. IPv4
    b. IPv6
    c. MPLS
    d. TCP

Answer: c

49. MPLS (Multiprotocol Label Switching) specifies a network architecture that uses labels attached to IP datagrams in order to provide Quality-of-Service (QoS).
    a. True
    b. False

Answer: a

CHAPTER 10

Cellular Networks

"Mobile phones are misnamed. They should be called gateways to human knowledge."

(Ray Kurzweil).

10.1 INTRODUCTION

Guglielmo Marconi demonstrated the feasibility of wireless communications in 1896 with his invention of the wireless telegraph. Ever since this time, the idea of communicating to anyone from anywhere without being physically tethered to an infrastructure has captured our imagination and interests as a society. Wireless communications, such as two-way push-to-talk (PTT) and citizen bands (CB) radios, have been around for decades; unfortunately they are limited in distance and easily intercepted by eavesdroppers. For most of us, wireless communications are only useful if it enables us to privately connect to anyone at any time. As such, an interface to the PSTN is necessary.

In 1946, AT&T offered the first mobile[1] radio-telephone service in St. Louis. Because only a single antenna was used to cover an entire metropolitan area, only 12 to 20 calls could be made simultaneously (AT&T). Maintaining the mobile telephone infrastructure to support a limited number of users meant that the costs, which were high, had to be passed on to the user. While this was a major milestone in the history of the mobile telephone, it was clear that technical advances were needed in order to increase the number of simultaneous calls while keeping costs affordable for the average subscriber.

A significant conceptual innovation came a year later in 1947 when *Bell Labs* engineers, Donald H. Ring and W. Rae Young, developed the concept of **cellular** telephone service. With the cellular concept, a service area was divided into separate radio communication *cells* vice a single large radio coverage area. By operating multiple smaller cells, frequency reuse could be achieved, thereby supporting greater numbers of simultaneous calls across the service area. However, the concept was ahead of the actual technology[2] needed to effectively implement cellular communications at the time. In addition, the necessary frequency spectrum to make cellular a reality had not yet been allocated for this purpose.

It should be pointed out that other wireless telephone efforts took place in different countries during this period of time. As an example, the *Dutch National* radio-telephone service began operations in

---

[1] "Mobile radio-telephones" were installed in automobiles. Considering the technology available at the time, handheld models would've been much too heavy.

[2] Technologies not yet available included low-cost transceivers, and technology needed for cells to handoff calls as users moved from one cell to another. In addition, the frequency spectrum needed was not yet available from the FCC.

1949, and the *Swedish Telecommunications Administration* developed an automatic mobile telephone system, *MTA*, in 1951. In 1952, the *Japanese Nippon Telephone and Telegraph* company began research into radio telephones. (Farley, 2005)

In April 1973, Joel Engel and Richard Frenkiel of *Bell Labs*, and Marty Cooper of *Motorola*, worked together to successfully demonstrate the cellular concept by making the first cellular call. By this time, solid-state circuitry and automated cell switch technologies had matured. While the prototype phone weighed 45 oz and had a battery life that only allowed 30 minutes of talk time, it proved the viability of the cellular concept. Although the demonstration got the attention of the FCC, it would take another 8 years before additional frequency spectrum was allocated for cellular communications. Finally in October 1981, the FCC identified two frequency bands within the 800 MHz range for dedicated mobile phone use.

As the popularity of cellular communications began to spread globally, numerous technical innovations were introduced to help service providers keep up with the ever-growing demand for services despite the limited frequency spectrum available. Over the years, the FCC has allocated more spectrum, however, considering consumer demands for multimedia services, available bandwidth is still an issue today. In addition, the lack of interoperability between cellular systems continues to present challenges for both providers and consumers. While numerous standards committees strive towards developing and adopting fully compatible standards, newer challenges for the cellular industry have emerged as a result of the popularity of the Internet.

Today, consumers desire access to multimedia rich applications and high-speed streaming. No longer are we satisfied with the basic voice call, as our smartphones now have the capability to combine communications, information, and entertainment into a single mobile handheld device. Meeting future demands efficiently will necessitate the convergence of Internet technologies with those innovations occurring within the mobile cellular industry, the PSTN, and the computer field.

10.2 REGULATION AND STANDARDIZATION

Each nation has regulatory authority over its telecommunication systems. In the United States, *FCC* is a federal agency in charge of regulating both wired and wireless communications within the country. However, considering the global nature of telecommunications, a coordinating entity such as the *ITU*, which falls under the authority of the United Nations, is essential in addressing any *information and communications technologies (ICT)* issues, especially those that impact more than one country. ICT encompasses numerous communications areas including wireless, Internet, satellite, radio astronomy, and maritime navigation. Therefore, ITU plays an important role in the coordination and assistance of both the regulatory and standardization efforts.

The allocation of frequency spectrum and the standardization of network interfaces are essential to achieving global telecommunications interoperability; however, the processes involved in any regulatory or standardization effort is arduous and time consuming. The cellular industry works closely with regulatory agencies to expand the availability of frequency spectrum and to ensure that government policies do not stifle growth or innovation. In addition, as communications capabilities converge the standardization process must ensure system interoperability. The cellular industry, once the domain of the telephone industry, has now converged with other domains such as the Internet, computer networking and wireless LANs.

There are numerous standardization organizations involved for every aspect of ICT. Below is a sample listing of standardization organizations involved with some aspect of the cellular industry.

Cellular Telecommunications and Internet Association (CTIA): Founded in 1984, CTIA represents the U.S. wireless industry comprised of manufacturers and service providers. CITA's primary purpose is to advocate policies to the federal government on behalf of industry partners.

Institute of Electrical and Electronics Engineers (IEEE): Dating back to 1884, IEEE has been involved in all aspects of the electronic, electrical and computing fields. They are actively involved in the research and standardization of digital communications, including Mobile WiMAX IEEE 802.16 which is a 4G cellular standard.

GSM Association(GSMA): Formed in 1982 by the Confederation of European Posts and Telecommunications (CEPT), GSMA represents over 200 companies comprised of manufacturers, Internet companies, and service operators in the development of the GSM standard.

Third-Generation Partnership Project (3GPP): 3GPP is comprised of seven telecommunications standard organizations intended to advance technologies and produce specifications in support of cellular network technologies. Technical specification groups include Radio Access Networks (RANs), Services & Systems Aspects (SA), and Core Network and Terminals (CT). While their name identifies 3G, the partnership has worked actively on 4G and future-generation cellular technologies.

Open Mobile Alliance (OMA): Formed by mobile operators, manufacturers, and IT companies, OMA is a nonprofit organization that develops open specifications to ensure interoperable communication systems around the world. In addition to supporting mobile communications, OMA is involved with machine-to-machine (M2M) and Internet-of-Things (IoT) device communications.

European Telecommunications Standards Institute (ETSI): ETSI is a non-for-profit organization recognized by the European Union, with membership from organizations based in 67 countries. ETSI produces ICT standards including GSM and Long Term Evolution[3] (LTE).

Telecommunications Industry Association (TIA): TIA is a global trade association in ICT focusing on standardization, policy initiatives, and business opportunities.

American National Standards Institute (ANSI): ANSI's heritage dates back to 1919 when it was called the American Engineering Standards Committee (AESC). Initially working on national safety codes, AESC actively participated in the creation of the International Standards Association (ISA) which eventually became the International Organization for Standardization (ISO). In 1987,

---

[3] LTE is a registered trademark owned by ETSI; however, many other organizations have played key roles in the development of the standard.

ANSI accepted administrative responsibility for ISO/IEC's Joint Technical Committee on Information Technology (JTC1).

European Conference of Postal and Telecommunications Administrations (CEPT): CEPT, which was established in 1959, is a consortium of 48 member countries across Europe. The organization collaborates on policy issues that include telecommunications, use of radio spectrum, and postal regulations.

International Organization for Standardization (ISO): ISO is an international nongovernmental organization dedicated to developing international standards on a broad scope of topics including ICT, food safety, agriculture, healthcare, and numerous other technologies. Consisting of membership from 163 countries, ISO is headquartered in Geneva, Switzerland.

The advancements made within the cellular industry from first-generation (1G) to fourth-generation (4G) systems demonstrates the need for a fully combined global effort involving technical innovation, policy making, and standardization.

10.3 THE CELLULAR CONCEPT

Prior to the creation of the cellular concept, the **mobile radio-telephone system** used a single large broadcast antenna to cover a given service area. In order for a mobile user to connect to the wired PSTN, an operator typically had to intervene to establish a connection for the user. In addition, some early systems provided only half-duplex communications requiring a push-to-talk (PTT) feature on the handset. Obviously, new technologies would have to be created to make these early systems viable. However, one of the biggest hurdles even in the early days was the lack of available frequency spectrum.

Let's consider an example of an early mobile radio-telephone system depicted in fig. 10.1. A single antenna is used to provide communications for an entire service area. In designing this system, you would have to take the following into consideration:

- To cover such a large area, powerful transmitters would be required by both the service provider base station and mobile user device. This would require mobile users to carry large power supplies, thus increasing both the size and weight of the handheld unit.

- Use of carriers at the lower frequency spectrum (e.g., low MHz range) would be required to lessen the impact of attenuation over distance. An added benefit is that lower frequencies (e.g., MHz range) do not require as strict a *line-of-sight (LOS)* requirement between transceivers compared to higher frequencies (e.g., GHz range). While these lower frequency systems can be impacted by obstacles, thus creating "shadow" areas of lower signal strength, it is not as big an impact when compared to higher frequency attenuation in the GHz range.

- In order to avoid interference between users, separate frequency channels are required per connection. For full-duplex communications, this means the allocation of separate transmit and receive channels (i.e., two channels per connection) are required.

- The availability of frequency spectrum for use on mobile communication systems is, and has always been, an issue. As such, only a limited number of users within the single service area can communicate simultaneously.

- Finally, the single antenna and transceiver equipment serving the entire service area would introduce a single point-of-failure.

Early mobile radio-telephone systems, to include first-generation (1G) cellular phone systems, operated using analog signals. The use of analog signals for voice communications results in an inefficient use of the limited frequency spectrum. This is because of inefficiencies inherent in voice communications, as well as the inability to virtually share send and receive frequency channels which must be dedicated for each analog call. In contrast, digital communications can take advantage of the many pauses, or empty spaces, of natural human speech, and fill them with voice data from other virtual calls, thus improving overall spectral efficiency. Further efficiencies can be gained using digital compression techniques. As we will see, the advantages of using digital techniques were the key drivers leading to fully digital 2G cellular standards.

In our example of the single antenna system in fig. 10.1, let's say that a service provider was allocated 20 channels in the 35 MHz range for mobile communications. Within the service area, the operator would only be able to simultaneously service 20 users in half-duplex mode, or 10 users in full-duplex mode (i.e., two channels per call). This limits the number of overall calls made on the system, thus limiting any revenue from these calls. Since the bottom line for all service providers is their return-on-investment (ROI), costs for operations and maintenance would be passed onto the

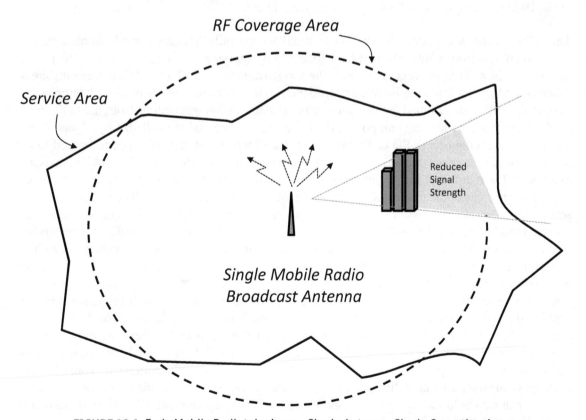

FIGURE 10.1 Early Mobile Radiotelephone—Single Antenna, Single Operating Area.

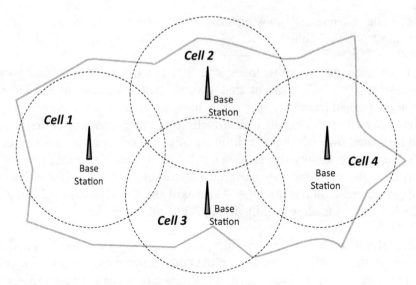

FIGURE 10.2 Cellular Concept.

users, who would be burdened with paying high prices for an inefficient system. This was the case in the 1940's when mobile radio-telephone services began.

The cellular concept improves the number of simultaneous calls that can be made within a service area without requiring additional frequency spectrum by applying the *frequency reuse* concept. The first step in the cellular concept is to divide the service area into smaller "cells" or operating areas. In the case of fig. 10.2, four cells have replaced the single service area of the previous example. The size of the cell is determined by the amount of transmit power emanating from the cell's main antenna. By reducing the transmit power, the RF coverage area and the cell size is reduced. Since the mobile user connects to the cell's main antenna, which is a shorter distance compared to the previous single antenna example, the power required to communicate using the mobile handset is much less. The reduced power required by the handheld device translates into longer on-air times. The coverage areas of the four cells overlap one another. As such, adjacent cells operating the same sets of frequency channels would interference with one another especially within the overlap areas. To avoid this, adjacent cells, such as cell 1 and 2 in fig. 10.2, must operate on different frequencies. However, since cell 1 and cell 4 are not adjacent, they can operate at the same frequencies without fear of interfering with one another. By being able to share the same frequencies within the overall area, service providers can support more subscribers. The reuse of frequency channels is termed ***frequency reuse***. In our example, the service provider was allocated enough frequency space to enable 10 simultaneous full-duplex calls. Cells 1, 2, and 3 operate on *channel pairs* 1 to 4, 5 to 7, and 8 to 10, respectively. Cell 4 can use the same channel pairs as cell 1, therefore the number of simultaneous calls that can be supported is 4 + 3 + 3 + 4 = 14. For this simple example, four additional calls are supported by dividing the service area into four cells, compared to only 10 calls with the single operating area. If we were to decrease the cell size and divide the service area even further, then we could increase the number of concurrent callers dramatically. We will see this in the next example (fig. 10.3).

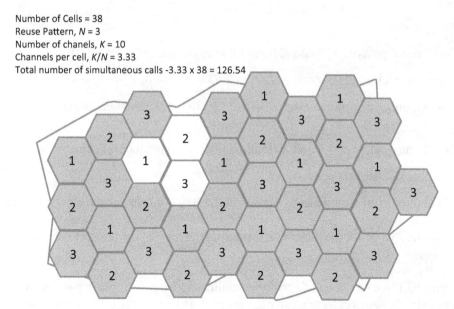

Number of Cells = 38
Reuse Pattern, N = 3
Number of chanels, K = 10
Channels per cell, K/N = 3.33
Total number of simultaneous calls -3.33 x 38 = 126.54

FIGURE 10.3 Service Area divided into 38 cells where $N = 3$. The cells in white represents a "cluster" of cells that is repeated over the entire service area. Cells are typically represented by hexagons.

Figure 10.3 demonstrates how increasing the number of cells increases *frequency reuse* and the number of subscribers supported. The service area has been divided into 38 smaller cells. The cell pattern for frequency reuse remains the same as before. In other words, the 10 full-duplex channels (one transmit and one receive channel per call) are divided into a three-cell pattern, or **cluster**, where each of the three cells are assigned unique channel frequencies. Therefore, the **frequency reuse pattern (N),**[4] in this case is $N = 3$. The total number of **channels available, K**, is $K = 10$. We can determine the number of channels per cell and the total number of simultaneous calls supported across the entire service area by doing the following calculations:

N (reuse pattern) $= 3$
K (total number of channel pairs available within the service area) $= 10$
K/N (number of channel pairs per cell) $= 10/3 = \underline{3.33}$
Number of simultaneous calls $= (K/N) \times$ number of cells $= 3.33 \times 38 = 126.54 \approx \underline{126}$

From these calculations, we see that dividing the service area further into 38 cells, that we have dramatically increased the number of simultaneous calls from 14 to 126. The smaller cells sizes also translate to smaller batteries and greater air time for user devices.

Example 10.1: A service provider is allocated $K = 28$ *full-duplex* channels to support calls within a busy urban area. The provider decides that the number of cells needed to cover the area is 50. You are asked to determine which cell repeating pattern should be select to enable the greatest number of simultaneous calls: $N = 3$ or $N = 7$?

---

[4] Frequency reuse pattern of N cells represents a "cluster." The cluster pattern is repeated across the service area.

Solution:

(a) For N (cell reuse pattern) = 3 and K (total number of channels available) = 28:

Number of channels per cell = K/N = 28/3 = 9.334 or $\approx$ 9

Total number of simultaneous calls = 50 (cells) $\times$ 9 (channels per cell) = <u>450</u>

(b) For N (cell reuse pattern) = 7 and K (total number of channels available) = 28:

Number of channels per cell = K/N = 28/7 = 4

Total number of simultaneous calls = 50 (cells) $\times$ 4 (channels per cell) = <u>200</u>

Therefore, you select a cell reuse pattern of 3, since this gives you the greatest number of simultaneous calls.

From example 10.1, we can conclude that the smaller the frequency reuse pattern (N), the greater the number of simultaneous calls that can be supported. However, the cell size, which is principally determined by the power and signal direction emanating from the cell's antenna, is not exact and can easily be influenced by propagation effects such as weather, multipath reflection, RFI, and other phenomena. As such, service providers may choose larger frequency reuse patterns, which in turn provide more distance between cells operating on the same sets of frequencies. Of course, innovation within the industry never ceases, and we will see how modern 4G cellular systems strive toward a reuse pattern of $N = 1$, which maximizes the number of calls for a given spectral allocation.

The cellular concept is a great solution when limited frequency spectrum is available, but it comes at the cost of increased overall system complexity. For instance, each cell has a main antenna and suite of equipment associated with it. All cell calls must be connected to the cellular providers' network through a ***backhaul*** connection, and eventually to the PSTN or other network such as the Internet. As a mobile user moves from one cell to another, the system must automatically disconnect and reconnect the user from cell to cell. Finally, the operations for such a complex system requires sophisticated switching and network management equipment, and highly skilled individuals to both operate and maintain it.

There are a few broad categorizations that describe the size of the cell itself. A ***macrocell*** covers a relatively large area that is approximately 60 miles wide. ***Small Cells*** is a general term used for smaller cell sizes such as ***microcell***, ***picocell***, and ***femtocell***. The *microcell* is approximately 4.3 miles wide, while the *picocell* covers just a few city blocks. The *femtocell* creates a wireless cell that can be as small as a home or the size of a floor in a large building. What differentiates the femtocell from other small cells is the backhaul connection to the service provider network. Since many homes and businesses have broadband connections to the Internet, the femtocell, which connects wirelessly to the mobile phone through cellular frequencies, uses the hosts connection as a backhaul to the service providers network. This enables the service provider to cover areas of poor cellular reception in a cost effective manner, while improving cellular coverage to the user.

The amount of transmit power from an *omnidirectional* antenna, which is typically depicted on paper as a hexagon,[5] is not the only way to shape cell coverage. Use of *directional smart antennas* enables service providers to divide the cell into pie-shaped sectors that operate on different frequencies. Smart antennas using electronic *beamforming* techniques can be programmed to modify coverage areas in response to changing traffic patterns during the day. So the cell dimensions and shape can be modified to match the coverage areas as needed.

As the concentration of users begin to increase in specific locations within the service area (e.g., development of high-rise apartments, business buildings, shopping and restaurant areas, etc.), the cells serving the area will need to increase their capacity to meet the growing mobile user base. Increasing call capacity can be accomplished by adding frequency channels, increasing the number of cells within an area, and by adopting technical solutions that maximize the use of limited channel resources. The following are ways that this can be achieved:

- Addition of new frequency channels. The service provider can request additional frequency spectrum, but this is extremely difficult to accomplish. Taking years of effort to go through the government's regulatory and legislative processes, lobbyists are hired by the wireless industries to work these issues on a full-time basis. The addition of new frequency bands is a strategic effort rather than one that can provide immediate relief for increased service demands.

- Dynamic frequency allocation. The concentration of calls within a service area is related to the concentration of mobile users. This concentration can be dynamic depending upon the time of day, as well as the day of the week. As an example, business offices will have much lower concentrations of calls during nonbusiness hours as opposed to business hours. Therefore, for a service provider, it would make sense to allocate the number of channels based upon call activity vice fixed cell allocations. However, dynamic allocation can be very difficult to accomplish because of the complexity it introduces when attempting to avoid the assignment of identical frequencies to adjacent cells. The *cell reuse pattern*, or *cluster*, and the *frequency reuse distances* are factors that must be taken into consideration when determining the effectiveness of implementing dynamic allocation.

- Frequency borrowing. Frequency borrowing is similar to *dynamic frequency allocation*, but is performed at a lower level between adjacent cells. As discussed, call activity concentrations can change throughout the service area, and with *frequency borrowing*, cells can borrow unused frequencies from their adjacent neighbors. To illustrate how this can be helpful, imagine that a cell serving a business district is adjacent to a cell serving the restaurant district. During normal business hours, call activity is greatest in the business cell. During extremely busy hours when the business cell's frequency allocation isn't enough, it can borrow unused frequencies from its neighbor, the restaurant cell. At the end of the work day, restaurant cell activity becomes greater than the business cell activity as patrons begin to arrive. If the restaurant cell becomes overloaded with call activity, it can borrow unused frequencies from the business cell. Under these types of circumstances, frequency borrowing can be an effective strategy. However, frequency borrowing can also be very complex since all cells involved in frequency borrowing must avoid interference with each of its adjacent neighbors.

---

[5] The hexagon is used to depict a cell created by an omnidirectional antenna; however, the actual physical pattern is circular resulting in overlapping coverage between adjacent cells.

- Network densification. One common method used to increase capacity within a cell is to divide the cell's area into smaller cells and/or sectors. Network *cell densification* enables providers to increase the *frequency reuse factor*, which in turn increases their capacity to support larger numbers of calls. However, as discussed previously, increasing the number of cells by decreasing cell size, translates into more cell handoffs as mobile users move inbetween smaller cells. This increases not only the complexity, but also the required number of cellular base stations, antennas, and backhaul connections to the main provider network.

- Use of femtocells. As described, femtocells are small cells that operate on cellular frequencies, but instead of using its own backhaul links, it uses the host's broadband connection (i.e., Internet) as a way to connect back to the service provider's network. This can be an effective strategy for supporting large businesses or hotels where a high concentration of call activity exists. Femtocells improve cellular connection within large buildings where foundational structures can negatively impact signal strength. Therefore, femtocells are a benefit to businesses as well as to the service provider.

- Technical solutions. An effective method to increase data capacity over a frequency channel is to implement digital data techniques designed to improve *spectral efficiency*.[6] Previous first-generation (1G) cellular systems were analog and required dedicated frequency channels per call. Obviously, this used up valuable frequency spectrum and severely limited the number of calls that could be made. With the introduction of digital communication techniques, single channels could be divided by time using TDMA, which meant that several calls could simultaneously operate on the same frequency channels. With direct sequence spread spectrum (DSSS) techniques such as CDMA, spectral efficiency improved as guard bands were no longer needed to separate channels resulting in increased throughput. Eventually, OFDM was adopted which improved spectral efficiency even further. The use of M'ary modulation techniques increased the number of bits per symbol, thus increasing data rates and overall system capacity. Of course, the adoption of sophisticated digital techniques requires more powerful and smart network devices, to include advanced antenna designs such as MIMO. Technical innovation in wireless communications continues to move forward, and its past implementations have helped service providers meet exponentially growing service demands.

- Inter-Cell Interference Coordination (ICIC). We learned that a frequency reuse pattern of $N = 1$ makes the greatest number of channels available to each cell. Of course, this means that each cell operates all of the service provider channels in the system, leading to adjacent cell interference near the edges of the cell. However, if the adjacent cells shared operating information, then the cells could coordinate ways to avoid channel interference within the overlap areas. This sharing of information and the algorithms designed to avoid interference is termed *Inter-cell Interference Coordination (ICIC)*. The basic idea is to ensure that users near the edges of the cell do not operate on channels used by other users near the edge of an adjacent cell. As an example, a user near an edge could be reassigned to a different channel if the possibility of interference was determined ahead of time.

---

[6] Spectral efficiency is measured in data rate over Hz.

WHY CELLS ARE DEPICTED BY HEXAGONS

It's obvious that the RF pattern emanating from an omnidirectional antenna is not shaped like a hexagon. However, when determining the distance between the center of adjacent cells, the geometry of the hexagon lends itself to an easy calculation for planning purposes. To illustrate, let's say "r" equals the radius of a circular cell, which also equals the propagation distance from an antenna located at the center. You want to determine the distance, "d", between cell centers. The idea is to eliminate any gaps in coverage. If we were to use circles, as in the figure below, the distance between cell centers is $d = 2r$, which creates a gap in coverage between all adjacent cells. Obviously, you'd want to reduce cell spacing to some distance less than $2r$ (i.e., $d < 2r$). The question becomes what distance to choose.

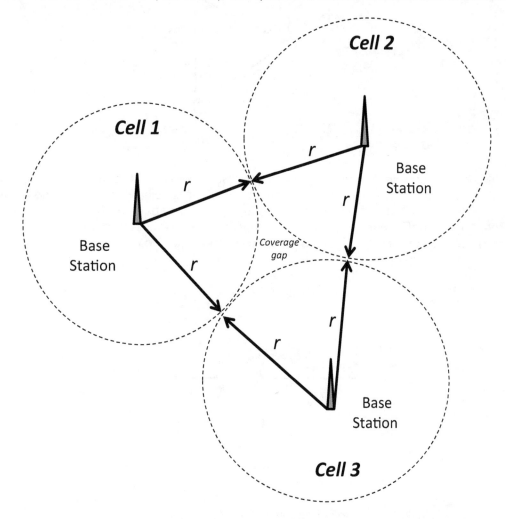

By using a hexagon, you have a shape that can be used for planning purposes to avoid potential gaps in coverage between cells (see figure below). A hexagon can be seen as six connected equilateral triangles where "r" is the distance from the center of the hexagon to a corner of one of the triangles. The height of the equilateral triangle is, $height = \dfrac{d}{2} = \dfrac{\sqrt{3}}{2} * r$, where "$d$" equals the distance between adjacent cell centers. Therefore, if two or more hexagons are adjacent to one another, using a distance between cell centers of "d" will prevent potential gaps in coverage.

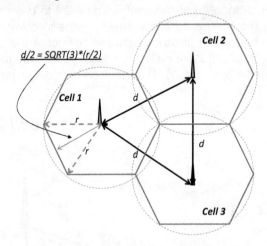

It is also critical for us to determine the spacing between cells operating on the same sets of frequencies in order to avoid adjacent cell interference. This spacing is termed the **frequency reuse distance, "D,"** and we will need to include the cell reuse pattern, "N."

The diagram below depicts our four cell service area operating with a cluster of three ($N = 3$). We want to know the distance "D" between the repeating cell #1.

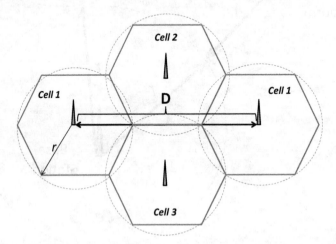

In this case, we include "N" into our equation: <u>Frequency Reuse Distance, $D = r * \sqrt{3N}$</u>

Therefore, for a cell repeating pattern of $N = 3$, the distance between cells operating the same sets of frequencies is "D." As the cluster size (N) increases, the distance between cells operating at the same frequencies also increases.

10.4 CELLULAR ARCHITECTURE

There are certain functions that all cellular phone systems must perform regardless of the specific standard[7] used. The most obvious function is an ability for the ***mobile station (MS)***, (a.k.a., ***mobile equipment, ME***), to connect wirelessly to a cellular ***base station subsystem (BSS)***, (a.k.a., ***base transceiver station, BTS***), which is comprised of the antenna and transceiver equipment. All of the *BS'* within the service area must have backhaul connections to the main service providers' network, which is called the ***network subsystem (NS)***. Within the *NS* is the ***mobile switch center (MSC)***, (a.k.a., ***mobile telecommunications switching office, MTSO***), whose function is to switch calls between the MS and PSTN or other network, and between MS'. In addition, the MSC is involved in the *handoff* of an MS as it moves from one cell to another. A final function is an ability for the cellular network to authenticate and identify users in order to bill and provide services.

10.4.1 Base Station Subsystem (BSS)

The MS connects wirelessly to the base station subsystem (BSS) through an "air interface." For ***first-generation (1G)*** analog systems, connection to the air interface was pretty straightforward, requiring knowledge of the control channel frequencies, assigned traffic frequencies, and modulation techniques. Digital techniques were introduced with ***second-generation (2G)*** systems, which involved a more sophisticated air interface that could support either TDMA time slot assignments or CDMA PN (*pseudorandom noise*) codes. In addition to supporting digital modulation techniques, 2G systems were also required to define and support digital protocols above the physical layer. With 2.5 ***generation (2.5G)*** and ***third generation (3G)*** systems, packet switching was introduced on some standards (i.e., *GSM's General Packet Radio Service or GPRS*), opening the path to Internet connectivity from the a user's MS. Today we have ***fourth-generation (4G)*** systems that use smart phones, and as such, require support for the entire OSI protocol stack (i.e., physical to applications layers).

Mobile users access the cellular system through ***demand assigned multiple access (DAMA)*** techniques that assigns available channels to users on a demand basis. However, since there are typically more subscribers than channels, *call blocking* can occur during times of emergencies or special events when unanticipated traffic volume causes system overload. With early analog systems, the only access technique was through frequency channel assignment or ***frequency division multiple access (FDMA)***. Digital technologies enabled the sharing of frequency channels by assigning time slots to each call using ***time division multiple access (TDMA)***. In this case, the combination of TDMA and FDMA helped to increase the number of calls that could be supported simultaneously. ***Code division multiple access (CDMA)***, still in use on 3G systems today, enables multiple users to share the same frequency bandwidth by assigning unique, orthogonal ***Pseudorandom Noise (PN) codes*** to each call. Finally, ***Orthogonal Frequency Division Multiple Access (OFDMA)*** assigns sets of orthogonal subcarriers to each call and is more spectrally efficient than CDMA.

The BSS is comprised of several components as shown in fig. 10.4. Each cell has a ***base station (BS)*** that contains one or more RF antennas with associated transceiver equipment. The power transmitted, as well as the RF pattern emitted from the antenna, defines the size and shape of the

---

[7] However, the description that follows is principally based upon the GSM architecture.

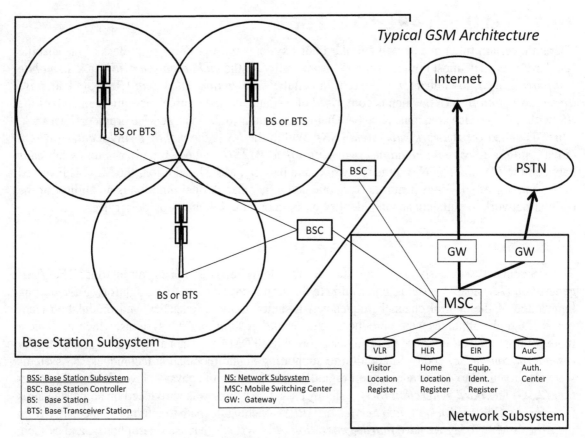

FIGURE 10.4 Basic GSM Cellular Architecture.

cell footprint. Each cell broadcasts control signals that are used throughout the cell for control and signaling purposes. An MS entering the service area will receive controls signals from all of the BS' within its range, and will then select the BS it intends to communicate with, typically based upon signal strength.

One or more BS' are controlled by a ***base station controller (BSC)***. The responsibility of the BSC is to allocate useable channel frequencies to the BS, track mobile user equipment (i.e., monitor signal strength) as it moves throughout the cells, and manage call hand-offs between the cells under its control. If, however, the MS departs the set of cells controlled by the BSC, the BSC must coordinate with the *mobile switching center (MSC)* to facilitate an inter-BSC hand-off. BSCs also serve to aggregate control and traffic information from cells for delivery to the MSC through backhaul channels. Backhaul channels are typically over fiber optic cables; however, broadband wireless systems such as WiMAX BWA are also used.

10.4.2 Network Subsystem (NS)

The NS is the service provider's wired network that controls and manages the cellular system. While the BSS provides the mobile user wireless access to the network, the NS essentially does the heavy lifting of switching calls, maintaining subscriber data bases, providing security, and establishing connections to external networks. It is comprised of several key components but the most important one is the ***mobile switching center (MSC)***. The MSC serves in all phases of support to the mobile user including initial logon to the system, establishment and termination of calls, and call handoffs between cells within the service area. There are several databases connected to the MSC that serve important functions. These databases are listed below.

Home Location Register (HLR). The HLR database contains subscriber information and is used on TDMA, CDMA, and GSM systems. For GSM systems, an ***International Mobile Subscriber Identity (IMSI)*** number that is associated with each user is stored in both the HLR database and the *Subscriber Identity Module (SIM)* card, which contains subscriber information and is placed into the phone. The HLR is also updated with the location of the mobile unit as it moves throughout the service area.

Visitor Location Register (VLR). The VLR database, which contains similar information as the HLR, is used to update the location of roaming users within the service area. The VLR database is updated with location information to help the MSC locate users without having to constantly query the HLR. The VLR also supports roaming subscribers from different service providers that have sharing agreements in place between the cellular providers.

Authentication Center (AuC). The AuC is used to authenticate subscribers when the MS is initially powered on. For GSM systems, this means authenticating the SIM cards attached to the mobile device. Failure to authenticate prevents the mobile equipment from being able to access cellular services. Once authenticated, the AuC provides encryption keys for secure voice, data, and message traffic.

Equipment Identity Register (EIR). Removable GSM SIM cards are placed into mobile phones to provide specific subscriber information including the IMSI. There is also a unique number associated with mobile hardware equipment called an ***International Mobile Equipment Identity (IMEI)*** number. The IMEI helps to identify legitimate devices on the network, and can also be used to stop stolen phones from accessing the network. The EIR maintains a list of all IMEI numbers used by subscribers within the system.

Finally, gateways are used to interconnect the cellular network to the PSTN and to other networks such as the Internet. *"Gateway"* is an often used, and general term that can be used to mean many things. As we have seen in this textbook, a gateway typically enables the interconnection of disparate networks operating on different protocols. In this way, a gateway is a highly intelligent device that is able to interface any protocol layer of the OSI reference model through protocol conversion or simple network tunneling techniques.

10.4.3 Mobile Call Process

Each cell base station communicates to mobile phones using control and traffic channels. ***Control channels*** are involved in mobile phone initialization, call setup and termination, and mobile user location registration. Once the mobile phone has been registered with the cellular provider, *control channels* communicate periodically with the mobile unit even if no calls are in progress. Once a call has been established between users, a ***traffic channel*** is assigned for the actual exchange of information between users. Both control and traffic channels operate in the ***forward*** (network to mobile user) and ***reverse*** (mobile unit to the network) directions.

As soon as an MS is turned on, it begins to scan for control signals emanating from nearby BS'. Cellular control channels are shared between all mobile units within the cell, and therefore in order to avoid interference, each mobile unit must ensure that the channel is clear prior to transmission. Control channels from adjacent cells operate at different frequencies and the MS selects the BS control channel that has the greatest signal strength. Once selected, a handshaking procedure takes place which involves participation by the MSC in order to identify the mobile user as an authorized subscriber eligible to receive services. After successful completion of the handshaking process, the control channel continues to periodically communicate with the mobile unit to monitor and register its location.

When a subscriber wishes to make a call, the control channel is used for call setup. The first step is to make sure that the shared control channel is clear. If it is, the mobile unit transmits a call setup request by sending the "called" phone number to the BS. The BS forwards this request to the MSC. If the call is to another MS within the same service area, the MSC checks the location registries (i.e., VLR and HLR) to determine its location. If information on the called unit is found, the MSC will send out a paging request to the BS where the mobile unit was last known to be. The paging request is broadcast throughout the cell, and if recognized and accepted, the called unit sends an acknowledgment back to the MSC. Upon call acceptance, the MSC allocates available send and receive traffic channels for use by the mobile units. In the event that no information regarding the called unit is found in the registries, the MSC instructs all BS' to page their mobile units within each cell in an attempt to find the called MS. If no response is received, then the call cannot be placed.

Finally, if a call from a mobile unit is made to a wired telephone on the PSTN, then the MSC sends the call request through an NS gateway to the PSTN. In reverse, a call from the PSTN will go through an NS gateway to the MSC, and the registry lookup and paging process is initiated.

During an active call, mobile subscribers typically move between cells requiring the departing BS to handoff the call to the arriving BS. With the older analog systems, handoffs between cells were abrupt, essentially terminating the connection to one BS prior to establishing a connection with the new BS. This was termed a ***hard handoff***, which was sufficient for analog voice calls since it did not significantly impact call quality. However, *hard handoffs* do not work well with digital communications, often leading to lost data and call disruption. As such, ***soft handoffs*** were designed to ensure that the outgoing BS did not terminate the call until the arriving BS had established a connection with the mobile unit. Handoffs between cells are based upon the measured signal strength emanating from the BS. There are several algorithms not discussed in this text, that are used with soft handoffs to prevent call drops in environments where multipath fading or other phenomena is of concern.

When the call is terminated, the MSC is notified and the traffic channels are made available to support the next call request.

10.5 CELLULAR GENERATIONS

Implementation of new technologies is captured as generational changes to the cellular system concept. It is a way to define how the newest technology innovations are introduced in order to meet exponentially increasing subscriber numbers, as well as to meet subscriber desires for services beyond the traditional voice call. The technology innovations implemented also address methods to improve spectral efficiencies in light of the constrained availability of frequency spectrum.

Figure 10.5 is a high-level description of the various cellular generations. It should be noted that during the historical development of mobile systems, other standards and specifications not indicated in the figure nor discussed in the following sections, were developed for region-specific cellular phone systems. The next several sections discuss some of the major standards adopted throughout the generations.

10.5.1 First Generation (1G)

Introduced in the late 1970s, first-generation cellular systems are consider analog systems although this mainly describes the RF interface between mobile phones and base stations. Most service providers incorporated digital control channels as well as digital switching within their network subsystem. Since initial subscriber numbers were manageable, analog systems easily met service

| 1G | 2G | 2.5G | 3G | 3.5G | 4G | 5G |

| Analog | Digital | | | | | |

| | | IMT-2000 | | | IMT-Advanced | |

AMPS FDMA 800 MHz	TDMA and Spread Spectrum Introduced	Packet Switching Introduced	CDMA	HSDPA High Speed	OFDM Introduced	2018 standards
TACS FDMA 900 MHz	D-AMPS TDMA/FDMA 800 MHz SMS 9600 bps	cdmaOne Packet switching 60-80 kbps	CDMA2000 1xEV-DO 1xEV-DV	Downlink Packet Access 14.4 Mbps	LTE-Advanced 3GPP OFDM OFDMA MIMO	MIMO Cognitive radios Smart antennas Ad Hoc networking
	GSM TDMA/FDMA 900/1800/1900 MHz SIM cards 9600 bps	GPRS/EDGE Packet Switching GPRS 30-40 kbps EDGE 90 kbps	UMTS W-CDMA 2 Mbps	HSUPA High Speed Uplink Packet Access 5.74 Mbps	Mobile WiMAX 802.16 OFDM OFDMA MIMO	
	CDMA IS95					

FIGURE 10.5 Generations of Cellular Advances. *Note: this is not an all inclusive list of cellular systems or standards.*

demands despite bandwidth inefficiencies, limited spectrum availability, and lack of wireless privacy. First-generation systems were monumental in that they introduced the world to cellular telephone technology, and demonstrated the feasibility of the cellular concept.

Several 1G standards were developed around the globe. In the United States, the **Advanced Mobile Phone System (AMPS)** was developed through a joint effort between AT&T and Motorola. Operating in the 850 MHz band, FCC allocated frequencies that consisted of two frequency blocks. *Forward* (*network to mobile user*) channel frequencies went from 869 MHz to 894 MHz, while *reverse* (*mobile user to network*) channel frequencies went from 824 MHz to 849 MHz. The bandwidth of each channel was 30 kHz wide, for a total availability of 832 channels; however, since both forward and reverse channels are needed for full-duplex communications, only half, or 416 channel pairs, were actually available. Of the 416 available channel pairs, 21 pairs were used for control signaling and 395 pairs allocated for user traffic. The assignment of a channel pair required that a 45 MHz separation exist between the forward and reverse channels. The digital control channels used FSK modulation, while analog traffic channels were modulated using FM.

The United Kingdom adopted the **Total Access Communications System (TACS)**, which was based upon AMPS. However, TACs differed from AMPS in that it operated in the 900 MHz band, and used smaller 25 kHz bandwidth channels, which increased the number of total channels available. TACS gained wide acceptance in Europe, with a version (JTACS) used in Japan.

The **Nordic Mobile Telephone (NMT)** system operated in Sweden, Denmark, Finland, and Iceland in the early 1980's. NMT operated in the 450 MHz band using FSK to modulate control channels, and FM for traffic channels. Security and privacy, like with all analog systems, were an issue.

Early 1G systems were developed mainly for local or regional markets, and therefore numerous incompatible standards that existed made roaming difficult if not impossible. Today, 1G analog systems have largely been replaced by digital systems.

10.5.2 Second Generation (2G)

As the popularity of mobile phones grew, the industry realized the need to increase communications capacity within the constraints of the allocated frequency spectrum. By the 1990's, with the advances made in computer technologies and integrated chip designs, cellular providers began to adopt digital communications as the solution to increase overall capacity. Dubbed "second generation" (2G) cellular, several incompatible standards were developed based upon TDMA or CDMA technologies. With TDMA, voice traffic was digitized and assigned specific TDM time slots within a frequency channel. By doing this, a single frequency channel could support several TDM digital voice calls. This was in comparison to the 1G analog systems using FDM where channels were fully dedicated to each communicating pair for the duration of each call. CDMA followed a method in which digitized voice calls went through a spread spectrum process, each call separated by unique PN code. While digital communications provided greater capacity, it also added more complexity, requiring voice coding and decoding and sophisticated modulation methods.

In North America, **Digital-AMPS (D-AMPS)**, described in TIA *Interim Standard IS-54*, which eventually became *IS-136*, was developed to enable backward compatibility with 1G AMPS.

By keeping the 1G frequency assignments and channel bandwidths, both AMPS and the newer 2G D-AMPS could be supported. This enabled a graceful upgrade for users transitioning from 1G to 2G systems. Each frequency channel was divided into six time slots each supporting 8 kbps. Four time slots were allocated per full-duplex call (i.e., two time slots each in the forward and reverse directions). Use of TDMA therefore increased the number of channels from 832 to 2496 (i.e., 3 $\times$ 832). Since D-AMPS used the same 21 control channels as AMPS, the number of full-duplex calls supported went from 395 to 1185. With *IS-136* came additional services such as text messaging and the use of TDMA on control channels. The modulation method used was termed π/4 DQPSK *(differential quarternary phase shift keying)*, which is a variant of QPSK.

The ***Global System for Mobile Communications (GSM)*** was adopted as a CEPT[8] standard primarily in Europe. GSM was compatible with ISDN and operated in both the 800 MHz and 900 MHz frequency bands. The frequency channel structure was different from D-AMPS, in that each channel was 200 kHz instead of 30 kHz wide. Each GSM frequency channel was divided into eight TDM time slots. A single call required one slot in the forward direction and one slot in the reverse direction for a total of two time slots per call. The modulation method used was a variant of *continuous-phase, frequency-shift*[9] *keying* called GMSK *(Gaussian minimum shift keying)*. Originally intended for digital voice communications, GSM expanded its services by introducing ***Short Message Service (SMS)*** and an *ETSI* packet switching standard called ***GPRS (General Packet Radio Service)***. Considered a *2.5G* capability, TDM time slots were dynamically allocated for use by GPRS packets in order to connect to the Internet. GPRS allowed the mobile user to maintain a persistent connection to the Internet at a bit rate of up to 21.4 kbps. The next phased upgrade to GPRS was called ***EDGE (enhanced data rates for GSM evolution)***, which provided higher data rates up to 68.4 kbps using 8PSK ($M = 8$) modulation over a single channel. In addition, multiple time slots could be combined increasing overall throughput.

In North America about the same time as the GSM effort, ***IS-95 CDMA***[10] ***(code division multiple access)***, also called ***cdmaOne***, replaced D-AMPS as a *2.5G* standard. With *IS-95 CDMA*, users shared the same forward and reverse frequency bandwidths which were both 1.228 MHz wide. The forward link was divided into 64 logical channels separated by unique PN codes. There were four types of logical channels. Channel 0 was the *pilot channel* that transmitted a continuous signal to provide phase, timing, and signal strength information to mobile units. Channels 1 through 7 were paging channels used for signaling purposes. Channel 23 provided synchronization, system time, and information regarding the protocols used. Finally, channels 8 to 31 and 33 to 63 were allocated for user traffic. Traffic channels initially supported 9600 bps, which was later revised to 14.4 kbps. On the reverse link, which was also 1.228 MHz wide, 94 total logical channels supported 32 access[11]

---

[8] ETSI is currently responsible for the GSM standard.

[9] Continuous-phase, frequency-shift keying was developed in the 1950s. In a nutshell, it is a modulation method in which the delta between highest and lowest carrier frequency shifts is identical to 1/2 of the bit rate. Doing this minimizes the modulation index.

[10] CDMA was developed by Qualcomm, who went on to develop 3G CDMA2000 in alignment with IMT-2000 requirements.

[11] Access channels were used as signaling channels similar to the forward link paging channels.

and 62 traffic channels. The use of CDMA spread spectrum technology had several advantages over TDMA systems:

- As a spread spectrum technology, signals were more immune to RFI and other RF impairments.
- CDMA had better multipath resistance, especially when specialized RAKE receivers were used. *Note - RAKE receivers essentially take the multiple signal copies received, and sends these copies through digital signal processors that adjusts their time and phase delays. This allowed copies to be constructively combined.*
- Since unique PN codes were required by each communicating pair, eavesdropping was extremely difficult, making data transmissions more secure.
- With FDMA/TDMA systems, once the maximum number of channels were allocated, all other attempted calls were blocked. However, with CDMA, additional calls can still be serviced, with a gradual degradation occurring in the form of increased bit errors. Eventually, system overload would be reached when bit errors became unmanageable. This was considered a *graceful degradation* of the system, vice the more abrupt call blocking scenario when the systems maximum number is reached.

To address the global incompatibility of 2G standards, the ITU-R published the ***International Mobile Telecommunications-2000 (IMT-2000)*** standard, intended for 3G systems but also covering 2.5G systems, in an attempt to produce a single compatible standard for all providers and manufacturers. GSM TDMA and cdmaOne (IS-95) CDMA were accepted as IMT-2000 alternative approaches and dubbed 2.5G standards. IMT-2000 3G standards would eventually adopt only CDMA approaches.

10.5.3 Third Generation (3G)

As 2000 approached and the popularity of the Internet and mobile phone continued to grow, the mobile phone industry recognized that users wanted support for multimedia data and Internet connectivity, as well as an ability to roam away from local cellular infrastructures. This meant that higher data rates needed to be supported, and a global standard was required that would allow users to connect through any cellular provider regardless of location.

IMT-2000 was intended to address the following needs:

- Support for higher data rates. Second-generation systems used first-generation frequency allocations in most cases. In order to increase data rates, greater spectrum allocations were needed along with technologies that could maximize spectral efficiency.
- Support for other forms of data beyond voice. It was clear that users wanted mobile access to the Internet and other data services using their mobile units. This meant that the cellular system, including mobile equipment, needed to be smarter. This also signaled the end of circuit switching in favor of packet switching techniques.
- Support for seamless roaming. Mobile users, especially international travelers, wanted to use a single mobile phone anywhere, vice having to own or rent specific phones designed to work with specific regions or service providers.

- Affordability. For the industry to continue to grow, 3G equipment and services needed to be affordable to both service providers and their users.

- Backward compatibility with existing 2G systems. While 3G represented the future at the time, it was understood that the migration from 2G might take a while. To ensure 2G continued to be supported, backward compatibility was needed.

- Modular design. The ability to upgrade and expand 3G was needed to enable system growth, and to enable the implementation of modern technologies over time.

- Data rates based upon user mobility. The data rates available to a user are dependent upon the user's mobility. IMT-2000 categorizes available data rates based upon fixed indoor connections up to 2.048 Mbps, slow moving users up to 384 kbps (e.g., walking), and high-speed users up to 144 kbps (e.g., vehicle).

While the effort by ITU captured in IMT-2000 was needed, 3G, like its predecessors 1G and 2G, continued to produce incompatible standards and systems. Part of this was intentional, since the various 3G alternatives were evolved from existing 2G systems, and complete system replacements were not the intent of IMT-2000.

We will discuss two major 3G standards that were derived from GSM and cdmaOne (i.e., WCDMA and CDMA2000, respectively). Today, both standards are in use, and smartphones typically support connectivity to either 3G or 4G systems.

As an upgrade to GSM in 1999, ETSI released the ***Universal Mobile Telecommunications System (UMTS)*** 3G wireless standard, which adopted ***Wideband CDMA (WCDMA)*** in partnership with the *3rd-Generation Partnership Project*[12] *(3GPP)*. UMTS WCDMA carriers are 5 MHz wide and operate in *frequency division duplex (FDD)* or *time division duplex (TDD)* modes. UMTS FDD is typically found in North America, and consists of separate forward and reverse frequencies allocated from 25 frequency bands ranging from 700 MHz to 2100 MHz. Forward and reverse logical channels separated by PN codes are assigned per call. UMTS TDD is used in Europe where forward and reverse logical channels are assigned according to time vice frequency. In this case, data exchange occurs on the same frequency, but at different times, which is advantageous for smaller cells, especially when adequate FDD separation between forward and reverse frequency channels is not possible.

Starting in 2006, UMTS improved *downlink* (forward link) speeds up to 14.4 Mbps by implementing ***High Speed Downlink Packet Access (HSDPA)***, using 16-QAM ($M = 16$) modulation vice the original QPSK (M-4) which was used on WCDMA. At the same time, UMTS introduced ***High Speed Uplink Packet Access (HSUPA)*** on the *uplink* (reverse link) side which improved bit rates up to 5.74 Mbps. Like HSDPA, HSUPA also used adaptive modulation schemes which improved the number of bits represented by a symbol (i.e., M'ary modulation).

CDMA2000 (IS-856) was the successor to cdmaOne (IS-95) and was approved by ITU-R as part of the IMT-2000 family of standards. Unlike WCDMA, CDMA2000 initially operated on a 1.25 MHz

---

[12] 3GPP was involved in the release of the original GSM standard.

channel. The air interface standard consisted of a data format called *1 × EV-DO (1 × Evolution-Data Only*[13]*)*, and a voice format called *1 × EV-DV (1 × Evolution—Voice Only)*. While the 1 × EV-DO data standard was successful, the voice 1 × EV-DV technology failed. The data 1 × EV-DO standard went through several versions, each providing improved uplink and downlink bit rates. *1 × EV-DO Revision A* enabled 1.8 Mbps uplink and 3.1 Mbps downlink rates. *1 × EV-DO Revision B* improved these bit rates to 5.4 Mbps uplink and 14.7 Mbps downlink rates by increasing the channel bandwidth from 1.25 MHz to 5 MHz. Similar to WCDMA, bit rate improvements were achieved using M'ary modulation techniques. Unfortunately, WCDMA and CDMA2000 are not compatible standards.

10.5.4 Fourth Generation (4G)

At an ITU assembly in January 2012 held in Geneva, *IMT-Advanced* goals were agreed to as an expansion to the *IMT-2000* requirements. IMT-Advanced emphasized global compatibility between mobile and fixed services, the ability to interoperate between disparate cellular access systems, a commonality of wireless user equipment, an ability to achieve worldwide roaming, and enhanced bit rates. Packet switching technologies were emphasized over traditional circuit switched concepts which had dominated previous cellular generations. Numerous service providers around the world began to evolve their systems toward the IMT-Advanced goals in 2013.

Two major 4G technologies emerged, 3GPP's *Long Term Evolution (LTE)* and IEEE 802.16 *Mobile WiMAX (Worldwide Interoperability of Microwave Access)*. Both technologies are based upon packet switching concepts that provide persistent connectivity to the Internet, and both replaced CDMA with the more spectrally efficient *OFDMA (Orthogonal Frequency Division Multiple Access)*. Unfortunately, LTE and WiMAX are not interoperable. Today, in North America, LTE is the predominant 4G technology used by most service providers.

10.5.4.1 Long Term Evolution (LTE)

Unlike 3G, LTE allowed for broadband wireless backhaul connectivity from base stations to mobile network switches using access methods such as WiMAX BWA. Both FDD and TDD are supported, although FDD is predominant in North America, while TDD is offered by China Mobile (Cory Beard, 2016). In addition, traditional circuit switched voice calls were replaced with IP-based packet switched voice. However, today's smartphones enables mobile users to connect to traditional circuit switched 3G voice as well as 4G IP voice services.

The initial LTE standard specified by 3GPP, *releases 8 and 9,* did not meet the original IMT-Advanced 4G bit rate requirements and was therefore considered by some as an enhanced 3.9G capability. However, despite the noncompliance, ITU allowed LTE to be called a 4G capability, understanding that follow-on releases would upgrade LTE to meet IMT-Advanced requirements.

LTE was developed to provide an upgrade path from 3G WCDMA and CDMA2000 systems. In order to meet global roaming requirements mobile smartphones were required to support multiple

---

[13] "1×" referred to the CDMA spreading rate which was 1.2288 Megachips per cycle.

carrier frequencies. Use of OFDMA and MIMO (multiple input multiple output) antenna systems were used as a way to increase spectral efficiency and to effectively deal with multipath fading. Peak bit rates specified were 75 Mbps uplink using SC-FDMA,[14] and 300 Mbps downlink using OFDMA.

To make LTE more compliant with the 4G requirements, 3GPP released LTE-Advanced *release 10* in 2011. LTE-Advance improved upon LTE in several ways:

- The number of LTE antennas used in a MIMO array was increased to a maximum 8 by 8 antenna array (8 × 8 pattern) for downlinks, and a maximum 4 by 4 antenna (4 × 4) array for uplinks.

- *Inter-Cell Interference Coordination (ICIC)* between cells which existed in LTE was improved.

- The LTE-Advanced SC-FDMA uplink was improved by applying a *clustering* concept to the SC-FDMA uplink. The older LTE SC-FDMA uplinks were allocated using contiguous frequency blocks, which tended to complicate the scheduling of uplink resource allocations to user devices. Clustered LTE-Advanced SC-FDMA allowed noncontiguous frequency blocks to be allocated instead, thus making resource scheduling more flexible.

- **Carrier Aggregation (CA)** was introduced to enable up to five carriers to be combined in both the uplink and downlink directions, in order to increase bit rates. *CA* enabled a maximum aggregated bandwidth of 100 MHz.

LTE-Advance is considered a *true 4G* standard that increases peak uplink and downlink bit rates to 500 Mbps and 1 Gbps, respectively.

The overall LTE and LTE-Advanced architectures have taken on several nomenclature changes when compared to the GSM architecture. Modified labels have replaced the traditional ones (e.g., BS, BSS MSC, and NS) although the basic functionalities of the subsystems and their components have remained, for the most part, unchanged. The LTE architecture is shown in fig. 10.6, with description provided below.

The LTE **Evolved UMTS Terrestrial Radio Access Network (E-UTRAN)** is similar to the GSM base station subsystem. User *mobile equipment (ME)* connects wirelessly to base stations called **evolved node B (eNodeB)** which differs from traditional 3G base stations, in that they perform cell control functions thus eliminating the need for separate base station controllers (BSCs). eNodeB base stations are connected to one another through an **X2 interface** that consists of two types, an **X2-C** for control and **X2-U** for user data. The X2-C (control) interface between base stations is used during mobile user hand offs between cells, as well as coordination between cells regarding potential frequency conflicts (i.e., *Inter-Cell Interference Coordination or ICIC*). The *X2-C* interface is used to enable a smooth handoff from one cell to another.

The **Evolved Packet Core (EPC)**, which is similar to the GSM Network Subsystem (NS), is the fixed cellular network that provides management, gateway connectivity to external networks, and switching. The EPC is connected to the E-UTRAN through the **S1 interface** which, like the X2

---

[14] SC-FDMA (single carrier FDMA) is used for uplinks (mobile user to network communications) because it enabled greater efficiency in terms of the transmitted power from a mobile device.

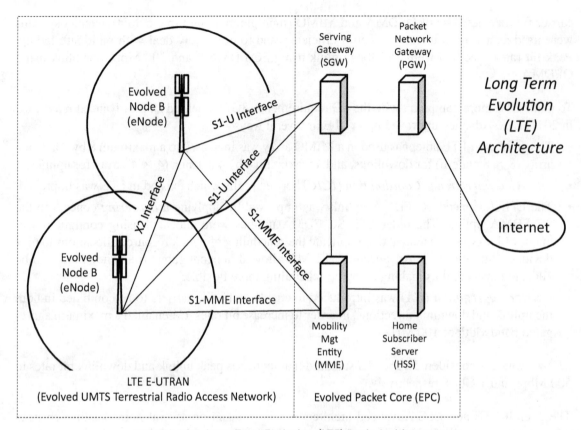

FIGURE 10.6 Long Term Evolution (LTE) Basic Architecture.

interface, is divided into *control* and *data* links. These control and data connections can be either wired (e.g., fiber optic) or wireless (e.g., WiMAX BWA). For control, the ***S1-MME*** interface is used to connect individual eNodeBs to the ***Mobility Management Entity (MME)*** system, which is responsible for managing control and signaling to the UEs. Because the MME is involved in user access, handoffs, and transfers to other networks such as 3G cellular, it must be capable of tracking UEs through the system, and executing required security procedures such as authentication and the negotiation of the security algorithms. Because the MME is responsible for UE control functions, it interacts with the ***Home Subscriber Server (HSS)***, which has a similar function as the GSM HLR and VLR databases. The *HSS* maintains database information on subscribers, and together with the MME, assists in authentication, call setup and security. User call traffic between the eNodeB and EPC is supported by the ***S1-U*** (user) interface, which connects the eNodeB to the ***Serving Gateway (SGW)***. The *SGW* routes user IP traffic between eNodeBs within the same service area, as well as to external networks such as the Internet by sending the IP packets to the ***Packet Data Network Gateway (PGW)***. The *PGW* acts as the external gateway for the service network, performing IP routing, filtering, and inspection of packets originating from external networks.

To increase capacity, LTE adopted a frequency reuse pattern of $N = 1$, which translates to the ability of all cells to operate on all allotted frequencies. Of course, this presents potential interference in the overlap regions of adjacent cells. To prevent potential interference between MEs, adjacent cell eNodeBs must coordinate the use of frequencies within shared overlap areas. *Inter-cell Interference Coordination (ICIC)* can be implemented using several methods. With ***ICI Coordination and Avoidance***, adjacent cells coordinate their intended use (i.e., schedule) of resource blocks defined by time, frequency, and transmit power levels. Restrictions are then applied in order to avoid mutual interference of scheduled resources. ***ICI randomization*** applies a pseudorandom sequence to transmitted codewords. If an adjacent cell operates on the same frequency, the interfering codewords can be separated. ***ICI cancellation*** can also be used through signal cancellation techniques; however, this would require specific information regarding the interfering signal which would be difficult to obtain.

10.5.4.2 Mobile Worldwide Interoperability of Microwave Access (WiMAX 802.16e)

The ***WiMAX Forum*** was established in 2001 to define a total wireless mobile system by adopting the IEEE 802.16e (2005) air interface standard. The WMAX Forum's *Network Working Group (NWG)* developed the standards that were intended for use by manufacturers and operators in building interoperable mobile WiMAX systems. The mobile WiMAX standard describes requirements for high bit rate IP connectivity which are in compliance with IMT-Advanced 4G requirements. Like LTE and LTE-Advanced, mobile WiMAX uses OFDMA as an access technology, MIMO technology, and supports both FDD and TDD operations.

The basic components of the WiMAX architecture are the ***Mobile Stations (MS)***, the ***Access Service Network (ASN)*** which encompasses the air interface to the MS, and the ***Connectivity Service Network (CSN)*** which covers the core network functions (see fig. 10.7).

The ASN consists of one or more base stations (BS) that are comprised of transceivers and antennas that connect to the MS through the cell's RF wireless links. Each BS connects to an ASN Gateway at the OSI RM physical (layer 1) and data link layers (layer 2). One or more ASN Gateways exist within the ASN. Through the ASN Gateway, control functions and data traffic are passed to and from the BS' from the CSN.

The CSN is the IP core network that provides similar functions as the GSM network subsystem. As an IP network, it provides interfaces to external networks including the Internet and other IP networks. There are a number of services that can be implemented within the CSN depending upon the service provider. Three key components include:

- ***Authentication, Authorization, and Accounting (AAA)*** server, which provides cellular network access to approved users.
- The ***Home Agent (HA)*** is a critical service that supports user mobility. Since mobile phones roam and may change IP addresses as it moves from one region or service area to another, the *HA* keeps track of the device's location so that data traffic intended for the user can be delivered.
- Multiple gateways and servers are used to connect to external networks such as the PSTN, Internet, etc. and to provide services such as DNS or DHCP.

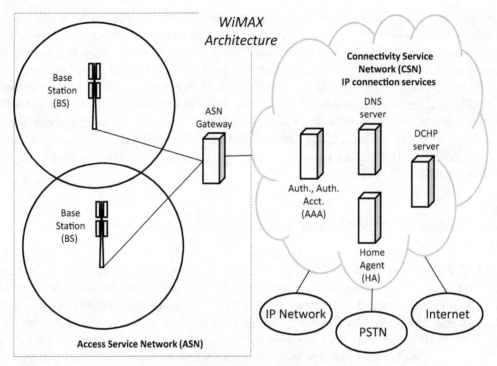

FIGURE 10.7 Mobile Worldwide Interoperability of Microwave Access (WiMAX 802.16e) Architecture.

Mobile WiMAX was released before 4G LTE; however, it was soon overtaken by LTE in many parts of the world. In 2012, the WiMAX Forum decided not to pursue WiMAX 2.0 in light of the popularity of 4G LTE. Part of the reason for LTE's popularity was that it offered a smooth transition from 3G UMTS, thus enabling service providers to upgrade their systems, vice adopting a new technology such as WiMAX. The global popularity of GSM and UMTS, also played a key factor in the competition, favoring LTE as the next natural step to 4G services. Sprint, who once championed WiMAX in 2010, announced just a year later in 2011 that it would phase out WiMAX in favor of LTE.

10.5.5 Fifth Generation (5G)

ITU-R is collaborating with industry manufacturers, service providers, standards organizations, and research institutions in developing the ***International Mobile Telecommunications-2020 (IMT-2020)*** standard framework for mobile communications. Built upon the previous *IMT-2000* and *IMT-Advanced* efforts, *IMT-2020* represents the next natural step towards building a truly global 5G mobile broadband network standard that promotes seamless connectivity of voice and data. Draft 5G performance requirements were agreed to during a working group meeting held in Geneva, Switzerland, in February 2017, with final approval anticipated in November 2017. Once these requirements are approved, detailed specifications will be reviewed, with the finished standards expected in 2020.

The requirements discussed in the February 2017 ITU-R meeting included:

- Minimum *peak* downlink and *peak* uplink speeds of 20 Gbps and 10 Gbps, respectively. Typical rates seen by users are lower, but must be a minimum of 100 Mbps for downlink and 50 Mbps for uplink.

- Improved peak spectral efficiency for downlink (30 bps per Hz) and uplink (15 bps per Hz).

- Mobile networks must be able to service a minimum of 1 million devices per square kilometer, with a latency of less than 4 ms. This latency requirement is reduced to 1 ms for critical system devices (e.g., medical system).

- Radio access networks (RANs) must be energy efficient to minimize network power consumption. This requirement also considers low energy devices that operate on wake/sleep cycles.

- Mobile user movement based on a defined QoS is categorized as *stationary* (0 km/h), *pedestrian* (0 to 10 km/h), *vehicular* (10 to 120 km/h) and *high-speed vehicular* (120 to 500 km/h). The later high-speed vehicular speeds represent high-speed trains.

Although detailed specifications and proposals have yet to be written and finalized as of the date of this writing, most experts agree that 5G will be based on OFDM, OFDMA, and MIMO technologies. Along with the current and additional frequency spectrum, 5G may also use *ISM* unlicensed bands in such a way as to avoid interference with 802.11 or 802.15 systems. Obviously, in order to improve spectral efficiencies and limit inter-cell interference, mobile systems will need to use smart technologies such as cognitive radios and smart antennas, as well as have an ability to form dynamic ad hoc networks.

Central to the excitement surrounding 5G are the potential applications that can be supported. These include the Internet-of-Things (IoT), driverless cars, remote robot-aided surgery, smart homes, robotics, and smart transportation. The ideas and concepts that can benefit from high-speed wireless systems are only limited by the imagination. The ever-increasing thirst for mobile data also places manufacturer and service providers in a good position for market creation and profit.

Even before the finalization of IMT2020 standards, many companies within the industry have already begun to work on their own 5G efforts. As examples, AT&T and Verizon plan initial deployments in 2019. In fact, Verizon expects some aspects of its 5G systems to be deployed as early as 2017. Qualcomm, who developed IS-95 CDMA, is working on a new 5G modem which will be used on the Snapdragon mobile platform in 2019. South Korea's KT mobile operator plans to unveil 5G capability during the Olympic Winter Games in 2018. There are many more initiatives and partnerships that are too numerous to cite here.

As the global market prepares for the arrival of 5G capability, industry giants are teaming up with one another on a global scale. The prize for being the first and most dominant version of a standard has historically been increased market share and return-on-investment (ROI). Like the cellular generations that preceded 5G, there will always be a certain amount of incompatibilities, as well as the identification of winners and losers. In the end however, the benefits of technology innovation to the average consumer will be great and ongoing. The past story and yet-to-be-future story of the cellular industry has been replayed throughout the entire telecommunication arena. For the technophile, it is a dynamic and interesting field full of adventure.

KEY TERMS

access service network (ASN)

Advanced Mobile Phone System (AMPS)

authentication center (AuC)

backhaul

base station (BS)

base station controller (BSC)

base transceiver station (BTS)

cell densification

cellular phone system

cdmaOne

CDMA2000

cluster

code division multiple access (CDMA)

connectivity service network (CSN)

control channel

demand assigned multiple access (DAMA)

Digital AMPS

Enhanced Data Rates for GSM Evolution (EDGE)

equipment Identity Register (EIR)

Evolved Node B (eNodeB)

Evolved Packet Core (EPC)

Evolved UMTS Terrestrial Radio Access Network (E-UTRAN)

femtocell

forward link

frequency division multiple access (FDMA)

frequency reuse pattern

General Packet Radio Service (GPRS)

Global System for Mobile Communications (GSM)

hard handoff

home location register (HLR)

home subscriber server (HSS)

inter-cell interference Coordination (ICIC)

International Mobile Equipment Identity (IMEI)

International Mobile Subscriber Identity (IMSI)

International Mobile Telecommunications-2000 (IMT-2000)

International Mobile Telecommunications-2020 (IMT-2020)

International Mobile Telecommunications-Advanced (IMT-Advanced)

Long Term Evolution (LTE)

macrocell

microcell

mobile radio-telephone system

mobile equipment (ME)

mobility management entity (MME)

mobile stations (MS)

mobile switch center (MSC)

mobile telecommunications switching office (MTSO)

network subsystem (NS)

orthogonal frequency division multiple access (OFDMA)

packet data network gateway (PGW)

picocell

reverse link

serving gateway (SGW)

small cells

soft handoff

time division multiple access (TDMA)

Total Access Communications System (TACS)

traffic channel

visitor location register (VLR)

Universal Mobile Telecommunications System (UMTS)

WCDMA

Worldwide Interoperability of Microwave Access (WiMAX)

CHAPTER PROBLEMS

1. Select the correct statement(s) regarding the single antenna mobile radio-telephone system offered by service providers prior to the wide-spread use of the cellular concept.
   a. Single antenna mobile systems had the simplicity and ability to reach out to large numbers of subscribers in urban areas.
   b. With a single antenna system, the mobile telephone power supplies were small and easily carried by users.
   c. Since available frequency channels were limited, a single antenna system could not easily support numerous simultaneous calls.
   d. Single antenna systems used high GHz frequencies in order to maximize data rates.

   Answer: c

2. Select the correct statement(s) regarding the cellular network concept.
   a. The number of mobile cellular users that can be supported within a single base station cell increases as the cell size (i.e., "footprint") increases.
   b. For areas where congestion occurs due to a high number of cellular users, base station transmit power should be increased in order to increase data throughput.
   c. Cell sizes ("footprint") can be decreased by decreasing base station transmit power.
   d. The only way to increase the number of mobile users that can be supported within a given cell, is to obtain additional frequency bandwidth.

   Answer: c

3. By dividing a mobile service area into smaller cells, *frequency reuse* can be achieved. As the cell size decreases, more cells cover a given area, and the ability to reuse frequency channels within the service area become greater.
   a. True
   b. False

   Answer: a

4. You are designing a cellular system where the available channels for the entire system is $K = 300$. The anticipated requirement per cell is 50 channels. You have a choice to choose a $N = 16$ or $N = 4$ reuse pattern. Which do you choose and why?
   a. $N = 16$, which equates to 18 channels per cell. This is insufficient to support requirements.
   b. $N = 16$, which equates to 75 channels per cell. This is more than sufficient to support anticipated use per cell.
   c. $N = 4$, which equates to 50 channels per cell. This meets the anticipated requirement.
   d. $N = 4$, which equates to 75 channels available per cell. This meets and exceeds the per cell requirement.

   Answer: d

5. As the *cell reuse pattern (N)* increases, the overall number of simultaneous calls that can be supported within the service area also increases.
   a. True
   b. False

   Answer: b

6. When designing a cellular system, a $N = 1$ cell reuse pattern means:
   a. Only one user will be allocated communication channels within a single cell
   b. All allocated frequency channels in the system can be used in each cell
   c. A minimum of one cell space must be used to separate cells that are allocated the same channels
   d. None of the above are correct

Answer: b

7. As the number of cells within a service area increases (i.e., the service area coverage remains the same, but the cells are decreased in size so that more cells support the service area), what will happen?
   a. Since each cell has a base station that must be connected to the main providers network, system complexity increases as the number of cells increase.
   b. If the service area remains the same and the cell sizes decrease, mobile users will experience more handoffs between cells.
   c. As the number of cells increase and cell size decreases, greater frequency reuse can be achieved
   d. All of the above

Answer: d

8. The _____ connects to the mobile user through cellular frequencies; however, backhaul connection to the service provider network is provided by the host broadband connection (e.g., Internet).
   a. Femtocell
   b. Picocell
   c. Macrocell
   d. None of the above

Answer: a

9. Identify some of the methods that can be implemented to meet increased subscriber numbers.
   a. Use of CDMA or OFDMA
   b. Borrowing channels from neighboring cells
   c. Use of ICIC methods
   d. All of the above

Answer: d

10. Select the correct statement(s) regarding cellular systems
    a. As cell sizes shrink, frequency reuse decreases significantly
    b. As cell sizes shrink, the complexities of switching mobile traffic between cells increases
    c. As cell sizes increase, frequency reuse increases
    d. As cell sizes increase, so does the complexities of switching mobile traffic between cells

Answer: b

11. Which of the following cellular concepts can be used to increase the number of subscribers within a single cell.
    a. Frequency borrowing
    b. Cell splitting
    c. Cell sectoring
    d. All of the above

Answer: d

12. In a GSM cellular architecture identify the components belonging to the Network Subsystem.
   a. VLR, HLR, AuC
   b. BSC, MSC, BTS
   c. BTS, BSC, PSTN
   d. PSTN, MSC, BSC

Answer: a

13. Identify the ways in which cellular providers address increasing subscriber numbers.
   a. Addition of new frequency channels
   b. Frequency borrowing between adjacent cells
   c. Network densification
   d. All of the above

Answer: d

14. OFDM is a spread spectrum technology similar to CDMA.
   a. True
   b. False

Answer: b

15. Which GSM system provides the air interface to the mobile station?
   a. BSS
   b. BSC
   c. MSC
   d. MS

Answer: a

16. Each base station broadcasts control signals that are used throughout the cell for control and signaling purposes.
   a. True
   b. False

Answer: a

17. If a mobile user departs the set of cells controlled by the BSC, the BSC must coordinate with the mobile switching center (MSC) to facilitate an inter-BSC hand-off.
   a. True
   b. False

Answer: a

18. During a network soft hand-off between cells, the ME (Mobile User) is continuously connected to both BTS' until the hand-off is complete.
   a. True
   b. False

Answer: a

19. Identify the components of a GSM *Network Subsystem*.
   a. HLR
   b. MSC
   c. EIR
   d. AuC
   e. VLR
   f. All of the above are components of the NS

Answer: f

20. In a GSM cellular network, when does the mobile equipment (ME) first connect to the Mobile Switching Center (MSC)?
   a. When the ME is turned on
   b. When the ME attempts to make a call
   c. Only if the called party is not within the same BSC area
   d. Only if the called party is not within the cellular service's network

Answer: a

21. Control channels in a cellular system have a dual purpose. Control channels provide the control and signaling to mobile user equipment, and they are used for user traffic when needed.
   a. True
   b. False

Answer: b

22. Describe the mobile call process when a mobile user places a call on a cellular network.

23. What was true about cellular first-generation (1G) systems?
   a. 1G used TDMA over FDM channels
   b. 1G introduced packet switching for analog circuits
   c. 1G traffic channels were analog
   d. 1G control and signaling channels were analog

Answer: c

24. Identify the 1G systems
   a. AMPS, TACS
   b. DAMPS, NMT, GSM
   c. CDMA2000, WCDMA
   d. LTE, WiMAX

Answer: a

25. Which cellular generation first introduced digital communications?
   a. 1G
   b. 2G
   c. 3G
   d. 4G

Answer: b

26. What was the significance of IMT-2000?
    a. Introduced international requirements for 2G
    b. Attempted to address the cellular system incompatibility issue by adopting CDMA and TDMA
    c. Introduced OFDMA and MIMO
    d. Officially introduced the cellular concept to mobile communications

Answer: b

27. CDMA2000 and WCDMA are both 3G standards that are fully compatible with one another because they both use direct sequence spread spectrum technologies.
    a. True
    b. False

Answer: b

28. Select the correct statement(s) regarding IMT-2000.
    a. IMT-2000 was an ITU attempt to define a single global standard for cellular communications
    b. TDMA and CDMA were selected as the global standard
    c. Greater spectral efficiency was one goal for IMT-2000
    d. All of the above

Answer: d

29. Select the correct statement(s) regarding IMT-Advanced.
    a. IMT-Advanced goals are an expansion to the IMT-2000 requirements
    b. Packet switching technologies were emphasized over traditional circuit switched concepts
    c. Long Term Evolution (LTE) and IEEE 802.16 Mobile WiMAX (Worldwide Interoperability of Microwave Access) were both 4G standards that addressed IMT-Advanced goals
    d. All of the above are correct

Answer: d

30. LTE was developed to provide an upgrade path from 3G WCDMA and CDMA2000 systems.
    a. True
    b. False

Answer: a

31. LTE-Advance is considered a true 4G standard.
    a. True
    b. False

Answer: a

32. The LTE Evolved Packet Core (EPC) is similar to the GSM Network Subsystem (NS) in function.
    a. True
    b. False

Answer: a

33. LTE adopted a frequency reuse pattern of $N = 1$. Therefore, ICIC is required to avoid channel interference between cells.
    a. True
    b. False

Answer: a

34. What does LTE-Advanced and mobile WiMAX have in common?
    a. Both support FDD and TDD
    b. Both operate using OFDMA as the access technology
    c. Both use MIMO technology
    d. All of the above

Answer: d

35. When implementing OFDM on either WiFi or ceullar RF link, the use of guard bands between subcarriers is not necessary.
    a. True
    b. False

Answer: a

36. Describe the role of the WiMAX *home agent*.

37. IMT-2020 follows IMT-2000 and IMT-Advanced as the next steps toward providing a fully interoperable and seamless voice and data communications system.
    a. True
    b. False

Answer: a

BIBLIOGRAPHY

(2017). Retrieved from Metro Ethernet Forum: WWW.MEF.NET

3GPP. (n.d.). *3rd Generation Partnership Project (3GPP).* Retrieved 2017, from http://www.3gpp .org/about-3gpp/about-3gpp

3M. (2015). *Passive Optical LAN Solutions.* Austini, TX: 3M Communication Market Division.

Ahamed, A. (2013, June 11). *RIP Vs. OSPF: Which is better for your network?* Retrieved 2017, from Intense School: http://resources.intenseschool.com/rip-vs-ospf-which-is-better-for-your-network/

Altera Corporation. (2012). *Implementing Next-Generation Passive Optical Network Designs with FPGAs.* San Jose, CA: Altera Corporation.

Alwayn, V. (2004). *Fiber-Optic Technologies.* Indianapolis: Pearson Education Cisco Press.

ANSI. (n.d.). *American Natioinal Standards Institute.* Retrieved 2017, from https://www.ansi.org/ about_ansi/overview/overview?menuid=1

AT&T. (n.d.). *Milestones in AT&T History.* Retrieved 2017, from AT&T: https://www.corp.att.com/ history/milestones.html

Beard, C., & Stallings, W. (2016). *Wireless Communicaation Networks and Systems.* Hoboken, NJ: Pearson Higher Education, Inc.

Berg, J. *The IEEE 802.11 Standardization, Its History, Specification, Implementations, and Future.* Fairfax, VA: George Mason University Technical Report Series.

Biography. (n.d.). Retrieved 2017, from James C. Maxwell: https://www.biography.com/people/ james-c-maxwell-9403463

California Cable & Telecommunications Association. (n.d.). *History of Cable.* Retrieved 2017, from https://www.calcable.org/learn/historyofcable/

Catherine Howell, D. M. (2016, November 7). *Brookings.* Retrieved 2017, from The Internet as a Human Right: https://www.brookings.edu/blog/techtank/2016/11/07/the-internet-as-a-human-right/

CEPT. (n.d.). *European Conference of Postal and Telecommunications Administrations.* Retrieved 2017, from CEPT: https://cept.org/

Cerf, V. (n.d.). *Internet Society (ISOC).* Retrieved 2017, from Technical Aspects of the Internet: https://www.internetsociety.org/internet/how-it-works/technical-aspects

Churchman, L. (1976). *Introduction to Circuits.* New York: Holt, Rinehart and Winston.

Cisco. (2005, June 14). *A Brief Overview of SONET Technology.* Retrieved 2017, from www. cisco.com/c/en/us/support/docs/optical/synchronous-optical-nework-sonet/13567-sonet-tech-tips.html

Cisco Networking Academy. (2014). *Introduction to Networks, Companion Guide.* Indianapolis, IN: Cisco Press.

CTIA. (2016). *Cellular Telecommunications Industry Association.* Retrieved 2017, from https://www.ctia.org/about

DARPA. (n.d.). *ARPANET and the Origins of the Internet.* Retrieved 2017, from Defense Advanced Research Projects Agency: https://www.darpa.mil/about-us/timeline/arpanet

Dean, T. (2003). *Guide to Telecommunications Technology.* Canada: Thomson Course Technology.

DEC, Intel Corp., Xerox. (1980). *The Ethernet, a Local Are Network and Physical Layer Specifications.* Maynard.

DOCSIS Resource Information for Cable Operators. (2017). Retrieved 2017, from docsis.org

Engineering and Technology History Wiki. (2016, September 22). *Telegraph.* Retrieved 2017, from http://ethw.org/Telegraph

Famous Scientists, The Art of Genius. (n.d.). Retrieved 2017, from Michael Faraday: https://www.famousscientists.org/michael-faraday/

Farley, T. (2005). *Private Line.* Retrieved 2017, from Moile Telephone History: http://www.privateline.com/wp-content/uploads/2016/01/TelenorPage_022-034.pdf

Frenkiel, R. (n.d.). *Rutgers University.* Retrieved 2017, from A Brief History of Mobile Communications: http://www.winlab.rutgers.edu/~narayan/Course/Wireless_Revolution/vts%20article.pdf

H. Takeuchi, I. N. (2000). Classic Work: Theory of Organizational Knowledge Creation. In M. M. D. Morey, *Knowledge Management, Classic and Contemporary Works.* London: The MIT Press.

Haykin, S. (1978). *Communication Systems.* New York: John Wiley & Sons.

History Channel. (n.d.). *The Invention of the Internet.* Retrieved 2017, from http://www.history.com/topics/inventions/invention-of-the-internet

Hogg, S. (2009). Ethernet on a Ring, Methods of using Ethernet in a ring topology. *Network World.*

Horak, R. (2007). *Telecommunications and Data Communications Handbook.* Hoboken, NJ: John Wiley & Son.

Hush-A-Phone Corporation v. United States, 238 F.2d 266 (D.C. Cir. 1956 1956).

IANA. (2017, July 26). *IANA.* Retrieved 2017, from Service Name and Transport Protocol Port Number Registry: https://www.iana.org/assignments/service-names-port-numbers/service-names-port-numbers.xml

IANA. (n.d.). *Root Zone Database.* Retrieved 2017, from Internet Assigned Numbers Authority: https://www.iana.org/domains/root/db

ICANN. (2011, March 4). *ICANN.* Retrieved 2017, from Beginner's Guide to Internet Protocol (IP) Addresses: https://www.icann.org/en/system/files/files/ip-addresses-beginners-guide-04mar11-en.pdf

ICANN. (n.d.). *ICANN History Project.* Retrieved 2017, from ICANN: https://www.icann.org/history

IEEE Computer Society. (2005). *802.15.1 Part 15.1: Wireless medium access (MAC) and physical layer (PHY) specifications for wireless personal area networks (WPAN).* New York: IEEE.

IEEE Computer Society and the IEEE Microwave Theory and Techniques Society. (2012). *IEEE Standard for Air Interface for Broadband Wireless Access Systems.* New York: IEEE.

IEEE. (2017). *The 40th Anniversary of Ethernet.* Retrieved 2017, from IEEE Standards Association: http://standards.ieee.org/events/ethernet/history.html

IEEE. (2017, March 1). *The Institute, IEEE News Source.* Retrieved 2017, from 5G: The Future of Communications Networks: http://theinstitute.ieee.org/technology-topics/communications/5g-the-future-of-communications-networks

IETF RFC 1883. (1995, December). *IETF.* Retrieved 2017, from Internet Protocol Version 6 (IPv6) Specification: https://tools.ietf.org/html/rfc1883

IETF RFC 2131. (1997, March). *IETF.* Retrieved 2017, from Dynamic Host Configuration Protocol: https://www.ietf.org/rfc/rfc2131.txt

IETF RFC 2460. (1998, December). *IETF.* Retrieved 2017, from Internet Protocol Version 6 (IPv6) Specifiction: https://www.ietf.org/rfc/rfc2460.txt

IETF RFC 3513. (2003, April). *IETF.* Retrieved 2017, from Internet Protocol Version 6 (IPv6) Addressing Architecture: https://tools.ietf.org/html/rfc3513

IETF RFC 4271. (2006). *Internet Engineering Task Force.* Retrieved 2017, from RFC 4271 A Border Gateway Protocol 4 (BGP-4): https://tools.ietf.org/html/rfc4271

IETF RFC 4884. (2007, April). *IETF.* Retrieved 2017, from Extended ICMP to Support Multi-Part Messages: https://tools.ietf.org/pdf/rfc4884.pdf

IETF RFC 792. (1981, September). *IETF.* Retrieved 2017, from Internet Control Message Protocol: https://tools.ietf.org/html/rfc792

International Telecommunication Union. (2011). *Chapter Seven: Case Study - How ITU's Broadband Standards Imrpove Access to the Internet.* Retrieved 2017, from International Telecommunication Union: www.itu.int/osg/spu/ip/chapter_seven.html

International Telecommunication Union, T. S. (2010, November). Series E: Overall Network Operation, Telephone Service, Service Operation and Human Factors. *Recommendation ITU-T E.164.*

Internet Assigned Numbers Authority. (n.d.). *IANA.* Retrieved 2017, from Domain Name Services: https://www.iana.org/domains

Internet World Stats. (2017, March 31). *Internet World Stats.* Retrieved 2017, from World Internet Usage and Population Statistics, March 31, 2017 Update: http://www.internetworldstats.com/stats.htm#links

ISDN & DSL Line Conditioning. (n.d.). Retrieved 2017, from Info Cellar: http://www.infocellar.com/cable-dsl/line-conditioning.htm

ISO. (n.d.). *International Organization for Standardization.* Retrieved 2017, from https://www.iso.org/about-us.html

ISO/IEC. (1994). *Information technology, Open Systems Interconnection, Basic Reference Model, Conventions for the definition of OSI services.* Retrieved July 20, 2016, from https://www.iso.org/obp/ui/#iso:std:iso-iec:10731:ed-1:v1:en

ISOC. (2015). *Internet Society.* Retrieved 2017, from Policy Brief: Internet Exchange Points: https://www.internetsociety.org/policybriefs/ixps?gclid=EAIaIQobChMIo7actauY1QIVj0wNCh1O_gl-EAAYAiAAEgINC_D_BwE

ITU. (2011). *International Telecommunications Unioin.* Retrieved 2017, from About Mobile Technology and IMT-2000: https://www.itu.int/osg/spu/imt-2000/technology.html

ITU. (2017). *ITU Global Standard for International Mobile Telecommunications IMT-Advanced.* Retrieved 2017, from http://www.itu.int/en/ITU-R/study-groups/rsg5/rwp5d/imt-adv/Pages/default.aspx

ITU-T Telecommunication Standardization Sector of ITU. (2016). *G.987.1 10-Gigabit-capable passive optical networks (XG-PON).* Retrieved 2017, from www.itu.net

ITU-T Telecommunication Standardization Sector of ITU. (2015). *G.989.3, 40-Gigabit-capable passive optical networks (NG-PON2).* Retrieved 2017, from www.itu.net

ITU-T Telecommunications Standardization Sector of ITU. (2014). *G.984.3 Gigabit-capable passive optical networks (GPON).* Retrieved 2017, from www.itu.net

J. L. LoCicero, B. P. (1999). *Mobile Communications Handbook, Line Coding.* Boca Raton: CRC Press LLC.

John w. Cook, R. H. (1999, May). The Noise and Crosstalk Environment for ADSL aand VDSL Systems. *IEEE Communications Magazine*, pp. 74–78.

Johnk, C. T. (1975). *Engineering Electromagnetic Field and Waves.* New York: John Wiley & Sons.

Jyoti Kataria, P. K. (April 2013). A Study and Survey of OFDM versus COFDM. *International Journal of Science and Modern Engineering*, 64–67.

Kennedy, G. (1977). *Elecronic Communication Systems, 2nd Ed.* New York: McGraw-Hill.

Luis F. Caro, D. P. (2017, June 5). Retrieved 2017, from Research Gate: www.researchgate.net

Mathias Hein, D. G. (1997). *Switching Technology in the Local Network, from LAN to Switched LAN to Virtual LAN.* London: United Kingdom.

MERIT. (2016). *A History of Excellence and Innovation.* Retrieved 2017, from https://www.merit.edu/about-us/merits-history/

Morikawa, R. (2004, July). A Framework for an Advanced XML Topic Map Knowledge Base. Fairfax, VA: ISBN/ISSN 0496834441.

NASA. (n.d.). *Sputnik and The Dawn of the Space Age.* Retrieved 2017, from NASA: https://history.nasa.gov/sputnik/

Neel Shah, D. K. (n.d.). *A Tutorial on DOCSIS: Protocol and Models.* Retrieved 2017, from clemson.edu: https://people.cs.clemson.edu/~jmarty/projects/papers/hetnet2005-tutorial.pdf

NETGEAR. (2016). *DOCSIS 3.1 Technology Whitepaper.* Retrieved 2017, from NETGEAR Inc.: https://www.netgear.com/images/pdf/DOCSIS31WhitePaper.pdf

OMA. (n.d.). *Open Mobile Alliance.* Retrieved 2017, from http://openmobilealliance.org/about-oma

PC Magazine. (2017, May 1). *What is 5G.* Retrieved 2017, from PC Magazine: https://www.pcmag.com/article/345387/what-is-5g

Pinheiro, J. (1987, September). AT&T Divestiture & Telecommunications Market. *Berkeley Technology Law Journal.*

Pratt, T. B. (2003). *Satellite Communications, 2nd Ed.* New York: John Wiley & Sons.

Roddy, D. (2006). *Satellite Communications, 4th Ed.* New York: McGraw-Hill.

Ross, E. (1977). *Professional Electrical Electronic Engineer's License Study Guide.* Blue Ridge Summit, Pa.: TAB Books.

Sampler, D. A. (1991). *Business Data Communications, Third Edition.* Redwood City, CA: The Benjamin/Cummings Publishing Company, Inc.

Schwartz, M. (1988). *Telecommunications Networks, Protocols, Modeling and Analysis.* Reading, MA: Addison-Wesley Publishing Company.

Scott Kipp, F. Y. (2012, February 27). Ethernet 102: The Physical Layer of Ethernet. *Ethernet Alliance.* Ethernet Alliance.

ShoreTel. (n.d.). *History of Telegraph in Communications.* Retrieved 2017, from https://www.shoretel.com/history-telegraph-communications

Stallings, W. (1997). *Data and Computer Communications.* Upper Saddle River, NJ: Prentice-Hall, Inc.

Tech Target. (2015, June 26). *Lossless and Lossy Compression.* Retrieved 2017, from http://whatis.techtarget.com/definition/lossless-and-lossy-compression?vgnextfmt=print

Telecommunications Act of 1996. (2013, June 20). Retrieved 2017, from Federal Communications Commission: https://www.fcc.gov/general/telecommunicationsact1996

The Economist. (2014). *A Brief History of Wi-Fi.* Retrieved 2017, from http://www.economist.com/node/2724397

The Fiber Optic Association, Inc. (2003). *Guide to Fiber Optics & Premises Cabling.* Retrieved 2017, from FOA Tech Topics: DWDM, Dense Wavelength Division Multiplexing: www.thefoa.org/tech/dwdm.htm

The Foundations of Mobile and Cellular Telephony. (2015). Retrieved 2017, from Engineering and Technology History Wiki: http://ethw.org/The_Foundations_of_Mobile_and_Cellular_Telephony

TIA. (2001). Commercial Building Telecommunications Cabling Standard, Prt 2: Balanced Twisted-pair Cabling Components. In TIA/EIA, *T1I/EIA Standard.* Arlington: Telecommunications Industry Association.

TIA. (2001). Commerial Building Telecommunications Cabling Standard, Part 1: General Requirements. In *TIA/EIA Standard.* Arlington: Telecommunications Industry Association.

TIA. (n.d.). *Telecommunications Industry Association.* Retrieved 2017, from https://www.tiaonline.org/about/

Webopedia. (2007, May 24). *Brief Timeline of the Internet.* Retrieved 2017, from Webopedia: http://www.webopedia.com/quick_ref/timeline.asp

White, C. (2013). *Data Communications & Computer Networks, A Business User's Approach 8th Ed.* Boston, MA: Cenage Learning.

White, C. M. (2013). *Data Communications and Computer Networks, A Business User's Approach.* Boston, MA: Cenage Learning.

Wood, M. C. (2006). *An Analysis of the Design and Implementation of QoS over IEEE 802.16.* Retrieved 2017, from Washington University in St. Louis, Schoole of Engineering & Applied Science: http://www.cse.wustl.edu/~jain/cse574-06/ftp/wimax_qos/

Wozniak, S. (n.d.). *Homebrew and How the Apple Came to be.* Retrieved 2017, from Atari Archives: http://www.atariarchives.org/deli/homebrew_and_how_the_apple.php

Yarbrough, R. (1990). *Electrical Engineering Reference Manual 5th Ed.* Belmont, CA: Professional Publications INC.

Youssef, M. A., & Miller, R. E. *Analyzing the Point Coordination Function of the IEEE 802.11 WLAN Protocol using a System of Communicating Machines Specification.* College Park, MD: University of Maryland, Department of Computer Science.

INDEX

Note: Page numbers followed by *f*, *t*, or *n* represent figures, tables, or foot notes respectively.

A

CPSIA information can be obtained
at www.ICGtesting.com
Printed in the USA
LVHW05s0734060718
582718LV00001B/1/P

9 781524 952075